'Written by experts in their fields and with a strong introduction, *Early Women Psychoanalysts: History, Biography, and Contemporary Relevance* is dedicated to the early European women psychoanalysts. Often ignored by males in their fields and, later, by historians, these women enhanced the study and practice of psychoanalysis, offering us invaluable histories of Jewishness, gender, World War II, the Holocaust, trauma, and memory studies. A must read!'

Marion Kaplan, *author of* Between Dignity and Despair: Jewish Life in Nazi Germany, *Professor Emerita of Hebrew and Judaic Studies, New York University*

'With an exemplary combination of scholarly originality and theoretical sophistication, the essays in this volume provide definitive introductions to the lives and legacies of fourteen women, from the famous to the forgotten, who forged psychoanalysis in the smithy of their souls. An invaluable resource for every serious student of the field.'

Peter L. Rudnytsky, *Head, Department of Academic and Professional Affairs, American Psychoanalytic Association*

'This wonderful, scholarly collection fills a hole in psychoanalysis's early history. Detailing the lives of little-known women psychoanalysts (nearly all of whom were Jewish), it provides a rich, in-depth glimpse of their personal evolution while beautifully explicating the impact of cultural, political (and especially antisemitic) forces on them.'

Joyce Slochower, PhD, ABPP, *NYU Postdoctoral Program, author of* Holding and Psychoanalysis: A Relational Perspective *(1996; 2014),* Psychoanalytic Collisions *(2006; 2014),* Elephants Under the Couch: Psychoanalysis and the Unspoken *(in press); co-editor, with Lew Aron and Sue Grand, 'De-Idealizing Relational Theory: A Critique From Within' and* Decentering Relational Theory: A Comparative Critique *(2018)*

'What is extraordinary about Klara Naszkowska's edited volume is not simply its focus on the lives and work of neglected, marginalized, and yet seminal women psychoanalysts. In addition, the chapters vivify ways in which a malignant mix of misogynistic, antisemitic, fascistic, and longtime sociocultural norms both hobbled, yet also galvanized some of the greatest psychoanalytic voices of all time.'

Emily A. Kuriloff, PsyD, *author of* Contemporary Psychoanalysis and the Legacy of the Third Reich: History, Memory, Tradition *(Routledge, 2016). Training and Supervising Psychoanalyst, Director of Clinical Education Emeritus, William Alanson White Institute, New York*

Early Women Psychoanalysts

Each life story is unique, yet each also entwines with other stories, sharing recurring themes linked to issues of gender, Jewishness, women's education, politics, and migration.

The book's first section discusses relatively known analysts such as Sabina Spielrein, Lou Andreas-Salomé, and Beata Rank, remembered largely as someone's wife, lover, or muse; and the second part sheds light on women such as Margarethe Hilferding, Tatiana Rosenthal, and Erzsébet Farkas, who took strong political stances. In the third section, the biographies of lesser-known analysts like Ludwika Karpińska-Woyczyńska, Nic Waal, Barbara Low, and Vilma Kovács are discussed in the context of their importance for the early Freudian movement; and in the final section, the lives of Eugenia Sokolnicka, Sophie Morgenstern, Alberta Szalita, and Olga Wermer are examined in relation to migration and exile, trauma, loss, and memory.

With a clear focus upon the continued importance of these women for psychoanalytic theory and practice, as well as discussion that engages with pertinent issues such as gendered discrimination, inhumane immigration laws, and antisemitism, this book is an important reading for students, scholars, and practitioners of psychoanalysis, as well as those involved in gender and women's studies, and Jewish and Holocaust studies.

Klara Naszkowska, PhD, is a cultural historian focusing on Jewish women and exploring intersections of gender, ethnicity, politics, emigration, and memory. In 2019, she received a Fulbright Fellowship for a research project about Sabina Spielrein.

RELATIONAL PERSPECTIVES BOOK SERIES
ADRIENNE HARRIS & EYAL ROZMARIN Series Editors
STEPHEN MITCHELL Founding Editor
LEWIS ARON Editor Emeritus

The Relational Perspectives Book Series (RPBS) publishes books that grow out of or contribute to the relational tradition in contemporary psychoanalysis. The term *relational psychoanalysis* was first used by Greenberg and Mitchell[1] to bridge the traditions of interpersonal relations, as developed within interpersonal psychoanalysis and object relations, as developed within contemporary British theory. But, under the seminal work of the late Stephen A. Mitchell, the term *relational psychoanalysis* grew and began to accrue to itself many other influences and developments. Various tributaries—interpersonal psychoanalysis, object relations theory, self psychology, empirical infancy research, feminism, queer theory, sociocultural studies and elements of contemporary Freudian and Kleinian thought—flow into this tradition, which understands relational configurations between self and others, both real and fantasied, as the primary subject of psychoanalytic investigation.

We refer to the relational tradition, rather than to a relational school, to highlight that we are identifying a trend, a tendency within contemporary psychoanalysis, not a more formally organized or coherent school or system of beliefs. Our use of the term *relational* signifies a dimension of theory and practice that has become salient across the wide spectrum of contemporary psychoanalysis. Now under the editorial supervision of Adrienne Harris and Eyal Rozmarin, the Relational Perspectives Book Series originated in 1990 under the editorial eye of the late Stephen A. Mitchell. Mitchell was the most prolific and influential of the originators of the relational tradition. Committed to dialogue among psychoanalysts, he abhorred the authoritarianism that dictated adherence to a rigid set of beliefs or technical restrictions. He championed open discussion, comparative and integrative approaches, and promoted new voices across the generations. Mitchell was later joined by the late Lewis Aron, also a visionary and influential writer, teacher and leading thinker in relational psychoanalysis.

Included in the Relational Perspectives Book Series are authors and works that come from within the relational tradition, those that extend and develop that tradition, and works that critique relational approaches or compare and contrast them with alternative points of view. The series includes our most distinguished senior psychoanalysts, along with younger contributors who bring fresh vision. Our aim is to enable a deepening of relational thinking while reaching across disciplinary and social boundaries in order to foster an inclusive and international literature.

A full list of titles in this series is available at www.routledge.com/Relational-Perspectives-Book-Series/book-series/LEARPBS.

Note

1 Greenberg, J. and Mitchell, S. (1983). *Object Relations in Psychoanalytic Theory*. Cambridge, MA: Harvard UP.

Early Women Psychoanalysts

History, Biography, and Contemporary Relevance

Edited by Klara Naszkowska

LONDON AND NEW YORK

Designed cover image: © Tola, Ada, and Joel

First published 2024
by Routledge
4 Park Square, Milton Park, Abingdon, Oxon OX14 4RN

and by Routledge
605 Third Avenue, New York, NY 10158

Routledge is an imprint of the Taylor & Francis Group, an informa business

© 2024 selection and editorial matter, Klara Naszkowska; individual chapters, the contributors

The right of Klara Naszkowska to be identified as the author of the editorial material, and of the authors for their individual chapters, has been asserted in accordance with sections 77 and 78 of the Copyright, Designs and Patents Act 1988.

With the exception of Chapter 8, no part of this book may be reprinted or reproduced or utilised in any form or by any electronic, mechanical, or other means, now known or hereafter invented, including photocopying and recording, or in any information storage or retrieval system, without permission in writing from the publishers.

Chapter 8 of this book is freely available as a downloadable Open Access PDF at http://www.taylorfrancis.com under a Creative Commons Attribution-Non Commercial-No Derivatives (CC-BY-NC-ND) 4.0 license.

The Open Access version of Chapter 8 was funded by Ostfold University College.

Trademark notice: Product or corporate names may be trademarks or registered trademarks, and are used only for identification and explanation without intent to infringe.

British Library Cataloguing-in-Publication Data
A catalogue record for this book is available from the British Library

Library of Congress Cataloging-in-Publication Data
Names: Naszkowska, Klara, editor.
Title: Early women psychoanalysts : history, biography, and contemporary relevance / edited by Klara Naszkowska.
Description: 1 Edition. | New York, NY : Routledge, 2024. | Series: Relational perspectives book series | Includes bibliographical references and index.
Identifiers: LCCN 2023041411 (print) | LCCN 2023041412 (ebook) | ISBN 9781032596938 (hardback) | ISBN 9781032595351 (paperback) | ISBN 9781003455844 (ebook)
Subjects: LCSH: Women psychoanalysts—Biography. | Women—Employment—Biography.
Classification: LCC BF109.A1 E37 2024 (print) | LCC BF109.A1 (ebook) | DDC 150.92082—dc23/eng/20231218
LC record available at https://lccn.loc.gov/2023041411
LC ebook record available at https://lccn.loc.gov/2023041412

ISBN: 978-1-032-59693-8 (hbk)
ISBN: 978-1-032-59535-1 (pbk)
ISBN: 978-1-003-45584-4 (ebk)

DOI: 10.4324/9781003455844

Typeset in Times New Roman
by Apex CoVantage, LLC

Contents

Acknowledgments   *xi*
List of Contributors   *xii*

Introduction: Progressives, in Their Day and in Ours   1
KLARA NASZKOWSKA

PART I
Beyond Wife, Lover, Muse   11

1   Sabina Spielrein: Pioneer of Medical Science   13
ANA TOMČIĆ AND JOHN LAUNER

2   Lou Andreas-Salomé: An Unacknowledged Psychoanalytic Theorist of Art   37
SHIRA DUSHY-BARR

3   Beata "Tola" Rank: Out From the Footnote   57
LENA MAGNONE

PART II
Beyond Psychoanalyst: Feminist, Marxist, Director of a Jewish Foster Home   77

4   Margarethe Hilferding: Women's Rights Activist Ahead of Her Time   79
CANDICE DUMAS

5   What Do We Know About Tatiana Rosenthal? An Interview With Leonid Kadis   104
PAMELA COOPER-WHITE AND LEONID KADIS

6 Erzsébet Farkas: An Unknown Heroine and Her Wartime Mission in a Jewish Foster Home DÓRA SZABÓ	129

PART III
Beyond the Homeland   153

7 Ludwika Karpińska-Woyczyńska: The Forgotten First Female Freudian EDYTA DEMBIŃSKA AND KRZYSZTOF RUTKOWSKI	155
8 Nic Waal: Speaking in Tongues HÅVARD FRIIS NILSEN	178
9 Barbara Low: "The Little Bit of Pioneering" or the Beginnings of British Psychoanalysis RICHARD THEISEN SIMANKE	204
10 Vilma Kovács and the Community of the Budapest School of Psychoanalysis ANNA BORGOS	223

PART IV
Beyond the Holocaust   247

11 Eugenia Sokolnicka and Sophie Morgenstern: The Intertwining of Life, Work, and Death URSULA PRAMESHUBER	249
12 Thinking Cure: Jewish Psychoanalyst Alberta Szalita, From Warsaw to New York EWA KOBYLIŃSKA-DEHE	270
13 Olga Wermer: From Galician Archives to Memory and Postmemory KLARA NASZKOWSKA	298

General Bibliography	*332*
Index	*341*

Acknowledgments

This book, *Early Women Psychoanalysts: History, Biography, and Contemporary Relevance*, was supported generously and in part by the Köhler-Stiftung Foundation and the Foundation for the Promotion of University Psychoanalysis (Stiftung zur Förderung der universitären Psychoanalyse). I want to also express my appreciation to Pamela Cooper-White, my Fulbright faculty advisor turned friend, for her insight and unwavering support. Finally, a huge thank you to my family: to Tola, to Ada, to Krysia, to Zbyszek, and to Joel.

Contributors

Anna Borgos, PhD, is a psychologist and women's historian, working as a research fellow in the Institute of Cognitive Neuroscience and Psychology, Hungary.

Pamela Cooper-White, PhD, is the Christiane Brooks Johnson Professor Emerita of Psychology and Religion at Union Theological Seminary, New York, author of *Old and Dirty Gods: Religion, Antisemitism, and the Origins of Psychoanalysis*, and co-editor of *Sabina Spielrein at the Beginnings of Psychoanalysis: Image, Thought, and Language*.

Edyta Dembińska, MD, PhD, is a senior psychiatrist, a psychodynamic and systemic psychotherapist, and an assistant professor in the Department of Psychotherapy at Jagiellonian University Medical College in Krakow, Poland.

Candice Dumas is a registered clinical psychologist based in Cape Town, South Africa, with a master of arts in clinical psychology.

Shira Dushy-Barr, MA in psychology (IPU Berlin) and in philosophy (Tel Aviv University), is a PhD student in the Psychoanalysis and Its Interfaces program at Tel Aviv University, researching aging from a psychoanalytic perspective.

Leonid Kadis is a specialist in criminal psychology and psychopathology from St. Petersburg, Russia; he is a member of the Leningrad Regional Forensic Psychiatric Team and also a psychotherapist at St. Basil the Great Center for rehabilitation of adolescent offenders.

Ewa Kobylińska-Dehe, PhD habil, is a psychoanalyst (IPA), philosopher, and cultural scientist, currently a professor at the Institute of Philosophy and Sociology of the Polish Academy of Science in Warsaw, a visiting professor at the International Psychoanalytic University in Berlin, and a member of the Frankfurt Psychoanalytic Institute.

John Launer, MD, is a family physician, family therapist, and Honorary Lifetime Consultant at the Tavistock Clinic, London UK.

Lena Magnone, PhD habil, is a research associate professor at the Institute for Slavic Studies at the University of Oldenburg, currently a visiting scholar at Paris-Sorbonne University.

Klara Naszkowska, PhD, is a cultural historian of Jewish women, founding director of the International Association for Spielrein Studies, and recipient of a Fulbright Fellowship at Union Theological Seminary in New York, currently a research fellow at Fordham University's Center for Jewish Studies.

Håvard Friis Nilsen, PhD, is a professor of social science at the University College of Ostfold, Norway, and a visiting professor at the Sigmund Freud University, Vienna.

Ursula Prameshuber, PhD, is a Jungian analyst with a background in English literature and psychology, a member of the Centro Italiano di Psicologia Analitica (CIPA) and of the International Association of Analytical Psychology (IAAP), in private practice in Rome.

Krzysztof Rutkowski, MD, PhD, is a professor of psychiatry, a senior psychiatrist, a Jungian analyst, a psychotherapy supervisor, and the Head of the Department of Psychotherapy at Jagiellonian University Medical College in Krakow, Poland.

Richard Theisen Simanke, PhD, is a professor of History and Philosophy of Psychology at the Department of Psychology of the Federal University of Juiz de Fora, Brazil.

Dóra Szabó, PhD, is a historian of psychology and psychoanalysis, and assistant lecturer at the Department of Personality and Clinical Psychology at the Pázmány Péter Catholic University (Hungary).

Ana Tomčić is a cultural historian, originally from Croatia, currently employed as a postdoctoral researcher with the project Free Clinics and a Psychoanalysis for the People (FREEPSY) at the University of Essex.

Introduction
Progressives, in Their Day and in Ours

Klara Naszkowska

The book in your hands is an edited collection of essays that emerged from the conference Sabina Spielrein and Early Female Pioneers of Psychoanalysis, organized in April 2022 by the International Association for Spielrein Studies. The event was chiefly dedicated to Spielrein, the brilliant Jewish Russian psychoanalyst, doctor, and medical scientist. Our goal was to comprehensively introduce her work and discuss its versatile, multifold tracks, many of which remain largely understudied. However, having received numerous groundbreaking proposals focused on other little-known foremothers of psychoanalysis or on neglected aspects of their work, the conference also dedicated three panels to them.

Early Women Psychoanalysts: History, Biography, and Contemporary Relevance is an in-depth exploration of 14 biographies. Each chapter reconstructs, retells, and reframes the personal and professional biography of one early psychoanalyst (born from the 1860s through the First World War), with the exception of Chapter 11, which tells the intertwined stories of Eugenia Sokolnicka and Sophie Morgenstern. Each life story in the book is unique and should be recognized as such, yet each also entwines with many other stories, sharing with them a number of themes, motives, and issues. Recurring topics and leitmotifs permeate the book, linked to issues of gender, Jewishness, women's education, politics, and migration. They are arranged into four sections to emphasize some of this interlinking. Many of the chapters include photographs that are almost unknown or even newly found.

Most recognizably, the early lives of these women, their career choices and paths, were affected, challenged, and derailed by sociopolitical circumstances and developments: the First World War, the rise of antisemitism in the interwar period, the Great Depression in the 1930s, the Second World

DOI: 10.4324/9781003455844-1

War, finally the Shoah. With the exceptions of Erzsébet Farkas and Vilma Kovács, two Hungarians, these New Women relocated often, in search of university educations, psychoanalytic training, and employment opportunities. They opted for vibrant and sociopolitically progressive intellectual centers, including Zurich, Vienna, and Berlin.

The situation of European Jews as the twentieth century gathered pace was impacted most obviously by the rise of Adolf Hitler's National Socialist German Workers' Party, the NSDAP. Only two of this book's subjects, Ludwika Karpińska-Woyczyńska and Nic Waal, were not born Jewish. The Nazi Party, bolstered by the brewing of isms in reaction to the terms of the Treaty of Versailles that had been imposed as harsh punitive measures, first gained considerable power in September 1930 after nominally democratic parliamentary elections. Shortly after Hitler was named chancellor on January 30, 1933, NSDAP policies unleashed a campaign of increasingly aggressive antisemitism, racism, and homophobia.

Nazi policies, spreading rapidly to neighboring countries, fell on fertile soil and readily took root, especially in Austria and Hungary. In the Austro-Hungarian Empire, the antisemitic Christian Social Party had already become dominant in Vienna as early as the 1890s. Party leader Karl Lueger, an influence on Hitler, was elected mayor in 1897 and held that position until his death in 1910. Following the First World War and the collapse of the Habsburg monarchy, the newly formed Austrian republic was a reduction by 90 percent from the broad-ranging extent of the empire. Within that conservative state, the capital became a socially progressive island, referred to as Red Vienna. Its tolerant norms enabled psychoanalysis to thrive as a social, cultural, and political project. Margarethe Hilferding had her practice in a working-class quarter during that period; she was only the fifth woman to receive a medical doctorate from the University of Vienna and the first to be elected a Vienna Psychoanalytic Society member. Hilferding, a social and feminist activist, is explored in Chapter 4, including her advocacy for access to contraception and abortion rights, as well as for providing medical services including sex education counseling for women.

But May 1933 marked the transition to Christian Austrofascism. Under Engelbert Dollfuss and his successor, Karl Schuschnigg, Austria was authoritarian, a one-party state. The ruling Fatherland Front party was a right-wing national-conservative organization modeled on Nazism. Regardless of the "collective amnesia" maintained in Austria through the postwar years and beyond, when German troops had marched into Vienna on March 11,

1938, to annex the country into the Third Reich, they were received with widespread and very public enthusiasm. And since early in that decade, the University of Vienna's renowned medical school, the alma mater of three of the women in this book, had been infested with antisemitism, eugenics, and exclusionary practices of racial hygiene.

After the Austro-Hungarian monarchy had been dismantled, the brief communist reign of the Hungarian Soviet Republic was led by Béla Kun. When that new regime collapsed after just four months, Kun's opponents carried out the two-year backlash now called the White Terror, a period of tortures and executions of communists, many of whom were Jews. In 1920, the conservative Kingdom of Hungary was (re)established, with Miklós Horthy as head of state. This marked the start of a rightist, Christian-nationalist regime, under which the Kingdom of Hungary gradually embraced Nazi-style anti-Jewish policies. In 1931, it aligned with the Third Reich, later joining the Axis powers during the Second World War. Both Farkas and Kovács, the Hungarian-born women focused on here, were forced to navigate this turbulent history in their country, with its increasingly antisemitic measures.

The Polish analysts, Beata "Tola" Rank, Ludwika Karpińska-Woyczyńska, Eugenia Sokolnicka, Sophie Morgenstern, Alberta Szalita, and Olga Wermer, were each born in a Poland that no longer existed as a country, with their families living in the respective partitions ruled by Russia, Prussia, and Austro-Hungary. Poland regained independence in 1918, in the aftermath of the First World War, and with the Treaty of Versailles in 1919 it received several formerly German territories: the western region around Posen (now Poznań), West Prussia near its north coast, and Upper Silesia to the south. Interwar Poland was home to the largest Jewish Ashkenazi community in the world, numbering some 2.8 million people in 1918 and 3.3 million by 1938. Both its dominant parties in this era were antisemitic: the nationalistic Sanacja (cleansing, in Polish) and the near-fascist Endecja, which advocated for expulsion of those millions of Jews. Following a May 1926 coup d'état, orchestrated by First Marshal Józef Piłsudzki, the authoritarian Sanacja regime was established, ending democratic rule. Brutal persecution of Piłsudzki's opponents started. Karpińska-Woyczyńska, the first woman to attend Freud's group meetings, was imprisoned and interrogated for weeks, accused of being a Russian spy. Though charges were dropped, the arrest deeply affected her life and career. Her story has been carefully reconstructed in Chapter 7.

In interwar Poland, the legal status of Jews was actively diminished, and economic boycotts of their businesses rose. After Piłsudzki's death, in 1935, right-wing radicalism and anti-Jewish boycott movements mounted further, with widespread violence and pogroms. Then, on September 1, 1939, Germany invaded Poland from the west, north, and south. Sixteen days later, the Soviet Union attacked, pursuing secret provisions in their Molotov-Ribbentrop Pact, signed with Germany that August, and occupied eastern Poland. By October 6, the Third Reich and the USSR had occupied or annexed all Polish territory. The Soviets also occupied Lithuania, Latvia, Estonia, and Bessarabia and northern Bukovina (now in Moldovia and Ukraine). The chapters about the Poles Wermer and Szalita also tell the story of the vibrant, multicultural, multireligious, multiethnic historic kingdoms of Galicia and Volhynia (the latter now in Ukraine), respectively, which by the end of the war had been violently transformed into the historian Timothy Snyder's "bloodlands." As well, they point to the almost untellable story of the entire interwar population of Polish Jews who perished in the Shoah, with the erasure or appropriation of their culture, customs, and religion.

The lives of Sabina Spielrein and Tatiana Rosenthal, two Russian-born analysts, both of whom would return to their homeland after living in the West, intertwine with Russia's turbulent history: the empire's fall in 1917 following the February Revolution and then Vladimir Lenin's Bolshevik Revolution that October, the brutal Civil War, and the creation of the Soviet Union in 1922. Many Bolshevik leaders were Jewish, entirely or in part, including Leon Trotsky, a supporter of psychoanalysis. In the early 1920s, the practice seemed to flourish in Bolshevik Russia. Rosenthal, until her death, in 1921, was reportedly trying to work out "a harmony" with "a combination of Freud and Marx." Spielrein also believed that "the teaching of Freud and Marx do not need to exclude each other and can co-exist perfectly well."

Following Lenin's death, in 1924, the unpredictable, paranoiac tyrant Joseph Stalin gradually took power, while the situation of Jews and of psychoanalysts deteriorated. During the cultural revolution and sociopolitical transformations as the USSR was being born, psychoanalysis served as a political-ideological tool. From the late 1920s, however, the practice came under attack; with its institutions dissolved by the early 1930s, it officially ceased to exist. The Stalinist era (1927–1953) brought the Great Purges:

mass arrests, tortures, imprisonments, and executions. Estimates show that up to one and a half million people were murdered from 1936 to 1938 by the secret police—the NKVD, precursors of the KGB. As the Great Terror peaked in 1937, scientists, wealthier citizens, and everyone suspected of disloyalty to Stalin could abruptly be declared enemies of the state and murdered. Spielrein's three brothers, Isaac, Jan, and Emil, were executed by firing squads, while her husband and father died of heart attacks. It is very likely that despite losing her family and the ban on psychoanalysis, Spielrein continued working in secret in Rostov-on-Don until her death at the hands of another aggressor, Germany, in 1942.

Many early women psychoanalysts also found themselves entangled in the Freudian movement's internal politics and conflicts. Eight years after the establishment of the Viennese Psychoanalytic Society, initially an exclusively male group and openly hostile to women's participation in medicine and science, it reluctantly accepted Hilferding as a member in April 1910. Due to her allegiance to Alfred Adler (who had supported women's membership), she was swiftly forced out in the fall of 1911. Other women were caught up in conflicts between pairs of "important" men: Beata Rank in the clash between her husband, Otto, and Freud, and Spielrein in another schism, between Carl Jung and Freud. In each case, the men involved tried forcing them to choose a side (with some success), while the women believed in possible reconciliation between the competing theorists and their theories. In another case, Sokolnicka was repeatedly refused Freud's endorsement and moral support, shunned and overlooked, despite having successfully transplanted his movement to France, as he wanted. Some among these first female analysts seemed to have internalized the misogyny of their colleagues. Some, including Beata Rank and Barbara Low, would understate their abilities and accomplishments. Others, including Karpińska-Woyczyńska, were pressured into competing with other women.

The Second World War was, in Alberta Szalita's words, "the abyss" or "the gulf" sharply dividing in half the lives of most of these Jewish women who would survive it. Regardless of how important their heritage and the Jewish religious, cultural, or familial identity components were to them, the war deeply affected their lives and often determined their fates. Hilferding and Spielrein perished in the Shoah, as did their families. Morgenstern took her own life as German forces approached Paris. In Békés, a Hungarian village, Farkas was a director of an orphanage for Jewish boys before and during the war. Rank, Szalita, and Wermer fled to the Unites States, where they contended with loss and trauma. Waal joined the Norwegian underground and was then honored as one of the Righteous among the Nations for having helped Jewish children escape German persecution and probable murder.

These daunting circumstances and other complex individual factors contributed to the fact that the women who are focused on in the coming chapters either have been left entirely out of the record, along with their contributions to psychoanalysis, or have been inadequately remembered.

The book's first section brings together chapters discussing three relatively known analysts: Sabina Spielrein, Lou Andreas-Salomé, and Beata Rank. Typically, each is remembered largely for reasons aside from their accomplishments, in connection to personal life: as someone else's wife, lover, or muse. In an attempt to flip such narratives, Ana Tomčić and John Launer introduce Spielrein's contributions to the field of medical science. They approach her work from an understudied angle, that of a scientifically oriented doctor, and position her ideas within the broad transdisciplinary context of advancing scientific thought in her time. Shira Dushy-Barr, instead of engaging with the famous-men narrative that typically hijacks Andreas-Salomé's fairly popular biography, discusses her as a profound independent thinker, with contributions to psychoanalytic theories of art. In her chapter on Rank, role-cast today as Otto's wife or as a social butterfly, Lena Magnone deploys archival materials in reconstructing her personal and professional biography. Magnone focuses on Rank modifying Freud's myth of the genesis of culture, as presented in *Totem and Taboo*, with results that can be seen as presaging feminist theories of the 1970s.

The second section sheds light on three women who, along with being psychoanalysts, took strong political stances and fought for a better future. Margarethe Hilferding's revolutionary ideas on the issues of motherhood and on her work as a women's rights activist are focused on by Candice Dumas. According to the historian Rosemary Balsam, it is only very recently that themes discussed by Hilferding in the 1910s, ranging from the absence of innate "motherly love" for an infant, destructive impulses of a new mother, and the sexual component of a mother-baby relationship, have been advanced by psychoanalysis. Then, Pamela Cooper-White interviews Leonid Kadis, who in unearthing new information about Tatiana Rosenthal's life and work has helped eliminate pervasive inaccuracies. Kadis and Cooper-White discuss Rosenthal's possible involvement with Russian politics and Marxism, which profoundly impacted her life and her decision to end it. Dóra Szabó reconstructs the story of Erzsébet Farkas, the entirely unacknowledged psychoanalytically-oriented who ran a foster home for Jewish boys from 1938 to 1942, in deeply antisemitic Hungary before it succumbed to German pressure. Szabó's chapter discusses the physically, mentally, and emotionally harrowing work, risks that Farkas took, and her postwar life.

The third section presents four biographies of psychoanalysts who played crucial roles in the early Freudian movement, but are now unknown beyond their home countries. While Hilferding is typically remembered for her "first" in joining the Freud circle's male membership, Ludwika Karpińska-Woyczyńska has too easily been left out of the record, though she was the first woman attending that circle's meetings. Her story is reconstructed utilizing archival information and her professional contributions by Edyta Dembińska and Krzysztof Rutkowski. After Karpińska-Woyczyńska fell victim to political circumstances in Poland's interwar shift to authoritarianism, her accomplishments then fell prey to the general erasure of psychoanalysis in communist-era Poland, where the field was seen as an "imperialist and bourgeois ideology," in Paweł Dybel's words. Håvard Friis Nilsen devotes his chapter to Nic Waal, yet another intellectually independent breaker of social mores. Waal, among the first Norwegian analysts, has remained acknowledged only in her native country yet merits broad recognition. Richard Theisen Simanke illuminates the overall accomplishments of Barbara Low, the first female analyst in the United Kingdom, who has remained too simply remembered for originating the Nirvana principle. Finally, Anna Borgos discusses the contributions of Vilma Kovács, a first-generation Hungarian analyst, a model New Woman as a strong-willed, educated professional and a divorcée in an epoch when that status ruffled the feathers of so-called good society. Borgos opens her chapter by examining the women-friendly psychoanalytic movement in Hungary and with brief biographies of the analysts Lilly Hajdu, Edit Gyömrői, and Alice Bálint.

The book's final section touches on issues of contemporary migration and exile. The intertwined lives of Eugenia Sokolnicka and Sophie Morgenstern, two psychoanalysts who worked in Paris, are explored by Ursula Prameshuber, including the impact their status had on them, after immigrating there from Poland. Ewa Kobylińska-Dehe tells of the Polish analyst Alberta Szalita, who was stranded in wartime Soviet Russia after her family was annihilated, then attempted to return home after the war and decided to immigrate to New York City. In her work, Szalita was among the very few mental-health professionals able to promptly take up Holocaust-related issues, specifically grief and bereavement. The concluding chapter is about Olga Wermer, who left for the US three weeks before Germany's invasion struck Poland, her home. Using long-overlooked archival materials, I reconstruct Wermer's familial, religious, and educational background, and track her career path, to provide insights into her relations with the past, her Jewish identity, and revealing aspects of her emigration experience.

These intertwining stories are complex, multilayered, multifaceted. They are stories both of success and of failure, of loss, rejection, reestablishment, of boldness and of bravery and of fighting for women's rights and children's safety, against Nazi Germany and against less militarized oppressors. Often for the bare needs of survival, then for recognition. Then for memory, and for postmemory.

The latter aspect is where our work comes in, and that of like-minded colleagues, and of interested readers. Many more women still merit our attention and deserve to be remembered. To end the book, and to extend and connect the results presented here, you'll find a bibliography of publications that address others among the first women psychoanalysts who are not subjects of book chapters but whose lives and works matter.

This book stems from my deep conviction that we can foster social and ethical change through taking responsibility for the past and through refocusing how we manage the education of it. Antisemitism and other forms of racism, gender violence, immigration laws, and the mental-health system remain red-hot topics. The past decade has seen history repeating itself in many places, including Poland, Hungary, India, Turkey, Brazil, Egypt, Italy, and Venezuela. Reemerging autocrats seem to be reading from the same playbook for hateful human-rights abuse and undemocratic strictures. This may be most notable in Russia's unprovoked war against Ukraine. In Poland, my home country, the rule of the right-wing nationalist Law and Justice Party (PIS) continues to replace constitutional democracy with an authoritarian one-party state. They undermine Poland's democratic institutions—the independence of judiciary and media and free and fair elections—and denounce LGBTQ+ rights. With the support from the nation's top court, the politically compromised Constitutional Tribunal, the PIS government approved a near-total abortion ban. When Belarus orchestrated a migration crisis in 2021, forcing Middle Eastern and African refugees out of Belarus, Polish authorities blocked the borders and prevented humanitarian aid organizations and individuals from helping. A year later, white, Christian Ukrainian refugees fleeing the war were greeted effusively.

In the US, recent years have shown that autocracy is possible here, too, where white supremacy is as prominent as it is endemic. And where far too many must endure inhumane immigration laws, xenophobia, antisemitism, racism, and misogyny, all of which mirror the experience of asylum seekers navigating the both Trump- and Biden-era immigration policies, and some 10.5 million undocumented immigrants living in the States today. Finally, *Early Women Psychoanalysts: History, Biography, and Contemporary Relevance* discusses individual and collective struggles to cope with trauma and loss. Once specific area of growing importance is the condition of mental-health care in the US, in its inaccessibility and in the deleterious role that structural racism has for so many people with daily needs. These are of grave relevance now, more than ever, in post-COVID reality, and they are reflected in the endeavors and in the needs of women recalled in these chapters.

At last, this book grew out of the realization that we are all at risk of becoming indifferent. Marian Turski, historian, journalist, and Shoah survivor, puts it powerfully in his speech given at the 75th anniversary of the liberation of the Auschwitz-Birkenau concentration camp, on January 27, 2020:

> Thou shall not be indifferent in the face of lies about history. Thou shall not be indifferent when the past is distorted for today's political needs. Thou shall not be indifferent when any minority faces discrimination. [. . .] Thou shall not be indifferent when any authority violates the existing social contract. [. . .] Because if you *are* indifferent, you will not even notice it when upon your own heads, and upon the heads of your descendants, another Auschwitz falls from the sky.
>
> Klara Naszkowska

Part I
Beyond Wife, Lover, Muse

Chapter 1

Sabina Spielrein
Pioneer of Medical Science

Ana Tomčić and John Launer

Since her death in the Holocaust, the Russian psychoanalyst and psychiatrist Sabina Spielrein (1885–1942) has been the subject of a remarkable succession of historical evaluations, reinventions, and reassessments. For around 40 years after her murder by the Nazis, she was virtually forgotten, except for her appearance in a footnote to Sigmund Freud's *Beyond the Pleasure Principle*, where he acknowledged her influence in ambivalent terms (Freud, 2001/1920, p. 55). Following the publication of the Freud–Jung letters in 1974 (McGuire, 1974), and then a selection of her own diaries and letters in the 1980s (Carotenuto, 1986), attention became focused on the erotic relationship she had with Carl Jung, who had been her hospital psychiatrist when she was in her late teens, and then her university mentor and supervisor. Contrary to common belief, it is arguable whether Jung carried out psychoanalysis on her in any meaningful sense (Graf-Nold, 2001; Minder, 2001; Launer, 2015). Her image as a *femme fatale* continues in popular culture to this day, in movies, in drama, and on websites. Since the turn of the twenty-first century, however, scholars have increasingly claimed a place for Spielrein as a key figure in early psychoanalytic thinking whose contributions significantly influenced Freud, Jung, and probably many others, including Anna Freud, Melanie Klein, and Sándor Ferenczi. Her writings are now recognized as highly prescient, anticipating more recent psychoanalytic thinkers like Jean Laplanche (Harris, 2019, p. 155).

In this chapter, we propose a further evolution in our collective understanding of Spielrein: as a rigorous, well-informed, and original medical scientist, whose contributions to psychoanalysis were made in a wider context of the advancing scientific thought of her time. Our view is based on her writings, but it also fits with the trajectory of her career. Spielrein first became engaged with psychoanalysis while a medical student, at a time when psychoanalysis was dominated by doctors and had only just begun to distinguish itself from Freud's original specialty of neurology and Jung's vocation in inpatient psychiatry. Her grounding at medical school was in the demanding scientific tradition of the German-speaking countries. For her final medical exam, she wrote an essay on puerperal sepsis, a life-threatening infection arising in the mother's genital tract following childbirth (Richebächer, 2008, pp. 159–169). The First World War broke out not long after she qualified, and she supported herself during that time by doing ophthalmology and general surgery.

Spielrein's first substantive institutional role was at the Rousseau Institute in Geneva in the early 1920s. It had been founded by the leading educationalist Edouard Claparède. Claparède started out as a natural scientist and laid the foundations of an approach to education that came to be known as "functionalist." It was in essence evolutionary. In Claparède's own words, he examined aspects of psychology "from the point of view of their role in life, their place within the overall behavior pattern at any given moment"

Figure 1.1 Sabina Spielrein, her parents, Eva and Nikolai, and brothers, Emil, Isaac, and Jan. Rostov-on-Don, 1909.

Reproduced with permission of Vladimir Shpilrain and the Spielrein Estate.

(Hameline, 1993, p. 162). He continued: "It amounts to asking what use they are for. After wondering what sleep is for, I tried to see what childhood is for, what intelligence was for, what the will was for" (p. 162). It was an entirely evolutionary manifesto, and it was one the Institute was centered on. While there, Spielrein worked closely with Jean Piaget (and also psychoanalyzed him). His own initial interest had been in biology rather than psychology, and he completed his doctoral dissertation on the evolution of mollusks. He shared with Spielrein an interest in childhood and the development of thought. They each saw how important it was for psychologists and psychoanalysts to learn from one another, and they did so within an overarching framework of evolutionary theory. Both Claparède and Piaget were sympathetic to psychoanalysis to an extent, but the focus of the Institute was on the study and teaching of developmental psychology.

Spielrein's work when she returned to Russia in 1923 reflected the same scientific interests. She worked not only in the State Psychoanalytic Institute but also at the First Moscow University and in pedology—an emerging discipline that combined medical, psychological, and educational approaches to the care of children. Although she continued to contribute to the psychoanalytic literature and (possibly) to see patients into the 1930s, her main occupation once she returned to her home town of Rostov-on-Don for the last 17 years of her life was as a pedologist. Thus, to characterize Spielrein as first and foremost a psychoanalyst may be more a consequence of the historiography that has developed around her rather than necessarily how she was seen by her contemporaries or indeed how she characterized herself. For example, in a questionnaire she completed in 1923, she listed her experience as follows:

> I worked in the Zürich Psychiatric Clinic (with Professor Bleuler) and in a domestic clinic (with Professor Eichhorst) but when I don't recall. I began to do research very early on, partly on topics I chose myself, partly on the topics proposed by Profs. Bleuler and Jung. Apart from my own work, I worked in a psychiatric clinic with Professor Bleuler, in a psychoneurological clinic with Professor Bonhöffer (Berlin) and in psychoanalysis with Doctor Jung in Zürich and Professor Freud in Vienna. In Munich I worked on mythology, and the history of art, and as a teaching-doctor in psychology in the Rousseau Institute of Professor Claparède in Geneva.
>
> (Ovcharenko, 1999, pp. 364–365)

If we approach Spielrein's work as that of a scientifically oriented doctor rather than solely as a pioneering psychoanalyst, what we find in her texts is somewhat different from what we might have expected. This is particularly the case in relation to two scientific fields: evolutionary theory and neurologically grounded linguistics. In the sections that follow, we examine her explorations of these fields, first with an overview of her thinking on evolution, followed by a more detailed consideration of her contributions to linguistics and neurology.

Spielrein as Evolutionist

While Jung and Freud had quite a good understanding of evolution for their time, they wanted to show that the laws of psychoanalysis were of a wider scope than those of biology. Therefore (especially in their later careers) they rejected attempts to combine psychoanalytic and evolutionary knowledge in potentially productive ways. Spielrein, on the other hand, was intent on doing just that. Her writings are shot through with signals that her wish was to anchor psychoanalysis within a biological and evolutionary framework. This is evident from early on in her career, and perhaps most strikingly in her best-known paper, "Destruction as the Cause of Coming into Being" (Spielrein, 2015a/1912).

The Destruction paper is her account of the inseparable relationship between sex and death, or what appears in her letters to Jung as a combined "sexual instinct–death instinct" (Carotenuto, 1986, p. 58). It can be read in many ways. As Adrienne Harris has pointed out, Spielrein throws out tantalizing hints, allusions or flashes of extraordinary perception that open up avenues of thinking that she does not explore fully herself but has left to others to do so (Harris, 2019, pp. 154–155). However, one of the themes that she spells out quite explicitly in her paper is a biological one. Indeed, the first section is headed simply "Biological facts." In it, she examines the power of the reproductive drive, emphasizing how people are drawn by an "inflexible urgency" (Spielrein, 2015a/1912, p. 186) to do something they do not want to do, even at the cost of immediate disappointment or disgust afterwards. She refers to the unavoidable dilemma, which all humans face, between ensuring their own individual survival and securing the continuity of their line through procreation. Most daringly, in the context of the psychoanalytic field of her time, she contradicts Sigmund Freud by speaking explicitly of reproduction rather than pleasure as our primary drive.

When Spielrein delivered an early version of the Destruction paper to the Vienna Psychoanalytic Society in November 1911, Freud and Jung had absolutely no doubt what she was attempting to do: to conceptualize psychoanalysis in biological terms. Both men profoundly opposed this idea. Indeed, Freud contradicted her in the discussion as soon as she had finished her presentation, as recorded in the minutes: "A psychological hypothesis," he stated, "must be determined by way of individual psychological investigation [. . .] however the speaker attempted to base the theory of instincts on biological presuppositions" (Nunberg and Federn, 1975, pp. 329–331). He reiterated the same point in a letter to Jung: "What troubles me most," he wrote, "is that Fräulein Spielrein wants to subordinate the psychological material to *biological* considerations; this dependency is no more acceptable than a dependence on philosophy, physiology or brain anatomy. PsA *fara da se*" (McGuire, 1974, p. 468, original emphasis). Jung replied, "I know of course that Spielrein operates too much with biology. But she didn't learn that from me. It is home-grown" (McGuire, 1974, p. 470). Spielrein, for her own part, apologized at the end of the evening for not having made the biological fundamentals of her argument clearer. Naively, she thought it would have made a difference.

In the published version of her paper (1912), Spielrein spoke of reproduction in the context of the psychological exploration of sexual masochism, clearly from her own personal experience of this:

> Do we not possess powerful drives that set our psychic contents in motion, untroubled by the welfare and misery of the ego? [. . .] I must dogmatically defend the viewpoint that the personal psyche is governed by unconscious impulses that lie deeper and, in their demands, are unconcerned with our feeling reactions. Pleasure is merely the affirmative reaction of the ego to these demands flowing from the depths.
> (Spielrein, 2015a/1912, p. 189)

In other words, the instinct for sex and reproduction comes first, even at the expense of huge risks. Pleasure is simply the lure that makes this level of risk acceptable.

Bearing in mind his earlier reaction, it may seem surprising that Freud's views on pleasure and the reproductive instinct underwent a radical shift only a couple of years later. When he first became acquainted with Spielrein's ideas, Freud still considered the pleasure principle to be the primary

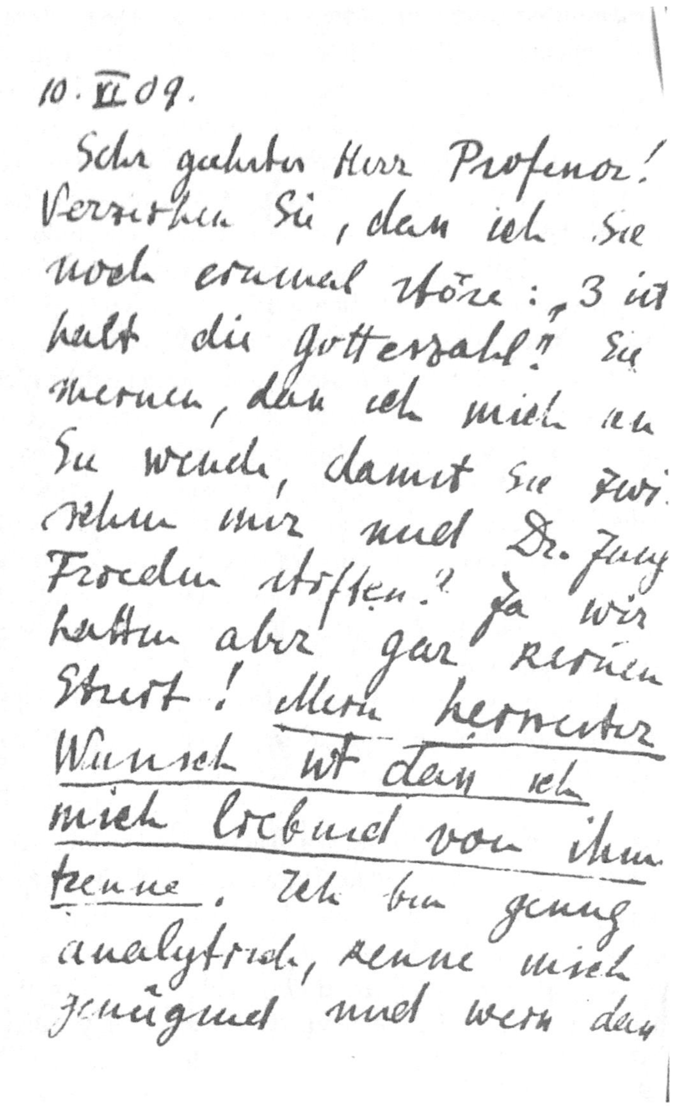

Figure 1.2 Letter from Sabina Spielrein to Sigmund Freud, June 10, 1909.
Reproduced with permission of Vladimir Shpilrain and the Spielrein Estate.

force in determining the individual's actions. However, by 1914, his views had edged much closer to Spielrein's. In his 1914 discussion of narcissism, for instance, we find the following statement:

> The individual does carry on a twofold existence: one to serve his own purposes and the other as a link in a chain, which he serves against his will, or at least involuntarily. The individual himself regards sexuality as one of his own ends; whereas from another point of view he is an appendage of his germ-plasm, at whose disposal he puts his energies in return for a bonus of pleasure.
> (Freud, 1957/1914, p. 78)

Here, we see Freud beginning to move "beyond the pleasure principle" and acknowledging, like Spielrein did before him, that there are more powerful drives related to sexuality (and the preservation of the species) that guide individual decisions. To what extent this change was motivated by Spielrein is difficult to say, but the Destruction paper may have been an important influence.

What is more, no modern evolutionary scholar would disagree with Spielrein's claim. Indeed, it is one of the fundamental principles of modern biology. The contemporary "Neo-Darwinist synthesis" is well summed up by the evolutionary scholar Barbara Low (not to be confused with the early psychoanalyst of the same name featured in Chapter 9 in this book):

> All living organisms have evolved to seek and use resources to enhance their reproductive success. They strive for matings, invest in children or help other genetic relatives, and build genetically profitable relationships. In biology, this is not a controversial proposition, and it follows that organisms will act as though they are able to calculate costs and benefits.
> (Low, 2001, p. xiii)

It is worth noting that evolutionists nowadays universally reject the idea of "genetic determinism" (i.e., the idea that our genes determine our fate). All recognize the constraints and opportunities for choice that arise from the interactions of a person's inherited constitution, development, and environment, just as most psychoanalysts would.

There are flaws in Spielrein's biological reasoning presented in the Destruction paper, both in terms of the evolutionary thought of her time and subsequently (Launer, 2014a, pp. 835–836). In spite of this, she succeeded in locating some essential truths about reproduction, sexuality, and the human mind that now lie at the center of evolutionary studies. She recognized the inseparable connection between death and sex: essentially, sex is irresistible only because death is inescapable. She realized that reproduction involves as much conflict between the sexes as it does love and collaboration. She knew that women and men have different reproductive interests that correspond with their different biological contributions to procreation, and these differences may be reflected in their feelings and behavior. She understood the tension in human lives between the pursuit of procreation and that of survival, a core concept in evolution that is now framed in terms of "trade-offs." Above all, she understood that the talking therapies would make no sense unless they could be harmonized with a theory that had earned—and still earns—almost universal credibility. Incidentally, it was this harmonization between biology and psychoanalysis that her own psychiatrist and mentor from the Burghölzli Clinic in Zurich, Eugen Bleuler, had devoutly wished for. Bleuler's disappointment over Freud's dogmatism in this respect was the reason he resigned from the Vienna Psychoanalytic Society. Whether by coincidence or not, he did so on the day that Spielrein delivered her Destruction paper.

Spielrein never articulated in writing a comprehensive vision of how psychoanalysis and evolutionary thinking might be harmonized. But she did indicate very clearly in two other places the direction of travel of her own ideas. One was in her final correspondence with Jung between 1917 and 1919. One of the main themes of Spielrein's later letters to Jung was her wish to tackle him on the differences between his approach to the mind and those of Freud and Adler. She tried to explore whether their three different views might be different perspectives on the same realities. She raised the possibility that the fundamental principles that Darwin set out might underlie the different drives that each of them described. She was, in effect, proposing an overarching biological theory that would make sense at a scientific level higher than any of the three men's personal and inductive systems. Putting forward her own view of their similarities, Spielrein wrote:

> Natural history recognizes only two drives, the drive for self-preservation and the drive for the preservation of the species. [. . .] To express my personal view, I would regard the instinct for self-preservation as contained within the instinct for the preservation of the species. [. . .] The need to

survive is thus inseparable from the need to die and be reborn again. At first, the instinct for self-preservation goes alongside the instinct for the preservation of the species. With tiny creatures you cannot yet say whether, for example, they love the mother's breast because it satisfies the need for nourishment, or whether this love is already so emancipated that the baby loves the breast "physically" for its own sake, or—what I think likeliest—because it satisfies hunger while providing warmth and calm. Thus, physical contact becomes pleasurable, and this is already the beginning of sexual feeling. And the feeling of power? What is it except the need to draw more love and attention to oneself? And the feeling of insufficiency? You suffer from a sense of inferiority if as a result you feel you have less right to recognition and love. Then you cannot survive and you also cannot procreate.

(Carotenuto, 1986, p. 141)

She is arguing here that all drives, whether for power, for love, for nourishment, or for warmth and peace, serve one single purpose: what she refers to (using Darwin's own language) as "the preservation of the species." Modern evolutionists would emphasize the preservation of genes through natural selection rather than species as such, but Spielrein's argument would also be valid in that context.

Some of what she says about the infant's desire for the breast, and for maternal attachment, anticipated the thinking of later psychoanalysts such as Anna Freud, Melanie Klein, and John Bowlby. In fact, Spielrein went further than any of them. She was arguing that all behavior is ultimately driven by the reproductive instinct, an idea that is increasingly favored among evolutionary thinkers today (for instance in the work of the evolutionary ecologist James Chisholm, 1999). From the perspective of modern biology, what she wrote was absolutely correct. Humans need to make conscious or unconscious decisions at different stages in their lives about whether to invest their energies and resources in self-preservation or procreation, but both impulses serve the same ends. To put it simply, we are all the descendants of an unbroken line of ancestors who made the right decisions in order to both survive and be able to reproduce or to invest in other ways in the well-being of our kin. Otherwise, not a single one of us would be here. There were parts of Spielrein's argument in these letters that were flawed too. She tried to fit parts of Jung's thinking into her schema in a way that would neither have satisfied him nor have made sense in Darwinian terms. Yet what she was doing was still enormously impressive: looking for commonalities rather than differences between the different emerging schools of psychoanalysis, and unity among them rather than exclusion. In this sense, Spielrein's efforts are reminiscent of Margarethe Hilferding, the first woman to join the Vienna Psychoanalytic Society, who also made an (unsuccessful) attempt at combining Adler's and Freud's thinking (about Margarethe Hilferding, see Chapter 4 in this book).

The other place where Spielrein demonstrates her grasp of evolutionary theory and her adherence to it as a framework for understanding human psychology is in her paper on the origin of the words "Papa" and "Mama," one of her most significant achievements (Spielrein, 2015b/1922). The paper goes far beyond addressing the origin of these two words. Indeed, it covers the entire nature of language and its relationship to the growth of the mind. What is most impressive here is her view of the reciprocal relationship between parental attachment, feelings, language, and cognition. Once again, her framework is explicitly an evolutionary one.

Spielrein describes in it how nature and nurture interact by explaining how mothers "encourage their children to develop the speech mechanisms for which they are prepared by heredity" (Spielrein, 2015b/1922, p. 235). The influences that help the child learn to speak are primed genetically and through selectively evolved neurological patterns. These are then reactivated in each generation by interaction with a mother whose behavioral instincts reflect back what she recalls from her own childhood. It is difficult to find anywhere a more accurate, or more subtle, account of the interplay between evolutionary selection and the growing child's environment than the following, from the "Papa and Mama" paper:

> Does the child himself make his language, or is it simply handed down from adults? In my opinion, this question should be formulated differently, thus: is the child by natural inclination a social being who has a need to communicate? If it has inherited a need to communicate, and if it belongs among people who speak, then it has inherited a need for language which leads it both to seek it and to invent it. Of course, the adults come to the aid of the young mind in its struggle; through their own talking and mimicry in the child's presence, they encourage it to develop the speech mechanisms for which it has been prepared by heredity; mothers and nurses adapt themselves instinctively to the kind of language that the child is ready to produce; they feel into the child's psyche, finding material in the depths of

Figure 1.3 Sabina Spielrein at the Rousseau Institute, Geneva, 1921.
Copyright: Archives Institut Jean-Jacques Rousseau (AIJJR).

their own minds, in their own earlier stages of development, and allowing this to speak to the child in an unconscious way.

(Spielrein, 2015b/1922, p. 235)

It is a wonderful passage, which clearly shows Spielrein's characteristic depth of feeling and insight and her directness of expression. But it also represents an extraordinary intellectual achievement: linking the subjectivity of psychoanalytic insight with a rigorous understanding of the objective biological processes by which this subjectivity is generated. In this sense, the "Papa and Mama" paper is representative of the mature phase in Spielrein's work, which was also characterized by the flourishing of her interest in neurology and child linguistics.

Spielrein, Linguistics, and Neurology

Although there have been some successful attempts to examine the later stages of Spielrein's career (Vidal, 2001; Santiago-Delafosse and Delafosse, 2002; Noth, 2015; Naszkowska, 2019; Caropreso, 2020; Faluvégi, 2021), the main focus among scholars is still on the Destruction paper. The reason for this unbalanced account is twofold. First, the paper was produced in the wake of the Freud/Jung controversy, which remains the most widely known part of Spielrein's biography. Second, Spielrein's mature work is more strictly medical than psychoanalytic and, to some extent, lacks the philosophical, artistic allure of the Destruction paper. Nevertheless, Spielrein's contribution to neurology and child linguistics is so important and original that, had it been given the credit it is due, it would have been proclaimed a key chapter in the history of linguistics and neurology (aphasiology in particular). In child linguistics, Spielrein explained language development through a combination of evolutionary and environmental factors. She grounded psychoanalytic terms in neurology by associating them with various parts of the brain, for example conscious functions with the cortex and the subconscious with subcortical regions (2019b/1931, pp. 331–332). Finally, she successfully combined neurological theories which explained speech disorders in terms of centers and pathways with those that looked at the brain's evolutional, chronological development. It was primarily this Spielrein that influenced thinkers like Jean Piaget, Lev Vygotsky, and Alexander Luria, rather than the Spielrein of the Destruction paper.

Spielrein's approach to language is close to what we might today call neurolinguistics. Perhaps this will strike some readers as peculiar in an early-twentieth-century scientist. In fact, the combination of linguistics, evolution, and neurology was not unique to Spielrein, but was fairly common among authors whose works she consulted. Consequently, Spielrein's neurological studies cannot be understood without first examining contemporary linguistic research.

The nineteenth century saw the establishment of linguistics as an independent science. This enabled a discovery that had vast ramifications in the fields of anthropology, biology, and psychology (including psychoanalysis): the exposition of the Indo-European language family, namely the idea that the peoples of India, the majority of Europe, and the Iranian plateau had common ancestry and had once spoken the same language. The discovery provoked a revival of interest in the original language of humankind. Artists and scientists began to wonder what this first language looked like and how humans came to speak at all. Between the 1860s and the 1880s, two main theories were fiercely contested and defended in linguistic circles: the origin of language from reflex sounds used to express emotions (various types of screams, cries, etc.) or alternatively from onomatopoeic sounds (sounds that imitate those present in nature). The same discussions resurfaced in the early twentieth century in the newly established branch of child linguistics, which studied the development of language and thought in young children. Here too it was predominantly claimed that the child's first words were either onomatopoetic or emotional in origin. What, then, was the connection between nineteenth-century studies on the origin of language and early-twentieth-century research into children's acquisition of their mother tongue?

The answer lies in a scientific concept that dominated nineteenth- and early-twentieth-century thought: Ernst Haeckel's theory of recapitulation. The seminal role of Darwin's evolution in Spielrein's oeuvre has already been discussed. Fewer scholars have observed the importance of Haeckel in Spielrein's approach to language and neurology.[1]

In the 1860s, the German biologist posited the claim that the development of the embryo in the womb repeats (recapitulates) the key evolutionary stages of that species. For instance, a human embryo would go through stages in which it resembled a fish or an amphibian, a reptile, a bird, and another mammal before finally assuming human form. Haeckel's famous formula "ontogeny (individual development) recapitulates phylogeny (species development)" had an immense influence on nineteenth- and early-twentieth-century science. Although discredited today, in Spielrein's time, recapitulation theory was almost universally accepted and was often fused with Darwinian ideas.

Within child linguistics, recapitulation was reflected in the claim that, as Spielrein put it, "the ancestor sleeps within the child" (2015b/1922, p. 235). The child's acquisition of language was seen as a reflection of how language was originally invented by humankind. Out of the linguists Spielrein quoted in her articles, recapitulation was most prominently discussed in the works of Clara and William Stern and Wilhelm Ament, whose books on child language were published in 1907 and 1899 respectively (she refers to these authors in Spielrein, 2015b/1922, pp. 235, 237, 240). Ament argued, "Haeckel's biogenetic law can be applied not only to the physical development of living beings, but also to the evolution of spoken language. The ontogenetic development of language is a brief repetition of phylogenetic development" (Ament, 1912/1899, p. 41).[2] The Sterns too agreed that child language recapitulates the initial stages of language acquisition in humans (Stern and Stern, 1907, p. 266). Crucially, analogies between child language and the original verbal expressions of humankind were also suggested by medical doctors studying speech disorders and brain anatomy, most prominently by Adolf Kussmaul (1885) and Hermann Gutzmann (1899). Psychologists and pedagogists researching children's behavior eagerly took up the studies written by doctors and neurologists. The consequence was a body of work that combined a neuro-medical, linguistic, and observational-pedagogical approach to children's thought and language. Spielrein and her Swiss collaborators at the Rousseau Institute in Geneva were very much a part of this trend.

References to recapitulation can be traced in two seminal papers Spielrein produced during her stay at the Rousseau Institute: "The Origin of the Child's Words Papa and Mama" (1922) and "Some Analogies between Thinking in Children, Aphasia and the Subconscious Mind" (1923). In both papers, Spielrein expressed agreement with the linguists who located the origins of language in reflex and onomatopoeic sounds. In the first paper, she refers to the historical origins of language: "We know a lot of theories for the origin of words of which it seems to me the reflex and onomatopoeic theories deserve the most consideration" (2015b/1922, p. 238). In her article on aphasia, on the other hand, she argued that the use of words as symbols distinct from objects is a skill that the child, like "primitive peoples" (2019a/1923, p. 301), only acquires in the course of its development. She then stated that, in the young child, the first words are reflexes and onomatopoeic phenomena (p. 301). Thus, in Spielrein's linguistic research of the early 1920s, the ontogenetic growth of the child's linguistic capacity was also a reflection of phylogenesis: reflex and onomatopoeic sounds formed the initial stage of the child's linguistic development *because* they constituted the beginning of the linguistic history of humankind.

Spielrein's reference to "primitive peoples" in the paper on aphasia might make us wonder about the political implications of the comparison between children and "primitive" societies. In order to answer this question fully, we first need to clarify what Spielrein meant by "primitive." In the early twentieth century, the adjective was generally used to refer to two things: our distant ancestors or contemporary nonindustrial nations. It is therefore crucial to stress that when Spielrein spoke of "primitive peoples," she referred exclusively to ancient communities, *not*—as some of her fellow psychoanalysts did—to nonindustrial cultures of the early twentieth century. In linguistics too, she refused the idea that the languages of other nations reflected the current state of their thought processes. In a paper on time in subliminal thought, for instance, she mentioned speaking to Charles Bally, a famous linguist residing in Geneva, who told her that there were some languages that did not possess a linear concept of time (according to Spielrein a characteristic of conscious thought). Spielrein was quick to note that this did not mean that the speakers of these languages did not have a fully developed concept of time. "Language," she explained, "is always more archaic than thought and preserves ways of thinking which we have long overcome" (2019c/1923, p. 286). Thus, for Spielrein, the characteristics of the world's languages were not an indication of the developmental level attained by their speakers, but merely a window into ancestral modes of thought.

But in what way did the child inherit the capacity to repeat the linguistic development of its ancestors? Spielrein and her forerunners thought that behaviors repeated in the course of generations eventually become inscribed into species memory. In her article on aphasia, she spoke of behaviors which we carry in ourselves as "acquired experience, organized, stabilized, organic I would say, as in the case of an instinct" (2019a/1923, p. 312). Initially acquired experiences, then, could cause permanent changes in the organism (become organic) and be transferred to future generations as instincts.[3] This was how the child inherited the desire for language as well as the drive to imitate the speech of people in its surroundings (2015b/1922, p. 235).

Today this might strike us as a rather Lamarckian idea: the French botanist and zoologist Jean-Baptiste Lamarck believed in the inheritance of acquired characteristics and learned behaviors, whereas Darwin claimed that the variations in nature were chance events and that those who happened to be best adapted to the environment survived. Although these two theories might seem incompatible to modern evolutionists, we must remember that, in Spielrein's time, such divisions were far from clear-cut and that Darwin himself at times spoke favorably of the inheritance of acquired characteristics.[4] While twenty-first-century scholars may not subscribe to recapitulation or even the inheritance of learned behaviors, they would certainly agree that humankind's linguistic evolution has left pathways in the brain which prepare the child for language acquisition.

Spielrein's studies of child language formed the basis of her neurological research into speech disorders. As we saw, her interest in neurology began while at medical school, where she assisted Jung in his association experiments. It developed during her work at a psychoneurological clinic in Berlin and culminated at the Rousseau Institute in Geneva, where her research was supported by Éduard Claparède. Here too, she showed great originality and ingenuity in uniting opposing schools of thought. Before we explain this in more detail, however, we need to give a brief outline of the medical context Spielrein was working in.

In the second half of the nineteenth century, a large number of neurologists believed in centers for reading, writing, and speaking located in various regions of the brain and connected by neural pathways. In 1861, in a suburban hospital for mental illness in Paris, the French anatomist Paul Broca was put in charge of a patient who suffered from extreme difficulties in producing articulated speech. He could only utter a single repeated syllable ("tan tan"). Following the patient's death, autopsy revealed extensive damage to the left posterior frontal lobe, which would later become known as Broca's area. Broca concluded that the correlation between the impaired function and physical brain damage could lead to the localization of a center responsible for that function. In other words, Broca's area would be the cerebral location of speech articulation. The question remained how a functional relationship between various centers was established. Karl Wernicke (whose name later became associated with another type of aphasia) provided an answer in terms of underlying pathways. In 1885, Louis Lichtheim expanded and systematized Wernicke's model and produced accessible diagrams that had a great didactic value but triggered fierce debates in the scientific world (cf. Graves, 2009, pp. 3–10). The localizationists—as adherents of this model are sometimes called—argued that brain injury causes either a destruction of "images" (visual, auditory, or motor representations of words) related to one center or a disconnection between various centers, creating a disturbance at one or both ends. For instance, in motor aphasia, either a destruction of motor images (images which tell us how speech organs should move in order to pronounce a word) takes place or the connection of motor images with other centers is ruptured.

Their view was disputed by scientists who favored an evolutionary approach to the mind. The evolutionists depicted language and thought as the product of the cooperation between evolutionarily earlier and later brain regions. The British neurologist John Hughlings Jackson was one of the first advocates of this model. He argued for a hierarchical brain structure, in which the cortex was the highest evolutionary level of the nervous system, which had the task of controlling the lower regions. In case of brain damage, the highest mental functions were the first to be affected. This resulted in the emergence of what psychoanalysts would call subconscious processes (cf. Jackson, 1884, pp. 660–663). Jackson's theory was upheld by the Russian scientist Constantin von Monakow, who developed his own evolutionary brain anatomy independently of Jackson. In her paper on aphasia, Spielrein stressed that Jackson and Monakow developed along similar lines without

MOTOR APHASIA ACCORDING TO LOCALIZATIONISTS

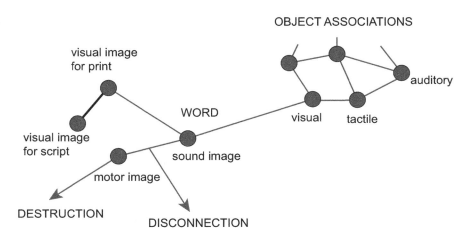

Figure 1.4 Motor aphasia (Broca's aphasia) according to the localizationists.
Image by Ana Tomčić (adapted from Freud's monograph on aphasia and Forrester, 1980, p. 73).

being aware of each other's work (2019a/1923, p. 314). Monakow shared some of Spielrein's sociocultural background: originally from Russia, he spent most of his scientific career in Zurich and even worked for a time at the Burghölzli Clinic. Spielrein was actually briefly his patient before she was admitted to the Burghölzli, but he considered her case too complex to be treated at his hospital (Launer, 2014b, pp. 26, 261).

Another fierce critic of the localizationist model was Henry Head, who worked with World War I soldiers who had suffered brain injury. What Head noticed was that nearly all of his patients (irrespective of the type of aphasia they were diagnosed with) could carry out operations demanding imitation, but difficulties arose when they needed to formulate a written or spoken statement themselves (Head, 1920, p. 98). Head concluded, "the more abstract the proposition, the more likely is the patient to fail" (p. 119). This was due to the fact that, evolutionarily speaking, the capacity for imitation developed earlier than abstract reasoning. In case of brain injury, imitation was thus more likely to remain intact. What the evolutionists shared was therefore the belief that, in aphasia, several linguistic functions (e.g., reading, writing, speech, or comprehension) regressed from the later acquired mechanisms of adult language (also referred to by some as direct,

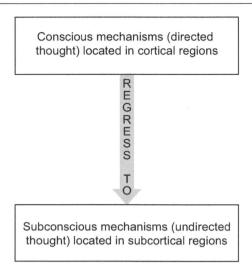

Figure 1.5 Motor aphasia (Broca's aphasia) according to the evolutionists. Image by Ana Tomčić.

verbal, or conscious thought) to the earlier modes of reasoning typical of children, which would later become subconscious in the adult. As we will see, Spielrein's explanation of aphasia had much in common with the views of these scientists.

In her 1923 paper on the similarities between aphasia, the subconscious, and child thought, Spielrein clearly expressed her agreement with the evolutionists:

> these are not the pure aphasias [. . .], but are mixed with alexia (an inability to read, of cerebral origin), agraphia (an inability to write, of cerebral origin), etc. In these cases, we find the same problems as are found in the domain of spoken language. This in fact supports Jackson, Monakow, Head, and their adherents. My own personal observations also appear to support these authors.
>
> (2019a/1923, p. 314)

For Jackson, Monakow, and Head, therefore, brain damage in aphasia nearly always affected more than one "center." For them, as for Spielrein, *all* of the patient's linguistic and cognitive mechanisms (reading, writing, speech, and even drawing) regressed to a lower evolutionary level. The patient's inability to use words as abstract symbols, combined with their readiness to imitate sounds and use interjections—similar to those of a young child, were seen as proof that, in case of brain injury, the mind regressed to earlier, more habitual modes of thought. In Geneva, in the early 1920s, Spielrein examined the parallels between the language of children and aphasic patients and assembled significant experimental and observational support for this hypothesis.

In order to detect the typical thought patterns of the child, Spielrein had meticulously recorded the sentences of her daughter Renata when—in 1916—the little girl was aged two years and four and a half months. In the 1920s, this material was extensively used in her research on aphasia. Spielrein's findings confirmed what she had already suspected: that a young child is unskilled in forming logical, linear sequences (what Spielrein, following Jung, called directed thinking) (cf. Jung, 2014/1912, p. 18 ff). Instead, the child's attention would be caught by an object, then drift back to what they were thinking about previously. The consequence were numerous sentences that contained a mixture of two subjects, "crossed" sentences as Spielrein named them. In another nod towards evolutionary theory, she adopted the term "crossing" from Gregor Mendel's genetic studies (2019a/1923, p. 304), which had been rediscovered in the early 1900s. According to Spielrein, this mental "crossing" was proof of the "stickiness" of children's thought processes (2019a/1923, p. 302). It was only slowly and with great difficulty that a young brain gave up its object of interest and would often return to it after it had moved on to something else.

Working with an aphasic patient at the Rousseau Institute (a 55-year-old man who had suffered a stroke), Spielrein was able to observe the same phenomenon in his speech and drawing. Asked to draw first a circle and then a triangle, the patient produced the following image: ◌. Spielrein explained that this was due to the patient's thought "persevering" with the previous symbol and fusing with one he was supposed to draw next. "Perseveration" is a term Jung adopted from contemporary neurological research and defined in his early association experiments as "the fact that the preceding association conditions the next reaction" (Jung and Riklin, 1973/1904, p. 34). The same tendencies were noted on the level of verbal language. When some of the patient's capacity for spoken expression returned, he would be asked to name surrounding objects as part of his medical examination. If Spielrein pointed first to the desk (Fr. *table*) and then to the entire room (Fr. *chambre*), the patient would merge the two words into one

(Fr. *timbre*) (Spielrein, 2019a/1923, p. 315). Spielrein concluded that, following brain injury, the patient's thought processes regressed to the level of a young child, where undirected thought and what, in the adult, would become subconscious processes prevailed. She was careful to warn, however, that this referred exclusively to the mechanisms of thought in aphasia and that the patient's rich life experience still made their mental capacity more complex than the child's (Spielrein, 2019a/1923, p. 318).

However, Spielrein did not entirely reject the disconnection theory of the localizationists. In 1923, she claimed that the loss of speech in Broca's aphasia (or motor aphasia) was due to a disconnection between subconscious motor images (memories of how a word is pronounced) and conscious thought. According to Spielrein, motor images were a part of the visual and kinesthetic imagery located in our subconscious. Once a disconnection between these images and conscious concepts occurred, conscious thought ran dry and regressed to the level of subconscious processes: the language of our early childhood years and of our distant ancestors (Spielrein, 2019a/1923, p. 318). In this way, Spielrein combined the disconnection theory—conscious images become disconnected from their subconscious counterparts—with the evolutionist approach—the disconnection causes a regression to the earlier evolutionary stage in the use of language. It was precisely this combination that was the original aspect of Spielrein's theory.

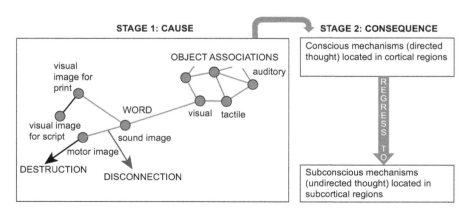

Figure 1.6 Sabina Spielrein's explanation of motor aphasia (Broca's aphasia). Image by Ana Tomčić.

Instead of siding with one of the existing neurological schools of thought, Spielrein showed that both the evolutionary and the disconnection theory were right, only none of them saw and embraced the full picture. In the field of neurology and the study of child language, Spielrein thus exhibited the same eclecticism and original synthesis that she had demonstrated earlier with respect to Freudian, Adlerian, and Jungian psychoanalysis. What we therefore see in both her thinking about evolution and her researches into neurolinguistics is a remarkable consistency in her approach to scholarship. She combined respect for all her intellectual forerunners with a determination to build bridges between them and to harmonize their findings. She displayed these qualities throughout her career. She had the courage to question others, challenge their certainties, teach them, and encourage them to learn from one another. She was never sectarian or interested in self-promotion (Launer, 2014b, p. 254). In our view, this goes a long way to explaining why it has taken so long to claim for her the historical stature she deserves.

Notes

1 A notable exception is Katalin Faluvégi's recently published article (2021, p. 65).
2 For texts where no English translation exists, such as this one, the quotations were translated by Ana Tomčić.
3 This refers to long-term processes repeated across generations and not to singular occurrences.
4 In Kussmaul's book on language disorders (read by Spielrein), Kussmaul referred to Darwin's *The Expression of the Emotions in Man and Animals* (1872, p. 36). In this work, Darwin himself claimed that reflex expressions of emotions in humans were originally purposeful (learned) behaviors in our animal ancestors (cf. pp. 33–54).

Reference List

Ament, W. (1912). *Die Entwicklung von Sprechen und Denken beim Kinde*. Leipzig: Verlag von Ernst Wunderlich. Online at https://archive.org/details/dieentwicklungv00amengoog/page/n5/mode/2up. Accessed Sept. 15, 2022. (Orig. publ. 1899).

Caropreso, F. (2020). Sabina Spielrein's Theory of the Origin and Development of Language. *The International Journal of Psychoanalysis*, 101(4), 706–723.

Carotenuto, A. (Ed.) (1986). *Tagebuch einer heimlichen Symmetrie: Sabina Spielrein zwischen Jung und Freud*. Freiburg: Kore.

Chisholm, J. (1999). *Death, Hope and Sex*. Cambridge: Cambridge UP.
Darwin, C. (1998). *The Expression of the Emotions in Man and Animals*. Oxford and New York: Oxford UP (Orig. publ. 1872).
Faluvégi, K. (2021). Psychiatry/Psychology and Linguistics Meeting in a Psychoanalytical and Developmental Psychology Framework. *Imago Budapest*, 10(1), 63–76.
Forrester, J. (1980). *Language and the Origin of Psychoanalysis*. London and Basingstoke: Macmillan Press LTD.
Freud, S. (1957). On Narcissism: An Introduction. J. Strachey (Trans.). In J. Strachey (Ed.), *SE, Vol. XIV: On the History of the Psycho-Analytic Movement* (pp. 67–103). London: Hogarth Press (Orig. publ. 1914).
Freud, S. (2001). Beyond the Pleasure Principle. J. Strachey (Trans.). In J. Strachey (Ed.), *SE, Vol. XVIII: Beyond the Pleasure Principle, Group Psychology and Other Works* (pp. 7–64). London: Hogarth Press (Orig. publ. 1920).
Graf-Nold, A. (2001). The Zürich School of Psychiatry in Theory and Practice. Sabina Spielrein's Treatment at the Burghölzli Clinic in Zürich. *Journal of Analytical Psychology*, 46, 73–104.
Graves, R. E. (2009). The Legacy of the Wernicke-Lichtheim Model. *Journal of the History of the Neurosciences*, 6(1), 3–20. https://doi.org/10.1080/09647049709525682. Accessed Sept. 15, 2022.
Gutzmann, H. (1899). Die Sprache des Kindes und der Naturvölker. *Zeitschrift für Pädagogische Psychologie*, 1(1), 28–40. Online at https://ia802703.us.archive.org/15/items/zeitschriftfrpd02unkngoog/zeitschriftfrpd02unkngoog.pdf. Accessed Sept. 15, 2022.
Hameline, D. (1993). Édouard Claparède (1873–1940). *Prospects: The Quarterly Review of Comparative Education*, 23(1), 159–171.
Harris, A. (2019). "Language Is There to Bewilder Itself and Others": Theoretical and Clinical Contributions of Sabina Spielrein. In P. Cooper-White and F. Kelcourse (Eds.), *Sabina Spielrein and the Beginnings of Psychoanalysis: Image, Thoughts, and Language* (pp. 151–194). London and New York: Routledge.
Head, H. (1920). Aphasia and Kindred Disorders of Speech. *Brain*, 43(2), 88–165. https://doi.org/10.1093/brain/43.2.87. Accessed Sept. 15, 2022.
Jackson, J. H. (1884). The Croonian Lectures on Evolution and the Dissolution of the Nervous System. *The British Medical Journal*, 1(1214), 660–663. https://doi.org/10.1136/bmj.1.1214.660. Accessed Sept. 15, 2022.
Jung, C. G. (2014). Symbols of Transformation. R. F. C. Hull (Trans.). In H. Read, M. Fordham and G. Adler (Eds.), *CW, Vol. V* (pp. 3–444). London and New York: Routledge (Orig. publ. 1912).
Jung, C. G. and Riklin, F. (1973). The Associations of Normal Subjects. L. Stein and D. Riviere (Trans.). In G. Adler and R. F. C. Hull (Eds.), *CW, Vol. II: Experimental Researches of C.G. Jung* (pp. 31–197). London: Routledge & Kegan Paul (Orig. publ. 1904).
Kussmaul, A. (1885). *Die Störungen der Sprache*. Leipzig: Verlag von F.C.W. Vogel. Online at https://archive.org/details/diestrungender00kussuoft/page/n5/mode/2up. Accessed Sept. 15, 2022.

Launer, J. (2014a). Sex and Sexuality: An Evolutionary View. *Psychoanalytic Inquiry*, 34(8), 831–846.
Launer, J. (2014b). *Sex Versus Survival: The Life and Ideas of Sabina Spielrein*. London and New York: Duckworth/Overlook.
Launer, J. (2015). Carl Jung's Relationship with Sabina Spielrein: A Reassessment. *International Journal of Jungian Studies*, 7(3), 179–193.
Low, B. (2001). *Why Sex Matters: A Darwinian Look at Human Behavior*. Princeton, NJ: Princeton UP.
McGuire, W. (Ed.) (1974). *The Freud/Jung Letters: The Correspondence between Sigmund Freud and C. G. Jung*. R. Manheim and R. F. C. Hull (Trans.). Princeton, NJ: Princeton UP.
Minder, B. (2001). Sabina Spielrein, Jung's Patient at the Burghölzli. *Journal of Analytical Psychology*, 46, 43–66.
Naszkowska, K. (2019). Passions, Politics, and Drives: Sabina Spielrein in Soviet Russia. In P. Cooper-White and F. Kelcourse (Eds.), *Sabina Spielrein and the Beginnings of Psychoanalysis: Image, Thought, and Language* (pp. 110–150). London and New York: Routledge.
Noth, I. (2015). "Beyond Freud and Jung": Sabina Spielrein's Contribution to Child Psychoanalysis and Developmental Psychology. *Pastoral Psychology*, 64(2), 279–286.
Nunberg, H. and Federn, E. (Eds.) (1975). *Minutes of the Vienna Psychoanalytic Society, Vol. III: 1910–1911*. M. Nunberg (Trans.). New York: International UP.
Ovcharenko, V. (1999). Love, Psychoanalysis and Destruction. *Journal of Analytical Psychology*, 44(3), 355–373.
Richebächer, S. (2008). *Eine fast grausame Liebe zur Wissenschaft*. Munich: BTB.
Santiago-Delafosse, M. J. and Delafosse, O. J. M. (2002). Spielrein, Piaget and Vygotsky: Three Positions on Child Thought and Language. *Theory and Psychology*, 12(6), 723–747.
Spielrein, S. (2015a). Destruction as the Cause of Coming into Being. B. Wharton (Trans.). In C. Covington and B. Wharton (Eds.), *Sabina Spielrein: Forgotten Pioneer of Psychoanalysis*. 2nd ed. (pp. 185–212). London and New York: Routledge (Orig. publ. 1912).
Spielrein, S. (2015b). The Origin of the Child's Words Papa and Mama. Some Observations on the Different Stages in Language Development. B. Wharton (Trans.). In C. Covington and B. Wharton (Eds.), *Sabina Spielrein: Forgotten Pioneer of Psychoanalysis* (pp. 233–248). London and New York: Routledge (Orig. publ. 1922).
Spielrein, S. (2019a). Some Analogies between Thinking in Children, Aphasia and the Subconscious Mind. J. Gresh et al. (Trans.). In P. Cooper-White and F. Kelcourse (Eds.), *Sabina Spielrein and the Beginnings of Psychoanalysis: Image, Thought, and Language* (pp. 301–322). London and New York: Routledge (Orig. publ. 1923).
Spielrein, S. (2019b). Children's Drawings with Eyes Open and Closed. J. Gresh et al. (Trans.). In P. Cooper-White and F. Kelcourse (Eds.), *Sabina Spielrein and the Beginnings of Psychoanalysis: Image, Thought, and Language* (pp. 330–367). London and New York: Routledge (Orig. publ. 1931).

Spielrein, S. (2019c). Time in Subliminal Psychic Life. J. Gresh et al. (Trans.). In P. Cooper-White and F. Kelcourse (Eds.), *Sabina Spielrein and the Beginnings of Psychoanalysis: Image, Thought, and Language* (pp. 279–294). London and New York: Routledge (Orig. publ. 1923).

Stern, C. and Stern, W. (1907). *Die Kindersprache*. Leipzig: Verlag von Johann Ambrosius Barth. Online at https://archive.org/details/diekindersprach00ster-goog/page/n4/mode/2up. Accessed Sept. 15, 2022.

Vidal, F. (2001). Sabina Spielrein, Jean Piaget—Going Their Own Ways. P. Bennett (Trans.). *Journal of Analytical Psychology*, 46(1), 139–153.

Chapter 2

Lou Andreas-Salomé
An Unacknowledged Psychoanalytic Theorist of Art

Shira Dushy-Barr

> Only *that* man who like Prometheus has created culture for himself and has thus created human existence anew as a second reality is at the same time Narcissus, fully evolved, standing before his own image. It is himself he gazes on. He is not the beaten slave forced against his will to escape from himself.
> (Andreas-Salomé, 1964, p. 147, original emphasis)

Lou Andreas-Salomé's personal biography does not demand reconstruction. In fact, her story has been told many times. She is relatively well known. She has been featured in several popular books and films, typically in the context of her liaisons with famous men and considered primarily as their muse (e.g., Peters, 1962; Yalom, 1992; Kablitz-Post, 2016). What is often overlooked however is her professional or intellectual biography. She is very rarely considered a serious thinker in her own right and even less frequently a "female pioneer of psychoanalysis." Notable exceptions I am deeply indebted to in gaining an understanding of Andreas-Salomé's ideas include Angela Livingstone's *Salomé, Her Life and Work* (1984), Biddy Martin's *Woman and Modernity* (1991), and Gisela Brinker-Gabler's *Image in Outline* (2012). These books are dedicated, even if not exclusively, to Andreas-Salomé's thought and her psychoanalytic writings. Further publications focused on her psychoanalytic concepts that contributed to my understanding of her ideas are Schultz (1994), Wang (2000), and Markotic (2001).

I too came to know Andreas-Salomé as a figure that inspired and allegedly brought together two exalted male figures she was close with: Friedrich Nietzsche and Sigmund Freud (cf. Borossa and Rooney, 2003). Intrigued by this intellectual female presence, I started to research her own writings. I discovered a rich and profound thinker, whose ideas had interesting implications for psychoanalytic theory, theory of art in particular. This chapter

DOI: 10.4324/9781003455844-4

will not discuss Andreas-Salomé's personal relations. Nor will it offer a comprehensive intellectual biography, which has already been provided by Livingstone (1984), Martin (1991), and Brinker-Gabler (2012). Instead, my goal is to reconstruct her thought as an early pioneer of psychoanalysis by presenting her ideas on the essence of artistic creativity and its significance to human life. These concepts crystallized during the period of her active involvement with psychoanalysis initiated in 1912.

Andreas-Salomé, born in 1861 in St. Petersburg, became acquainted with psychoanalysis in her fifties. By then, she was already an accomplished author of over 50 literary and theoretical works. Her publication record included a book on Henry Ibsen's female characters (1985/1892); a celebrated intellectual psychobiography of Nietzsche (2001/1894); her monography on eroticism and femininity written in response to Martin Buber's request (2012/1910); several novels, stories, and poems; and many scholarly and newspaper articles and theater and book reviews (cf. Livingstone, 1984). In 1912, after an acquaintance had introduced her to psychoanalysis and after attending the 1911 Psychoanalytic Weimar Congress, Andreas-Salomé wrote Freud: "the study of psychoanalysis has not let me go, and the deeper I get into it, the more firmly it holds to me" (Andreas-Salomé, 1964, p. 31). She then asked for his permission to attend his lectures and discussions in Vienna, to which he delightedly agreed. Hence, on October 25, 1912, Andreas-Salomé moved to Vienna to join the Wednesday discussion evenings of the Vienna Psychoanalytic Society (VPS) and to attend Freud's university lectures. She stayed in Vienna for six months, until April of 1913 when she headed back to her home in Göttingen. Her thoughts and experiences of studying with Freud and his circle, as well as her professional and personal exchanges—in particular with Freud, Viktor Tausk, Alfred Adler, and Sándor Ferenczi—were documented in her diary, published posthumously in 1958 and translated into English as *The Freud Journal* (1964).

The psychoanalytic way of thinking about human life suited Andreas-Salomé's worldviews and her lifelong interest in psychological reflection and "the inner life." Psychoanalysis made her joyous like a "sort of Christmas present" (Andreas-Salomé, 1964, p. 90). After leaving Vienna, she devoted much of the following 25 years of her life to it, until her death in 1937. Encouraged by Freud, she practiced as a lay analyst. She saw patients at her home in Göttingen and occasionally in clinics, such as Eitingon's psychoanalytic Polyclinic in Berlin. She had never had a personal analysis

(Livingstone, 1984, p. 173). She held a close personal and professional relationship with Sigmund and Anna Freud, which included long correspondences and mutual visits, and became Anna's confidante and counselor (Freud and Andreas-Salomé, 1966; Andreas-Salomé and A. Freud, 2001; Young-Bruehl, 2008). Finally, she published a number of theoretical papers in psychoanalytic journals. The most notable publications include her paper on anal eroticism (Andreas-Salomé, 2022/1916), praised by Freud, and her paper on narcissism (Andreas-Salomé, 1962/1921), both in *Imago* (cf. Livingstone, 1984; Andreas-Salomé, 1991). Though not a political thinker *per se*, she embedded in her psychoanalytic writings a critical aspect of personal liberation from oppressive social forces, aligned with the psychoanalytic approach. Her concepts of art and creativity were no exception.

Andreas-Salomé's writings are interspersed with discussions of artistic activity and its unique and central role in human life (e.g., Andreas-Salomé, 2012/1910, 1962/1921, 1964). All in all, she wrote over 50 texts related to art. What intrigued her in the arts had little to do with formalism or literary theory. Instead, she perceived art in a philosophical, even metaphysical, sense and examined it side by side with religion, psychology, and sexuality (Livingstone, 1984, p. 228). On several occasions, she attributed to art an inherent connection to the very essence of our humanness, to what it essentially means to be human. For instance, she referred to art as a "mode of expression serving a great power within us, the insufficiency of what is immediately available" (Andreas-Salomé, 2003, p. 121), while assigning to the figure of a creative artist a special position of "the guard of man's primal impressions" (Andreas-Salomé, 1931, p. 74).[1] What I initially found fascinating in Andreas-Salomé's writings was her understanding of art. However, in order to grasp her concept of art, one must first become familiar with her views on human nature and psyche. One component of her views, the most fundamental one in my opinion, is the concept of "primary narcissism." I will thus begin by presenting her understanding of this idea, setting the stage for the explanation of the special status she gave to artistic creativity.

Andreas-Salomé's Concept of Primary Narcissism

Andreas-Salomé borrowed the term "primary narcissism" from psychoanalytic theory, yet it existed in her thought as a concept much earlier. In both her personal and scholarly writings, usually blended together,

Andreas-Salomé's thought revolved around four main themes. The first, already mentioned, was art and artistic creation. The second, religion and the religious feeling. The third, sexuality and love. Finally, femininity and "the woman question." What seemed to have attracted her to these four topics was their association with states, in which a subject experienced a sense of unity with the world. The split between "I" and "the world," or "self" and "the other," was less pronounced. For this reason, Freud's concept of primary narcissism, developed, perhaps not coincidently, during the period of Andreas-Salomé's stay in Vienna, was especially appealing to her.

Freud officially introduced the term "narcissism" into psychoanalytic theory with his "On Narcissism: An Introduction" from 1914 (1957/1914). It denoted the possibility of directing sexual psychic energy or libido to oneself or to one's own body instead of external objects. In his introductory lectures on psychoanalysis given in 1917, Freud explained this discovery as "the notion that the libido, which we find attached to objects and which is the expression of an effort to obtain satisfaction in connection with those objects, can also leave the objects and set the subject's own ego in their place" (Freud, 1963/1917, pp. 415–416).

From this, he inferred the existence of an early developmental stage of "primary narcissism." While narcissism in adult life, the "secondary narcissism," was pathological and associated with psychotic states such as megalomania, primary narcissism was normal for all people (Freud, 1957/1914, pp. 74–75). It is probable, he claimed, that "narcissism is the universal and original state of things, from which object-love is only later developed" (Freud, 1963/1917, p. 416). In this stage, the entire libido is concentrated in the ego, which in fact becomes the first love object. The ego at the stage of primary narcissism is a sufficient source of pleasure, just as Narcissus from the myth indulges in his own reflection in the pond, indifferent to the world.

Freud further distinguished in his paper between two types of libido: ego- or narcissistic-libido and object-libido. Their relationship is antithetical, or that of a "zero-sum game": "the more of the one is employed, the more the other becomes depleted" (p. 76). Freud provided examples of extreme states to demonstrate the relationship between the two types of libido. The state of being in love increases the object-libido to the maximum at the expense of the feeling of self-worth. In paranoid fantasies of "the end of the world," the opposite is true: the object-libido is dwindled due to the intensification of ego-libido (Freud, 1957/1914, p. 76). According to Freud's theory of narcissism, being absorbed with oneself comes at the expense of being involved with the outer world, or in the words of philosopher Paul Ricœur, "self-attention is inattention to the other" (1970, p. 277).

As documented in her *Freud Journal* (1964) and in her correspondence with Freud (cf. Freud and Andreas-Salomé, 1966, pp. 22–26), Andreas-Salomé was very enthusiastic about Freud's new concept, even prior to its official introduction into the theory in 1914. She became greatly preoccupied with it and debated the nuances of its definition with Freud and others, as well as with herself. Her engagement with primary narcissism led to her own publication on the subject in 1921, "The Dual Orientation of Narcissism" (1962/1921). In her paper, she transformed Freud's concept of "narcissism" almost completely. Her intention was to undermine the dichotomous logic between self-love and object-love, characteristic to the popular interpretation of the Narcissus myth. She perceived this popular interpretation as oppressive and pessimistic.

In order to illustrate her understanding of primary narcissism, Andreas-Salomé retold the myth of Narcissus. In her version, Narcissus was still gazing at his own image in erotic self-enjoyment. However, the emphasis was placed on the fact that his image was reflected not by a man-made mirror, but by a natural one: a pond in the midst of the woods. "Perhaps," Andreas-Salomé suggested, "it was not just himself that he beheld in the mirror, but himself as if he were still All: would he not otherwise have fled from the image, instead of lingering before it?" (1962/1921, p. 9). She then offered an interpretation of Narcissus's fixation on his reflection. According to her, it was not directed at his own image chosen by him over the rest of the world, but at his image as reflected by nature, against the background of nature, as if he was still an inseparable part of the universe as a whole. Andreas-Salomé's Narcissus does not favor himself over external objects. He favors himself as an integral part of the world. The image he fell in love with was his ego still united with the All. It was an embodiment of the undifferentiated unity between himself and the world, a balanced, unbiased merge of the ego and the outside world, where neither is left out (p. 9).

Andreas-Salomé thus reconceptualizes Freud's primary narcissism into an inherent opposed movement. On the one hand, it consists of a tendency towards the formation of the ego as the first love object, representing the desire for individuality. On the other, a tendency toward the dissolution of the ego. This is the idea of primary narcissism's "dual-orientation" or "double-tendency" (Germ. *Doppelrichtung*), developed by her in the 1921 paper "Narzißmus als Doppelrichtung" or "The Dual Orientation of Narcissism."

She claimed that to understand narcissism one must go beyond the discussion of self-love. She asked to bring to the fore "its other, less obvious aspect: the persistent feeling of identification with the totality" (p. 5). Andreas-Salomé associated primary narcissism as a developmental stage in infancy with the state preceding the full development of language and rational thought. The ego is then in the process of formation but is not entirely stable yet. In this early state, the narcissistic-libido and the object-libido are not yet in a zero-sum game relationship because the differentiation between the self and the world is not yet sharp and absolute. Only with the establishment of the ego and entrance into language, and thus into subjecthood and individuality, an alienating cleft is created in the mind. It appears, at first, between the subject and the world, now posed against the subject as an object. Second, the split occurs within the subject themself, as they begin to reject elements which hitherto were experienced as a continuation of themself.

Inevitably, the primal unified state is rendered as unavailable to the mind. According to Andreas-Salomé, this original unity is not an actual memory. Yet she believed that its loss is tangible and painful. It leaves a lasting mark on us and becomes the main driving force of everything we do, in an attempt to restore the lost unity. This idea was expressed in the opening lines of her memoirs:

> Our first experience, remarkably enough, is that of loss. A moment before, we were everything, undifferentiated, indivisibly part of some kind of being—only to be pressed into birth. Henceforth a tiny residue of the whole must strive to avoid contracting into even less and less, must stand up to a world which rises before it with ever-increasing substantiality, a world into which is has fallen, from universal fullness, as into a deprivating void.
> (Andreas-Salomé, 1991, p. 1)

Albeit painful, the emergence out of the stage of primary narcissism is thus valuable: it sets us in motion as we try to recreate the unified state.

So far, I have discussed primary narcissism as a developmental stage. This brings me to the other aspect Andreas-Salomé attributed to it, when she referred to it as "a part of our self-love which accompanies all phases" (Andreas-Salomé, 1962/1921, p. 3). She described primary narcissism as an integral, constitutive force of the human psyche, manifested in adult, socialized life in a positive way. She did not see human nature and culture as excluding opposites. In fact, according to her, rationality and civilization, typically contrasted with narcissism as primal unity, are in fact its delegates and, as such, do not necessarily contradict it. Seeing them as mutually exclusive opposites, as did Freud, is problematic. It removes humans further away from the possibility of living a full life that enables expression of and participation in all aspects of humanhood.

Thus, I would suggest that despite designating the loss of primal unity as the breaking point, Andreas-Salomé's concept places the human mind on a spectrum between two modes of consciousness. The first, narcissistic-unified, is able to continue experiencing identification with the surrounding world. The second, rational-split, marks a growing separation and individuation. Andreas-Salomé showed the possibility of getting closer to each of the poles throughout life. She viewed the mid-area of the scale that maintains a meaningful connection to both ends of it as the most valuable position. She argued that the dual-orientation or double-tendency of self-assertion and self-abandonment is inherent to the human condition.

Figure 2.1 Lou Andreas-Salomé around the age of 40, ca. 1900.
Copyright: Freud Museum London.

The Historical Dimension of Narcissism

Interestingly, Andreas-Salomé believed that the human position on the scale of modes of consciousness, between unified and split, is subjected to sociohistorical influences and fluctuates with time. As a result, although the loss of primary narcissism is unavoidable and inseparable from human experience, our proximity to it throughout our lives is contingent upon historical changes. Thus, primary narcissism's twofold orientation, its essential double tendency to merge and to separate, is more or less available to humans, depending on a society they live in or period in history. Andreas-Salomé identified modernity as an especially detrimental time for the narcissistic mode of consciousness (cf. Brinker-Gabler, 2012; Martin, 1991; Wang, 2000). It would be interesting to compare her critique of modernity with a number of prominent thinkers, such as Nietzsche or the theorists from the Frankfurt School. I, however, choose to stay in the framework of her own thought. I believe that understanding her ideas within her own world of reference is an important part of reestablishing her as a thinker.

According to Andreas-Salomé, at first the aforementioned loss was tempered by religious belief. God served as a mediator, a bridge between the subject and the world. He enabled humans to keep feeling "at home" despite the cleft that had occurred between them and their surroundings (Andreas-Salomé, 1991, p. 1). As she wrote in her essay on narcissism:

> In the religious experience [. . .], object libido originally directed to the parents flows into the narcissistic stream,—so producing narcissism's most brilliant performance: the two energies unite to the glory of God, ruler of all, and at the same time nearest and dearest of all.
> (Andreas-Salomé, 1962/1921, pp. 18–19)

Due to its duality between omnipotence and intimacy, power and love, devotion and self-affirmation, a religious feeling is a form of an extension of primary narcissism. It is, thus, a force that softens the sharpness of distinction between self and world. It provides the final membrane enveloping humans, protecting them from feeling complete isolation.

Andreas-Salomé described the loss of religious faith in modern times as a phylogenetic process analogous to the personal, ontogenetic process of growing out of primary narcissism. With this loss, the human condition changes. The availability of the double tendency inherent to primary narcissism is at stake. She experienced her own crisis of faith, as did many of her contemporaries, as a psychic wound but nevertheless believed that disillusionment from religious mysticism was inevitable (Andreas-Salomé, 1962/1921, pp. 18–19, 1964, pp. 191–192, 1991, pp. 1–11).

Despite the "death of God," the seminal moment in the history of humanity, Andreas-Salomé still believed that human beings are capable of maintaining their relationship with primary narcissism. She identified, however, a few more factors that keep humans away from it in modern times. She did not present them in an organized, systematic way. They appear sporadically in her writings. Examining them together, I divided these factors into two categories: modern epistemology and modern ethics.

I will begin with the first group: modern epistemology. On many separate occasions, Andreas-Salomé described her times as characterized by features of epistemology harmful to the essential link between humans and primary narcissism. She pointed specifically to the cult of rationality and science specific to her times as a problematic epistemological tendency. The over-rationality of the modern era was dangerous to humans because it reinforced dichotomous thinking. It also positioned impulsive, irrational, and incontrollable aspects of life in opposition to knowledge and truth. As a result, it drove people away from their experiential, bodily aspects (Andreas-Salomé, 1964, p. 118; cf. Brinker-Gabler, 2012, p. 145). It left them fatigued and listless, in *Weltschmerz*. For instance, Andreas-Salomé viewed the youth's dropping interest in philosophy and art as a sign of "not only weariness but actually a kind of self-stupefaction that results from devotion to absorbing activities of a scientific or practical kind" (Andreas-Salomé, 1964, p. 105).

Unlike the reactionaries of her time, including Nietzsche (as perceived by her), she did not advocate for giving up on reason altogether or on the differentiated ego. Instead, she aspired to enable them to coexist side by side with other aspects of humanity. Her understanding of mental health was not of a strong, stable, rational ego, in contrast to other psychoanalytic concepts of mental health, including the late Freudian theory presented in his *The Ego and the Id* (Freud, 1961a/1923). She preferred a flexible, lively ego instead:

> Just as illness needs to reach out for cure, so the healthy mind should confidently submit to the risk of loosening and transformation. For our inner vitality is no less endangered by the walls that confine it than by the abyss beneath; petrification is death just as surely as disintegration.
>
> (Andreas-Salomé, 1964, p. 72)

Modern epistemology, by encouraging rigid thinking and rejecting all irrationality, put people in danger of stagnation.

I will now proceed to the second group of factors: modern ethics. Andreas-Salomé criticized the unnecessarily oppressive attitudes towards drives as the ethical aspects of modernity. This oppression did not derive from conservative morals regarding sexuality. Instead, it stemmed from the utilitarian and practical approaches that prevail in a modern society, as well as from oppressive social structures such as the patriarchal family. As a result, society and culture are perceived as externally imposed on humans. They are positioned in contrast to human nature and to satisfaction of drives, instead of being presented as a potential realm for expression and fulfillment. Andreas-Salomé referred to Freud's concept of sublimation presented, for instance, in his 1908 *"Civilized" Sexual Morality and Modern Nervous Illness* and later in his *Civilization and Its Discontents* from 1930, where culture is "standing in opposition to the natural" and superseding it (Freud, 1959a/1908, 1961b/1930; Andreas-Salomé, 1964, p. 146; cf. Wang, 2000). "In most of Freud's writing," she wrote, "civilized man appears as a sadly domesticated savage, and his sublimation by the aid of his repressed savagery assumes an essentially negative quality—drive and culture being contrasted like the inner and outer value" (Andreas-Salomé, 1964, p. 56). Sublimation, thus, is viewed as foreign to humans and forced upon their impulses, the rejected "lower" or "primitive" aspects of the psyche. In such a constellation, the civilized subject is bound to be discontent.

Contrary, again, to reactionary thinkers and those she perceived as "depressive," such as Freud himself, Andreas-Salomé wished to see culture and civilization as driven by the fundamental narcissistic strive and not in contrast to it. She viewed culture and civilization as enabling rather than inhibiting. Sublimation was not as an oppressive mechanism for her, as it was for Freud, but a means for potential narcissistic self-fulfillment of drives through cultural means. As mentioned earlier, Andreas-Salomé was cautious with sharp divisions and dichotomous thinking; in this case, with the dichotomy between nature and culture, sensuality and rationality. She also rejected a linear view of human development, which treats early stages of life as phases that should be overcome and replaced by later, more appropriate ones. She preferred using the word "elaboration" instead of sublimation, which she had borrowed from Victor Tausk (Andreas-Salomé, 1964, p. 146). This implied a continuous horizontal movement of the drives from humans into the social-cultural sphere, rather than the vertical movement implied by the term sublimation. To her, any binary understanding of human nature and culture leads to a loss of euphoria in human life.

> Anyone who is creatively gifted and not pathologically inhibited [would find] anchorage in cultural activity, no matter how much narcissistic satisfaction he may seek in himself. So America was discovered when the intended goal of the journey was its opposite, the dreamland of India.
>
> (p. 146)

Culture, creation, intellectual inquiry, according to her, should be seen as means for the subject's libidinal fulfillment, and not for its inhibition or oppressive control. "It is our own self realization" (p. 146).

Andreas-Salomé further criticized narrow modern views on sexuality as genital sex and the demand that a subject sublimated their sexuality into love and affection within the confines of a modern family. She, on the other hand, advocated for an understanding of sexuality in a broad sense, as continuous with the cultural field and incorporated into it (Wang, 2000, p. 231). Andreas-Salomé saw the modern worldview as a desexualization of life. It prevented people from seeing themselves reflected in culture, from duplicating their own nature in cultural means, as a plant duplicates itself in its shadow:

> It is wrong to see nature and culture opposed like sunlight and shadow in respect to our natural desire for happiness and the ego's fulfillment. It is wrong to think that the increase of the shadow coincides with the slanting of the sunlight; it is a false and contrived picture. The right picture is rather that of the plant around high noon: then it casts its own shadow straight down beneath it, a self-duplication wherein it gazes on its own repeated outline, its finest safeguard from the great flame that would consume it before its fruiting.
>
> (Andreas-Salomé, 1964, p. 147)

For modernity, libidinal fulfillment meant decent family life. The social-cultural sphere was seen as a space of rational, practical activity, to which human beings must accommodate even at the price of their own mental health. Moreover, Andreas-Salomé claimed that women maintained a stronger proximity to primary narcissism than men. However, as presented in her paper "What Follows from the Fact That It Was Not the Woman Who

Killed the Father," in modern times women's subjugation to the house and family was harmful to this privileged connection (Andreas-Salomé, 1928).

These analyses of modernity, though not meticulous or fact-based, interestingly depict it as an era when an increase of individuation and pragmatism comes at a psychological price of a growing distance between humans and the world. By historicizing the concept of primary narcissism, Andreas-Salomé added a thought-provoking aspect to this theoretical concept, which is most often referred to in universal, timeless terms.

The Artist as Narcissus: Narcissism and Its Relation to Artistic Creation

Let us now return to my initial question regarding the meaningfulness of artistic creation. Andreas-Salomé indicated two main occurrences of primary narcissism, or two occasions on which it is encountered. The dual orientation of self-abandonment and self-assertion comes into play in adult life in (1) erotic love and (2) artistic activity. According to Andreas-Salomé, sexual encounter and artistic creation had a "profound kinship" and grew "from a single root" (Andreas-Salomé, 2012/1910, pp. 67–68). They are moments in which human capacities creatively collaborate to cause a dissolution of boundaries, where the physical aspect and the spiritual one are equally involved. Both, sex and art, ease the rational, split mode of consciousness and reconnect humans to their narcissistic ground of life, making them "drunk" on life.

In a letter to Freud following his publication of "On Narcissism" in 1914, Andreas-Salomé discussed an inherent relationship between artistic creation and narcissism. She emphasized its particular connection to primary narcissism, as opposed to narcissism commonly understood as a sense of vanity or self-admiration:

> [W]hile creating, the artist is completely absorbed in his creation, and is quite unaware of the extremely personal and decisive relationship of his work to his own most intimate and infantile nature. It is only when he has awakened from this "unconscious" explosion or else has not properly entered into it that he is thrown back into personal vanity, i.e., into the surplus libido directed towards himself as a person.
> (Freud and Andreas-Salomé, 1966, p. 23)

Only in the awakened state, the ego simply becomes an object of the libido. In the process of creation, however, "it would be equally true to say that the frontiers of the ego are totally eliminated, affording in this way an escape from its subjectivity and from the opposition of the ego and the external world" (p. 24).

What is it about art that ties it to a more unified mode of the mind? And is this view compatible with the stereotypical image of an artist, present also in psychoanalysis, as egoistic and self-involved?

Andreas-Salomé listed a number of capacities at work in the process of creation that enable a bridging of the split in consciousness. Artwork brings these capacities to their fullest. First, she attributed "recollection" (Germ. *Erinnerung*) to an artist. It is a unique form of remembering, distinguished from "memory" (Germ. *Gedächtnis*). While memory is conscious and associated with the rational ego, recollection is the ability to remember past experiences in a live, sensuous, affective manner. Through recollection, "we can [. . .] reach back to the realm where inner experience and external event represented the same occurrence" (Andreas-Salomé, 1962/1921, p. 22). Recollection leads us back to where a subject can identify themself in external objects, while the separation between inside and outside is not experienced as alienation. Recollection enables access to the narcissistic experience by conjuring up the feelings that accompanied the experiences in the past, not through an exact reconstruction of objective events. We all have recollections; it is the "only bit of poetical talent preserved to every one of us" (p. 23). However, an artist actively works to give them form. For this reason, "poetry is perfected recollection" (p. 23). Poetry and artistic creation in general are an extension and revival of childhood, sacrificed by an adult for the sake of practical living.

Artists' capacity for symbolization is the second important factor in bringing an artist closer to narcissism. Unlike non-artists, artists have to translate their recollections into an outside expression, in a process driven by a "compulsion towards objectification" (p. 28). However, creation of an art object is not merely a matter of craftsmanship. Artists treat their artefacts like children treat their toys, positioning them as symbols of more than themselves. They thus modify their fixed, ordinary meanings and enable an imaginative activity. The work of art becomes a symbol of the "one that is all" (Livingstone, 1984, p. 228). The form given by an artist to an artistic object forces objects in practical, logical reality to represent more than themselves.

The libido is the third element in Andreas-Salomé's theory, at work in the artistic activity. However, it is not used by artists for its adult, genital aims but remains infantile and dispersed. Andreas-Salomé wrote accordingly, "artistic production strips away the husk of corporeality from the fruitful seed, which then reaches full growth in the work itself" (Andreas-Salomé, 1962/1921, p. 26). Fantasies and desires are pursued in the creative process. However, again, not the conscious personal desires, but primal transsubjective ones. The latter seem to be forced upon artists, impelling them to put their own personal wishes and needs on hold. Sexuality is thus directed from the physical plane to the creative one.

Regarding the second question, Andreas-Salomé argued that the essence of artistic activity is not personal gratification or self-glorification. It requires a complete involvement and absorption, and hence does not allow for such self-consciousness. In the creative process, an artist least of all strives to fulfill their private, conscious wishes. "On account of their temporary withdrawal into that primal enclosure which is otherwise cleft into subject and object, they are more abstracted from solipsistic privacy in their creative work than anywhere else" (p. 24). In retracting into themselves and simultaneously identifying with the All, an artist does not attain an extreme form of personal subjectivity. On the contrary, they achieve a form of transsubjectivity and neutrality. Thus, the artist often "awakens from his abstracted state as if from a compulsion, feeling liberated to turn his thoughts where he pleases, and to return unhindered to his own personal [. . .] desires" (p. 25).

The modern way of thinking condemns art as a useless, non-pragmatic, and egoistic illusion, which may even be harmful. For Andreas-Salomé, this conception is biased and false. It overlooks the true metaphysical-psychological essence of art. According to her understanding, artists mobilize their ability to dive into the primordial states of the psyche. Still, they don't give up on their subjecthood or ego, necessary for creation of an art object. They are regressive, in a positive, non-pathological sense, in their ability to retreat to the state to the primary narcissism. They are able to hold on to both ends of the spectrum of consciousness: the rational-split one and the narcissistic-unified one. Artists have both the capability of being receptive to impressions and to master them into form, into a piece of art. Andreas-Salomé described art, poetry in particular, as a bridge between the realms of the effable and ineffable (Germ. *Sagliche* and *Unsagliche*, respectively). The position of an artist is therefore midway between childish and adult, infantile and adult, preverbal and articulate, neurotic and psychotic, as well as feminine and masculine. This hybrid, inclusive middle position is capable of bringing human potential to its highest fulfilment.

Andreas-Salomé Versus Freud on Artistic Creation

Clearly, Andreas-Salomé's views on art and artists bear affinity to Freud's ideas, expressed, for example, in his "Creative Writers and Day-Dreaming" (1959b/1908). She agreed with his general view on the psychodynamics of artistic creation. She sided with him on seeing it as a libidinal, narcissistic activity which resembles a child at play. I will not provide an elaborate comparative analysis of their concepts; instead, I will present the points of disagreement, as discussed by Andreas-Salomé explicitly in her Open Letter to Freud on his 75th birthday (Andreas-Salomé, 1931).

First, she believed that in his understanding of the artist's work, Freud overemphasized the connection with daydreaming. According to him, the purpose of daydreaming for an adult was the same as creation for an artist: to fulfill concealed wishes. In this context, he remarked, "His Majesty the Ego [was] the hero alike of every day-dream and of every story" (Freud, 1959b/1908, p. 149). The link to daydreaming thus portrays artwork as narcissistic in the Freudian sense, that is, as serving the desire for power and grandeur. This point of disagreement was crucial to Andreas-Salomé, since, unlike Freud, she did not believe that artistic work served as gratification of conscious wishes of aggrandizement that prioritize the ego over other objects. On the contrary, she understood artistic creation as a manifestation of primary narcissism seen as a dual state, where the ego and the surroundings are not yet entirely separated (Andreas-Salomé, 1931, p. 76).

Second, Andreas-Salomé objected to Freud's understanding of creativity as a derivative of repression. While he interpreted creation as stemming from the need to express and fulfill forbidden or immoral wishes, she described it as an emanation of an involuntary, impersonal force of fulfillment. Thus, this origin of creativity is in complete contradiction to Freud's idea of locked-up passions or to any notion of pathology or immorality. For Andreas-Salomé, artistic creation is founded on a universal, positive force. The artwork "assists a primal sense of experience to become more conscious" (p. 77). Lastly, Andreas-Salomé took issue with Freud's emphasis on the social factor as the driving motivation for an artist, such as the desire for professional recognition, fame, or profit. She did not believe in any connection between artists' relations with other people, erotic or ethical, and their artistic activity (p. 78). According to her, an artist is driven solely by their impulse for creation and pleasure derived from work. The origins of artwork are deep in the past, in infantile sexual development, on the threshold of subjecthood and individuality.

Rainer Maria Rilke and the Artist's Struggles

Despite her objection to viewing artists in pathological terms, Andreas-Salomé did see them as prone to pathologies. Their privileged position, midway between differentiation and unity, puts artists at risk. While art itself is a secure sphere for an artist to remain in, their repeated transitioning into and out of the creative state, between practical life and poetic existence, is difficult and entails struggles. Falling out of the creative state, artists might find themselves "fearfully suspended between nothingness and nothingness: he is protected neither by his work nor by the real world, and he becomes questionable in the criteria of others as well as in his own, that is, in the practical judgment of his own inner world" (Andreas-Salomé, 1962/1921, p. 27). She sees the artist as reexperiencing the pangs of becoming a subject. Between the pulses of creation, "[i]t is as if the artist must come again to live through childhood's heaven and childhood's hell" (p. 27).

The artist was positioned by Andreas-Salomé as oscillating between neurotic and psychotic tendencies. When they are unable to create, they are anxious and restless and seem neurotic. However, during the creation itself they approach a psychotic state. "The basic predisposition of all [artistic] productivity dangerously approximates the psychotic organization" (p. 27). An entire field of pathologies thus lurk for the artist, "like a spiderweb, lies in wait for the exhausted fly" (Andreas-Salomé, 1931, p. 79). If not for the hardship, artistic creation would be "a guide to blessedness like nothing else on earth, a rejoicing in the incredible fullness of union between intoxication and peace" (Andreas-Salomé, 1962/1921, p. 9).

In the context of her theories on artistic creation, it is interesting to briefly present Andreas-Salomé's discussion of a figure considered by her the model artist: her close friend, the poet Rainer Maria Rilke. In her collection of memoirs, published posthumously in 1951 (1991) and in her book, *You Alone Are Real to Me, Remembering Rainer Maria Rilke*, written after his death (2003), she presented Rilke's creation as epitomizing her theories on art and narcissism in modern times. She claimed that his poetry grew out of his position on the borders of subjecthood, from the dual tendency to merge and to separate. Andreas-Salomé believed that God was the object of Rilke's art. To both, her and Rilke, God symbolized the link connecting the subject with the world and enabling a restoration of the primal unity. He was an "ultimate anonymity beyond all conscious limits of the ego" (Andreas-Salomé, 1991, p. 75), inspiring humans with intimate confidence in the world.

The challenge faced by Rilke, in her view, was that during the poet's lifetime in modern times, God did not exist anymore as a given object. Rilke lived at a time "when viable images for 'religious art' were no longer provided, indeed dictated, by a generally accepted belief system" (p. 75). Yet he continued to be driven by a religious impulse to give form to the missing God. He was impelled to reach the foundational narcissistic unity, increasingly less accessible, and to create in his poetry the mediating object with which people could feel at home again. Andreas-Salomé stressed the ensuing conflicted demands placed on Rilke, as a modern poet. On the one hand, to be receptive to God in passive devotion, to be sensitive enough to feel his growingly elusive presence. On the other hand, to control these impressions of God as mediating object, and to mold them into a poetic form (pp. 87–88). This conflict between receptivity and expression in art, between devotion and testimony, grew with time, making it increasingly difficult for Rilke to carry out his artistic work. It led to extreme mental states, while the moments of creative bliss became increasingly scarcer. Despite the metaphysical and psychological hope provided to him by his poetry, he was tormented. His position at the threshold of subjecthood was unbearable in the modern era.

Regardless of Rilke's personal struggles, Andreas-Salomé identified the pinnacle of modern artistic achievement in his poetry (Andreas-Salomé, 2003, p. 29). She believed that, like Narcissus gazing into the pond, acknowledging the separation between himself and the world, and longing for the unified image, only a poet "can name a whole picture of the unity of joy and sorrow, departure from self and absorption in self, devotion and self-assertion" (Andreas-Salomé, 1962/1921, p. 9). Only a poet, like Rilke, in the unique middle position, is capable of expressing the fundamental duality of the human psyche, conflicted between declaring "I" and aspiring to be at-one-with-the-world. To return to the epigraph of this chapter: poets, and artists in general, are thus simultaneously Narcissus in love and Prometheus the creator. They delve into the depths of the mind to create a culture in their own image and then stand proudly in front of it.

Conclusion

The objective of this chapter was to give a taste of Andreas-Salomé's psychoanalytic theories concerning the intriguing topic of artistic creation in relation to the concept of primary narcissism, fundamental to her. Her ideas provide an interesting psychoanalytic conceptualization of an artist's work, focused on the very experience of an artistic mind in the process of creation. I found Andreas-Salomé's views on artistic creation insightful and liberating. They offer fresh non-dichotomous understanding of social life where nature and culture, and rationality and irrationality, are not excluding opposites but potential continuations of one another. She provided a critical approach to modernity, stressing that overly pragmatic and logocentric views cost humans a price. Yet, by pointing at moments where primary narcissism may be recovered throughout life, her critique remained optimistic in the face of growing individuation and alienation.

Acknowledgments

The author would like to thank the Ariane de Rothschild Women Doctoral Program and the Healthy Longevity Research Center at Tel Aviv University for their support during the composition of this chapter. I am also grateful to Ilit Ferber from the Department of Philosophy at Tel Aviv University for her guidance and feedback as I worked on the research project on Andreas-Salomé.

Note

1 For texts where no English translation exists, such as this one, the quotations were translated by Shira Dushy-Barr.

Reference List

Andreas-Salomé, L. (1928). Was daraus folgt, daß es nicht die Frau gewesen ist, die den Vater totgeschlagen hat. *Almanach der Psychoanalyse*, 3, 25–30.

Andreas-Salomé, L. (1931). *Mein Dank an Freud: Offener Brief an Professor Sigmund Freud zu seinem 75. Geburtstag*. Wien: Internationaler Psychoanalytischer Verlag.

Andreas-Salomé, L. (1962). The Dual Orientation of Narcissism. *The Psychoanalytic Quarterly*, 31(1), 1–30. (Orig. publ. 1921).

Andreas-Salomé, L. (1964). *The Freud Journal of Lou Andreas-Salomé*. S. A. Leavy (Trans.). New York: Basic Book Publishers.

Andreas-Salomé, L. (1985). *Ibsen's Heroines*. S. Mandel (Trans.). Redding Ridge, CT: Black Swan Books (Orig. publ. 1892).

Andreas-Salomé, L. (1991). *Looking Back, Memoirs*. B. Mitchell (Trans.). New York: Paragon House.

Andreas-Salomé, L. (2001). *Nietzsche*. S. Mandel (Trans.). Chicago: University of Illinois Press (Orig. publ. 1894).

Andreas-Salomé, L. (2003). *You Alone Are Real to Me, Remembering Rainer Maria Rilke*. A. von der Lippe (Trans.). Rochester: BOA Editions.

Andreas-Salomé, L. (2012). *The Erotic*. J. Crisp (Trans.). New Brunswick: Transaction Publishers (Orig. publ. 1910).
Andreas-Salomé, L. (2022). "Anal" and "Sexual". *Psychoanalysis and History*, 24(1), 19–40. (Orig. publ. 1916).
Andreas-Salomé, L. and Freud, A. (2001). *". . . als käm ich heim zu Vater und Schwester": Lou Andreas-Salome—Anna Freud, Briefwechsel 1919–1937*. Göttingen: Wallstein.
Borossa, J. and Rooney, C. (2003). Suffering, Transience and Immortal Longings: Salomé between Nietzsche and Freud. *Journal of European Studies*, 33(3–4), 287–304.
Brinker-Gabler, G. (2012). *Image in Outline, Reading Lou Andreas-Salomé*. New York and London: Continuum International Publishing Group.
Freud, S. (1957). On Narcissism: An Introduction. J. Strachey (Trans.). In J. Strachey (Ed.), *SE, Vol. XIV: On the History of the Psycho-Analytic Movement, Papers on Metapsychology and Other Works* (pp. 67–102). London: Hogarth Press (Orig. publ. 1914).
Freud, S. (1959a). "Civilized" Sexual Morality and Modern Nervous Illness. J. Strachey (Trans.). In J. Strachey (Ed.), *SE, Vol. IX: Jensen's "Gradiva" and Other Works* (pp. 177–204). London: Hogarth Press (Orig. publ. 1908).
Freud, S. (1959b). Creative Writers and Day-Dreaming. J. Strachey (Trans.). In J. Strachey (Ed.), *SE, Vol. IX: Jensen's "Gradiva" and Other Works* (pp. 141–154). London: Hogarth Press (Orig. publ. 1908).
Freud, S. (1961a). The Ego and the Id. J. Strachey (Trans.). In J. Strachey (Ed.), *SE, Vol. XIX: The Ego and the Id and Other Works* (pp. 1–66). London: Hogarth Press (Orig. publ. 1923).
Freud, S. (1961b). Civilization and Its Discontents. J. Strachey (Trans.). In J. Strachey (Ed.), *SE, Vol. XXI: The Future of an Illusion, Civilization and its Discontents, and Other Works* (pp. 57–146). London: Hogarth Press (Orig. publ. 1930).
Freud, S. (1963). The Libido Theory and Narcissism. J. Strachey (Trans.). In J. Strachey (Ed.), *SE, Vol. XV: Introductory Lectures on Psycho-Analysis (Parts I and II)* (pp. 412–430). London: Hogarth Press (Orig. publ. 1917).
Freud, S. and Andreas-Salomé, L. (1966). *Sigmund Freud and Lou Andreas-Salomé Letters*. E. Pfeiffer (Ed.). W. Robson-Scott and E. Robson-Scott (Trans.). London: The Hogarth Press and the Institute of Psycho-Analysis.
Kablitz-Post, C. (Dir.) (2016). *Lou Andreas-Salomé, The Audacity to be Free*. Kablitz-Post and Kranzelbinder: Reidinger & Sasse.
Livingstone, A. (1984). *Salomé, Her Life and Work*. New York: Moyer Bell Limited.
Markotic, L. (2001). Where Primary Narcissism Was, I Must Become: The Inception of the Ego in Andreas-Salomé, Lacan, and Kristeva. *American Imago: Psychoanalysis and the Human Sciences*, 58(4), 813–836.
Martin, B. (1991). *Woman and Modernity: The (Life)Styles of Lou Andreas-Salomé*. Ithaca, NY: Cornell UP.
Peters, H. F. (1962). *My Sister, My Spouse: A Biography of Lou Andreas-Salomé*. London: V. Gollancz.

Ricœur, P. (1970). *Freud and Philosophy, An Essay on Interpretation*. D. Savage (Trans.). New Haven and London: Yale UP.

Schultz, K. (1994). In Defense of Narcissus: Lou Andreas-Salomé and Julia Kristeva. *The German Quarterly*, 67(2), 185–196.

Wang, B. (2000). Memory, Narcissism, and Sublimation: Reading Lou Andreas-Salomé's Freud Journal. *American Imago*, 57(2), 215–234.

Yalom, I. (1992). *When Nietzsche Wept: A Novel of Obsession*. New York: Harper Perennial.

Young-Bruehl, E. (2008). *Anna Freud: A Biography*. 2nd ed. New Haven and London: Yale UP.

Chapter 3

Beata "Tola" Rank
Out From the Footnote

Lena Magnone

When I was writing the book about the cultural transfer of psychoanalysis to the Polish intelligentsia before the Second World War (Magnone, 2016, 2023), the chapter about Beata Rank seemed indispensable. At the same time, compared to those dedicated to better-documented figures, such as Ludwik Jekels, Helene Deutsch, and Gustav Bychowski, it presented as particularly challenging.

Beata Rank's name has been a footnote in the history of psychoanalysis. Her close friendship with Sigmund Freud has left a single trace: in his 1919 essay "The Uncanny," Freud thanked "Frau Dr. Rank" for a useful suggestion (Freud, 1955a/1919, p. 23). The history of psychoanalysis remembers her chiefly in the context of Otto Rank's break with Freud. The only article dedicated exclusively to Beata Rank treated her biography as a story of failure (Roazen, 1990, p. 247). Literary scholars come across her name on the margins of various biographies of Anaïs Nin, who had a passionate love affair with Otto Rank. Beata never recorded her version of the story. It is known only from Nin's diaries, where she appears as "the cold, snippy, frostbitten Mrs. Rank" (Nin, 1993, p. 320). A Polish author of a study on Nin, discussing the affair, not only overlooked Beata's Polish roots but even failed to remember her last name, as she recalled Rank's "first wife, the outstanding analyst Beata Toller" (Derc, 2010, p. 160).

As shown by the civil status records of the Jewish Metropolitan District in Nowy Sącz (then Neu-Sandez) in the Austrian Galicia, the region annexed from the Polish-Lithuanian Commonwealth by the Habsburg Empire, she was born in 1896 as Betty (Beata) Münzer, daughter of Salomon and Debora (née Hoffmann). She signed her work "Beata," but her friends and colleagues typically called her "Tola." A short bio by her daughter, published in the *International Dictionary of Psychoanalysis* (Rank-Veltfort, 2005,

DOI: 10.4324/9781003455844-5

p. 1443), falsely claimed that she was born in 1886. This year was thoughtlessly cited by many other scholars, including those who mention that Beata was more than ten years younger than her husband, born in 1884 (Lieberman and Kramer, 2012, pp. 77, 326). Unsure as to the correct spelling of her maiden name, moreover, Beata's daughter gave two versions—Minzer or Munzer. These also reappeared in many other publications.

Unlike other first female disciples of Freud, whose life trajectories share a clear pattern—Helene Deutsch's path into psychoanalysis seems here in many respects paradigmatic (cf. Magnone, 2016, pp. 325–440)—Beata Münzer's entrance into the Freudian movement could be said to result from coincidence.

The year Beata was born, the first private high school or *Gymnasium* for girls in Austrian Galicia opened in Kraków (then Krakau). It ended with the *matura* examination required to apply to university. Until 1896 this kind of education was offered exclusively to boys. The girl's high school in Kraków was the third school of this kind in the Austro-Hungarian Empire, following Prague in 1891 and Vienna in 1893 (Bilewicz, 1997, p. 44). By the time she reached the age of 14 and could attend secondary school, there were 11 high schools to choose from in Galicia (Kramarz, 1986, pp. 367–368). The one established in Nowy Sącz in 1907 was one of the last to open before World War I (Dybiec, 1993, p. 387). The students were predominantly Jewish daughters of the members of the intelligentsia and the liberal professions (Czajecka, 1990, p. 125). It is safe to assume that Beata's parents were wealthy enough to pay for her education, for no public high school for girls was ever established in Galician times.

Beata claimed to have been a psychology student (Eissler, 1954, p. 1); however, it is most likely that if she studied at all, it was at the philosophy department of the Jagiellonian University in Kraków, as psychology had not been established as a separate course until the 1950s. Her choice would have been another indicator of her family's wealth. While medicine was a pragmatic choice for those who intended to pursue a career, philosophy had more to do with personal preferences and thirst for knowledge. A woman with a degree in the humanities could become a secondary school teacher. Still, it was difficult to achieve for Jewish women who had to navigate the antisemitic Austrian educational system. Another obstacle to being a teacher was a law that stated that female teachers had to give up their posts immediately after getting married (in force in 1873–1919). Examining a group of 460 educated Central-European Jewish women, Harriet Pass

Freidenreich found that very few of them managed to find employment in the educational sector, and most of those who succeeded had converted to Christianity. Meanwhile, almost all women students who took their medical degrees before 1930 went on to work as doctors (2002, p. 58). Statistically, women who enrolled in philosophy departments came from wealthier families than future physicians and were less determined to graduate. They were more likely to drop out, get married, and become mothers.

The data presented in Urszula Perkowska's book on the first female students at the Jagiellonian University confirms Freidenreich's findings. In Kraków, Jewish women were much less likely to enroll in the philosophy department than their Christian counterparts. Before limitations were imposed on women and Jews, in 1918 and 1938, respectively, only 22.3 percent of all female students in the philosophy department were Jewish, compared to 56.1 percent in medicine. Women students in philosophy were also more likely to drop out or transfer to another department (Perkowska, 1994, p. 143). In total, between 1894 and 1939, 401 women dropped out from medicine, compared to 2,250 from philosophy—29.9 percent and 46.5 percent of all women enrolled in the two departments, respectively (p. 144). Moreover, only 27 percent of female students at the philosophy department of the Jagiellonian University managed to graduate, compared to 44 percent of the women studying to be doctors (p. 153). Beata Münzer's career trajectory seems to be a typical case: in 1918, at the age of 22, she possibly interrupted her studies to get married; her daughter Helena was born one year later.

The precise day Beata met her future husband, Otto Rank, is unknown, for he didn't mention her in any of his letters. It happened during the war while he, called up to the army for two years, was stationed in Kraków. The wedding took place in 1918, four days before the war ended. At the time, the "little Rank" (Falzeder, 2002, p. 133) had a closer relationship with Freud than any of Freud's three biological sons (Roazen, 1990, p. 255). When Rank was called up to the army, Freud wrote to Ernest Jones that it was the saddest news related to the war. In 1919 he wrote again: "I am nearly helpless and maimed when Rank is away" (Paskauskas, 1993, pp. 314, 360). Until the young couple settled in Vienna, Freud remained highly suspicious of Rank's decision to marry Beata and was quick to judge her. In a letter to Karl Abraham, he wrote: "Rank seems to have done himself a great deal of harm with his marriage. A little Polish-Jewish woman whom nobody likes, and who does not seem to have any higher interests. It is quite sad and scarcely comprehensible" (Falzeder, 2002, p. 389).

Freud noticed with relief that Otto returned to his work with even greater zeal, as if he wanted "to rehabilitate himself for his marriage" (Brabant et al., 1993, vol. II, p. 321). Freud soon changed his mind about Beata. She supported Otto in his tasks as the editor-in-chief of *Imago*, the first journal dedicated to the psychoanalysis of culture, founded in 1912. She also worked at the Internationaler Psychoanalytischer Verlag publishing house, headed by Otto Rank since 1919. She participated in the meetings of the Vienna Psychoanalytic Society (VPS) and attended the 1920 Sixth International Psychoanalytic Congress in The Hague. Freud admired how this "hospitable and fun-loving little Polish woman" managed to adjust to the spartan conditions the couple was forced to live in (Freud and Eitingon, 2004, p. 254). Otto's monthly salary at the time was 48,000 Austrian Kronen, and Beata received a compensation of 6,000 Kronen (Fallend, 1995, p. 83), while the minimum wage for one person to go by in Vienna at the time was estimated at around 30,000 Kronen. Despite the adverse conditions that the young family lived in in the apartment at Grünangergasse 3, Beata hosted a "psychoanalytical salon" for Freud and his most eminent guests (Lieberman, 1985, p. 158). She also helped organize the International Psychoanalytic Congress in Salzburg in April 1924, taking on such tasks as reserving hotel rooms for the attendees (Freud and Ossipow, 2009, p. 59; Wittenberger and Tögel, 1999, vol. IV, pp. 98, 182, 186).

Beata's role was not limited to being her husband's wife. She translated Freud's "On Dreams" from German into Polish as "O marzeniu sennem" (Freud, 1923). It came out in 1923 as the first volume of the "Polish Psychoanalytic Library" (Polska Biblioteka Psychoanalityczna) launched by the Verlag on her initiative, as the second of only two foreign-language series (the first was the Italian "Biblioteca Psicoanalitica Italiana" founded by the psychiatrist Marco Levi-Bianchini). The following year, two more translations were published in the "Polish Psychoanalytic Library": the *Psychopathology of Everyday Life* (Freud, 1924a) and *Three Essays on the Theory of Sexuality* (Freud, 1924b). It was also Rank's accomplishment that 1924 editions of the journal, *Internationale Zeitschrift für Psychoanalyse*, included a section devoted to Poland (B. Rank, 1924a, 1924b). These achievements alone should secure her an important place in the history of the cultural transfer of psychoanalysis.

In 1923 she was admitted to the VPS based on her presentation on the role of women in the development of societies. She indicated that her lecture was meant as an introduction to future research on the topic. The first part of the study was to focus on women in mythical tradition, the second was on women in prehistoric societies, and the third was on the role of women in history. Her article "Zur Rolle der Frau in der Entwicklung der menschlichen Gesellschaft" or "On the Role of Women in the Development of Human Society," published in *Imago* a year later, outlined the methodological framework of her project (B. Rank, 1924c). When interviewed by Kurt R. Eissler in 1953, Beata affirmed having almost completed her research, but it was never published in full (Eissler, 1953, p. 4).

In this remarkable text, Beata Rank boldly modified Freud's myth of the genesis of culture, as presented in his *Totem and Taboo* from 1913. Drawing on a theory of the matriarchy proposed by a Swiss thinker, Johann Jakob Bachofen, in *Das Mutterrecht* (Bachofen, 1992), she offered two hypotheses: first, that matricide preceded patricide described by Freud; and second, that after the death of the primal father, women tried to regain power and were eventually defeated by a clan of brothers. As a result, there were not two but four stages in the development of human society: the primal rule of the mother, the law of the father, a period marked by the rule of "masculine daughters," and finally, the seizure of power by the sons.

Beata Rank's point of departure was Freud's *Group Psychology and the Analysis of the Ego* (Freud, 1955b/1921). She was uncomfortable with the fact that the yielding of total control from a group to a leader was seen exclusively from a male perspective. She asked about possible differences in the case of female communities, and if a woman could take on the role of a leader, as defined by Freud. She made no secret of the fact that her argument was inspired by Jules Michelet's *The Women of the French Revolution* (1855). She found it especially striking that the women who actively participated in the revolution were said to possess many traits typically seen as masculine, such as bloodthirstiness, feistiness, and bravery. She also discussed the woman's role as "instigator" of violence, which Freud had examined in the context of the heroic myth (Freud, 1955b, p. 136).

Just as Freud founded his anthropological concept on the Oedipus complex and the assumption that ontogeny recapitulates phylogeny, Beata Rank bolstered her argument with the research findings in the field of individual psychology. According to Freud, in the oedipal phase, a mother ceases to be a child's primary object and the father, previously an embodiment of the incest taboo, becomes a model to emulate. Mirroring Freud's designation of the ego ideal, Beata Rank introduced the term "id ideal" to signify the moment when a child identifies with its mother, preceding the identification with the father. This moment occurs before the ego is formed and before the discovery of sexual difference. Thus, the mother cannot become the ego ideal. As a result, the desire for the mother becomes part of the unconscious. The process of idealization of the libidinally charged mother is a mechanism of denial and of not passing through the Oedipus phase. The mother is both an erotic object and an object of identification; she is therefore a "phallic mother," a mother who does not lack anything.

As Freud argues, the mother is the first object for children of all genders. Beata Rank closely discussed a case of a little girl who not only has to transpose her erotic feelings from her mother onto other women (as is the case for boys) but also has to direct her libido to the other sex. She pointed out that girls who fail to complete this milestone in their development have been described in psychoanalysis in pathologizing terms in the context of the castration complex or female homosexuality. According to Beata, this psychological structure of not passing through the Oedipus phase can occur in girls when they make the mother into their original ego ideal. On the level of phylogeny, this process corresponds with the aforementioned second period in the rule of women (the rule of "masculine daughters") while the corresponding figure on the mythological level is the female instigator whose agency is repressed, for the center stage is taken by the battle between the hero and his opponent. Still, the figure of the female instigator represents a residuum of the original female agency.

According to Freud, a society is made up of individuals who have installed the same object in the place of their ego ideal. In a situation where a woman is the leader, she must replace the father, becoming masculine like the warlike Amazons or the frenzied women of the French Revolution. At the same time, she draws her strength from the earlier, motherly id ideal, thus exerting power "through a crossing of identifications" (B. Rank, 1924c, p. 283). Beata Rank refers to the myths cited by Bachofen based on the same pattern: the hero vanquishes the valiant Amazons, and then one of them betrays her sisters and becomes a mother. She discovers a similar structure in the Oedipus myth. After murdering his father, but before he is made king of Thebes, Oedipus must defeat the Sphinx, a representation of the masculine mother (the mother as the ego ideal). Beata argues that the Sphinx is put to death in the transitional, matriarchal phase, between the rule of the father and the rule of the son. However, there is an earlier crime: the murder of the primal mother who is later deified as a female totem. (Beata discusses in some detail the totemic feast highlighted by Freud in *Totem and Taboo*, which in her opinion is an act of "devouring the mother," a return to the incorporation of the mother's body proper to the newborn.) This mother is the id ideal that has no masculine features. She is the caring and nurturing mother, an embodiment of exclusively feminine maternal power. It is her son who, having overcome his own dependency, becomes the father of the primal horde. He is the tyrant, described by Freud as monopolizing all women. After killing his mother, he raises her to the rank of goddess as a form of compensation. When the father is put to death by his frustrated sons, and before they come to rule, it is the women who, freed from the control of the father, assume power for some time. However, they cannot hold the father's position unless they identify with him. Such a female leader is the product of a compromise, a hermaphrodite, a woman with a phallus who, in the mythical tradition, is exaggerated to appear like a monster. The brothers come to power by forcing her into the traditionally feminine role of wife and mother.

There are unexpected parallels between Beata Rank's article and the work of feminist writers of the 1970s and beyond who draw on psychoanalysis, especially Luce Irigaray and her theory of primal matricide (Irigaray, 1993; cf. Jacobs, 2007). At the same time, Beata's theories were firmly embedded in some of the key debates of her time. The 1924 issue of *Imago*, which included her article on the role of women in the development of societies was dedicated to psychoanalysis and anthropology. It also contained Bronisław Malinowski's study "Mutterrechtliche Familie und Ödipus-Komplex," a German version of the paper "Psycho-Analysis and Anthropology" (1924a), three years later incorporated in his book *Sex and Repression in Savage Society* (1927). Based on his research on the Trobriand Islands, Malinowski argued against the universality of the Oedipus complex. In his view, psychoanalysis should instead discuss unique complexes pertaining to each type of civilization.

Malinowski met Beata and Otto Rank in 1923, and consulted his theory with his "Viennese friends" (Stocking, 1986, pp. 33, 35). In his role of the editor of *Imago*, Otto accepted Malinowski's article; as the director of the Verlag, he decided to publish it in book form (Malinowski, 1924b). Malinowski's arguments, just as Beata's, supported Otto's theory alternative to Freud's. In 1924, Otto Rank's book *The Trauma of Birth* already questioned the importance of the Oedipus complex, shifting the original trauma from the discovery of sexual difference to the very moment of birth. Beata extensively quoted from her husband's writings, such as *The Don*

Juan Legend, Art and Artist, and most importantly *The Myth of the Birth of the Hero* (O. Rank, 1975, 1932, 1952); Malinowski also cited Rank at length in his work. On the other hand, *Sex and Repression* indicated that by 1927 Malinowski had overcome his dalliance with psychoanalysis. In a footnote added to the shorter version of the text published in *Imago*, he distanced himself from Rank's *The Trauma of Birth*: "Needless to say, the conclusions of Dr. Rank's book are entirely unacceptable to the present writer, who is not able to adopt any of the recent developments of psychoanalysis nor even to understand their meaning" (Malinowski, 1927, p. 22).

We might surmise that Beata exerted a considerable influence on her husband's theory. First, through her pregnancy and motherhood. In March 1919, when she was four months pregnant, Otto was preoccupied with the primacy of the mother-child relationship. Second, through the dynamics of their relationship as a couple. Ernest Jones noted that shortly after the wedding Otto Rank argued in one of his presentations that, in a way, marriage inevitably repeats the mother-child relationship (Lieberman, 1985, p. 195; Lieberman and Kramer, 2012, p. 157).

Furthermore, Beata's findings proved inspiring to her husband's later research. In a posthumously published essay, "Feminine Psychology and Masculine Ideology" (O. Rank, 1941), Otto Rank wrote about men casting women as the other and as the embodiment of the irrational. He examined their status as a tabooed totem that is cursed and venerated, avoided and desired, inspiring fear and love at the same time. He explored the consequences of replacing the primordial goddess-mother by a self-sufficient male hero in the myths of Greece and Asia Minor. He recognized the repression of femininity in the development of civilization, present only in myths, religion, and art.

Although Otto Rank got Freud interested in the "childhood of humanity" (Freud, 1955c/1916–1917, p. 168) and inspired him to write *Totem and Taboo*, his departure from the theoretical orthodoxy in psychoanalysis and the desire for an independent career led to the dramatic break between the two men in 1926, confirmed by Rank's resignation from the VPS in 1929.

Some commentators blamed Beata Rank for this turn of events. For example, Anna Freud believed that Beata's ambitions were responsible for her husband's actions (Rothe and Weber, 2004, p. 379). In reality, Beata was torn between her loyalty to Freud and the well-being of her own family. Otto's conflict with Freud deepened the already existing marital crisis between Beata and Otto. In 1925, upon realizing that her marriage was struggling, Beata asked Sándor Ferenczi to take her on as an analysand. Ferenczi immediately informed Freud (Brabant et al., 1993, vol. III, p. 202). The father of psychoanalysis was overjoyed. He had hoped to learn about Otto Rank's motivation. He also believed that Ferenczi would get detailed insight into the whole affair, as he was counting on his Hungarian colleague's opinion and support (p. 203). Beata's analysis with Ferenczi never came to be. Instead, she decided to save her marriage by leaving Vienna and following Otto to Paris (Brabant et al., 1993, vol. III, pp. 256, 304). In a letter to Max Eitingon, Freud expressed a skeptical view as to the couple's future:

> Rank's wife paid me a farewell visit. She fully shares our point of view. [. . .]. She says he is all but hoping to be "sent away," that he cannot stand any objections from her and never lets himself be held back when an idea comes to him. The poor woman, she still wishes to be with him—but is finding it hard to bear—she should be assured of our discretion. It seems very doubtful to me how this marriage will end.
> (Freud and Eitingon, 2004, p. 462)

While Beata remained a member of the VPS until its dissolution in 1938, Otto Rank's conflict with Freud impacted the series "Polska Biblioteka Psychoanalityczna": no new publications appeared beyond 1924. Beata's accounts of the reception of psychoanalysis in Poland also disappeared from the *Internationale Zeitschrift für Psychoanalyse* after her husband had lost his editorial position.

Meanwhile, in Paris, Otto ran a successful psychoanalytical practice. In 1933 he was contacted by Henry Miller, riveted by Rank's *Art and Artist* published in New York the previous year (O. Rank, 1932). Soon afterward, Anaïs Nin lay down on Rank's couch, beginning her analysis by declaring, "I am one of the artists you are writing about, Dr Rank" (1966, p. 270). She had hoped Rank could cure her inability to create literary fiction, "help the writer to be born" (p. 305). In this regard, the therapy was successful: she wrote all of her fiction after the analysis was complete, and Nin said on many occasions that she owed her literary development to Rank, for he had convinced her to "write as a woman" (cf. Spencer, 1982).

Anaïs became not only the patient of Beata's husband but also his lover. She reported him saying: "I denied myself life before, or it was denied me—first by my parents, then Freud, then my wife" (1993, p. 370). Like many psychoanalysts of the first generation, Otto Rank never underwent an analysis, despite having analysands and training future analysts since 1919. It was only with Nin that he opened up completely. He told her in detail about the harrowing experiences of his childhood and adolescence and of his longing for artistic creativity. Her interest in his story moved him deeply ("Nobody ever asked me this before. I have to listen to others all the time," Nin, 1995, p. 7). With Nin, Otto shed the role of "Dr Rank." Instead, he called himself Huck, identifying with Mark Twain's resolute little tramp, Huckleberry Finn, who was, like Otto, the son of a brutal alcoholic forced to grow up quickly and take his life into his own hands. It soon became clear to Anaïs that Beata Rank was a caregiving type, like Twain's Widow Douglas, devotedly looking after the neglected boy but unable to relieve his loneliness and alienation. Nin did not take on the maternal role but became Otto Rank's female companion, his twin, his soulmate, the one who understood him, for they were both similarly abandoned and unhappy, as well as equally creative and curious.

The love affair led directly to the breakup of Beata and Otto's marriage. In 1934 Otto left his family and immigrated to the United States. He was soon joined by Anaïs, who also tried her skills as a psychoanalyst, despite having no qualifications whatsoever. The idyll was short-lived. In June 1935, Nin returned to France. But memories of "Mrs Rank" haunted her long after the separation, for instance, when she mistakenly recognized Beata in women she encountered while traveling (Nin, 1995, p. 93). When she thought about how to keep a man she loved, the relationship between Beata and Otto served as a negative example (p. 163).

However, these two women meet not only as soap-opera rivals, fighting over a man as they fight for their right to tell their own story, but also as feminist theorists well ahead of their time. A careful reading of Nin's diary reveals that she owed her view of women's art to Otto Rank who was, in turn, deeply indebted to his wife's feminist theories. As if repeating his conclusions from the essay "Feminine Psychology and Masculine Ideology," an important part of which is a discussion of women's inability to express themselves in a language created by and for men (O. Rank, 1941), Nin wrote that "woman's creation far from being like man's must be exactly like her creation of children, that is it must come out of her own blood, englobed by her womb, nourished with her own milk. It must be a human creation, of flesh, it must be different from man's abstractions" (Nin, 1967, p. 233). Anaïs didn't know Beata's work but, since she knew Otto's so well, it is not surprising to hear her speak in Beata's voice. In 1937, convinced that she had discovered a model of creativity to which she should aspire, she made a diary entry that could have come from Beata Rank's essay, if not for the more radical tone:

> She [a female artist] has to sever herself from the myth man creates, from being created by him, [. . .] recover the original paradise. [. . .] Most women painted and wrote nothing but imitations of phalluses. The world was filled with phalluses, like totem poles, and no womb anywhere [. . .]. My work must be the closest to the life flow. I must install myself inside of the seed, growth, mysteries. [. . .] My art must be like a miracle. Before it goes through the conduits of the brain and becomes an abstraction, a fiction, a lie. It must be for woman, more like a personified ancient ritual, where every spiritual thought was made visible, enacted, represented.
>
> (Nin, 1967, p. 235)

The Ranks got officially divorced in 1939, shortly before Otto's death. At that time Beata was also already living in the United States. She settled in the Boston area in 1936, where she soon fitted into the lively psychoanalytical community mainly made up of immigrants, including Helene and Felix Deutsch, her friends from Vienna, who had arrived in Boston in 1935 and 1936, respectively. Deutsch wrote in her autobiography that she and Beata first met as young mothers (Rank's daughter Helena was two years younger than Deutsch's son Martin): "We were both Polish and both very interested in our small children" (Deutsch, 1973, p. 145). In a touching letter written in Polish in Vienna on March 28, 1933, Helene called Beata her "dearest Tolunia" (a loving diminutive of the nickname Tola) and "a guardian spirit." When discussing her plans to immigrate to Boston, she encouraged her friend to also put her "American plans to fruition" (Deutsch, 1933).

We can make an informed assumption that Beata didn't plan to become a psychoanalyst. She didn't have a personal or training analysis in Vienna; she didn't see patients there (Roazen, 1966, p. 2). She decided to become a psychoanalyst after her marriage started to fall apart and she sought financial independence. Taking advantage of her trips to Switzerland, where her daughter went to school, she underwent psychoanalysis with another Polish disciple of Freud, Mira Gincburg-Oberholzer (sometime between 1926 and 1936). The two women became close friends. Beata Rank even considered

Figure 3.1 Beata "Tola" Rank, probably in the 1950s.
Copyright: Boston Psychoanalytic Society & Institute Archives.

moving in with the Oberholzers when she first arrived in the States (Planta, 2010, p. 94). She also regularly traveled to Vienna to participate in Anna Freud's seminars on child analysis.

Beata's brilliant career as a specialist in psychotic disorders in children began after the separation from her husband. Despite not having any medical background, typically required of psychoanalysts in the US, Beata became a respected training analyst for child psychoanalysts. She was chair of the Educational Committee at the Boston Psychoanalytic Institute and received an honorary professorship at the Boston University School of Psychiatry. Among her most outstanding achievements in the States was co-founding (with Marian Putnam) the James Jackson Putnam Children's Center in 1943, co-chaired by the two women for many years. There, Beata Rank worked with autistic children, adapting the principles of psychoanalytic therapy to their needs. She also worked as a consultant and supervisor for the Judge Baker Guidance Center. She continued to host a popular "European style" salon for psychoanalysts in her Cambridge home where she "introduced [them] to elegant Viennese cuisine" (Gifford, 2003, p. 170). She remained an orthodox Freudian until her death in 1967.

Despite her successes, her contemporaries remember Beata Rank to be suffering from a chronic depression (Roazen, 1990, p. 259). Like all newly arrived Jewish psychoanalysts in the United States, she faced many struggles and suffered from survivor syndrome (cf. Prince, 2006; Kuriloff, 2014). When Siegfried Bernfeld, then still in France, inquired about emigration prospects, she bitterly admitted that, based on her own experiences with American antisemitism, her only advice could be to stay where he was (B. Rank, 1937, p. 1). In the eulogy given at her funeral, Boston psychiatrist and psychoanalyst, John M. Murray, spoke of the impact the Holocaust had on her:

> The helplessness and uncertainty of the unspeakable horrors continued [. . .] until in the late forties it was certain none of the loved ones has survived.[1] In the face of all of these cruelties Tola carried on. Life was not the same, but her devotion to her life's purpose and endeavors never flagged. [. . .] Her productivity in her clinical work, her training and teaching activities, her devotion to the development of the use of analytic methods in the areas of her competency never faltered—though it was so often evident how heavy was her heart.
>
> (Murray, 1967, p. 2)

There could have also been another reason for her depression, dating back to before the war and emigration. Helene Deutsch wrote about her friend in terms that could be summarized as impostor syndrome: "Beata Rank was extremely gifted in her work, but a certain weakness in her personality structure caused psychological problems. [. . .] Although she was loved and admired by many, she suffered from a painful though unjustified sense of inferiority" (Deutsch, 1973, p. 145).

A sense of inadequacy can be felt in the only text she published in her native tongue, the moving translator's introduction to Freud's *On Dreams* from 1923. Here, Beata Rank's own voice can be heard. This voice is muffled in the article she wrote for *Imago* in elegant German, probably proofread by her husband, nor can it be heard in her postwar American publications, mostly brief reports or case descriptions written in the simple English of an émigré.

Beata Rank's two-page introduction to *On Dreams* begins with an admission that she "feels it is her responsibility to provide, even if only in a few words, an explanation and justification for the following translation" (Freud, 1923, p. 3). These words seem to be directed not at the general readership but at the psychoanalytical community. This hypothesis is supported by Freud's note to Beata, appended to his letter to Otto Rank. Freud wrote in it that he would be highly grieved if she gave up on her translation project on account of the "harsh criticism." Though he is unable to assess the quality of her work, he added, he believes that with the help of Polish-language experts in the field, Beata would live up to the challenge. "Don't lose courage: that would not be like you" (Lieberman and Kramer, 2012, p. 142). The draft of her translation had probably garnered negative reviews from other Poles in Freud's circle, most possibly Ludwig Jekels, the first Polish translator of Freud's writings (cf. Freud, 1911, 1913, 1924a, 1924b). We might assume that Beata Rank revised her translation following Jekels's critical feedback. She indicated that she used his translations as a source for "a great majority of terms" (Freud, 1923, p. 4).

In the final paragraph, she implied that if readers have to focus particularly hard to understand the book, her translation would not be the only thing to blame, since the book is merely an "essence" or an "extract of Freud's scholarship on dreams." Still, in her introduction she repeatedly stated that she "hoped for a kind treatment," as if she was questioning the value of her work and almost begging for forgiveness for daring to undertake it.

Beata's disarming introduction can be just an example of a quite typical tendency among women to belittle and dismiss the fruits of their labor, resulting in an impulse to apologize or justify themselves. In Beata's case, however, there is an additional trace that we must not overlook. In the course of my research, I stumbled upon an unexpected difficulty when I tried to confirm biographical information on Beata Rank found in reference works on the psychoanalytical movement. They all asserted that she was a student at the Jagiellonian University when she met Otto Rank (Mühlleitner, 1992, p. 248; Rank-Veltfort, 2005, p. 1443; Roudinesco and Plon, 2000, p. 893), but her name is not in the admissions records (Kulczykowski, 1995; Stopka, 2011) or on the lists of graduates (Suchmiel, 1997). According to the institution's archivists, without formal enrolment, it was impossible to even audit a single lecture. This means that Beata never even crossed the university's threshold.

What is more, I was unable to find Beata Münzer's name on a list of graduates of any of the girls' high schools in Kraków in 1900–1918 (Dutkowa, 1995, pp. 88–109). Regarding the girl's high school in her hometown of Nowy Sącz, there is very little information available besides that 355 girls were studying there before the First World War (Bilewicz, 1997, p. 119). However, the local newspaper, *Ziemia Sądecka*, does not list Beata among the first 13 young women who obtained their *matura* exit exam at the girl's high school in Nowy Sącz in 1913 (Egzamin, 1913, p. 3). She was 17 at the time; no further documents have survived.

It is also worth noting that in the aforementioned footnote to *The Uncanny*, Freud thanks "Frau Doktor Rank," following the German-language tradition of a woman assuming her husband's name as well as his title. This tradition led the first women with doctoral degrees to continue calling themselves "Fräulein Doktor" (Miss Doctor), even after getting married, to emphasize that they had earned their degrees via education (Nipperdey, 1994, p. 52).

It is likely that Beata's aunt, a fellow student of Otto Rank's at the Vienna University who supposedly introduced the two of them in Kraków (Lieberman, 1985, p. 155), presented her niece as a student with the best intentions in mind. Perhaps Beata had considered enrolling at the Jagiellonian University but was unable to do so when the institution shut down during the First World War (Perkowska, 1990, pp. 24–53). Perhaps her plans got thwarted when she married young, became pregnant, and left for Vienna. Perhaps when she arrived with Otto in the vibrant intellectual avant-garde former Imperial capital, Beata felt compelled to pretend to be as highly educated as the other psychoanalysts' wives. Did Freud's trust in her abilities and the fact that she was coping quite well with the successive responsibilities she was given at the publishing house, make her believe that gaps in her formal education or complete lack thereof could be concealed?

The deficiency of academic training would make her achievements even more impressive, making her one of Freud's most talented disciples. It could also account for her lifetime of self-doubt. Sanford Gifford recalled after her death: "Mrs. Rank was known for her uncanny intuition, her sensitivity in observing and synthesizing complex events. At the same time she was remarkably inarticulate in communicating her insights [. . .]. Mrs. Rank also had difficulty writing papers, and needed close collaborators to interpret what she meant" (Gifford, 1996, p. 29). Gifford quotes Helene Deutsch on that Beata had the same difficulty when communicating in her native Polish. Another colleague from Boston, Gregory Rochlin, supposedly called her "a very cultivated, very well-read woman, although I suspect, self-educated" (p. 29).

At this stage of my archival research, I am inclined to assume that the lack of education was Beata Rank's deeply hidden, guilt-causing secret. It is about time to liberate her from its weight and to tell her story, not in terms of failure but empowerment. Indeed, I cannot think of any better illustration of how psychoanalysis enabled women's emancipation than the biography of Beata Rank: Polish Jewish girl from a small Galician town who, thanks to a lucky break (meeting her future husband) and a lot of hard work, achieved incredible professional success and made a name for herself beyond the last name shared with the infamous Otto.

Note

1 It is unclear whom Murray refers to here.

Archival Materials

Birth certificate of Beata Münzer. Akta stanu cywilnego Izraelickiego Okręgu Metrykalnego w Nowym Sączu. Archiwum Narodowe w Krakowie, oddział w Nowym Sączu, 31/494/0/2/34/55.

Deutsch, H. (1933). Letter to Tola Rank from March 28, 1933 (manuscript in Polish), Schlesinger Library, Radcliffe Institute for Advanced Study, Harvard University; Papers of Helene Deutsch, MC 578 10.11.

Eissler, K. R. (1953). Interview with Beata Rank from May 30, 1953 (typescript in German). Library of Congress, Sigmund Freud Papers, MSS39990, Interviews and Recollections, Box 120.

Eissler, K. R. (1954). Interview with Beata Rank from February 13, 1954 (typescript in English). Library of Congress, Sigmund Freud Papers, MSS39990, Interviews and Recollections, Box 120.

Gifford, S. (1996). "Oral History Workshop #44: Women in Psychoanalysis, Part III" (transcript). The American Psychoanalytic Association. The Boston Psychoanalytic Society and Institute; Oral History Transcripts, MS—N029, Box 8, f. 09, pp. 22–34.

Murray, J. M. (1967). Eulogy of Tola Rank (typescript in English). Schlesinger Library, Radcliffe Institute for Advanced Study, Harvard University; Papers of Helene Deutsch, 82—M143-85—M247.

Rank, B. (1937). Letter to Siegfried Bernfeld from April 2, 1937 (manuscript in German). Library of Congress, Siegfried Bernfeld Papers, MSS41897, Box 3.

Roazen, P. (1966). Interview with Beata Rank from February 12, 1966 (manuscript notes in English). Boston University; Howard Gotlieb Archival Research Center; Paul Roazen Collection #1623, Box 12, folder 10.

Reference List

Bachofen, J. J. (1992). Mother Right. In *Myth, Religion, and Mother Right. Selected Writings of J.J. Bachofen.* R. Manheim (Trans.). Princeton, NJ: Princeton UP, pp. 67–207 (Orig. publ. 1861).

Bilewicz, A. (1997). *Prywatne średnie ogólnokształcące szkolnictwo żeńskie w Galicji w latach 1867–1914.* Wrocław: Uniwersytet Wrocławski.

Brabant, E., Falzeder, E. and Giampieri-Deutsch, P. (Eds.) (1993). *The Correspondence of Sigmund Freud and Sándor Ferenczi.* P. T. Hoffer (Trans.). Cambridge and London: Belknap Press.

Czajecka, B. (1990). *"Z domu w szeroki świat": Drogi kobiet do niezależności w zaborze austriackim w latach 1890–1914.* Kraków: Universitas.

Derc, M. (2010). *Anaïs Nin: Studium życia i twórczości.* Toruń: Adam Marszałek.

Deutsch, H. (1973). *Confrontations with Myself: An Epilogue.* New York: W.W. Norton.

Dutkowa, R. (1995). *Żeńskie gimnazja Krakowa w procesie emancypacji kobiet (1896–1918).* Kraków: Księgarnia Akademicka.

Dybiec, J. (1993). *Dzieje miasta Nowego Sącza w czasach Autonomii Galicyjskiej (1867–1918).* Kraków: Secesja.

Egzamin dojrzałości w prywatnym gimnazyum żeńskiem w Nowym Sączu (1913). *Ziemia Sądecka,* 8, 3.

Fallend, K. (1995). *Sonderlinge, Träumer, Sensitive. Psychoanalyse auf dem Weg zur Institution und Profession. Protokolle der Wiener Psychoanalytischen Vereinigung und biographische Studien.* Wien: Jugend & Volk.

Falzeder, E. (Ed.) (2002). *The Complete Correspondence of Sigmund Freud and Karl Abraham, 1907–1925.* C. Schwarzacher (Trans.). London and New York: Karnac.

Freidenreich, H. P. (2002). *Female, Jewish, and Educated: The Lives of Central European University Women.* Bloomington: Indiana UP.

Freud, S. (1911). *O psychoanalizie.* L. Jekels (Trans.). Lwów: Altenberg (Orig. publ. 1910).

Freud, S. (1913). *Psychopatologia życia codziennego.* L. Jekels and H. Ivànka (Trans.). Lwów: Altenberg (Orig. publ. 1904).

Freud, S. (1923). *O marzeniu sennem.* B. Rank (Trans.). Wien: Internationaler Psychoanalytischer Verlag (Orig. publ. 1901).

Freud, S. (1924a). *Psychopatologia życia codziennego.* L. Jekels and H. Ivànka (Trans.). Wien: Internationaler Psychoanalytischer Verlag (Orig. publ. 1904).

Freud, S. (1924b). *Trzy rozprawy z teorii seksualnej.* L. Jekels and M. Albiński (Trans.). Wien: Internationaler Psychoanalytischer Verlag (Orig. publ. 1905).

Freud, S. (1955a). The Uncanny. J. Strachey (Trans.). In J. Strachey (Ed.), *SE, Vol. XVII: An Infantile Neurosis and Other Works* (pp. 217–253). London: The Hogarth Press (Orig. Publ. 1919).

Freud, S. (1955b). Group Psychology and the Analysis of the Ego. J. Strachey (Trans.). In J. Strachey (Ed.), *SE, Vol. XVIII: Beyond the Pleasure Principle, Group Psychology and Other Works* (pp. 67–145). London: The Hogarth Press (Orig. publ. 1921).
Freud, S. (1955c). New Introductory Lectures on Psycho-Analysis. J. Strachey (Trans.). In J. Strachey (Ed.), *SE, Vol. XXII: New Introductory Lectures on Psycho-Analysis and Other Works* (pp. 5–185). London: The Hogarth Press (Orig. publ. 1916–1917).
Freud, S. and Eitingon, M. (2004). *Briefwechsel 1906–1939*. M. Schröter (Ed.). Tübingen: Diskord.
Freud, S. and Ossipow, N. J. (2009). *Briefwechsel 1921–1929*. E. Fischer (Ed.). Frankfurt am Main: Brandes & Apsel.
Gifford, S. (2003). Émigré Analysts in Boston, 1930–1940. *International Forum of Psychoanalysis*, 12, 164–172.
Irigaray, L. (1993). Body Against Body: In Relation to the Mother. In *Sexes and Genealogies* (pp. 7–23). G. C. Gill (Trans.). New York: Columbia UP.
Jacobs, A. (2007). *On Matricide: Myth, Psychoanalysis, and the Law of the Mother*. New York: Columbia UP.
Kramarz, H. (1986). Stan ilościowy gimnazjów galicyjskich w latach 1867–1914. *Studia Historyczne*, 29(3), 359–383.
Kulczykowski, M. (1995). *Żydzi-studenci Uniwersytetu Jagiellońskiego w dobie autonomicznej Galicji (1867–1918)*. Kraków: Księgarnia Akademicka.
Kuriloff, E. A. (2014). *Contemporary Psychoanalysis and the Legacy of the Third Reich. History, Memory, Tradition*. New York: Routledge.
Lieberman, E. J. (1985). *Acts of Will: The Life and Work of Otto Rank*. New York: Free Press.
Lieberman, E. J. and Kramer, R. (Eds.) (2012). *Inside Psychoanalysis: The Letters of Sigmund Freud & Otto Rank*. Baltimore: Hopkins UP.
Magnone, L. (2016). *Emisariusze Freuda. Transfer psychoanalizy do polskich sfer inteligenckich przed drugą wojną światową*. Kraków: Universitas.
Magnone, L. (2023). *Freud's Emissaries: The Transfer of Psychoanalysis Through the Polish Intelligentsia to Europe 1900–1939*. T. Bhambry (Trans.). Lausanne: Sdvig Press.
Malinowski, B. (1924a). Psycho-Analysis and Anthropology. *Psyche*, 4, 293–332.
Malinowski, B. (1924b). *Mutterrechtliche Familie und Ödipus-Komplex: Eine psychoanalytische Studie*. Wien: Internationaler Psychoanalytischer Verlag.
Malinowski, B. (1927). *Sex and Repression in Savage Society*. London: Kegan Paul.
Michelet, J. (1855). *The Women of the French Revolution*. Meta Roberts Pennington (Trans.). Philadelphia: Baird (Orig. publ. 1854).
Mühlleitner, E. (1992). *Biographisches Lexikon der Psychoanalyse. Die Mitglieder der Psychologischen Mittwoch-Gesellschaft und der Wiener Psychoanalytischen Vereinigung 1902–1938*. Tübingen: Diskord.
Nin, A. (1966). *The Diary of Anaïs Nin 1931–1934*. G. Stuhlmann (Ed.). New York: The Swallow Press.

Nin, A. (1967). *The Diary of Anaïs Nin, 1934–1939.* G. Stuhlmann (Ed.). New York: The Swallow Press.
Nin, A. (1993). *Incest: From a Journal of Love: The Unexpurgated Diary of Anaïs Nin 1932–1934.* London: Peter Owen.
Nin, A. (1995). *Fire. From "A Journal of Love". The Unexpurgated Diary of Anaïs Nin, 1934–1937.* R. Pole and G. Stuhlmann (Eds.). New York: Harcourt Brace.
Nipperdey, T. (1994). *Deutsche Geschichte 1866–1918, Vol. I: Arbeitswelt und Bürgergeist.* Munich: C. H. Beck.
Paskauskas, R. A. (Ed.). (1993). *The Complete Correspondence of Sigmund Freud and Ernest Jones, 1908–1939.* Cambridge, MA: Harvard UP.
Perkowska, U. (1990). *Uniwersytet Jagielloński w latach I wojny światowej.* Kraków: Universitas.
Perkowska, U. (1994). *Studentki Uniwersytetu Jagiellońskiego w latach 1894–1939: w stulecie immatrykulacji pierwszych studentek.* Kraków: Secesja.
Planta von, V. (2010). Analysiere nie wieder einen jungen Menschen wie mich . . . Emil Oberholzer und Mira Oberholzer-Gincburg, ein russisch-schweizerisches Analytikerpaar in der ersten Hälfte des 20. Jahrhunderts. *Luzifer-Amor*, 45, 70–104.
Prince, R. (2006). Psychoanalysis Traumatized: The Legacy of the Holocaust. *The American Journal of Psychoanalysis*, 69, 179–194.
Rank, B. (1924a). Polen. *Internationale Zeitschrift für Psychoanalyse*, 1, 101–102.
Rank, B. (1924b). Polen. *Internationale Zeitschrift für Psychoanalyse*, 4, 485–486.
Rank, B. (1924c). Zur Rolle der Frau in der Entwicklung der menschlichen Gesellschaft. *Imago*, 2/3, 278–295.
Rank, O. (1929). *The Trauma of Birth.* London: Kegan Paul, Trench, Trubner & Co., Ltd. (Orig. publ. 1924).
Rank, O. (1932). *Art and Artist. Creative Urge and Personality Development.* Ch. F. Atkinson (Trans.). New York: A. A. Knopf (Orig. publ. 1907).
Rank, O. (1941). Feminine Psychology and Masculine Ideology. In *Beyond Psychology* (pp. 235–270). New York: Dover Publications.
Rank, O. (1952). *The Myth of the Birth of the Hero. The Psychological Interpretation of Mythology.* F. Robbins and S. E. Jelliffe (Trans.). New York: Brunner (Orig. publ. 1909).
Rank, O. (1975). *The Don Juan Legend.* D. G. Winter (Trans.). Princeton: Princeton UP (Orig. publ. 1922).
Rank-Veltfort, H. (2005). Beata Rank-Minzer. In A. de Mijolla et al. (Eds.), *International Dictionary of Psychoanalysis* (pp. 1443–1444). Detroit: Macmillan Reference.
Roazen, P. (1990). Tola Rank. *Journal of the American Academy of Psychoanalysis and Dynamic Psychiatry*, 18, 247–259.
Rothe, D. A. and Weber, I. (Eds.) (2004). *". . . als käm ich heim zu Vater und Schwester": Lou Andreas-Salomé—Anna Freud, Briefwechsel 1919–1937.* München: Deutscher Taschenbuch Verlag.

Roudinesco, E. and Plon, M. (2000). *Dictionnaire de la psychanalyse*. Paris: Fayard.
Spencer, S. (1982). Delivering the Woman Artist from the Silence of the Womb: Otto Rank's Influence on Anaïs Nin. *Psychoanalytic Review*, 69(1), 111–129.
Stocking, G. W. (1986). Anthropology and the Science of the Irrational: Malinowski's Encounter with Freudian Psychoanalysis. *History of Anthropology*, 4, 13–49.
Stopka, K. (2011). *Corpus studiosorum Universitatis Iagellonicae in saeculis XVIII—XX, Tomus III: 1850/1851–1917/1918, M—N*. Kraków: Historia Iagellonica.
Suchmiel, J. (1997). *Żydówki ze stopniem doktora wszech nauk lekarskich oraz doktora filozofii w Uniwersytecie Jagiellońskim do czasów II Rzeczypospolitej*. Częstochowa: WSP.
Wittenberger, G. and Tögel, C. (1999). *Die Rundbriefe des "Geheimen Komitees"*. Tübingen: Diskord.

Part II

Beyond Psychoanalyst
Feminist, Marxist, Director of a Jewish Foster Home

Chapter 4

Margarethe Hilferding
Women's Rights Activist Ahead of Her Time

Candice Dumas

Margarethe Hilferding was the very definition of an emancipated woman. Her life was centered on three basic issues: her identity as a Jew, women's rights, and her commitment to the socialist cause. She was one of the first women to graduate from the medical school in Vienna and the first woman to join Freud's circle. Despite a life fraught with personal and political ruptures, she was a fighter. She fought for women's rights to work and to sexual freedom, and she advocated for access to contraception and the right to abortion. In the end, she fought to save her own life in the Holocaust. She was a truly inspirational woman, who has sadly been mostly marginalized in history.

Both Remembered and Forgotten

Nazi persecution, the war, and the Holocaust not only led to Hilferding's death, but also destroyed all of her possessions and traces of her life. Only one suitcase remained, containing documents and papers, including notes for lectures and sketches of articles, primarily on policies concerning women and family. The suitcase had been left with her sister's family before she was deported and was retrieved by her son Peter Milford (List, 2006, p. 229).

With her death in the Holocaust, Hilferding's professional contributions and her psychoanalytic publications were largely forgotten. By siding with Adler and leaving the Vienna Psychoanalytic Society, she found herself on the margins of mainstream psychoanalysis, even ignored. When psychoanalysis was banned in Austria, many documents and records were lost, leaving a gap in her biography, and she plunged even deeper into oblivion. Hilferding's psychoanalytic contribution only became publicly available in the 1960s when the *Minutes of the Vienna Psychoanalytic Society* were

DOI: 10.4324/9781003455844-7

published. However, for reasons unknown, interest in Hilferding only seemed to start growing in the 1990s. Several books, chapters, and dictionary entries in German were dedicated to her in the 1990s and 2000s, albeit not always remembering her original work. These include Mühlleitner (1992), Cremerius (1992), Roudinesco and Plon (1997), Stipsits (2000), and List (2016). A book with a section on Hilferding by Handlbauer was translated from German to English (Handlbauer, 1998). Mühlleitner also contributed an entry to a French dictionary of psychoanalysis (Mühlleitner, 2002), translated into English in 2005. There is a largely unknown book in Portuguese on motherly love with a chapter devoted to Hilferding, which recognizes the originality of her contributions (Pinheiro, 1991). The most recent book publication is in French (Wilder, 2015). The most comprehensive and informative work encompassing Hilferding's personal and professional life is Eveline List's *Motherly Love and Birth Control* (2006), written in German with the help of Hilferding's son, Peter Milford. Few of the publications appreciated the importance of her contributions to the psychoanalytic theory of maternal love. Most notable examples are the writings in English of Rosemary Balsam (Balsam, 2003, 2013). Another example is Jean Laplanche's text *The Theory of Seduction and the Problem of the Other* (1997), where he recognized her extraordinary contribution to psychoanalytic theory building. Her name is also briefly mentioned in a book on the first women psychoanalysts (Appignanesi and Forrester, 1992, p. 194).

The city of Vienna commemorated her and her family in 2003 by naming a footpath on the outskirts of Vienna, Hilferdingweg, dedicated to Margarethe, Rudolf, and Karl (Autengruber, 2014, p. 133). In 2006, a residential building from 1928–1929 at Leebgasse 100, in the district of Favoriten where Hilferding worked as a district councilor, doctor, and social activist for decades, was named after her, as Margarethe-Hilferding-Hof. The inscription on the memorial plaque reads: She was the first woman to complete a medical degree in Vienna, a doctor and district councilor in Favoriten, and the first female member of the Psychoanalytic Association. She was murdered in a concentration camp in 1942. An inscription on the building reads: Margarethe-Hilferding-Hof. Residential complex built by the Municipality of Vienna in 1928–1929.

Early Life and Jewish Identity

For centuries Jewish people in Austria experienced segregation and discrimination and were excluded from politics, professions, and institutions, keeping them impotent. Rights of Jewish people in Austria were restricted until the late 1860s when they were granted full freedom of movement, travel, and land acquisition. They also achieved freedom of belief and increased civil rights (List, 2006, pp. 8–9). These changes paved the way for Margarethe.

Margarethe Hönigsberg[1] was born on June 20, 1871, in Vienna, Austria, to a Jewish family ("Hönigsberg, Margarethe," Vienna Births, 1856). Despite its minority status, her family was wealthy, well established, and privileged. Her ancestors were respected members of the Viennese community. Her parents' marriage was unusual in that it was the first marriage for love in the history of both families. Until then, all marriages had been for economic or class purposes. Her father, Paul, was a doctor, and her mother, Emma (née Breuer), was a legal counsellor and women's rights activist. They had four children: Otto (b. 1870), Margarethe (b. 1871), Adele (b. 1873), and Clara (b. 1879). The Hönigsberg children had an unusual childhood. They moved between three different places in 1875–1896, which made it difficult to maintain friendships. Ottakring in Vienna was their permanent residence; they spent the summer in Bad Gleichenberg and the winter in Meran. Bad Gleichenberg and Meran were spa towns. The spa guests paid the children special attention because their father was a respected doctor. Margarethe Hilferding seemed to have a happy childhood, with close family ties and identification with both parents (List, 2006, pp. 40–48, 53–65).

The Hönigsbergs were liberal yet observant Jews. They were active in the Jewish community and observed Jewish rituals at home. Emma ran a traditional Jewish household, followed the Jewish laws and customs related to the kosher dietary regulations and observance of the Sabbath. The Hönigsbergs' choice to follow the Judaic traditions was probably informed by both their religiosity and an effort to honor their Jewish origins and the religious views of their social circle (List, 2006, p. 62).

Regardless of her Jewish roots and upbringing, it seems that the Jewish component of her identity was not very important to the adult Hilferding. The part she seemed to relate to, as did most middle-class Central European Jewish families of that time, was the concept of *Bildung* (education), the fusion of the values of the enlightenment and emancipation (Beller, 2008, p. 20; Freidenreich, 1996, p. 83). This was evidenced by Hilferding prioritizing education and her career above conventions like marriage and children in her twenties. It seemed that she had emancipated herself from the more religious constraints of being Jewish for long periods of her life before the 1930s. The main reason being that the gender and class issues were more central to her. It might have also been related to the fact that she believed that education and social emancipation would eradicate antisemitism. She believed that one could build a reputation and become prosperous despite adverse circumstances, through hard work, discipline, and solidarity, as well as intellectual and humanitarian achievements. Still, she was unable to ignore or escape her Jewish identity that determined her tragic fate and death (List, 2006, p. 7).

Education

Before the Austro-Hungarian universities opened their doors to women in 1895 (medical schools in 1900), access to education and employment opportunities for women were very limited (Weinzierl, 2003, p. 12). In the early 1880s, when Hilferding was growing up, there were only two options for women to get an education in Vienna: a teacher training institute or a preparatory high school or a *Gymnasium*. For women who wanted to study without having to move abroad, teacher training was the highest qualification available at the time (Freidenreich, 2002, pp. 5–6).

The Jewish community placed a high value on academic education (Soukop and Rosner, 2019, p. 963), and so did Hilferding's parents who encouraged each of their children to pursue a professional career of their choice. Jewish families were more likely to provide higher education for girls, likely due to the declining Central European Jewish birthrate, thus they could afford to educate their daughters (Freidenreich, 1996, p. 83). Hilferding enrolled in the teacher training institute in Vienna in 1888, at the age of 18 (List, 2006, p. 67). Her choice was untypical. At that time, most women in Austria did not pursue higher education and professional careers (Weinzierl, 2003, p. 13). Most women in Austria were homemakers, like their mothers before them. They ran a household, raised children, tended to their husbands' needs, organized religious events, and supported their children's education and careers (Weinzierl, 2003, p. 14). But not Margarethe Hilferding. She worked hard at the teacher training institute, despite teaching not being the career of her dreams (List, 2006, pp. 68–72).

Hilferding graduated from the teacher's training college in 1893 with honors. She then had to fulfil the requirement of two years of practical experience. Due to the rise of antisemitism and discriminatory civil service regulations towards Jewish women in Vienna, she was unable to get a position at one of the municipal schools (List, 2006, pp. 70–72). The rise of antisemitism at that time was likely linked to the Christian Social Party's coming into power in Vienna, which attributed secularization and modernization of society to Jewish influence (Perry and Schweitzer, 2002, p. 6). Hilferding found a position at a newly opened relatively poor rural school in the Bad Gleichenberg municipality. After a year, she accepted an unpaid teaching position at a private school in Vienna. Hilferding was fortunate to be in a privileged position that allowed her to accept a volunteer job, due to the financial support of her parents. She passed the teaching qualification examination and received her qualification in 1897 (List, 2006, pp. 70–72).

Socialist and Feminist

Hilferding's parents, Paul and Emma Hönigsberg, were socialists. Their socialist views were reflected by their decision to live in a working-class Viennese neighborhood that was not Jewish. It can be deduced from this that they foregrounded the class question above the Jewish question. The rest of their family lived in more affluent areas (List, 2006, p. 42).

Being a medical doctor came with financial security, social recognition, and personal independence. Paul Hönigsberg was known for enjoying treating the working class at his practice in Vienna, rather than enjoying the social recognition that came with being a medical doctor. Due to the unsustainable income that came with treating the working class, he also worked as a spa doctor for the wealthier. He was a progressive social physician, committed to his patients and to improving the health and social policies (List, 2006, pp. 42–44).

Emma Hönigsberg was actively involved in the women's rights movement. She reportedly advocated for women's legal rights, women's suffrage, and full equality in education, work, and associations. She was a member of the organization for women's suffrage, the General Austrian Women's Association, as well as a member of the legal commission of the National Council of Women in Austria since 1902. She also encouraged her daughters, Margarethe, Adele, and Clara, to become politically active and engage in social change (List, 2006, p. 66, 74). Hilferding followed in her parents' footsteps in terms of education, social service, and political views. They must have been impressive authorities for her.

By the time Hilferding graduated from the teacher's training college in 1897, she already had a strong socialist and feminist identity. It stemmed both from her own experiences of being disadvantaged as a woman and from her exposure to the social misery of the lower classes in the rural Austria. She read socialist literature, including the journal of the Socialist Democratic Party of Germany, *Die Neue Zeit* or *The New Times*. It is not documented when she joined the Social Democratic Worker's Party of Austria, but she reportedly gave lectures there from 1901 and joined the Social Democratic Women in 1902 (List, 2006, pp. 73–74).

Hilferding's writings over the years centered on social and political issues, particularly those related to women. She attended lectures of the Libertas reading and discussion group for social democrats. The Libertas intended to prepare future public speakers for political debates. Occasionally Hilferding and her mother, Emma, worked together, for example in their fight for women to gain access to the consumer associations that controlled the food prices (List, 2006, pp. 72–74). Throughout her life, women's rights were Hilferding's main concern, and the participation in the women's movement was the most important one of her political involvements.

Creative Life

The biweekly Austrian magazine *Dokumente der Frauen* or *Women's Documents* focused on politics, literature, and women's emancipation and was edited by women's rights activists. When it first came out in 1899, it included Hilferding's fictional work, *Hanna*, an unhappy love story. In it, when a doctor proposes to Hanna, she initially rejects him, despite being past the customary age for women to marry at the time. Upon discovering that he has a son from a previous relationship, whom he gave up for an adoption, Hanna gives the doctor an ultimatum: she will marry him only if his son comes to live with them. The doctor, in fear of losing his social status due to having an illegitimate child, replies in a letter: "I can't" (Hönigsberg, 1899a, pp. 252–254).[2] It is likely that Hilferding, then 28 and unmarried, was writing from her own disappointing romantic experiences.

Hilferding had a rich imagination and was very creative. She wrote a volume of poetry, *Rot und andere Gedichte* (Red and other poems) (Hönigsberg, 1899b). Some of her poems had a sociocultural focus, especially on poverty, suffering, and oppression of the lower classes (List, 2006, pp. 81–88). For example, a poem titled "Hunger" opened with the following verse:

I am the hunger that holds
The world together with a grip firmer

Than iron clamps.
My arm is strong and my tooth is sharp,
I spare neither woman nor man,
No pleading and whining will help.
             (Hönigsberg, 1899b, p. 13)

Other poems dealt with spiritual life or were a critique of the Catholic Church, its ignorance and hypocrisy (List, 2006, p. 83).

The people have long borne the yoke.
Lulled by the sound of pious bells.
[. . .] But the voice of the people will grow stronger,
The lullaby of the bells
Will drown out all the pious fairy tales.
             (Hönigsberg, 1899b, p. 5)

A few poems concerned Hilferding's inner world and described her emotional states. Some were love poems revealing disappointments in Hilferding's relationships (List, 2006, pp. 81–88).

Medicine—Her True Passion

Despite the fact that women were permitted to study in Austro-Hungary since 1895, they experienced a fierce resistance from the clergy and conservative parents who feared that education may affect their daughters' marriageability. There was also a social stigma associated with the pursuit of university education by women (Freidenreich, 2002, p. 13). Austria and Germany were behind Switzerland, which admitted first female students in 1864 (Holmes, 1984, pp. 243–245). Typically, one of two main arguments was brought up against women's education. The first insinuated that women were physically and mentally unfit for intellectual achievements at university level. Women were believed to be incapable of studying science due to their "cerebral incapacity" (List, 2006, pp. 92–93; Albrecht, 2021). The second argument suggested that intellectual exercise would destroy "feminineness," spoil the female form, and make women's hair fall out. These ideas were presented as "scientific evidence" (List, 2006, p. 92). There was also opposition toward women and men sharing educational institutions, especially in medicine. It was believed that women should be taught separately for reasons of "morality" and "sense of shame," so that the "minds" of women were not offended (List, 2006, p. 92).

Hilferding passed her *matura* exit exam at 25 years old, in 1897. She enrolled in the Department of Philosophy at the University of Vienna, which opened its doors to women that year. Ambitious and determined, Hilferding and two handfuls of other like-minded women found a way to study the discipline they were really interested in: medicine. They started attending medical courses as "extraordinary students" with special permission from professors to participate in each course (Albrecht, 2021; List, 2006, pp. 89–93). At that time, many female "undercover" medical students in Europe had to fulfil this requirement, for example Irma Cronheim (née Klausner) at the University of Halle, Germany, or Rachel Straus (née Goitein) at the University of Heidelberg, Germany (Freidenreich, 1996, pp. 86–87). When in 1900 women were officially permitted to study medicine at the University of Vienna, Hilferding immediately switched faculties. Along with ten other women, including her younger sister, Clara, she received credits for the several semesters she had already completed as an "extraordinary student" (List, 2006, pp. 95–96).

There is no available information regarding Hilferding being affected by misogyny, but we do know that female students of the period were often provoked and disrespected (Freidenreich, 1996, p. 87). Jewish students in Vienna were also regularly targeted by antisemitic attacks when Hilferding was a student (List, 2006, p. 98).

In 1903 Margarethe Hilferding received her medical doctorate from the University of Vienna, as the fifth woman. She was very likely the first to do so after completing her entire studies in Vienna. The magazine *Neues Frauenleben* or *New Women's Life* celebrated her success with the following announcement: "On December 24 [. . .] Miss Margarete Hönigsberg received her doctorate in medicine from the local university. She is the first to acquire a doctorate as a regular student of medicine at the University of Vienna. All previous doctorates in medicine were validations of doctorates acquired abroad" (qt. in List, 2006, p. 100).

Marriage and Motherhood

Typically for the educated professional women of the time, Hilferding was "late" in the making of personal decisions concerning marriage and motherhood. She married in 1904, at 33 years old. Her marriage to Rudolf

Hilferding was somewhat unconventional. First, he was seven years her junior. Second, despite their shared Jewish ancestry, the couple did not marry in a synagogue. The fact that they had a civil marriage indicated that they were not religious and most likely attached little significance to their Jewish identities. It was a marriage of intellectual partners, actively involved in politics (List, 2006, pp. 101–116).

Rudolf Hilferding (1877–1941) was a Marxist economist, theorist, and politician, as well as medical doctor. They met in the Free Association of Socialist Students at the University of Vienna. Rudolf practiced medicine for a brief time, while writing part-time for the German socialist journal *Die Neue Zeit* or *The New Times* on the issues of economics and politics. He eventually left medicine to pursue a career in politics and economics and went on to become the German Finance Minister in 1923 and again in 1928–1929. Margarethe and Rudolf had two sons, Karl in 1905 and Peter (later Milford) in 1908. They moved to Berlin when Rudolf was offered a position as an editor at *Die Neue Zeit* and a lectureship (Nölleke, 2007–2023). They separated in 1909. One reason was that Hilferding was not permitted to work in Germany as a doctor because she did not graduate from a state-controlled university. It must have been devastating, given her determination to pursue a career in medicine. Hilferding moved back to Vienna with her children, where she opened a private medical practice in the city's working-class district. She specialized in gynecology, women's health, and counseling (List, 2006, pp. 101–116).

Psychoanalysis

Hilferding's turn to psychoanalysis coincided with Rudolf's decision to prioritize economics over medicine. Clearly neither of them was satisfied with the medical profession, likely due to the fact that the prevailing medical perspective was narrow and paid little attention to psychosocial factors and conditions (List, 2006, p. 117).

Hilferding had several lines of connection to psychoanalysis. One was her distant relative, Anna von Lieben (List, 2006, pp. 117–133), a cousin of Freud's earliest collaborator, Josef Breuer, included in Freud's and Breuer's *Studies on Hysteria* under the pseudonym "Cecilia M." (Breuer and Freud, 1953/1895, pp. 69–70, 76). Freud even described her as his "teacher" (Freud and Fliess, 1985, p. 229). Another connection was Emma Eckstein, one of Freud's earliest patients. Emma and Hilferding knew each other well via their shared ties to the social democratic bourgeoisie. Hilferding also enjoyed a lifelong friendship with Otto Bauer, the brother of Ida Bauer, better known as "Dora" from Freud's case study (Freud, 1953/1905; List, 2006, pp. 118–119). Finally, Hilferding likely met one of the very first child psychoanalysts, Hermine Hug-Hellmuth, at the university, as they were studying around the same time. Hilferding and Freud both knew the Federn and Heller families through their ties to the social democratic community (List, 2006, pp. 118–119).

In 1885, Freud was appointed lecturer in neuropathology at the University of Vienna. Following his studies of hysteria under Jean-Martin Charcot in Paris, he delivered a lecture on male hysteria to the Vienna Society of Physicians in 1886 (Ellenberger, 1993, pp. 119–136). He then went on to develop his theory of unconscious processes and a dynamic model of the human psyche. His theory on the importance of sexual development was not easy to uphold in conservative Christian, antisemitic Vienna. In 1902, he spearheaded the Psychological Wednesday Society. The group mostly consisted of Jewish intellectuals, including physicians, educators, and writers (Nunberg and Federn, 1962, p. xx). From 1906 onward, the discussions were recorded as the *Minutes of the Vienna Psychoanalytic Society* (p. xviii). At that time, they were still developing a common understanding of fundamental psychoanalytic concepts, such as drive theory, the unconscious, repression, and the Oedipus concept. In 1908 the Wednesday Society was renamed the Vienna Psychoanalytic Society (VPS) (p. xviii).

In April 1910 Paul Federn recommended Hilferding to be the first woman admitted to the all-male group, after almost a decade of existence of VPS (Balsam, 2003, pp. 306–308; Nunberg and Federn, 1974, p. xv). Isidor Sadger was openly opposed to the admission of women. Alfred Adler was in favor of admitting female physicians and laywomen interested in psychoanalysis. Freud felt it would be a "gross inconsistency" if women were excluded on principle (Nunberg and Federn, 1974, p. 477). At the end, there were only two votes against admitting Hilferding and 12 votes in support of it. On May 4, 1910, she joined the group as its first female member (p. 507). She attended meetings regularly and actively contributed to discussions (Balsam, 2003, p. 314).

Thanks to her university experiences, Hilferding knew how to handle the burden of being the first, but prejudices and misogyny of her new colleagues likely affected her. We may assume that their chauvinistic worldviews and ways of speaking must have at least made her uncomfortable. Two main misogynists in the group were Sadger and Fritz Wittels. The former reportedly repeatedly provoked Hilferding. The latter believed that women were hysterical and inferior and their entry into the field of medicine was "a danger for others" (Balsam, 2003, p. 306; Nunberg and Federn, 1962, p. 196). According to Wittels's earlier paper, women's "true profession" was to merely attract men; additionally, they were incapable of understanding the male psyche (Nunberg and Federn, 1962, p. 196). Hilferding was described by her other male colleagues as down-to-earth, an astute observer, and a good listener (Balsam, 2003, p. 314).

Motherly Love

It was customary for new VPS members to present a paper. In January 1911, nine months after becoming a member, Hilferding gave her first, and only, formal presentation, "On the Basis of Mother Love" (Nunberg and Federn, 1974, pp. 113–116). She proved to be a self-confident, clear thinker with excellent observational skills. She used the material collected during her earlier work as a gynecologist and women's counselor, as well as her own experiences of motherhood, and analyzed them through the lens of psychoanalysis (Balsam, 2003, pp. 308–314). Hilferding discovered that it was not uncommon for mothers who had recently given birth to feel disappointed by their newborn and lack the feelings identified as motherly love, even if they had been looking forward to motherhood. After a while, a "sympathy" may develop, based on the "convention that demands love on the part of the mother." The tendency for "psychological factors" to substitute for "physiological mother love" was found mostly in well-educated circles (Nunberg and Federn, 1974, p. 113).

The absence of motherly love manifested itself in refusal to breastfeed, thoughts of giving the baby away, and hostile behavior against the newborn, ranging from maltreatment to infanticide. The first children typically evoked the most hostility in the mother, especially if the father had abandoned her or the child was illegitimate or brought up by someone besides the biological mother. The children growing up in these circumstances were often brought up in a strict way. As a rule, the youngest children elicited the opposite response. They were pampered and spoiled. Hilferding understood this behavior as exaggerated mother love aimed at overcompensating for and repressing the hostile impulses. She also observed that if the mother succeeded in nursing after initial problems, she often did not want to let go of her baby (Nunberg and Federn, 1974, p. 114).

Hilferding drew two conclusions: first, there is no such thing as innate motherly love. Second, motherly love can be triggered by physical contact with the child. In the case of subsequent children, motherly love may be innate. If the mother is capable of recalling the feelings that accompanied the care and nursing of her first child, motherly love may emerge without delay (p. 114).

Hilferding believed that motherly love had a sexual component. She claimed, "certain changes in the mother's sexual life are brought on through the child" (p. 114). From the moment the first fetal movements are experienced, motherly love is awakened. The sensations are pleasurable, even sexual. After birth, the loss of this pleasure may cause an aversion toward the baby. However, milk shooting into the breast may also be pleasurable. Hilferding believed that the sexual sensations of the infant must find "a correlate in the corresponding sensations of the mother" (p. 115).

She observed that mothers often refrain from sex until after they have finished breastfeeding, due to afterpains, as well as frigidity during the nursing period. She concluded that an infant naturally represents a sexual object for the mother. This coincides with the period of the infant's need for care: "If we assume an Oedipus complex in the child, it finds its origin in sexual excitation by way of the mother, the prerequisite for which is an equally erotic feeling on the mother's part" (p. 115). After the period is over, the child should make way for the husband, or the next child. Mothers who don't receive sexual gratification from their sexual partners may hold on to their children as sexual objects longer. This decision should not be seen as a perversion but a prolongation of a natural state (p. 116).

Finally, Hilferding introduced the issue of the role of the father in this situation. She proposed to explore

> under what conditions the father comes to be the child's sexual object (homosexual attitude); under what modalities the child's detachment from this first sexual object occurs; and, further, in what way the period of asexuality (before puberty) is connected with detachment from the mother.
> (p. 116)

Unfortunately, she did not have the time to elaborate on these issues in more detail during the meeting.

Her presentation was intellectually complex, but specific and practical. She did not hesitate to address sexual components. It discussed the mythically and romantically overloaded subject of maternal love, but it inadvertently focused on the sexuality of women, who, while being mothers, remained sexual beings. Hilferding advocated for a psychological approach that saw interpersonal relationships as determined by sexual experiences and pleasurable/unpleasurable sensations.

The responses from the all-male group were ambivalent. The idea of a sexual mother and her destructive impulses was perhaps too taboo, even for this otherwise revolutionary group. They generally believed that motherly love is anchored in the satisfactory experience of conception, and that love for a baby is a continuation of the love for a man. There was some resistance to her ideas, as the men were unable to be part of the discussion of bodily sensations experienced by women prior to and after birth (Balsam, 2013, pp. 310–314; Nunberg and Federn, 1974, pp. 116–125). Instead, much of the discussion was devoted to the natural relationships between mother and child, with references to animals and primitive civilizations, for example Aboriginal Australian and Inuit cultures, eating their young. The terms "degenerate mothers" and "less gifted mothers" were used for those who lacked motherly love (Nunberg and Federn, 1974, pp. 116–125). There was also much focus in the discussion on fatherly love or the absence thereof. Hilferding felt misunderstood. In her concluding remarks after the discussion, she stated that many incidental facts had been overemphasized and the actual key idea had not been dealt with (p. 125).

It took at least two decades for other psychoanalysts to produce significant work on motherhood and the importance of sexuality in the mother-infant relationship. She foresaw the development of a two-person psychology and the psychic reciprocity between mother and child, later developed further by the next generation of psychoanalysts such as Donald Winnicott, John Bowlby, Hans Loewald, and Jean Laplanche (Balsam, 2013, p. 461).

Early psychoanalysis failed to pick up on the revolutionary theories she proposed. The issues and themes of the centrality of the female body, conception, the pregnant body, and childbirth were explored much later by Julia Kristeva (1977) and Rosemary Balsam (2012). Psychoanalysis also failed to investigate the fact that some mothers are not overjoyed with motherhood and reject their babies, and that motherhood is not an instinct and cannot be reduced to a desire to have a child, all linking with Hilferding's proposition that motherly love is not innate (Kristeva, 2005). In the world today it is generally assumed that a mother "should" love her baby from the start and "should" experience the pregnancy and childbirth as a joyous gift, while for many women it is a very different experience. Motherhood and motherly love is a very complex experience, which is precisely what Hilferding was trying to prove in her presentation.

Around the time of Hilferding's presentation in January 1911, Alfred Adler, one of the founders of the psychoanalytic movement and the first president of the VPS, started proposing ideas on sexuality, psychology, and sociology that differed considerably from Freud's and his followers. For example, Adler increasingly disagreed with the basic elements of Freud's theory, such as the emphasis on sexuality and the past. Differences in opinion started escalating. Freud identified Adler's theories as opposed to his own, which was unacceptable. Adler attended his last meeting of the VPS on May 24, 1911. Shortly afterward, he and three other members resigned from the Society. Hilferding did not comment on Adler's theories, nor did she participate in the discussions that led to his resignation. However, when he left, she and five other members signed a letter that criticized the treatment of Adler, while emphasizing their desire to remain in the VPS. After being forced to choose between Adler and Freud, the signatories left the group (Nunberg and Federn, 1974, pp. 279–283).

Adler went on to establish his own Association for Individual Psychology in 1912. Hilferding joined it in the mid-1920s to eventually become the president of the Vienna Association for Individual Psychology after World War I (p. xv). She did not work as a psychoanalyst and never underwent her own personal psychoanalysis. According to her son, Peter, she held the view that psychoanalysis was interesting but too complicated for practice (personal communication, qt. in List, 2006, p. 170).

Adler's ideas fit in with Hilferding's political social democratic views and were ideologically closer to hers than Freudian psychoanalysis. Adler's theory focused on social interactions, the need for connection, community, and belonging. It stressed the power of personal choice, the importance of a positive, encouraging life focus, and the eradication of social inequality. Its two cornerstones of human development, the improvement of worldviews and of living conditions, turned individual psychology into a political pedagogy. Adler was one of the leading advocates for women's rights, children's rights, and the rights of other marginalized communities (Carlson and Englar-Carlson, 2017, pp. 4–8).

Many individual psychologists worked for the Vienna municipal administration, including Hilferding. Her involvement in public health and welfare institutions gradually increased. In 1910 she started working as a doctor in the proletarian 10th district of Vienna with working-class patients. Since 1927 she headed several educational counseling centers in Vienna associated with individual psychology established as part of the Vienna school reform (Mühlleitner, 1992, pp. 145–146). She was also a district councilor in the 1927–1934 period. In addition, she worked as a physician at the Clinic for Nervous Diseases at the Mariahilfer day hospital (or Franz-Josef Ambulatorium) in Vienna, established by Adler (Albrecht, 2021).

Hilferding wrote several articles for the *Arbeiter-Zeitung* or *Worker's Newspaper* as well as the Social Democratic weekly journal, *Sozialdemokratische Wochenschrift*. She addressed the current topics, such as the cost of adequate nutrition and the smuggling trade (Hilferding, 1919a, 1919b, 1920). Her writings were influenced by the suffering of her working-class patients. In the interwar period in Vienna, frustrations were high for the working-class population due to food and fuel shortages, inflation, overcrowding, and housing shortages (Gruber, 1991, pp. 15–16).

Figure 4.1 Margarethe Hilferding, ca. 1930.
Copyright: Dokumentationsarchiv des Österreichischen Widerstandes.

Birth Control and Abortion

Vienna occupied a special position after World War I. As the so-called Red Vienna in 1918–1934, under the Social Democratic Workers' Party (SDAP), it was a socially progressive island within a conservative nation (McEwen, 2012, p. 5). SDAP's views were based on the theories of Austro-Marxism that combined idealistic philosophy, materialistic conception of history, and Marxist economics (Gruber, 1991, pp. 29–44).

In Red Vienna, birth control was seen as a social policy measure in tandem with health care, housing issues, emancipation of women, and education policies. The SDAP promoted access to birth control and adequate sexual education and counseling and worked to lift the abortion ban. Family planning, specifically for the working-class population, was framed as a political duty and seen as a way of increasing earning capacity and economic profitability of the nation (Nemec, 2019, pp. 273–289). The public health councilor of Vienna after World War I and one of the architects of Red Vienna, Julius Tandler, advocated for a "productive population policy"—a specific form of eugenics based on state-prescribed sexual hygiene (McEwen, 2012, p. 44). He founded eugenic-oriented premarital counseling centers that provided selective birth control, venereal disease testing and treatment, and maternity benefits (McEwen, 2010, p. 174). His welfare system was primarily designed to produce physically healthy children (Gruber, 1991, p. 68).

In the 1920s, as a doctor and socialist, Hilferding dealt with women's issues, sexual education, and health policy. In 1922 she published a series of articles titled "Motherhood" in the social democratic worker's newspaper, *Arbeiterinnen-Zeitung* (Hilferding, 1922a, 1922b, 1922c, 1922d, 1922e, 2020/1922). Motherhood was a leitmotif in her professional, political, and personal life. The series of articles discussed planned parenthood for working women and advocated for contraception above abortion as a form of birth control. For Hilferding, birth control was not merely a population policy. It was a real issue encountered daily in her work with female patients who faced health, socioeconomic, and psychological problems associated with having many children and who were forced to make difficult decisions. Hilferding believed that motherhood should be a conscious choice (Hilferding, 1922a). Women with many children often lived in difficult conditions. The children had an increased risk of morbidity and mortality due to malnutrition, illness, insufficient care, and the mother's inability to nurse. Hilferding was also concerned about the impact of multiple pregnancies and childbearing on the mother's body and psyche, and referred to it as exploitation (Hilferding, 1922a, 1922b).

In reality, regular use of contraceptives was not affordable to most working-class women. Additionally, it was often incorrectly used, due to lack of sexual education and counseling and because men resisted it (Gruber, 1987, pp. 57–58). Hilferding also observed that intercourse was often accompanied by fear of unwanted pregnancies and sexually transmitted diseases and was thus not enjoyable for women. She rejected abstinence and *coitus interruptus* as too stressful and a source of nervous disorders (Hilferding, 1922c). Hilferding advocated for greater sexual freedom of women. She taught her patients that intercourse and pregnancy is not a marital obligation, God's will, or inevitable fate. Women don't have to accept them without objection.

Despite being a proponent of contraceptives over abortions, the poor economic and psychosocial circumstances of most of her patients prompted Hilferding to assist with illegal abortions. She viewed abortion as a social problem. In absence of adequate sex education and contraception, it was a prevalent form of birth control among the working-class women (List, 2006, pp. 176–181).

At the 1924 congress of the Association of Social Democratic Doctors devoted to abortion, Hilferding gave a presentation which drew attention to the social and financial costs of having a child. Many doctors were afraid to perform abortions as it was still illegal, forcing women to have dangerous self-induced or "back-alley" abortions (List, 2006, p. 180). In 1924 and 1925 she published a series of essays in a newly founded magazine *Die Mutter* or *Mother* entitled "Birth Control Issues" (Hilferding, 1924, 1925). In 1926 she published a brochure, *Birth Control: Discussions on Section 144* (Hilferding, 1926). In her writings she called for access to birth control and to legal and safe abortions (Hilferding, 1924, 1925). In the interests of socialized medicine, she demanded that health insurance companies cover the costs of contraceptives. She argued that society could control how many children a woman has only if it assumed the costs and responsibility for the offspring (Hilferding, 1926).

In Red Vienna abortion remained an unresolved issue until 1926 when the SDAP permitted abortions in public hospitals in one of three situations: the risk to the health of a pregnant woman, the risk of fetal defect, or when it would put the mother and her other children in economic risk (Gruber, 1987,

p. 43). At the same time, the Social Democratic Workers' Party called for the creation of public birth control clinics and the dispensing of contraceptives through public health services. But neither the SDAP nor municipality turned this into a reality. Instead, the municipality created mothers' consultation clinics throughout Vienna which focused on the problems of childbirth, mother's pre- and postpartum health, and infant care (Gruber, 1987, p. 44).

In 1930, at the World League for Sexual Reform, Hilferding, one of 11 women among 87 speakers, once again lectured on free access to contraceptives and the impunity of abortion (List, 2006, p. 189). With her speech, she anticipated the demands of the 1970s feminists. Almost 100 years later, women's movements are still fighting this battle. Just recently, on June 24, 2022, the US Supreme Court overturned the landmark 1973 *Roe v. Wade* ruling that recognized the constitutional right to abortion. It was immediately followed by several state abortion restrictions. Abortion is currently banned in 24 countries around the world, while many other only allow it in certain cases, such as rape.

Additionally, Hilferding supported women's right to work and financial independence. She encouraged people to consider the ways to improve their circumstances, to build a supportive community, and replace old-fashioned views on marriage (Hilferding, 1928, p. 180).

End of Life

When Engelbert Dollfuss was named Chancellor of Austria in 1932, he formed a right-wing government. Parliamentarian democracy in Austria was replaced with authoritarian rule. The next year, he founded the Fatherland Front (Germ. *Vaterländische Front*, VF), a right-wing conservative, nationalistic political organization. In 1934, the SDAP was declared illegal and was dissolved (Solsten, 1994, p. 191). The next year the VF military and police crushed a workers' uprising. Many participants were arrested, including Hilferding. She was released a week later but lost her job as a school doctor. Like all Jews and non-Catholics, she had her health insurance contract revoked. Her name, amongst others, was smeared in an article (List, 2006, p. 174). She found herself politically and academically sidelined and increasingly isolated.

The rise of antisemitism was followed by a reversal of secularization. The Catholic Church was becoming increasingly authoritarian. The gains of the women's movement were undermined. The labor movement and trade unions were destroyed. Reforms in education, health care, and housing were reversed. Additionally, Hilferding's older son, Karl, converted to Catholicism, joined a Catholic youth organization, and finally joined the priesthood. Interestingly, his baptism and confirmation coincided with her presentation to the Association of Social Democratic Doctors in 1924, during which she particularly criticized the role of the Catholic Church in relation to abortion laws (List, 2006, pp. 199–201).

The Anschluss of March 13, 1938, changed the situation of Jews in Austria dramatically overnight. The Nazis made immediate arrests, and riots began. Identification cards with questions about race, religion, political affiliation, and family roots were introduced. They were later used by the Nazis to organize persecution. Hilferding's younger son, Peter, was interrogated several times following the annexation, in 1938, mainly about his father. His bookstore was ransacked and closed, like many other Jewish businesses (List, 2006, pp. 207–208).

When the abuse of Viennese Jews intensified after the Anschluss, many realized it was time to leave the country, including many of Hilferding's friends. However, according to her son, Peter, she did not consider emigration (List, 2006, p. 209). Her reluctance to flee suggests that she had had a strong attachment to Austria, and more specifically to Vienna. During the violent riots of November 1938, Margarethe and Peter's apartment was searched by the Gestapo, while they were held at gunpoint. They were then taken with hundreds of other Jews to a district police station, arrested and separated. Hilferding was released a week later, only to find that most of her belongings had been stolen or damaged. Jewish men were loaded onto trucks and taken to a concentration camp. One of the Gestapo officers, who was a former friend of Karl's, recognized Peter and he was spared from the concentration camp. He remained in prison until January 1939, when he was released under condition of leaving the German Reich within three weeks. He immigrated to New Zealand on January 30, 1939, where he changed his name to Milford (List, 2006, pp. 210–211).

In 1939 Hilferding turned down a French visa in order to work at the neurology department of the only Jewish hospital in Vienna, the Rothschild Hospital headed by psychotherapist Viktor Frankl. In the fall of 1939, she completed a course in orthopedics to expand her job opportunities in Austria and abroad. She maintained regular contact with Peter until she was transported to Theresienstadt in 1942 (personal communication from Peter Milford, qt. in List, 2006, pp. 213, 219–229). She reportedly wrote in her 1939 letter that work, despite being taxing, made her feel useful.

Figure 4.2 Margarethe Hilferding (second from the left) and Viktor Frankl (fourth from the left) at the Rothschild Hospital, in the 1939–1942 period.
Copyright: Dokumentationsarchiv des Österreichischen Widerstandes.

In February 1941, when exit permits were no longer issued to Viennese Jews, Hilferding finally realized she had to leave the city. She tried to secure a visa and transport abroad but to no avail. Shortly after, Jews were banned from leaving Nazi-occupied territories. Hilferding spent time with the few friends she had left. She looked after relatives of concentration camp prisoners and provided them with financial support (List, 2006, pp. 219–222). In September 1941, when the number of Jewish employees of the Rothschild Hospital had to be reduced, she was let go. With the loss of this fulfilling job also came the loss of the freedom of movement enjoyed by hospital doctors. She was no longer permitted to take her beloved long walks (pp. 222–225).

Shortly after Hitler formulated the Final Solution on January 20, 1942, Hilferding found herself living in a Jewish old people's home in Vienna (List, 2006, pp. 226–229). Deportations to camps in Eastern Europe started a few weeks earlier (*Holocaust Encyclopedia*). She wrote farewell letters to her sons on her 71 birthday, on June 20, 1942 (List, 2006, p. 227). Eight days later she was deported to Theresienstadt in an overcrowded train (p. 228). Her brother, Otto, arrived a few days later. The siblings had a close relationship; her family had always been the strongest source of security for them, as it was for most people in Theresienstadt (pp. 14–15). In 1942 Theresienstadt became a ghetto labor camp for additional 30,000 Jews deported from the German Reich, including about 15,000 from Nazi Austria. The Nazis called Theresienstadt an "old-age ghetto" for the elderly and disabled, and used targeted misinformation to hide the nature of deportations (*Holocaust Encyclopedia*). Medical care was grossly inadequate in Theresienstadt. Hilferding began to provide medical and psychological assistance to other prisoners. The buildings were overcrowded, and people were sick and starving. She didn't have appropriate medication, tools, or help. We may assume that she found relief in her new duty, since work had always been of great importance to her (List, 2006, pp. 12–13).

"Of the approximately 140,000 Jews transferred to Theresienstadt, nearly 90,000 were deported to points further east and almost certain death. Roughly 33,000 died in Theresienstadt itself" (*Holocaust Encyclopedia*). Between September 19 and October 22, 1942, 19,000 people, most over 65, were deported from Theresienstadt to the Treblinka and Maly Trostinec extermination camps, where almost all of them were murdered. Hilferding was taken to Treblinka on September 23, 1942. She died the next day (Jewish Gen). Freud's three sisters, Rosa Graf, Marie Freud, and Pauline Winternitz, were deported to Treblinka in the same transport as Hilferding, where they were executed in gas chambers. Adolfine Freud died in Theresienstadt in 1943 (Gottwaldt, 2004). Hilferding's brother, Otto, died in Theresienstadt on September 27, 1942 (pp. 228–229).

Karl Hilferding tried to escape to Switzerland in 1942, but was arrested and deported to Auschwitz in September that year and then to Niederkirch subcamp where he died on December 2, 1942 (pp. 203–205). Her ex-husband, Rudolf, died in Paris in 1941, in the Gestapo prison La Santé (p. 206).

Conclusion

Throughout her life Margarethe Hilferding continued to use her privileged position of a wealthy educated woman to advocate for those who had less power and whose voices were less heard. She searched for practical solutions to social problems of the working classes. Regardless of how we describe her—a socialist, a feminist, or an activist, her professional persona was certainly her strongest identity. Her work was likely what kept her going without regard to gendered discrimination and antisemitic persecution. She was the forerunner in the fight for women's rights that continues today.

Notes

1 I have come across several different spellings of her name in the various texts consulted: Margret, Margaret, and Margarete. It is likely her name was Germanized and Anglicized over the years. I am using the spelling "Margarethe" following her birth certificate.
2 For texts where no English translation exists, such as this one, the quotations were translated by Candice Dumas.

Archival Materials

Vienna Births. (1856). "Hönigsberg, Margarethe," Book E1 1870–72, Vol. E, no. 1856.

Reference List

Albrecht, H. (2021). *Zum 150. Geburtstag von: Hilferding-Hönigsberg, Margarethe: Zur Behandlung der Schwangerschaftsbeschwerden. Vortrag, gehalten in der Gesellschaft für innere Medizin in Wien*. Wien: Moritz Perez. Online at https://ub.meduniwien.ac.at/blog/?p=37159. Accessed Jan. 20, 2023.

Appignanesi, L. and Forrester, J. (1992). *Freud's Women*. London: Weidenfeld & Nicolson.

Autengruber, P. (2014). *Lexikon der Wiener Straßennamen. Bedeutung, Herkunft, Hintergrundinformation frühere Bezeichnung(en)*. Wien: Pichler-Verlag.

Balsam, R. (2003). Women of the Wednesday Society: The Presentations of Drs. Hilferding, Spielrein, and Hug-Hellmuth. *American Imago*, 60(3), 303–342.

Balsam, R. (2012). *Women's Bodies in Psychoanalysis*. New York: Routledge.

Balsam, R. (2013). Freud, Females, Childbirth, and Dissidence. Margarete Hilferding, Karen Horney, and Otto Rank. *Psychoanalytic Review*, 100(5), 695–716.

Beller, S. (2008). How Modern Were Vienna's Jews? Preconditions of "Vienna 1900" in the World-View of Vienna Jewry, 1860–90. *Austrian Studies*, 16, 19–31.

Breuer, J. and Freud, S. (1953). Studies on Hysteria. In J. Strachey (Ed.), *SE, Vol. II: Studies on Hysteria*. London: The Hogarth Press (Orig. publ. 1985).

Carlson, J. and Englar-Carlson, M. (2017). *Adlerian Psychotherapy*. Washington, DC: American Psychological Association.

Cremerius, J. (1992). Margarete Hilferding (1876–1942). In E. Federn and G. Wittenberger (Eds.), *Aus dem Kreis um Sigmund Freud* (pp. 117–120). Frankfurt: Fischer.

Ellenberger, H. (1993). *Beyond the Unconscious: The Essays of Henri F. Ellenberger in the History of Psychiatry*. F. Dubor and M. Micale (Trans.). Princeton, NJ: Princeton UP.

Freidenreich, H. P. (1996). Jewish Women Physicians in Central Europe in the Early Twentieth Century. *Contemporary Jewry*, 17(1), 79–105.

Freidenreich, H. P. (2002). *Female, Jewish, and Educated*. Bloomington: Indiana UP.

Freud, S. (1953). Fragments of an Analysis of a Case of Hysteria. J. Strachey (Trans.). In J. Strachey (Ed.), *SE, Vol. VII: A Case of Historia, Three Essays on Sexuality and Other Works* (pp. 1–122). New York: Penguin Books (Orig. publ. 1905).

Freud, S. and Fliess, W. (1985). *The Complete Letters of Sigmund Freud to Wilhelm Fliess: 1887–1904*. Ed. M. Masson. London: The Belknap Press of the Harvard UP.

Gottwaldt, A. (2004). Sigmund Freud's Sisters and Death. Notes on Their Fate in Deportation and Mass-Murder. *Psyche*, 58(6), 533–543.

Gruber, H. (1987). Sexuality in "Red Vienna": Socialist Party Conceptions and Programs and Working-Class Life. *International Labor and Working-Class History*, 31, 37–68.

Gruber, H. (1991). *Red Vienna: Experiment in Working Class Culture, 1919–1934*. Oxford: Oxford UP.

Handlbauer, B. (1998). *The Freud-Adler Controversy*. Oxford: OneWorld Publications.

Hilferding, M. (1919a). Wie groß ist unser Lebensmittelbedarf? *Arbeiterinnen-Zeitung*, 6, 14.

Hilferding, M. (1919b). Was kostet eine auskömmliche Ernährung? *Der Kampf, Sozialdemokratische Wochenschrift*, 12(35), 101–105.

Hilferding, M. (1920). Der Schleichhandel. *Der Kampf, Sozialdemokratische Wochenschrift*, 13(4), 300–303.

Hilferding, M. (1922a). Mutterschaft. *Arbeiterinnen-Zeitung*, 31(1), 6–7.

Hilferding, M. (1922b). Mutterschaft. *Arbeiterinnen-Zeitung*, 31(2), 4–5.

Hilferding, M. (1922c). Mutterschaft. *Arbeiterinnen-Zeitung*, 31(4), 4–6.

Hilferding, M. (1922d). Mutterschaft. *Arbeiterinnen-Zeitung*, 31(6), 3–4.

Hilferding, M. (1922e). Mutterschaft. *Arbeiterinnen-Zeitung*, 31(7), 4.

Hilferding, M. (1924). Probleme der Geburtenregelung. *Die Mutter*, 1(2), 4.

Hilferding, M. (1925). Probleme der Geburtenregelung. *Die Mutter*, 2(9), 6–7.

Hilferding, M. (1926). *Geburtenregelung: Erörterungen zum § 144*. Wien and Leipzig: Perles.

Hilferding, M. (1928). Zum Eheproblem. *Der Kampf, Sozialdemokratische Wochenschrift*, 21(4), 180.

Hilferding, M. (2020). Motherhood. P. Woods (Trans.). In R. McFarland, G. Spitaler and I. Zechner (Eds.), *The Red Vienna Sourcebook* (pp. 287–288). New York: Boydell & Brewer (Orig. publ. 1922).

Holmes, M. (1984). Go to Switzerland, Young Women, If You Want to Study Medicine. *Women's Studies International Forum*, 7(4), 243–245.

Hönigsberg [Hilferding], M. (1899a). Hanna. *Dokumente der Frauen*, 1(9), 252–254.

Hönigsberg [Hilferding], M. (1899b). *Rot und andere Gedichte*. Wien: Meyer und Comp.

Kristeva, J. (1977). Sabat Mater. In T. Moi (Ed.), *The Kristeva Reader* (pp. 160–186). Oxford: Blackwell.

Kristeva, J. (2005). *Motherhood Today*. Online at www.kristeva.fr/motherhood.html. Accessed Nov. 5, 2022.

Laplanche, J. (1997). The Theory of Seduction and the Problem of the Other. *International Journal of Psycho-Analysis*, 78, 653–666.

List, E. (2006). *Mutterliebe und Geburtenkontrolle—zwischen Psychoanalyse und Sozialismus. Die Geschichte der Margarethe Hilferding-Hönigsberg*. Wien: Mandelbaum.

List, E. (2016). Margarethe Hilferding-Hönigsberg: Die erste psychoanalytische Theorie der Mutterliebe. In C.-P. Heidel (Ed.), *Jüdinnen und Psyche* (pp. 29–37). Frankfurt am Main: Mabuse-Verlag.

McEwen, B. I. (2010). Welfare and Eugenics: Julius Tandler's Rassenhygienische Vision for Interwar Vienna. *Austrian History Yearbook*, 41, 170–190.

McEwen, B. I. (2012). *Sexual Knowledge: Feeling, Fact and Social Reform in Vienna, 1900–1934*. New York: Berghahn Books.

Mühlleitner, E. (1992). Hilferding-Hönigsberg, Margarethe. In *Biographisches Lexikon der Psychoanalyse: Die Mitglieder der Psychologischen Mittwoch-Gesellschaft und der Wiener Psychoanalytischen Vereinigung 1902–1938* (pp. 145–146). Tübingen: Ed. Diskord.

Mühlleitner, E. (2002). Hilferding-Hönigsberg, Margarethe. In A. de Mijolla (Ed.), *Dictionnaire International de la psychoanalyse* (p. 778). Paris: Ed. Calmann-Lévy.

Nemec, B. (2019). Health Care and Social Hygiene. In R. McFarland, G. Spitaler and I. Zechner (Eds.), *The Red Vienna Sourcebook* (pp. 273–289). New York: Boydell & Brewer.

Nölleke, B. (2007–2023). *Psychoanalytikerinnen. Biografisches Lexikon*. Online at www.psychoanalytikerinnen.de/. Accessed Dec. 26, 2022.

Nunberg, H. and Federn, E. (1962). *Minutes of the Vienna Psychoanalytic Society. Volume I: 1906–1908*. New York: International Universities Press.

Nunberg, H. and Federn, E. (1974). *Minutes of the Vienna Psychoanalytic Society. Volume III: 1910–1911*. New York: International Universities Press.

Perry, M. and Schweitzer, F. M. (2002). *Antisemitism: Myth and Hate from Antiquity to Present*. New York: Palgrave MacMillan.

Pinheiro, T. (1991). Reflexões sobre as bases do amor materno. In T. Pinheiro and H. B. Vianna (Eds.), *As bases do amor materno* (pp. 102–134). Sao Paulo: Escuta.

Roudinesco, É. and Plon, M. (1997). *Wörterbuch der Psychoanalyse: Namen, Länder, Werke, Begriffe*. Wien: Springer-Verlag.

Solsten, E. (1994). *Austria: A Country Study*. Washington, DC: GPO for the Library of Congress.
Soukop, R. W. and Rosner, R. (2019). Scientific Contributions of the First Female Chemists at the University of Vienna Mirrored in Publications in Chemical Monthly 1902–1919. *Monatshefte für Chemie—Chemical Monthly*, 150, 961–974. https://doi.org/10.1007/s00706-019-02408-4
Stipsits, S. (2000). Margarete Hönigsberg. Aus dem Leben einer Pionierin. Unter Einbeziehung der lebensgeschichtlichen Erinnerung ihres Sohnes Peter Milford. In B. Bolognese-Leuchtenmüller (Ed.), *Töchter des Hippokrates. 100 Jahre akademische Ärztinnen in Österreich* (pp. 45–53). Wien: Verlag der Österreichischen Ärztekammer.
Weinzierl, E. (2003). *The Jewish Middle Class in Vienna in the Late Nineteenth and Early Twentieth Centuries*. Center for Austrian Studies (Working Paper 01–1). Online at https://conservancy.umn.edu/bitstream/handle/11299/60664/WP011.pdf?sequence=1&isAllowed=y. Accessed June 5, 2022.
Wilder, F. (2015). *Margarethe Hilferding. Une femme chez les premiers psychanalystes*. Paris: Editions Epel.

Websites

Holocaust Encyclopedia, United States Holocaust Memorial Museum. Washington, DC. Online at https://encyclopedia.ushmm.org/content/en/article/theresienstadt. Accessed Dec. 23, 2022.

Chapter 5

What Do We Know About Tatiana Rosenthal? An Interview With Leonid Kadis

Pamela Cooper-White and Leonid Kadis

This interview was recorded on March 13, 2022, in preparation for the online conference "Sabina Spielrein and the Early Female Pioneers of Psychoanalysis," April 10, 2022, organized by Klara Naszkowska and a conference committee of the International Association for Spielrein Studies, and edited for this publication.

Pamela Cooper-White (PCW): It's my very great pleasure to introduce Dr. Leonid Kadis, who is the most recent and most important biographer of Tatiana Rosenthal. Through a variety of pathways, my Russian translator, Sergey Trostyanskiy, and I were able to find Dr. Kadis and his wonderful book about Tatiana Rosenthal published in Russian (Kadis, 2018). My attention to Rosenthal was drawn because I was already interested in the early history of Freud's inner circle in Vienna, and especially the little-known women members, and because much of Rosenthal's life—at least as we knew it before Kadis did his comprehensive research—seemed so closely to parallel that of Sabina Spielrein. Spielrein's personal story is now well-known, but her important scholarly contributions to psychoanalytic theory are still just being translated and examined thoroughly by scholars of psychoanalysis (e.g., Carotenuto, 1982; Kerr, 1994; Richebächer, 2003; Hensch, 2006; Covington and Wharton, 2015; Launer, 2015; Lothane, 2016; Cooper-White and Kelcourse, 2017; Spielrein, 2002/1987, 2018; about Sabina Spielrein, see Chapter 1 in this book).

Rosenthal, like Spielrein, was a young Jewish woman from Russia who sought medical training in Switzerland

DOI: 10.4324/9781003455844-8

and became involved in the earliest developments of psychoanalysis. Secondary sources (e.g., Van der Veer, 2011) have speculated that she studied at the Burghölzli Hospital in Zurich (where Spielrein was treated for hysteria and subsequently trained as an analyst under C. G. Jung), however there is no documentary evidence to support that suggestion. Both women were medical students at the Zurich University, and both were well trained in biology and medical science, as well as in psychology. Like Spielrein, Rosenthal traveled to Vienna for a short time and joined Freud's Vienna Psychoanalytic Society in 1911 (Mühlleitner and Reichmayr, 1997; Nunberg and Federn, 1979), where they attended four of the same meetings (Nunberg and Federn, 1979, pp. 23, 28, 32–33, 35, 43). Like Spielrein, Rosenthal returned to Russia to disseminate psychoanalytic ideas and practices there, and she also worked in the area of child analysis. Finally, also like Spielrein, she wrote an essay introducing ideas that only later were taken up by Freud—a psychobiographical investigation of Fyodor Dostoevsky (Rosenthal, 1919c). Unlike Spielrein, she was an ardent social democrat and welcomed the 1917 February Revolution in Russia and the very brief period of democratic reform that followed. She rejected the later Bolshevik coup, as her poems attest, and bloodshed was alien to her (Kadis, 2018, pp. 30–31). Her life's work was to forge a synthesis between psychoanalysis and Marxist social reform (Neiditsch, 1921b). Like Spielrein, Rosenthal died tragically—but of suicide, not as a victim of the Holocaust. The cause of her suicide was a mystery until now. Dr. Kadis's (2018) biography provides clues that were previously unknown.

Until now, Rosenthal has remained one of the shadowy figures among the many women pioneers of psychoanalysis (and almost no scholarship has been available in English). The only available brief summaries in English ([n.a.], n.d.a, n.d.b; Leo, 2018) were based heavily on a brief contemporaneous biographical source—an obituary written by one of Rosenthal's close Russian colleagues, Sara Neiditsch (1921b). Rosenthal's known writings consisted of two articles, published in German (Rosenthal, 1911) and Russian (Rosenthal, 1919c), respectively, as well as the existence of a collection of unpublished poetry (Kadis, 2018). Secondary source articles were written about Rosenthal in recent years in French ([n.a.], n.d.c; Accerboni [Pavanello], 1992, 2019; Roudinesco, 1998), Italian (Leo, 2010), and Russian (Meier, 2011), as well as very brief mentions in several articles and books on the history of psychoanalysis in Russia (Angelini, 2008; Etkind, 1997; Marti, 1976; Miller, 1986, 1998; Nölleke, 2019; Rice, 1993; Van der Veer, 2011; Wermuth-Atkinson, 2018). Given the lack of primary sources until now, all the secondary sources leaned on the Neiditsch obituary, and longer articles were highly speculative.

As initial research, I engaged a Russian colleague in New York, Sergey Trostyanskiy, to translate Rosenthal's Russian paper (the Dostoevsky study) and a recent Russian biographical essay (Meier, 2011). Then, Dr. Trostyanskiy, too, became captivated by Rosenthal's story, and during a trip back to Russia he came upon Dr. Kadis's (2018) critical biography of Rosenthal based entirely on new archival resources. In this book, Dr. Kadis, a psychotherapist and forensic clinician, has uncovered a wealth of new information based on previously unknown documentary evidence. The three of us are now working on an edited translation of Kadis's biography into English, together with translations of Rosenthal's two published papers and selected poetry (Kadis, [2024]). This has been a truly international and multilingual scholarly detective story!

Leonid Kadis (LK): I'm very pleased to have an opportunity to talk to you about Tatiana Rosenthal, one of the female pioneers in the history of the psychoanalytic movement, and to share some results of my research. It was presented in my book, *"I Am Young, I Live, I Love . . .": The Tragedy of Tatiana Rosenthal*, published in Russian in 2018.

Rosenthal was one of the most enigmatic figures in early Russian psychoanalysis. Yet she was considered among scholars of Russian psychoanalysis to be the first psychoanalyst in St. Petersburg if not the entire Russia, despite the scarcity of facts about her professional activities or her life in general that could be supported by documents. By the time I took up the study of Rosenthal's life, I had already had some experience in reconstructing biographies, including Dr. Pevnitsky's, who was really the first Russian psychoanalyst (Kadis, 2013), and one more Russian specialist whose name is not well-known even in Russian psychoanalytic circles, Dr. Khaletsky (Kadis, 2014). However, this previous research did not require such an in-depth and extensive search and reconstruction. Rosenthal's story was particularly obscure. She seemed to have been willing to leave no traces of the papers she wrote and reports she made, family life, political views, photos, or the book of poems. For decades there used to be only a cursory outline of her biography, while huge parts of it were missing altogether, largely based on an obituary written by Sara Neiditsch (1921b), Rosenthal's close friend and colleague. It was the only and insufficient source of information about Rosenthal, reproduced over and over again in the works of historians and psychoanalysts. So, this project posed a challenge for me. I was extremely enthusiastic when looking for bits and pieces of information that could help me reconstruct Rosenthal's lifeline, political and professional activities, and the tragic end. I started by searching for all potential published sources in which Rosenthal might have been mentioned to gather clues for further inquiries. I then expanded the search to her relatives: parents, brothers, and sisters. At the same time, I approached archival institutions to uncover potential documentary information about her studies, professional and scholarly work, and records pertaining to the members of her family. Overall, I collected data from 25 archives in seven countries:

108 Pamela Cooper-White and Leonid Kadis

Figure 5.1 Tatiana Rosenthal, before April 1902.
Copyright: State Archive of the Tomsk Region.

	Russia, Belarus, Latvia, Estonia, Austria, Germany, and Switzerland.
PCW:	You really put so much effort into this! And it's remarkable that the photograph on the cover of your book is the only known photograph of her, at least that I had ever seen before!
LK:	There are two photographs. There is also one more portrait inside my book.
PCW:	So, what facts were you able to discover about Rosenthal's life during your archival research that we didn't know before?
LK:	I have been able to reconstruct the story of Tatiana Rosenthal quite fully. She was born in Minsk, then part of the Russian Empire (in present-day Belarus) on July

3, 1884, in a Jewish family. She was the first of five children of Chonel (Conrad) Gilelevich Rosenthal, a merchant, and his wife, Anna Abramovna (née Shabad). In 1900, Tatiana graduated with a silver medal from the Vilna Mariinsky Higher Women's School, and then attended a special pedagogical class to receive the title of a French home tutor. Yet, opting for medical profession, she traveled to Europe. There she attended lectures at the Universities of Halle-Wittenberg, Berlin, and Freiburg. On October 13, 1902, she enrolled in the Medical Faculty of the University of Zurich, yet her studies were frequently interrupted by trips to Russia. After she obtained her doctorate in medicine from the University of Zurich, she passed her final examination at the Imperial Tomsk University in Siberia, and in November 1909, she was awarded the title of *lekar* or practitioner, with distinction.

From that moment on, at the Clinic of Mental and Nervous Diseases in St. Petersburg, Rosenthal's professional activities began. Vladimir Bekhterev was the head of this Clinic that was a part of the Imperial Military Medical Academy. There, back in 1899, he was elected an academician and received a gold medal from the Academy of Sciences of Russia. He was one of the leading Russian psychiatrists and neurologists of that time. For three years Rosenthal served as a resident doctor of the Clinic and several years had a private practice.

As a student she was fascinated by psychoanalysis. So, in 1911–1912, she participated in meetings of the Berlin and Vienna Psychoanalytic Societies, traveling from Russia. In Russia, Rosenthal also became involved in scientific life. Her polemical remarks in the discussions of the St. Petersburg Society of Psychiatrists and at the congresses of the Society of Russian Physicians in memory of N. I. Pirogov demonstrate her broad outlook and ability to formulate her thoughts in a succinct and clear way. From 1915 to 1919, she worked at the Military Hospital and in the neurological department of the Physiotherapeutic Institute. Her works on endocrine pathology published at that period were not known before I managed to unearth them (Rosenthal, 1917, 1919b). They give an idea of her comprehensive scientific interests, embracing not only psychiatric treatment but also internal medicine. Since 1919, Rosenthal worked at several institutions in St. Petersburg together with Bekhterev. She was the head of the Outpatient Clinic and Psychotherapeutic Laboratory of the Institute for the Study of Brain and Mental Activity. She also worked as a senior physician at the Educational and Clinical Institute for Children with Nervous Diseases. This period of her life can be considered the most productive. She became a respected specialist, who practiced psychotherapy with both children and adults, participated in significant events in the psychiatric community, and gave oral reports at conferences and meetings.

Fortunately, her work on Dostoevsky was published (Rosenthal, 1919c), but most of her writings were not. After a long search, I finally found some of them. These works, either unknown or thought to have been lost, reinforce our understanding of the nature of Rosenthal's pioneering work. In them, she presents herself as a sensitive interpreter of Freud. At the same time, she establishes herself as an independent thinker, who develops some of the implications of Freud's doctrine and adapts them for therapeutic and pedagogical practice. Importantly, the events that led Rosenthal to suicide also came to light. I also discovered that she had two brothers and two sisters, found some information about them, along with photos. And I was very happy to find her enigmatic book of poems published under a pseudonym Tatiana Riesen (1918).

PCW: It's notable that Rosenthal was already studying child psychotherapy and analysis and practicing several years prior to Anna Freud's own first published work in child psychoanalysis when she joined the Vienna Psychoanalytic Society in 1922, "Beating Fantasies and Daydreams" (A. Freud, 1923); Melanie Klein's (1975/1932)

Figure 5.2 Tatiana Rosenthal, before September 1909.
Copyright: State Archive of the Tomsk Region.

Psycho-Analysis of Children was not published until 1932 (although both were working with children for some time prior to these publications). Yet we know so much more about Anna Freud and Klein than we do about Rosenthal!

What are some of the myths and misconceptions in the previously published secondary sources on Rosenthal that you had to correct? There were some speculative writings about her in recent years, especially with regard to her possible motivations for committing suicide. Was there anything that you found was particularly incorrect?

LK: Yes, I've been able to refute some erroneous judgments made about Rosenthal's life. From the newly found documents it became apparent that previously available works contained numerous inaccuracies and omissions. Some authors claimed that Rosenthal immigrated to Zurich at an early age and returned to Russia after the revolution; others were mistaken about the year she graduated from the University of Zurich, the date of her return to St. Petersburg, and the year of her death. A number of sources incorrectly stated that she was born and received her primary education in St. Petersburg. Such ungrounded statements abound. Now it has become possible to eliminate a lot of inaccuracies in Rosenthal's biography.

PCW: There were many young Jewish women studying medicine in Zurich because it was a more hospitable place for women to earn a medical degree (Launer, 2015, p. 54). We know that Rosenthal and Spielrein were both there and also both briefly in Vienna in Freud's psychoanalytic society (VPS) during the same year (1911). Rosenthal is listed as a member of the Society in the Society's minutes and membership records (Nunberg and Federn, 1979; Mühlleitner and Reichmayr, 1997), and both are listed as attending the same meetings of VPS on January 24 and 31, 1912, and February 7 and 14, 1912 (as noted earlier). Rosenthal is not at all shy about speaking up at these meetings, as recorded in the minutes. Do you think Rosenthal ever had much direct contact with Spielrein? In her diary in 1910 Spielrein records having helped a Jewish woman friend in Zurich to "overcome her ennui with life" (Carotenuto, 1982, p. 30) and in another entry, she herself wants to find some respite from the "Weltschmerz [world weariness] which I am always trying to help my women colleagues to overcome" (p. 30). Is it at all possible that she is referring there, at least in part, to Rosenthal, since we know from your work that Rosenthal was afflicted with depression? Do you think that Spielrein could have been referring to or including Rosenthal in those comments (as Anna Maria Accerboni [Pavanello] had wondered, 1992, p. 100), since all the Russian students in Zurich were part of a kind of separate colony? (Launer, 2015, p. 55).

LK: Of course, there is a great temptation to intertwine the lifelines of Spielrein and Rosenthal. Both were Russian students at the University of Zurich's Faculty of Medicine during some of the same years where they became interested in psychoanalysis. However, even though their paths had crossed at several meetings of the VPS, there is no documentary evidence of any close contact. At the same time judging by Rosenthal's poetry, she did have a "restless spirit" (Neiditsch, 1921b) or *Weltschmerz*, that you have mentioned in a quote from Spielrein. Spielrein writes about her women colleagues whom she helped to overcome this state, but many other Jewish women from Russia, including Fanny Chalewsky and Esther Aptekman, studied medicine in Zurich around the same time. John Launer states that "large numbers of Russian women" followed the example of Nadezhda Suslova, the first woman student at the university, who matriculated in 1867: "By 1910 there were 362 Russian students at Zurich University. The majority were women, and more than half were studying medicine. Out of 84 students who qualified in medicine there at the same time as Spielrein, no fewer than 52 were Russian women" (Launer, 2015, p. 54). Therefore, we cannot be sure that Spielrein's diary refers to Rosenthal, unless new archival documents were to be discovered to clarify this reference.

PCW: We also know from Neiditsch's obituary that Rosenthal's passionate desire was to create a synthesis between psychoanalysis and Marxist theory. This is supported by Spielrein's letter to Max Eitingon from August 1927 where she cited Rosenthal, alongside Reissner and Luria, stating, "the theories of Freud and Marx do not need to be mutually exclusive: they can exist peacefully side by side" (Spielrein, 2015, p. 222). Rosenthal was also a strong and outspoken advocate for the well-being of the common people from an early age. In what ways was Rosenthal involved in the Revolution(s) in Russia—we have some documentation for that—and how did she try to bring her interest in psychoanalysis together with her political idealism?

LK: We do learn about Rosenthal's fascination with ideas of equality from the obituary, and I was able to track down documents confirming her studies at the Law School of the Higher Women's Courses in St. Petersburg during a pause she made in her medical studies in Zurich in 1906–1908. From 1912 to 1917, she also worked at the Society for the Health Protection of the Jewish Population, a public organization that dealt with medical care for Jews, especially in shtetls. She was a member of the Sanitary Committee and of the Publishing Committee there. She supervised cooperation with doctors and publishers and planned to systematize the society's library. Among people who were close to her, her husband, Mikhail Rosen, and an acquaintance, Vladimir Kantorovich, were prominent leaders of the General Jewish Labor Bund in Lithuania, Poland, and Russia. However, the archival resources have not confirmed the information that Rosenthal was a member of any political party.

At the same time, as we learn from her poetry, Rosenthal was passionate about social democratic and revolutionary ideas. She welcomed the February Revolution of 1917 with enthusiasm. Yet, an extremely brief period of democratic transformations in Russia was followed by the Bolshevik Revolution in October the same year. As far as I know, Rosenthal never spoke openly about her political views, but her poems indicate that she was against the usurpation of political power, the restriction of freedom, violence, and terrorism. I would like to quote from an untitled poem:

> Booming, evil days.
> People have turned into beasts.
> All the same—cry or refrain:
> The line has been crossed.
> "But yet it moves"—
> Galileo said . . .
> There will be many days,
> Many black nights.

> From beastly faces,
> From black claws,
> From slaves' slime,
> From a ravenous toad
> Another face will arise, an unknown one . . .
> This distant vision is far away,
> A long way, like sadness,
> Love this distance,
> Betray or judge it not.
> . . . .
> . . . .
> It is hopeless to measure it . . .
> God, let me believe
> In the sanctity of movement—
> In Transfiguration.
>   (Riesen, 1918, p. 97, trans. A. Atlas)

So, I tend to think that she can hardly be called a communist or a Lenin activist as some publications previously assumed.

PCW: At least one secondary source (Miller, 1998, p. 187n2) reports that she enthusiastically was present to greet Lenin when he returned from exile to Petrograd (now St. Petersburg)? Is that true?

LK: I don't think it's true.

PCW: What do you think are Rosenthal's most important contributions to psychoanalysis, especially after she returned to Russia and began working at the institution headed by Bekhterev?

LK: In my opinion, the most significant one is Rosenthal's contribution to child medical psychoanalysis that was not so much a theoretical as a practical one. Child psychoanalysis began to develop quickly in Russia after the October Revolution. Already in the first post-revolutionary years, the health care system faced grave problems. There was a considerable growth in the number of homeless children, an increase of child and adolescent dissociality, and rising frequency of various forms of developmental disorders and sexual anomalies. Therefore, the practical psychoanalytic work in the field of paedopsychiatry (the branch of psychiatric science and practice devoted to the study and treatment of mental disorders in children) had a strong social orientation. It was assumed that this work would become one of the means of creating healthy "human units," members of a new, that is communist, society. After the October Revolution, academician Vladimir Bekhterev organized one of the first specialized children's psychiatric hospitals, the Educational and Clinical Institute for Children with Nervous Diseases. Tatiana Rosenthal worked there as a chief physician from 1919 until her death in 1921.

The institution was intended for neuropaths, persons with constitutional anomalies of neuropsychic activity, and patients with neuroses, children for whom there was no place in medical institutions of that time. The approach to the organization of the Institute's therapeutic activities was also different from traditional ones, as medical treatment was combined with pedagogical influence on children. This was of paramount importance since the institution had a preventative function. Working at the Institute, Rosenthal had the opportunity to test in practice the validity of Freud's theories of mental development and also to apply the technique of child psychoanalysis in the context of a specialized medical institution. This experience enabled her to participate in the 1919 conference on sexual education in Petrograd. Her report was not published, but I managed to find it in the archive among typewritten summaries of the participants' contributions (Rosenthal, 1919a). From them we learn that Rosenthal put forward a number of fundamental points on which sexual pedagogy should be based. She recommended providing children with truthful answers about sexuality and to encourage them not to share a bed with their parents. She also focused on the necessity of moderation in fondling children. She emphasized the harmful effect of frightening children who masturbate and the sexualizing effect of corporal punishment. Her ideas on sexual education foreshadowed the research of Soviet scholars, such as Vera Schmidt and Rosa Awerbuch. I would like to emphasize that, to the best of my knowledge, Rosenthal's report was the first attempt by a Russian author to create a sex education program based on psychoanalytic theory. At the First All-Russian Congress of Activists against Childhood Deficiency in the summer of 1920, Rosenthal gave a talk entitled "Psychoanalysis and Pedagogy." Proceedings of the congress were published, yet Rosenthal's paper wasn't included in the book. However, I was fortunate to find the abstract of the talk, with a slightly different title, in one of the archives. In her congress presentation, Rosenthal stressed the importance of childhood experiences in which unconscious processes play a large part. She wrote that knowledge of the processes of reaction formation, displacement, and sublimation in the normal and the neurotic child is essential for the pedagogue. According to her, by identifying mental conflicts, psychoanalysis can establish the mechanisms of hysteria and compulsions in children (Rosenthal, 1920). To summarize: Rosenthal's work was groundbreaking for that time. In Russia, it reflected the first experience of systematic treatment and education of children based on the principles of psychoanalysis and conducted in a state institution. Thus, Rosenthal was a pioneer of Russian child psychoanalysis and the first specialist in Russia to practice psychoanalytic therapy not in a private office but in the setting of clinic.

PCW: It strikes me that when you think about the development of child analysis in the western European institutes, what she was doing foreshadows much more the work of Anna Freud and her psycho-educational work at the Hampstead Clinic, as opposed to Melanie Klein's doing strictly interpretive psychoanalysis of children. Anna Freud believed that children didn't have a fully developed unconscious at that point in their development, so it was important to do psycho-education. Nevertheless, Rosenthal's work really precedes by quite some time the work that Anna Freud was doing, and it's again an example of how these women's work can be lost in the mists of history. They actually were laying down some work that was taken up by others much later, whether the later theorists knew of their work or not. For example, with regard to strict Freudian analysis, in addition to working with concepts such as the sexual drive (libido), she also used educational methods, hypnosis, catharsis, and even Jung's association test, so she was willing to work much more eclectically than in a narrowly orthodox "Freudian" approach. And, of course, in the early days of Freudian psychoanalysis, nobody was working as strictly in ways that Freud later insisted upon, especially in the later 1920s. So, Rosenthal was part of that flowering of creativity in psychoanalysis at that time.

I'd like to turn now to what is probably her most important published work, which we're working on translating (Kadis, [2024]), which is her psychobiographical essay in Russian entitled "Dostoevsky's Suffering and Creativity." I'm wondering in what ways this was an important work in terms of so-called applied psychoanalysis, where rather than being purely scientific clinical work, psychoanalysis was applied to literature, history, biography, and culture. Rosenthal called it a "psychogenetic approach to creativity" and was truly pioneering that method. It predates Freud's own published essay on Dostoevsky (Freud, 1961/1928) by nine or ten years. What can you tell us briefly about that paper and its importance?

LK: Rosenthal's unfinished essay on Dostoevsky is indeed an important work, despite the lack of translation into German or, until recently, English (Kadis, [2024]). In it, Rosenthal attempted to develop a particular "psychogenetic" method of investigating artistic creation. The method consists in comparing two sets of data: characters created in the literary work with information about the author's life and her or his experiences, including the pathological ones. In this way, it is possible to establish individual patterns of the creative act, the pathways of the author's imagination. Unlike other psychoanalysts, Rosenthal focused on the differences, not similarities, between the mechanisms of the creativity of the artist and that of children and neurotics. She emphasized that an author creates first and foremost for herself or himself, acting out her or his own negative emotional states. An author embodies in the image the shadowy, unacceptable sides of her or his personality and own dramatic experiences. Inner conflicts are overcome through creativity. After applying this approach to Dostoyevsky's work, Rosenthal concluded that his inner suffering was not only responsible for his creative activity but also provoked his epileptic seizures. With her publication, Rosenthal was ahead of Freud in substantiating the psychogenic and, one might say, pseudo-epileptic nature of the writer's seizures. She identified the individual traumatic experiences framed in vivid and surprisingly realistic descriptions of his literary characters.

There is every reason to believe that Freud was aware of Rosenthal's work on Dostoyevsky. Yet, he passed over it in silence. James L. Rice suggested that Freud would have been familiar with the gist of Rosenthal's article from the summary of Russian papers on psychoanalysis published by Neiditsch (1921a): "The report of her work should have come to Freud's attention a few weeks before he wrote to Zweig about Dostoevsky" (Rice, 1993, p. 143). The explanations why the founder of psychoanalysis neglected to reference Tatiana Rosenthal's work are sufficiently convincing. Firstly, she criticized Freudian pansexualism; secondly, she appealed to the concepts of Alfred Adler, who was ultimately expelled by Freud from the Vienna Society in 1911. (**PCW**: In the same year Rosenthal joined it!) Adler went on to establish his own school of individual psychology and one of Rosenthal's unpublished papers was, in fact, entitled "On Adler's Individual Psychology" (Neiditsch, 1921b,

p. 385). Nonetheless, despite lack of Freud's recognition, Rosenthal's work on the psychogenesis of Dostoevsky's creativity was groundbreaking.

PCW: Freud did cite Spielrein on the death instinct in his *Beyond the Pleasure Principle*—and although he said that he didn't really understand her point of view, he at least acknowledged her (Freud, 1955/1920, p. 55n). In the case of Rosenthal, he didn't acknowledge her at all.

The final mystery surrounding Rosenthal's story until now has, of course, to do with her suicide. Since the only biographical source previously available was the obituary in German by Sara Neiditsch (1921b), scholars who have studied Rosenthal have hypothesized—and I would say maybe even engaged in a bit of "wild analysis." They suggested a number of reasons for her suicide, including her passionate or restless nature (Neiditsch, 1921b) or her inability to face menopause (Leo, 2010, 2018; Accerboni [Pavanello], 1992, p. 103n1). This far-reaching speculation was linked to Rosenthal's psychobiographical essay "Karen Michäelis: The Dangerous Age in Light of Psychoanalysis," in which the protagonist of Michaëlis's novel, *The Dangerous Age*, feels oppressed by sexual frustration and society's repressiveness toward women at midlife, though she does *not* become suicidal (Rosenthal's paper is translated in Kadis, [2024]). The most plausible hypothesis for the suicide was of a sense of foreboding that psychoanalysis and Rosenthal's life's work would eventually be crushed by the already-increasing political repression (Marti, 1976, p. 208; Accerboni [Pavanello], 1992, p. 103). Psychoanalysis was already in a state of disarray after the Revolution (Neiditsch, 1921a; Neiditsch et al., 1922), and political opposition would culminate with Stalin a few years after her death. Maybe she foresaw it. Neiditsch (1921b) mysteriously wrote that Rosenthal's suicide was "fate," and "she was a victim of her own will and power" (p. 384). You were able to view actual psychiatric records and also to consider previously unknown facts about her husband's arrest as a "counter-revolutionary" by the Petrograd section of the Soviet secret police, the Cheka, a forerunner of the KGB, and consignment to a hard labor camp. So, what do your discoveries tell us about the possible reasons for her suicide, leaving behind a son, Adrian, who according to Neiditsch was "tenderly loved and gifted" (Neiditsch, 1921b)?

LK: First of all, I agree with you about "a bit of wild analysis": when there is no objective information about the reasons behind a crucial decision in a person's life, such as suicide, it is rather presumptuous, I believe, to make any hypothesis. In fact, 1920 was a turning point in the life of Tatiana Rosenthal. At the beginning of January her husband, Mikhail Rosen, who was a revolutionary, was arrested by the Cheka. Rosenthal fought to save him for about a year, but she failed, and Rosen was sentenced to 15 years in a hard labor camp. This was the last straw. Utterly exhausted, Rosenthal found herself in the psychiatric clinic of Moscow State University, where she was treated by the famous psychiatrist, Pyotr Borisovich Gannushkin. He was the so-called Red Professor, loyal to the Soviet authorities. Yet, he already had a solid reputation before the revolution as an outstanding specialist in personality disorders. He diagnosed Rosenthal with "severe psychasthenia." According to Gannushkin, it is a personality disorder characterized by heightened anxiety and mistrustfulness, propensity for obsessive introspection and doubts, and dissatisfaction with oneself. I think he was mistaken. Rosenthal's life story, as well as her poetic work, indicate that her dominant personality traits did not match his diagnosis. Moreover, for a diagnosis of a personality disorder to be made, a patient must satisfy several criteria, such as rigidity of character traits, presence of deviations from cultural norms of behavior, affective response, thinking, and communication, and symptoms of social maladjustment. To the best of my knowledge, none of these were present in Rosenthal's case. I am inclined to assume that she was suffering from a psychogenic depression: a state of low mood combined with inhibition of intellectual and motor activity caused by traumatic events in one's life.

Accordingly, Gannushkin's recommendations were, in my opinion, incorrect: he ordered a change of ordinary surroundings and abstinence from work for three to four months. Work—and we shouldn't forget that she was a highly qualified and respected doctor—was probably one of the few factors that had kept Rosenthal from committing suicide up to that point.

Neiditsch was right in that Rosenthal was a very complex and fragile person, carrying a heavy burden of inner contradictions and dissatisfaction with herself. But at the time of her husband's arrest the inner conflict and the external conflict converged. Contrary to Sabina Spielrein's (2019/1912) now best-known thesis, destruction wasn't the cause of coming into being: in spring 1921, Rosenthal took her own life. Thus, her death was a result of a combination of factors. All of them taken together—the collapse of hopes and dreams about social democratic reforms in Russia, disillusionment in the ideals of youth, hunger in Petrograd (present-day St. Petersburg), tuberculosis, having to leave her job, her husband's arrest and imprisonment, and staying all alone with her five-year old son—led her to that final step.

PCW: It's a tragic loss indeed, because she still had much to contribute, and the second part of her Dostoevsky research, where she would have analyzed some of his best-known works, remained unfinished at the time of her suicide. At that time, in their report to the International Psycho-Analytical Association in 1922, Sara Neiditsch along with Ossipow and Pappenheim state that it was "more than unusually difficult" to gather information about the state of psychoanalysis after the revolution, and that in Petrograd in particular, progress in psychoanalysis was mainly due to Rosenthal herself (whose suicide is noted in the article). In recent times, Alexander Etkind (1997) in his well-known survey of the history of psychoanalysis in Russia states that psychoanalysis was already under threat—Trotsky had supported it, but when he lost to Stalin, was it no longer supported? As a result, was Rosenthal no longer able to work entirely in the way that she wished at that time?

LK: The point is, at that period of time psychoanalysis was not beginning threatened yet. On the contrary, it had about seven or eight more years of flourishing, until the end of the 1920s. Many psychoanalytically oriented papers and books were published during that period, including translations of Freud's works and of his followers. The Russian Psychoanalytic Society was established only after the October Revolution, in 1922, and quickly launched its activities. Actually, if she hadn't committed suicide, Rosenthal could have worked as psychoanalyst during that entire period. The idea that psychoanalysis developed in Soviet Russia thanks to Trotsky's support and that Stalin stopped supporting it is a simplification. This supposition, suggested by Alexander Etkind about 30 years ago, is highly hypothetic. Stalin intervened with its development a full decade later.

PCW: And what do we know about the son Rosenthal left behind?

LK: Adrian was raised by his father. After completing a trade school, he graduated from the Moscow Institute of Chemical Engineering *summa cum laude* in 1936. He was deputy chief of staff in the Artillery Brigade in World War II. After getting wounded in 1943, he was demobilized in the rank of major. He then became professor of chemistry at the All-Russian Scientific Research Institute for Inorganic Materials. The Russian Academy of Sciences rewarded him with the title of Honored Worker of Science and Technology of the Russian Federation and the Khlopin Prize for his outstanding contributions to radiochemistry. He inherited the best qualities of the Rosenthal family: he was a brilliant scientist and a

	learned intellectual. He lived a long life until his death in Moscow in 2001.
PCW:	It's also a tragedy for us, as historians, that had we been able to contact him and talk with him before he died, we might have learned even more. So finally, I know that you were very taken with Rosenthal's poetry, and you found a lot of it. What do you think her poetry reveals about her to us today?
LK:	First of all, I was very impressed by the magnetism of her personality, the power of thought, and her erudition. When you learn a lot about Rosenthal and her family, you begin to treat them as very close to you, as if you were acquainted with them. I should mention that there are not many poems in her small book, and some of them are translations of Nietzsche and Richard Dehmel from German. Yet, after discovering her poetry I began to understand that by reading her poems alone, one is able to reconstruct the tragic logic of her life, without taking all the facts about her life into consideration. And even though she was a private person and kept, as I take it, many things to herself, one can learn quite a lot about her inner conflict and her death drive from her poems. I tend to think that her poetry confirms the ideas she expressed in her scientific papers about the genetic connection of creative work with inner suffering. Or probably her awareness about where her own poems came from made her formulate the claim about the origin of Dostoevsky's literary work.
PCW:	You close your biography of Rosenthal with one of her poems. We will also close our dialogue with an English rendering of Rosenthal's own Russian translation of Friedrich Nietzsche's poem "Yorick as a Gypsy" about death and immortality (Nietzsche, 2019/1884). As you have pointed out, she selected for translation only those poems that were in many ways close to her personality and her worldview. There are some differences between Rosenthal's rendering and Nietzsche's original, which

also contains images of death on gallows, and a hanged man screaming at an uncomprehending crowd that they will die, but he will live on forever.

> Just know my covenant:
> There is no corruptible death for me!
> I will turn into smoke or light,
> I'll come back in the form of air!
> You should know my covenant well:
> There is no death, no death for me!
> ~ Tatiana Rosenthal, translation
> from Nietzsche's "Yorick as
> a Gypsy" (Riesen, 1918,
> p. 58, trans. S. Trostyanskiy
> and A. Atlas)

Archival Materials

Rosenthal, T. (1919a). Доклад о половом воспитании детей—Doklad o polovom vospitanii detei. Tsentral'nyi gosudarstvennyi istoricheskiy arkhiv Sankt-Peterburga. F. 2265. Op. 1. D. 820. L. 24–25ob.

Rosenthal, T. (1920). Психоанализ во врачебной педагогике—Psikhoanaliz vo vrachebnoi pedagogike. Tsentral'nyi gosudarstvennyi istoricheskiy arkhiv Sankt-Peterburga. F. 2265. Op. 1. D. 829. L. 38.

Reference List

[n.a.] (n.d.a). *Psychoanalysis: Tatiana Rosenthal*. Online at www.answers.com/topic/rosenthal-tatiana. Accessed Aug. 29, 2022.

[n.a.] (n.d.b). *Tatiana Rosenthal or Rozenthal (1885–1921)*. Online at https://en.wikipedia.org/wiki/Tatiana_Rosenthal. Accessed Aug. 29, 2022.

[n.a.] (n.d.c). *Tatiana Rosenthal, Encyclopédie sur la mort*. Online at http://agora.qc.ca/thematiques/mort/dossiers/rosenthal_tatiana. Accessed Aug. 29, 2022.

Accerboni [Pavanello], A. M. (1992). Tatiana Rosenthal: Une brève saison analytique. *Revue internationale d'histoire de la psychanalyse*, 5, 95–109.

Accerboni [Pavanello], A. M. (2019). Rosenthal, Tatiana (1885–1921). In A. de Mijolla (Ed.), *International Dictionary of Psychoanalysis, Vol. III*. Farmington Hills, MI: Thomas Gale Publ. Online at www.encyclopedia.com. Accessed April 15, 2019.

Angelini, A. (2008). History of the Unconscious in Soviet Russia: From Its Origins to the Fall of the Soviet Union. *International Journal of Psychoanalysis*, 89(2), 369–388.

Carotenuto, A. (1982). *A Secret Symmetry: Sabina Spielrein between Jung and Freud*. A. Pomerans (Trans.). New York: Pantheon.

Cooper-White, P. and Kelcourse, F. (Eds.) (2017). *Sabina Spielrein and the Beginnings of Psychoanalysis: Image, Thought, and Language*. London and New York: Routledge.

Covington, C. and Wharton, B. (Eds.) (2015). *Sabina Spielrein: Forgotten Pioneer of Psychoanalysis*. 2nd ed. New York: Brunner-Routledge.

Etkind, A. (1997). *Eros of the Impossible: The History of Psychoanalysis in Russia*. New York: Routledge.

Freud, A. (1923). Beating Fantasies and Daydreams. *International Journal of Psycho-Analysis*, 4, 89–102.

Freud, S. (1955). Beyond the Pleasure Principle. J. Strachey (Trans.). In J. Strachey (Ed.), *SE, Vol. XVIII: Beyond the Pleasure Principle, Group Psychology and Other Works* (pp. 7–64). London: The Hogarth Press (Orig. publ. 1920).

Freud, S. (1961). Dostoyevsky and Parricide. J. Strachey (Trans.). In J. Strachey (Ed.), *SE, Vol. XXI: The Future of an Illusion, Civilization and its Discontents, and Other Works* (pp. 175–194). London: The Hogarth Press (Orig. publ. 1928).

Hensch, T. (Ed.) (2006). *Sabina Spielrein: Nimm meine Seele—Tagebücher und Schriften*. Freiburg: Freitag.

Kadis, L. R. (2013). Алексей Александрович Певницкий. Краткий очерк жизни и творчества—Aleksei Aleksandrovich Pevnitskiy. Kratkiy ocherk zhizni i tvorchestva. In A. A. Pevnitskiy (Ed.), *Naviazchivosti. Fobii. Alkogolizm: Psikhoanaliticheskie trudy* (pp. 103–111). Izhevsk: ERGO.

Kadis, L. R. (2014). Жизнь и труд А.М. Халецкого—Zhizn' i trud A.M. Khaletskogo. In A. M. Khaletskiy (Ed.), *Iskusstvo. Shizofreniia. Prestupnost': Psikhoanaliticheskie trudy* (pp. 167–179). Izhevsk: ERGO.

Kadis, L. R. (2018). "*Я молода, я живу, я люблю . . .": Трагедия Татьяны Розенталь—"Ia moloda, ia zhivu, ia liubliu . . .": Tragediia Tatiany Rozental*. Izhevsk: ERGO.

Kadis, L. R. [2024]. *Tatiana Rosenthal: Suffering and Creativity*. P. Cooper-White (Ed.), S. Trostyanskiy (Trans.). London: Routledge.

Kerr, J. (1994). *A Most Dangerous Method: The Story of Jung, Freud, and Sabina Spielrein*. New York: Vintage.

Klein, M. (1975). *Psycho-Analysis of Children*. A. Strachey (Trans.). New York: Delacorte Press/Seymour Lawrence (Orig. publ. 1932).

Launer, J. (2015). *Sex vs. Survival: The Life and Ideas of Sabina Spielrein*. New York: Overlook Duckworth.

Leo, G. (2010). La honte et l'âge dangereux. In C. Trono and E. Bidaud (Eds.), *Il n'y a plus de honte dans la culture* (pp. 103–118). Paris: Penta Éditions.

Leo, G. (2018). *Tatiana Rosenthal*. Online at http://web.tiscali.it/tatianarosenthal/biography.htm. Accessed June 5, 2023.

Lothane, H. Z. (2016). Sabina Spielrein's Siegfried and Other Myths: Facts versus Fictions. *International Forum of Psychoanalysis*, 25, 40–49.

Marti, J. (1976). La psychanalyse en Russie et en Union soviétique de 1909 à 1930. *Critique*, 32(346), 199–236.

Meier, S. (2011). Предисловие—Predislovie. In T. K. Rosenthal (Ed.), *Stradanie i vorchestvo Dostoevskogo*. Izhevsk: ERGO.
Miller, M. A. (1986). The Origins and Development of Russian Psychoanalysis, 1909–1930. *Journal of the American Academy of Psychoanalysis*, 14(1), 125–135.
Miller, M. A. (1998). *Freud and the Bolsheviks: Psychoanalysis in Imperial Russia and the Soviet Union*. New Haven: Yale UP.
Mühlleitner, E. and Reichmayr, J. (1997). Following Freud in Vienna: The Psychological Wednesday Society and the Viennese Psychoanalytical Society 1902–1938. *International Forum of Psychoanalysis*, 6, 73–102.
Neiditsch, S. (1921a). Die Psychoanalyse in Russland wahrend der letzten Jahre. *Internationale Zeitschrift für Psychoanalyse*, 7(3), 381–384.
Neiditsch, S. (1921b). Dr Tatiana Rosenthal, Petersburg. *Internationale Zeitschrift für Psychoanalyse*, 7(3), 384–385.
Neiditsch, S., Ossipow, N. and Pappenheim, M. (1922). Psychoanalysis in Russia. *Bulletin of the International Psycho-Analytical Association*, 3, 513–520.
Nietzsche, F. (2019). Unpublished Fragments from the Period of "Thus Spoke Zarathustra" (Spring 1884—Winter 1884/1885). In *The Complete Works of Friedrich Nietzsche, Vol. XV*. P. S. Loeb and D. E. Tinsley (Trans.). Stanford, CA: University of Stanford Press.
Nölleke, B. (2019). *Geschichte der Psychoanalyse in Russland*. Online at www.psychoanalytikerinnen.de/russland_geschichte.html. Accessed June 13, 2023.
Nunberg, H. and Federn, E. (Eds.) (1979). *Minutes of the Vienna Psychoanalytic Society, Vol. IV: 1912–1918*. M. Nunberg (Trans.). New York: International Universities Press.
Rice, J. L. (1993). *Freud's Russia: National Identity in the Evolution of Psychoanalysis*. London: Routledge.
Richebächer, S. (2003). *Eine fast grausame Liebe zur Wissenschaft*. Munich: BTB.
Riesen, T. [Rosenthal, Т.] (1918). *Руки слепой—Ruki slepoi*. Petrograd: M. I. Semenov.
Rosenthal, T. (1911). Karin Michaëlis: "Das gefährliche Alter" im Lichte der Psychoanalyse. *Zentralblatt für Psychoanalyse*, 7–8, 277–284. [Lecture presented to the Berlin Psychoanalytic Society, Jan. 5, 1911].
Rosenthal, T. (1917). Случай комбинированного расстройства внутренней секреции—Sluchai kombinirovannogo rasstroistva vnutrennei sekretsii. *Psikhiatricheskaya gazeta*, 1, 10–13.
Rosenthal, T. (1919b). К вопросу о конституциональном гипогенитализме—K voprosu o konstitutsional'nom gipogenitalizme. *Nauchnaya meditsina*, 3, 325–331.
Rosenthal, T. (1919c). Страдание и творчество Достоевского. Психогенетическое исследование—Stradanie i tvortchestvo Dostoevskogo. *Voprosy izucheniya i vospitaniya lichnosti*, I.
Roudinesco, É. (1998). Les premières femmes psychanalystes. *Mil neuf cent*, 16(16), 27–41. Online at www.persee.fr/web/revues/home/prescript/article/mcm_1146-1225_1998_num_16_1_1182. Accessed June 13, 2023.

Spielrein, S. (2002). *Sabina Spielrein: Sämtliche Schriften*, 2nd ed. Hensch, T. (Ed.). Gießen: Psychosozial-Verlag/Edition Kore.

Spielrein, S. (2015). Letter to Max Eitingon. B. Walton (Trans.). In C. Covington and B. Wharton (Eds.), *Sabina Spielrein: Forgotten Pioneer of Psychoanalysis*, 2nd ed. (p. 222). London: Routledge. [Orig. unpubl. manuscript 1927.]

Spielrein, S. (2018). *The Essential Writings of Sabina Spielrein*. R. Cape and R. Burt (Trans.). London: Routledge.

Spielrein, S. (2019). Destruction as a Cause of Becoming. B. Mathes with P. Cooper-White (Trans.). In P. Cooper-White and F. Kelcourse (Eds.), *Sabina Spielrein and the Beginnings of Psychoanalysis: Image, Thought, and Language* (pp. 209–253). London and New York: Routledge (Orig. publ. 1912).

Van der Veer, R. (2011). Tatyana on the Couch: The Vicissitudes of Psychoanalysis in Russia. In S. Salvatore and T. Zittoun (Eds.), *Cultural Psychology and Psychoanalysis: Pathways to Synthesis* (p. 53). Charlotte, NC: Information Age Publishing.

Wermuth-Atkinson, J. (2018). Petersburg and the New Science of Psychology. In L. Livak (Ed.), *A Reader's Guide to Andrei Bely's "Petersburg"* (p. 111). Madison, WI: University of Wisconsin Press.

Chapter 6

Erzsébet Farkas
An Unknown Heroine and Her Wartime Mission in a Jewish Foster Home

Dóra Szabó

To the Memory of Ferenc Erős, one of the founders of the Theoretical Psychoanalysis Doctoral Program at the University of Pécs, Hungary, and my mentor who called my attention to the work of Erzsébet Farkas's granddaughter, Mária Hódos, and introduced me to her personally.

Introduction

There has recently been an increased interest among researchers in the role women played in the history and development of psychoanalysis (Thompson, 1987; Appignanesi and Forrester, 1992; Perelberg and Leff, 1997; Sayers, 1991; Freidenreich, 2002; Borgos, 2010, 2021; Borgos, Chapter 10 in this book; Naszkowska, 2022). Thanks to their studies we have learned in the past few decades about the theoretical and practical contribution of female patients, analysts, and financial supporters to this new psy- discipline dealing with "people's mental health, behavior, cognitive capacities, personalities, and social functionality" (McAvoy, 2014, pp. 1527–1529) in the first half of the twentieth century. Most of the prior investigations focused on women pioneers who successfully introduced new psychoanalytic concepts and methodologies (Thompson, 1987; Appignanesi and Forrester, 1992; Perelberg and Leff, 1997; Sayers, 1991; Quinodoz, 2007; Graham, 2009; Covington and Wharton, 2015; Borgos, 2021) or criticized the classical Freudian theory of psychosexual development of children and its approach to girls (Chasseguet-Smirgel, 1970; Balsam, 2015; Chodorow, 1989). As a result, professional contributions of women psychoanalysts, who were not members of any psychoanalytic societies or associations and did not teach at institutes or universities or publish in professional journals, are still understudied and not part of the psychoanalytical discourse. This chapter aims to contribute to an inclusion of the completely unknown work of a Hungarian female "analyst," Erzsébet Farkas, to the broad scientific audiences, by exploring her unique professional life.

Erzsébet Farkas was the director of a Jewish foster home that operated in 1938–1942 in Békés, a small village in southeastern Kingdom of Hungary (the name was used in 1920–1946 for the conservative and nationalist country ruled by Miklós Horthy). With time she served as a foster parent to six to ten foundling Jewish boys (their number was constantly changing) who found themselves in the home. Some of the reasons behind their stay in the home were poor financial situation of their families, being born out of wedlock, and Jewish ancestry. When Farkas accepted the job in 1938, she did not know how physically, mentally, and emotionally challenging her position would be. She had to raise the boys on her own, while performing all of the housework (Vajda, 2019). Despite the everyday exhausting routine of physical and mental work, she was able to find the time to record her observations in her diary. In years, she wrote several hundred pages preserving in writing the information on the intellectual and emotional development of the foster children and the difficulties of everyday life in rural Kingdom of Hungary on the eve of and during the Second World War. The detailed records reveal the social divisions in the late 1930s and early 1940s, with particular regard to the difficulties of the coexistence of Jews and Christians, and the rising antisemitism (Hódos and Farkas, 2019). This chapter is based two historical sources: the previously unpublished diary of Erzsébet Farkas, first published in 2019 by her granddaughter, Mária Hódos, as *Fiaim, hol vagytok?* (Eng. My Boys, Where Are You?). Hódos supplemented the diary with the results of a comprehensive investigation conducted with the goal of identifying the children from the Békés foster home. She tried to contact and interview those of them who were still alive and fill in the gaps from the diary with their individual perspectives. Although seven of the boys survived the Holocaust, only one could be reached in person who immigrated to Israel in 1948. The second source used in the chapter is Farkas's correspondence with Kata Lévy, member of the Hungarian Psychoanalytical Society (Hódos and Farkas, 2019).

Erzsébet Farkas's knowledge of psychoanalytical theory and practice defined her observational perspective and analysis of the behavioral issues experienced by the foster children and their intellectual and emotional development. Her interest in psychoanalysis stemmed from her participation in seminars organized by female members of the Budapest School of Psychoanalysis, such as Kata Lévy, Edit Gyömrői, Vilma Kovács, and

Alice Bálint. Budapest was then the third hub of psychoanalysis in Europe after Vienna and Berlin. The Hungarian Psychoanalytical Society, founded in 1913 and chaired by Sándor Ferenczi, informally called "the Budapest School," represented specific views on the theory and practice of psychoanalysis, strongly influenced by Ferenczi (cf. Mészáros, 2014; Borgos, 2021). During the seminars, besides acquiring theoretical knowledge, she became part of the Hungarian psychoanalytic community to some extent (Hódos and Farkas, 2019, p. 512). She made personal and professional connections with other female psychoanalysts, especially Kata Lévy, a prominent member of the Hungarian Psychoanalytical Society. The contact with Lévy proved very helpful during the years Farkas spent in Békés: she would regularly send Lévy a copy of her diary to consult on the issues she encountered with the boys (p. 501).

This present chapter is divided into three sections. The first part provides an overview of the history and operation of the Békés foster home and its specific connection to the Hungarian psychoanalytical community. It also explores the influence of psychoanalytic theory on Farkas's pedagogical approach to the disturbed children. The second part concentrates on Farkas's values in relation to women's emancipation. It also considers the importance of her being a woman to her pedagogical work. The third part investigates the role of Judaism in the everyday life of foster children, and the nature of their Jewish identities in reference to the religiosity of the local people.

The Family Background and Career Path of Erzsébet Farkas

Erzsébet Farkas was born in 1907, Budapest, in Hungary. Her father, Ignác Farkas, worked at the Franklin Literary and Printing Corporation for almost 40 years as a printing worker. As a working-class representative, he belonged to the local labor union and was an activist in the Social Democratic Party of Hungary. Erzsébet Farkas's mother, Róza Klein, was an orphan. To support herself financially, Róza Klein had to work in a clothing workshop since she was very young, 12 or 13. Farkas remembered that her mother was clever and resourceful but unable to get an education due to their difficult financial situation caused by the First World War. Farkas's two siblings, Pál and Magda, both perished in the Holocaust. Her older brother, Pál, starved to death in 1944 in the labor camp of Sopronbálfalva during forced labor service. Her younger sister, Magda, was deported and murdered in Bergen-Belsen concentration camp in 1944 (Hódos and Farkas, 2019, pp. 509–510).

Erzsébet Farkas's enormous enthusiasm for learning became evident in her teenage years. According to her own statement, what she wanted most at that time was to go to school (p. 510). Her wish was fulfilled when her mother enrolled her in a trade school at the age of 14. The reason behind this decision was to allow Farkas to find a job as soon as possible. After graduating at the age of 15 in 1922, she started working at the Hungarian Italian Bank. Then, in the 1920s, she worked as an accountant at a number of companies. At 16, an opportunity presented itself to participate in free English classes at the so-called English Medical and Psychological Laboratory (pp. 510–511). She studied the English language and participated in lectures in various fields given by young medical students, such as biology, philosophy, pedagogy, and psychology. During the two years she spent in the Laboratory, Farkas gained an extensive theoretical knowledge. It also strengthened her ambition to become a teacher. The career path she had chosen was in sharp contrast to her mother's idea that a young girl should marry and her plan to arrange a beneficial marriage for her daughter. Despite her mother's disapproval, after completing the trade school, Farkas continued her education in a preparatory high school or a *Gymnasium*. She supported herself by doing bookkeeping in the evenings. However, her proletarian background impeded her graduation, because Kálmán Bernolák, the director of her *Gymnasium*, allowed only children of university-educated parents to graduate. She dealt with the obstacle with the help of her employer, Imre N. Balog, who influenced the decision by pressuring Bernolák to finally allow her to graduate in 1930 (p. 511).

In 1931, Erzsébet Farkas married Rezső Holczer, from a similar socio-economic background. Holczer, an ironworker actively involved in a trade union, contributed to the formation of the Budapest workers' movement. Their only son, Mátyás, was born in 1933. After their divorce, Mátyás remained with Farkas and then moved with her to Békés in 1938 (p. 512).

Farkas knew what she wanted in terms of her career path: she wanted to become an educator. However, she was unable to realize this dream because of the antisemitic Hungarian laws of the period, including the introduction of the *numerus clausus* in 1920. She could not get a higher education and, hence, could not obtain a pedagogical certificate. Regardless of her exclusion from academia, she remained well informed of the new educational trends of the time and became deeply interested in psychoanalytic theory.

Figure 6.1 The Farkas family, 1926. From the left: Pál, Róza, Erzsébet, Ignác, Magda. Reproduced with permission of Mária Hódos.

The Origins of the Foster Home

In 1910, an unusual Hungarian child welfare institution, the Israelite Patronage Association, was established with the goal of providing care for the Jewish children who had been orphaned or lived in inadequate socioeconomic conditions. Since 1937, the Patronage was more concerned with the generational transition of the Jewish cultural and religious traditions, increasingly threatened with extinction. The Patronage argued that children with Jewish roots should exclusively be raised in family of the Jewish denomination (p. 12).

The foster home in Békés was established in response to this appeal. It was founded by a local pharmacist, Lajos Goldberger, in 1938. The funds came from two sources: the Royal Hungarian State Children's Shelter and the Patronage, who then controlled and supervised the running of the home. Their financial contributions were insufficient to cover the everyday functioning of the home. Goldberger was forced to make considerate financial sacrifices to provide basic living conditions (pp. 11–16): he had to use his own savings. An advertisement was placed in a Budapest-based social democratic daily newspaper, *Népszava*, in search of dedicated employees to run a rural children's home. Erzsébet Farkas likely applied for the position of a home manager through the advertisement (p. 497).

During the prime ministership of Pál Teleki, in 1920, the number of Jewish students in higher education was severely limited. The *numerus clausus* capped the proportion of Jews admitted to a university at 6 percent. Although the *numerus clausus* did not mention Jews directly, it was clear that the law was created specifically for them. Then, the First Jewish Law of 1938, modelled on the Germany's Nuremberg Laws, passed by the parliament when Béla Imrédy was prime minister, limited the number of Jews to 20 percent in liberal professions and in commercial, financial, and industrial companies that employed more than ten intellectuals. Many professions were affected by this law: lawyers, physicians, engineers, journalists, and actors (Don, 1986). At first, the anti-Jewish laws in the Kingdom of Hungary defined "Jews" in religious way, but the restrictions affected also Jews who had been baptized after 1919. The comprehensive Second Jewish Law of 1939, designed by the Imrédy government but passed by his successor, Pál Teleki, redefined "Jewishness" as a race. It eliminated people with Jewish ancestry from the administrative and judicial public sector and drastically limited their economic involvement. The implementation of the Third Jewish Law was initiated by the Bárdossy government in 1941. It extended the definition of "Jewishness" to anyone with two grandparents born Jewish. It is also prohibited "interracial" Jewish-Christian marriages and sexual relations between them (Kovács, 2016, pp. 37–44).

To compensate for the discriminative anti-Jewish laws in Hungary, Patronage hoped to preserve in the Békés foster home the Jewish identities of the children and Judaic traditions through education. However, the initiative had some serious downfalls. In some cases, children who had lived in Christian foster homes were separated from their foster families and placed in an entirely unfamiliar environment. It also turned out that some of the children had been unaware of their Jewish origin. As a result, they had to adopt to a new cultural tradition, rituals, and customs they had been unacquainted with. This, in turn, often led to severe identity crises that manifested in behavioral disorders. Goldberger and Farkas both found the mandatory Jewish education problematic and causing a number of obstacles in their work with the troubled children (Hódos and Farkas, 2019).

Despite the financial difficulties, Goldberger had grandiose ideas for the operation of the foster home. He wanted to build a lasting bond between the children and Judaism. His other goal was to teach the boys a profession, such as agriculture or handcraft, that would help them sustain themselves after leaving the home at 18 (p. 56). It was Farkas who was usually charged with the implementation of Goldberger's ideas. The method of implementation of his visions was often a subject of their disputes. Farkas saw the issues of boy's occupation from much more professional and practical perspective. She often confronted Goldberger pointing out the impracticality and inconsistency of his idealistic concepts (pp. 331, 425, 441–443).

Connection With Psychoanalysis

In order to provide a broader historical context to my research, I need to add a brief overview of the extraordinary role of Hungarian women analysts in the history of the application of psychoanalysis in education. In the 1920s and 1930s, the psychoanalytical community became interested in this new research field. The field was dominated by female members of the Hungarian Psychoanalytical Society, most of whom were non-physicians, usually educators (Vajda, 1996; Borgos, 2021). For example, Alice Hermann, Alice Bálint, Kata Lévy, Rotter Lillian, and Edit Gyömrői from the Budapest School of Psychoanalysis tried to introduce psychoanalytic theory to lay audience. In 1936–1938 they organized so-called Wednesday seminars offering lectures, symposiums, and discussions of case studies. They were addressed to nonprofessionals interested in psychoanalysis and focused predominantly on the issues of child rearing and the psychological aspects of the mother-child relationship. In 1935, a new psychoanalytic journal, *Gyermeknevelés*, was founded with the goal of publishing articles on various aspects of psychoanalytically oriented pedagogy (Vajda, 1996, p. 329). In its four years of operation, until 1939, the journal grew to become the most influential scientific forum for reform pedagogical ideas and child psychology. In addition to *Gyermeknevelés*, another important Hungarian journal, *A Jövő Útjain*, founded in 1926, published articles on the application of psychoanalytic theory in education. Both journals were important professional forums for female analysts.

Erzsébet Farkas was associated with the Hungarian psychoanalytical community in a number of ways. For almost two years, between 1936 and 1938, she regularly attended the Wednesday seminars (Hódos and Farkas, 2019, p. 512). In this period, she learned about the basic psychoanalytic concepts and internalized the psychoanalytic understanding of human behavior. As a result, she became an admirer of the Hungarian psychoanalytic movement.

At that time, she met Kata Lévy, who was one of the lecturers and a full member of the Hungarian Psychoanalytical Society (cf. Borgos, 2017a).

Farkas and Lévy had a professional and a personal relationship. Lévy analyzed Farkas's son, Mátyás, who began to suffer from a number of symptoms considered neurotic at the time, when his parents' relationship started to sour. These included zoophobia, dysphemia, and bed-wetting (p. 448). The connection between Farkas and Lévy became even more significant when the former was at the Békés foster home. At that time, Farkas regularly sent Lévy copies of her diary entries for consultation. Lévy tried to help by providing psychoanalytic interpretations of behavioral problems and reflections on the educational methods used by Farkas.

Farkas's nonprofessional interest in psychoanalytic theory is manifested in many of her diary entries. It shaped the composition and structure of the text and the nature of the recurring topics. Her psychoanalytical knowledge determined the topics and issues she had considered worth discussing. Second, she consistently used psychoanalytic terminology, such as castration anxiety and sublimation, and psychopathological terminology, such as neurosis, sadism, and persecution mania. She interpreted the penis and female genitalia in psychoanalytic terms. Third, psychoanalytic theory shaped her attitude toward the children and her choice of pedagogical methods concerning their behavioral issues (Hódos and Farkas, 2019, pp. 44, 53–54, 57, 84, 89, 114, 131, 268, 278, 365, 484).

Regarding behavioral issues, Farkas most frequently referred to the work of an Austrian psychoanalyst, August Aichhorn. In her diary, she suggested that Aichhorn's approach was discussed during the Wednesday seminars (Aichhorn, 1925/1951). Her claim was supported by the fact that Kata Lévy had a personal relationship with Aichhorn. Her son, Vilmos Lévy, was living with Aichhorn in Vienna in the 1920s (Borgos, 2021, pp. 152–156). Kata Lévy was probably up to date on Aichhorn's educational and therapeutic practices at a welfare school for delinquent boys (Aichhorn, 1951/1925). Farkas mentioned Aichhorn (with a typo in his name) and his method of dealing with new members of his educational institution in her letter to Lévy from November 8, 1939. She also referred to his approach in a letter to a physician and regular participant of the Wednesday seminars, Emma Gál, written on the same day (Hódos and Farkas, 2019, pp. 43–44). Aichhorn recognized that acting out was an important aspect of the treatment of juvenile delinquents, which could reveal their hidden emotions and anxieties (Aichhorn, 1951/1925). This idea attracted Farkas's attention and helped her understand the latent meaning of the boys' lack of impulse control. Unfortunately, the constrained living conditions of the home and the bad opinion of the locals precluded her from practicing Aichhorn's technique and allowing her pupils to act out. She and Goldberger agreed that if their living conditions improved, they would use an empty room to apply Aichhorn's method (Hódos and Farkas, 2019, p. 45).

It is not surprising that one of the most often recurring topics in Farkas's diary was the dynamics of a mother-child relationship and its connection to behavioral problems of the foster children. Farkas was aware of Alice Bálint's analytical work with children. She even suggested one of Bálint's books, probably *The Psycho-Analysis of the Nursery* (Bálint, 2017/1931), to the Békés rabbi. Bálint was a Hungarian anthropologist turned analyst who focused on the role of the mother in child development. Contrary to Sigmund Freud, Bálint argued that the early mother-child relationship is not exclusively driven by biological drives, such as the death drive or sexual instincts. Its foundation was the so-called archaic love: unconditional and mutually satisfactory. We may identify this special connection between mother and infant as a primary object relation. Therefore, Bálint's concept is one of the first attempts to define an object relation theory (Bálint, 1941; Vajda, 1996, p. 334).

In October 1938, Erzsébet Farkas started to work in the foster home that housed six boys aged four to six. All of her pupils came from a low socioeconomic background. Their reading and writing skills were significantly below their age level. The boys also struggled with socialization. Their perceived behavioral control was unsatisfactory, and they were verbally and physically aggressive (Hódos and Farkas, 2019, pp. 23–24).

Although Farkas did not always use the correct psychoanalytic terminology employed by her colleagues, such as Kata Lévy or Alice Bálint, to describe mother-child relations, she recognized the defense mechanism of projection and understood how it worked. She instinctively detected the source of the projection in the mother-child relationship. She believed that projection occurred when children tried to rid themselves of unwanted feelings towards their mother. One of the boys was not an orphan, but his mother had to entrust him to the Patronage Association because of financial reasons. According to Farkas, this mother also had mental problems, which made her constantly project her emotional life onto the child. Therefore, she paid special attention to manipulative, guilt-causing maternal behavior, which proved her extraordinary ability to analyze the dynamics of mother-child relationship (pp. 119, 282).

Figure 6.2 Foster children in Erzsébet Farkas's care in Békés, 1939.
Reproduced with permission of Mária Hódos.

Working With Troubled Children

At first, Farkas gathered information about the personal backgrounds of the children and wrote brief case studies on the psychological and intellectual states they were in upon arrival. Her notes focused on describing symptoms, which might have a psychological background (pp. 479–489). The purpose of the notes was to send them to Budapest, to have them discussed during the "Wednesday seminars." Farkas had hoped that seminar participants would provide helpful insights facilitating her pedagogical work at the foster home. Unfortunately, her plan did not come to fruition. There was not enough time during the seminars to discuss her cases. Time was limited and there was a large number of cases waiting to be analyzed (pp. 51–52). This clearly indicates that the number of mothers interested in getting professional psychological counseling was growing. Second, personal attendance was required during the counseling given during the seminars in order to provide adequate feedback to the client. Farkas obviously could not personally attend the seminars. As a result, she was unable to get the professional assistance she had hoped for (pp. 51–52). However, the correspondence with Kata Lévy continued for four years, in 1938–1942.

The latter continuously reflected on diary entries sent by Farkas and provided her professional advice.

In her diary, several remarks of a sociopsychological nature can be found regarding shifts in the group dynamic. Farkas noticed a decrease in her son's sense of responsibility within the group (p. 30). She observed that it was accompanied by a more disrespectful and insolent behavior. Newly arrived children also played an important role in modifying the group structure because their arrival caused interpersonal conflicts. Another phenomenon frequently described throughout the diary was sibling rivalry, which often manifested itself in aggressive behavior. She interpreted it using psychoanalytic theory, as a form of repetition compulsion (p. 58).

Apart from aggression, the most frequently recurring symptom in children was inability to control one's sphincters, such as urinary retention. The issues not only made the domestic work harder for Farkas (there was an insufficient number of bedclothes) and radically reduced the comfort in the rooms, but also was a serious health risk. The boys' beds made of straw could quickly start to rot, and the wet underclothing could cause cystitis. When unannounced health official investigators, for example the health officer of Gyula, a town near Békés, visited the home, they repeatedly threatened to close it because of this issue (pp. 61, 64). The investigators typically visited the home when Farkas was absent, so she was unable to argue with their opinions. The medical officers criticized not only the conditions of the home but also the Jewish dietary regulations followed there, seen as an obstacle to assimilation (pp. 38–39, 81–82).

According to Kata Lévy, the boys' behavioral problems described in Farkas's letters originated predominantly from the lack of identification. During the identification process, a child identifies with the moral values of her or his parents or other parental figures and begins to imitate their behavior. Parents mediate the social norms and expectations that children should internalize in order to adapt to the society. The continuous presence of a role model with whom emotional attachment can be built is essential to the successful identification process. In the case of foster care, this requirement is rarely fulfilled because parent figures change frequently. Lévy believed that the solution was to provide a substitute for the absent unconditional maternal love (pp. 42, 54). One of the milestones in building an emotional bond with the boys was the time Farkas took to talk with them privately about their problems. As a result, she became familiar with the unique emotional needs of each child.

Despite many serious difficulties, Farkas observed in her diary that the emotional bond she was able to build with the boys functioned as a reparative experience. In their relationship with Farkas they experienced a mother representative as a simultaneously good and bad love object. Farkas was strict in the imposition of discipline, but she was also affectionate, empathic, and caring. The formation of the mutual attachment was also informed by her psychoanalytic orientation. I would argue that in her role as a mother figure, Farkas provided a corrective emotional experience. Her psychoanalytic knowledge enabled her to understand the psychological reasons behind the hostile and violent behaviors of the boys as a form of projection. She believed that they were not innately aggressive, but rather reacted in a violent way to their experiences of being abandoned by their biological parents and uprooted from their Christian foster homes. She also recognized their individual emotional needs.

According to the correspondence of Farkas and Lévy, the most controversial topic was the implementation of corporal punishment as a form of discipline in education. As a psychoanalyst, Lévy firmly objected to using physical punishment as a pedagogical tool. She strongly argued that it is ineffective and destructive in the context of building relationships between the boys and Farkas. Farkas self-reflected on the issue. Theoretically, she agreed with Lévy and rejected corporal punishment in childrearing. She acknowledged that by inflicting physical pain, she was disrespectful towards the rights of the children. She did however reach for this tool in desperation, caused by exhaustion, lack of professional support, and poor housing conditions (pp. 41–45). As she acquainted herself with the boys' sociocultural backgrounds and the dynamics of their biological families or previous foster families, she changed her methods of teaching. She gradually replaced punishment with reward-based learning, especially since 1940 (Hódos and Farkas, 2019). The diary clearly proves that Farkas constantly reflected on the pedagogical methods she was using and was significantly developing her approach to child rearing and education. Despite the fact that Farkas had a large number of children in her care, she tried to pay special attention to each of them. As a result, she successfully built relationships based on mutual trust. This, in turn, created the space to discuss the boys' individual problems privately, granting that the daily struggles allowed her to (pp. 55, 59, 65, 76, 153–154, 244, 311, 450).

Farkas's professional approach to raising foster children, drawing on her psychological and psychoanalytic knowledge and Levy's advice, was criticized by Géza Varsányi, the secretary of the home's founder, the Israelite Patronage Association. Varsányi's hostile attitude and incompetence were a constant problem for Farkas. They were in conflict with regards to many issues. For example, Varsányi strongly opposed the idea of sexual education for children (p. 158). Furthermore, according to Varsányi, running a foster home required skillfulness in performing housework rather than a pedagogical knowledge. An ideal director of a shelter should represent values traditionally attributed to women: be a good housewife rather than a professional caretaker (pp. 156, 164–166). Farkas did not have a degree in pedagogy or any other official teaching qualification, but she identified as a professional. She distanced herself from Varsányi and Goldberger, whom she defined as a layman with reference to both pedagogy and psychology (p. 442).

Farkas's desire for intellectual independence and her uncompromising, almost combative behavior led to many interpersonal conflicts. She confronted Lajos Goldberger about his superficial pedagogical views and disagreed with her mentor, Kata Lévy, who suggested how to reconcile the local Christian population with the existence of the home (pp. 67, 71–72, 331, 425, 441–443). One of the sources of the conflict was their different perspective. As an intellectual living in the country's capital, unaware of the divided nature of rural society, Lévy gave advice that was not always feasible. Erzsébet Farkas described Békés in her diary as an extremely divided society and did not believe that communication between the Christian and the Jewish population was at all possible. The local Jewish community was also internally divided and conflicted. Farkas did not sympathize with the local Jewry because they did not support the cause of the home. The dislike was mutual: the members of the Jewish community were averse to the foster home partly because its director, Erzsébet Farkas, came from the capital (pp. 67–71, 497).

Farkas's son, Mátyás, remembered that the Békés society saw the pupils of the foster home as outsiders. In his opinion, this situation resulted predominantly from the fact that the foster boys existed between the two cultures. For the local Jewish community, they were not Jewish enough; for the Christians, they were too Jewish (p. 497). The rejection of the home by the local Jewry is interesting in the light of the fact that Békés Jews were mostly nonobservant, especially the younger generation. In the 1930s and 1940s only the grandparents' generation attended the synagogue regularly (p. 403). Hence, Judaism did not unify them into a homogeneous religious community.

Erzsébet Farkas and the Emancipation of Women

In the early twentieth century, as a new field of psy- sciences, psychoanalysis provided opportunities for women to enter a community of psy- disciplines and be successful (Chodorow, 1989; Appignanesi and Forrester, 1992; Borgos, 2010, 2021; Naszkowska, 2022). First, the establishment of psychoanalysis in Hungary overlapped with an era of expanding opportunities for women. Since 1895 women could enroll in university studies at the faculties of medicine and humanities. The First World War radically increased the participation of women in economic life. Furthermore, the first wave of Hungarian feminism took place in the first decade of the last century. In 1904, the Association of Feminists was founded in Budapest (Borgos, 2021, pp. 13–14). Second, psychoanalysis was relatively inclusive compared to other fields of science at the time. As an entirely new phenomenon, it did not have a fixed hierarchy. It was easier for women to enter the uncrystallized structure and compete for the still unfilled positions. Third, psychoanalysis attracted women because values traditionally attributed to women, such as empathy, emotional attachment, and caring, were important psychoanalytical concepts in personality development. Not surprisingly, the first female analysts typically worked with children and studied topics connected to the concepts of womanliness, such as the psychological nature of motherhood, the importance of the mother-child relationship, and female sexuality (Zaretsky, 2005; Borgos, 2010, 2017b, p. 158).

As a result, many women seeking personal fulfillment in a professional career joined the psychoanalytic movement in the early twentieth century. By the 1930s the proportion of women in the field of psychoanalysis was higher than in any other discipline in Europe. The same tendency can be detected in the development of Hungarian psychoanalysis. The proportion of women in psychoanalysis dramatically increased: by 1937, 48 percent of psychoanalysts were women in Hungary (Borgos, 2017b, pp. 156–160). The relative overrepresentation of women in the Hungarian psychoanalytical movement was connected to the work of Sándor Ferenczi. His theory and technique of intersubjectivity, which emphasized equality and reciprocity, provided an ideological basis for the inclusion of female analysts. Ferenczi had a strong opinion on this issue: he stated that female professionals are fully equal to men (Borgos, 2021, p. 15). On the other hand, the vast majority of women who could afford a university education and a career in psychoanalysis came from very similar sociocultural backgrounds: wealthy culturally assimilated Jewish families (Chodorow, 1989; Borgos, 2017b; Naszkowska, 2022).

Erzsébet Farkas was born into a family with a socioeconomic background that is atypical compared to that of most second-generation female analysts. Differently from her peers, she did not have her parents' financial and emotional support to study and become a professional woman analyst. Without it, she was forced to work against the social expectations of women on her own. She studied in high school against her mother's wishes, only to be legally excluded from university education. She then built her career at the foster home as a form of self-fulfillment. Finally, she divorced her husband and raised her son as a single working mother (Hódos and Farkas, 2019, pp. 510–512).

Since Farkas's diary was written from a woman's point of view, it offers the opportunity to discuss neglected issues that at that time especially affected women in particular. The fact that there were orphans revealed challenges faced by single mothers and options available to them in the late 1930s and the early 1940s. As a single mother herself, Farkas understood first-hand the socioeconomic difficulties a young, single mother had typically struggled with. For example, she reflects on the difficult social and economic situation of a woman who became pregnant out of wedlock.

An entry from 1940 is an example of how Farkas tried to explain to one of the certain boys—who experienced the feelings of intense hatred towards his biological mother who had abandoned him—that it was not only his mother's responsibility to take care of him, it was also his father's (pp. 379, 446). Farkas wanted to give a different interpretational perspective to the boy that could help him to better understand the decision of his biological mother. While mother figures are frequently represented in the diary, father figures are conspicuously absent. Their absence suggested to Farkas that the father representations had not played a significant role in the children's lives. Farkas made several critical statements regarding this issue. According to her, in most cases, the mother was solely responsible for childcare, while men were insufficiently involved in raising their children (p. 446).

Another recurring theme from the diary was sexuality of children. It deserves special attention in the context of psychoanalytic theory, as well as the emancipation of women. Farkas believed that sexual issues should be discussed with children openly because they are naturally curious about their sexualities. In line with the psychoanalytical approach, she argued that sexuality should not be treated as a taboo, to prevent children from filling the gaps in their knowledge with fantasies leading, in turn, to anxiety (pp. 172–173, 257–258). Farkas believed that, in general, open conversations help deepen the relationships between adults and children by creating a sense of security. She essentially provided sexual education to her pupils. Her liberal viewpoint is clearly visible in her approach to contraception. She brought up the issue with the boys when they inquired about pregnancy and childbirth. In the conversations that followed, she purposefully drew the boys' attention to the fact that responsibility for preventing pregnancies is shared by men and women (p. 409).

Religious Traditions

Farkas approached religion and religiousness in an equally liberal and untraditional way, as gender and sexual issues. The issue of boys engaging in Jewish religious practices and traditions was a recurring topic in her discussions with Goldberger. The requirement of providing boys with meals in accordance with the dietary laws of *Kashrut* was the main source of conflict. Farkas objected to following the kosher tradition for economical and practical reasons. First, it was more expensive to comply with the *Kashrut* regulations. Second, preparation of kosher meals required considerably more time and physical work of Farkas who had to manage on her own, without any assistance (pp. 123, 498). The issue of implementation of dietary laws also emphasized the differences in the pedagogical approach of Farkas and Goldberger. According to Farkas's diary, he demanded kosher meals of her, but then he regularly broke the rules in the presence of the children. Farkas found his behavior very inconsistent. She believed that one of the most important elements of education, especially in the case of religious education, was learning from role models. Consequently, she sharply criticized Goldberger's inconsistent behavior regarding the religious education of the boys from a pedagogical point of view. She argued that Goldberger is a father representation to the boys and, as such, should serve as an exemplar (pp. 405, 443–445).

Against the demands of the Israelite Patronage Association and Goldberger, Farkas strove to include Jewish religious and cultural traditions into the boys' lives in a natural way. Hence, she placed a strong emphasis on treating the celebration of main Jewish holidays as a social experience that could strengthen the bonds between the children, and not just as the obligatory observation of rituals (pp. 29, 384–385, 435–436, 445). For

Figure 6.3 Lajos Goldberger with the foster children, ca. 1939.
Reproduced with permission of Mária Hódos.

example, they celebrated Seder together at home in an intimate atmosphere instead of accepting the invitation of the local rabbi. Although they were less focused on following the exact dietary rules, Farkas managed to make the boys understand the significance of the holiday by reading and singing the Haggadah together (p. 385).

Despite Farkas's efforts, not all of the boys internalized their Jewish cultural heritage easily. It was particularly difficult in the case of the oldest, ten-year-old boy, Feri. He was an illegitimate child who never knew his biological Jewish parents and was placed in foster care since early infancy. He was raised Christian by his foster parents who did not inform him of his Jewish ancestry. On the one hand, he was a victim of the Israelite Patronage Association's child welfare program. Not only was he separated from his loving foster mother, but the sudden discovery of his Jewish roots also led to a serious identity crisis. The shocking confrontation with his ancestry induced a persistent ambivalence towards Judaism. On the personal level,

Feri showed an interest in the Jewish culture and religion, but it seems that he had hardly accepted his Jewish identity. He willingly attended the local synagogue and learned the Hebrew alphabet, while making antisemitic statements at home. Farkas even noted that Feri's comments suggested he hated his peers because they were Jewish (pp. 56–57). She handled his case with empathy and did not try to force Feri to accept her Jewishness. For example, she tried to counterbalance his reluctance to the bar mitzvah and the anxiety it caused by emphasizing that the ritual will endow him with an exceptional role of an adult among the group. The special attention and care Farkas gave him during the preparation for the bar mitzvah strengthened his self-esteem, while the ceremony itself became a milestone in the process of accepting his Jewish identity (p. 396).

Rise of Antisemitism

Apart from following the everyday lives of the boys, Farkas's diary also recorded the rising influence of antisemitism in Hungary in the late 1930s and early 1940s. It clearly illustrated the gradual escalation of the antisemitic violence from prejudice and verbal aggression to physical, life-threatening assaults, and finally to the mass deportation of Jews. The diary also documented the extent to which the Jewish community was aware of the seriousness of the danger it was in.

The first attack on the foster home took place in December 1938, just four months after it was opened. A parliamentarian of the National Unity Party and state secretary to the minister of agriculture, Ferenc Marschall, in participation with a local health officer, ordered Lajos Goldberger to close the institution immediately. Marschall's decision was informed by his apparent antipathy towards Jews. According to the diary, he declared that he did not want Jewish children in his district (pp. 63–65).

Around the time of Marschall's order, a sense of defenselessness regarding the social and economic situation of Jewish people in Hungary crept into the diary. Farkas assumed, and rightly so, that the Hungarian pro-Nazi authorities would eventually find a reason to shut down the home. She believed that the only solution to the situation would be to find an intermediary who could discuss the issue with Marschall (pp. 63–64). This situation describes well the everyday experience of Jews that their legal protection was not provided. Therefore, they were forced into finding alternative ways to protect their interests.

As a result of the First Jewish Law and the First Vienna Award in 1938, the political orientation of the Hungarian government shifted even more toward the right. Even before this first attempt at shutting down the home, in the end of 1938, Farkas and other members of the Békés Jewish community seriously considered emigration (p. 72). They tried to prepare for this scenario by organizing an English language course. They didn't make specific plans regarding a destination, but England was likely considered. Unfortunately, they were unable to find a teacher and the plan was not realized. In January 1939, Farkas considered emigration once more because of the increasingly open antisemitic policy in Hungary. England seemed to be a possible destination for Farkas, because her sister-in-law worked as a housemaid there (p. 82). In the end, the emigration plan did not come to fruition. Farkas failed to secure employment and find housing for herself and her son abroad.

We know from the diary that since 1939, the boys were harassed more frequently in the form of insults, teasing, and fighting by the locals because of their Jewish ancestry. They were also forced to join the local nationalistic paramilitary youth organization, Levente, founded in 1921 (Laine-Frigren, 2022) where they suffered racial discrimination in a less drastic form. For example, while the Christian students participated in classes, their Jewish counterparts performed physical work outside, in the cold (Hódos and Farkas, 2019, pp. 346, 445).

The year 1941 was the turning point with regards to the antisemitic violence in Békés. In January 1941, Lajos Goldberger's younger brother, physician Izsó Goldberger, died in a bicycle accident. Goldberger was refused information concerning the circumstances of the event. Not surprisingly, Farkas believed that he was murdered by Hungarian Nazis (p. 368). At the end of 1941, Goldberger's nephew and the son of Izsó Goldberger, Tamás Goldberger, committed suicide in Karcag, a town northwest of Békés. The tragic death of this young brilliant medical student took a toll on Erzsébet Farkas. She questioned her qualifications as a mother, foster mother, and educator. If a young man with a family took his own life, how could she protect the troubled boys from the foster home (p. 435)?

Termination of the Foster Home

After a long bureaucratic struggle, a decree of the Ministry of the Interior shut down the foster home in February 1942. The Israelite Patronage Association was made responsible for finding homes for the children.

Figure 6.4 Erzsébet Farkas (third from left) with her son, Mátyás (fourth from left), the last group photo, 1942.
Reproduced with permission of Mária Hódos.

Unfortunately, they operated like every bureaucratic machinery. The children were for them just paperwork that had to be handled, not individuals. As a result, the Patronage did not help solve the crisis. It was Farkas who set about to find a Jewish community that would take the boys in. She tried collaborating with the Jewish community in a nearly city of Csaba, but they refused to help (p. 449).

In March 1942, shortly after the Békés home was shut down, the Patronage founded another institution for delinquent Jewish children with serious behavior problems in Budapest. Pursuant to the treaty, First Vienna Award, in 1938, the Hungarian-populated part of Czechoslovakia, the region of Upper Hungary (*Felvidék*, now mostly present-day Slovakia) was reattached to the Kingdom of Hungary (Komjathy, 1979, p. 131). After the First Vienna Award, many of the local Jewish population was deported from Slovakia to the new territory of the Kingdom of Hungary. Many did not survive the measure. As a result, a large number of orphaned Jewish children arrived in Budapest in poor physical and mental state, many later found themselves in the new foster home. Farkas moved to the new foster home with her son and four remaining boys from Békés in March 1942. In inadequate living conditions, she developed severe arthritis (Hódos and Farkas, 2019, pp. 512–513). Farkas worked in the home for about a year, but due to serious health issues, she was unable to continue the stressful work. In 1943, the second home closed as well and the boys from Békés had to be separated. From the autumn of 1943 Erzsébet Farkas worked as a private governess. She was forced to entrust the care of her son to his father (p. 513).

The next ordeal in Farkas's life resulted from the change in Hungary's position in the Second World War. The Kingdom of Hungary was the fourth member of the Axis powers, with Germany, Japan, and Italy. Still, in March 1944 Hitler launched Operation Margarethe and ordered his forces to occupy Hungary. During the Nazi occupation, 550,000 Jews were deported from Hungary to extermination camps.

In October 1944, Farkas was forced into compulsory labor in Vecsés, a village near Budapest, by the fascist Government of National Unity led by Ferenc Szálasi, who overthrew the government of Miklós Horthy in October 16, 1944. Ten days later, the deportations to Auschwitz started. Farkas managed to escape and was hiding for several weeks on the outskirts of the capital, unaware of her son's whereabouts. Fortunately, both of them survived the siege of Budapest by the Soviet forces between December 1944 and February 1945. They reunited in January 1945, at the Red Cross in Budapest (p. 513). It remains unknown when Farkas learned of the tragic fate of her siblings. However, in a letter dated March 1946, she stated that her sister was probably no longer alive (p. 472). In the course of her extensive research, Mária Hódos uncovered that Lajos Goldberger was deported to Auschwitz and murdered in 1944. She believed that the four residents of the Békés foster home, who were later in the second home in Budapest, probably survived the Shoah.

When the Second World War ended in 1945, Farkas joined the Hungarian Communist Party (MKP) (pp. 513–514). Her tasks were mainly propagandist and administrative. Later on, despite her working-class background, she was discriminated against by a party secretary as an intellectual and was not allowed to engage in political activities (p. 515). Despite the tragedies endured, she maintained her desire to learn. She completed a philosophy course at the workers' academy. In addition, she educated herself through various publications (p. 515). As far as her health condition allowed, she lived an active intellectual and physical life even in the last stages of her life. She maintained a good relationship with her grandchildren. Erzsébet Farkas passed away in 1991 (p. 18).

As a result of the years spent in the foster home of Békés, she came to serious conclusions about the process of socialization. Farkas argued that political and social views are determined by early experiences of children. The collective experiences, such as cohesion, working and playing together, cooperation, emotional issues associated with being part of a group, and adaptation, impact the way that adults later define their roles and positions in the society. She attributed her son's socialist identity to the fact that he spent his formative years in a community of children (p. 515).

Conclusions

Erzsébet Farkas had several reasons why she might have felt she had been left alone in a challenging situation. In the absence of adequate pedagogical knowledge, Lajos Goldberger set extremely high expectations for the development of the boys that could not be fulfilled. However, despite their arguments about the effectiveness of their pedagogical methods, Goldberger always stood up for Farkas against the illegitimate critiques of the Patronage.

The case of the boys' development also illustrates the gap between the regulations of a public organization—such as the administrators of the Patronage—and the real needs of a child welfare institution. As a result of the trauma of the Holocaust, and because it was closed in February 1942, the history of the Békés foster home was eradicated from the collective memory of the town for over 80 years, until Mária Hódos began to uncover her grandmother's biography and published her diary in 2019. The act of remembering the story of the home, as written by Erzsébet Farkas in her diary, could be interpreted as a reparational attempt.

Reference List

Aichhorn, A. (1951). *Wayward Youth*. London: Imago Publishing (Orig. publ. 1925).
Appignanesi, L. and Forrester, J. (1992). *Freud's Women*. New York: Basic Books.
Bálint, A. (1941). *Anya és gyermek*. Budapest: Pantheon.
Bálint, A. (2017). *The Psycho-Analysis of the Nursery*. London: Routledge (Orig. publ. 1931).
Balsam, R. H. (2015). The War on Women in Psychoanalytic Theory Building: Past to Present. *Psychoanalytic Study of the Child*, 69(1), 83–107.

Borgos, A. (2010). Woman as Theory and Theory-Maker in the Early Years of Psychoanalysis. In A. Schwartz and J. Szapor (Eds.), *Gender and Modernity in Central Europe: The Austro-Hungarian Monarchy and Its Legacy* (pp. 153–168.) Ottawa: University of Ottawa Press.
Borgos, A. (2017a). Lévy (Freund) Katáról. *Imágó Budapest*, 6(3), 149–164.
Borgos, A. (2017b). Women in the History of Hungarian Psychoanalysis. *European Yearbook of the History of Psychology*, 3, 155–180.
Borgos, A. (2021). *Women in the Budapest School of Psychoanalysis: Girls of Tomorrow*. A. Borgos and K. Rácz (Trans.). New York and Abingdon: Routledge.
Chasseguet-Smirgel, C. (1970). *Female Sexuality: New Psychoanalytic Views*. London and New York: Routledge.
Chodorow, N. (1989). Seventies Questions for Thirties Women: Gender and Generation in a Study of Early Women Psychoanalysts. In N. Chodorow (Ed.), *Feminism and Psychoanalytic Theory* (pp. 199–218). New Haven and London: Yale UP.
Covington, C. and Wharton, B. (2015). *Sabina Spielrein: Forgotten Pioneer of Psychoanalysis*. London and New York: Routledge.
Don, Y. (1986). The Economic Effect of Antisemitic Discrimination: Hungarian Anti-Jewish Legislation 1938–1944. *Jewish Social Studies*, 48(1), 63–82.
Freidenreich, H. P. (2002). *Female, Jewish, and Educated: The Lives of Central European University Women*. Bloomington and Indianapolis: Indiana UP.
Graham, P. (2009). *Susan Isaacs: A Life Freeing the Minds of Children*. London and New York: Routledge.
Hódos, M. and Farkas, E. (2019). *Fiaim, hol vagytok?* Tinta: Budapest.
Komjathy, A. (1979). The First Vienna Award (November 2, 1938). *Austrian History Yearbook*, 15, 130–156.
Kovács, M. M. (2016). The Numerus Clausus and the Anti-Jewish Laws. In R. L. Braham and A. Kovács (Eds.), *The Holocaust in Hungary: Seventy Years Later* (pp. 37–44). Budapest and New York: Central European UP.
Laine-Frigren, T. (2022). Traumatized Children in Hungary after World War II. In V. Kivimäki and P. Leese (Eds.), *Trauma, Experience and Narrative in Europe after World War II* (pp. 149–176). London: Palgrave Macmillan.
McAvoy, J. (2014). Psy Disciplines. In T. Teo (Ed.), *Encyclopedia of Critical Psychology* (pp. 1527–1529). New York: Springer.
Mészáros, J. (2014). *Exile of the Budapest School and Solidarity in the Psychoanalytic Movement During the Nazi Years*. London: Karnac Books.
Naszkowska, K. (2022). Psychoanalyst, Jew, Woman, Wife, Mother, Emigrant: The Émigré Foremothers of Psychoanalysis in the United States. *European Judaism*, 55(1), 112–137.
Perelberg, R. J. and Raphael-Leff, J. (Eds.) (1997). *Female Experience: Three Generations of British Women Psychoanalysts on Work with Women*. London and New York: Routledge.
Quinodoz, J. M. (2007). *Listening to Hanna Segal: Her Contribution to Psychoanalysis*. D. Alcorn (Trans.). London and New York: Routledge.

Sayers, J. (1991). *Mothers of Psychoanalysis: Helene Deutsch, Karen Horney, Anna Freud, Melanie Klein*. New York: W. W. Norton & Company.
Thompson, L. N. (1987). Early Women Psychoanalysts. *International Review of Psycho-Analysis*, 14, 391–406.
Vajda, Z. (1996). A Budapesti Pszichoanalitikusok rendhagyó nézetei a gyermeki természetről és a nevelésről. *Magyar Pedagógia*, 96(4), 329–339.
Vajda, Z. (2019). Hódos Mária—Farkas Erzsébet: Fiaim, hol vagytok? *Imágó Budapest*, 8(2), 76–80.
Zaretsky, E. (2005). *Secrets of the Soul. A Social and Cultural History of Psychoanalysis*. New York: Vintage Books.

Part III

Beyond the Homeland

Chapter 7

Ludwika Karpińska-Woyczyńska
The Forgotten First Female Freudian

Edyta Dembińska and Krzysztof Rutkowski

Figure 7.1 Ludwika Karpińska-Woyczyńska, posthumous tribute by Maria Więckowska, *Polskie Archiwum Psychologii*, September–November 1936/1937, 9(1), p. 185.
Copyright: Polona, public domain.

Ludwika Karpińska-Woyczyńska was born 150 years ago. She was an associate professor of applied psychology and psychotechnics at the Free Polish University, one of the first Polish psychologists, a proponent of psychoanalysis in Poland, and the creator of the foundations of psychotechnical testing.

DOI: 10.4324/9781003455844-11

Her personal life and research were both notably impacted by the sociopolitical situation in Europe at the turn of the twentieth century. At the time of her birth, the Polish state (the Polish-Lithuanian Commonwealth) was under occupation, split between the Russian Empire, the Austro-Hungarian Empire, and the Kingdom of Prussia. Each partition had its own character. Each had its own degree of civil, political, and religious freedoms and various limitations of the use of the Polish language at educational institutions. In the Russian partition, called the Congress Kingdom or simply Russian Poland, where Karpińska-Woyczyńska spent her formative years, Poles were subjected to many repressions implemented in response to their endless efforts to regain independence. Many educational institutions were shut down by the Russian authorities. The quality of education in the ones that remained open dropped significantly, and the Polish language was banned. In Congress Kingdom, women were not allowed to study at universities. The quality of education at girls' elementary and secondary schools was even lower than at the schools for boys. Another form of repression was 25-year-long military service in the Russian army, mandatory for all young Polish men. The goal was to Russify Poles and to discourage them from organizing future uprisings.

Karpińska-Woyczyńska's family was directly targeted by the repressions. Her father, Kazimierz, and his older brother, Aleksander, were convicted of participating in pro-Polish patriotic activities. Russia's educational policy hindered the development of Polish science in the Congress Kingdom. Karpińska-Woyczyńska's achievements are even more remarkable when one fully comprehends the number of obstacles she had had to overcome.

Origins: Płock and Warsaw (1872–1897)

Ludwika Zofia Karpińska-Woyczyńska was born on August 25, 1872, as the daughter of Kazimierz Nestor Karpiński and Katarzyna or Catherine (née Fearey). She was baptized in the Roman Catholic parish of St. Bartholomew in a mid-size town of Płock in April the following year. Despite the accessibility of original documents, it was difficult to determine her date of birth due to an error in recording the date according to the Julian calendar (Dembińska and Rutkowski, 2016). Her father came from a noble family. At the time of Ludwika's birth, he was a merchant in Płock. Her mother's descent was more unusual. In the course of extensive inquiries, we established that Catherine was an Englishwoman born in Weston Favell village near Northampton. She came from a family of craftsmen. Her father, Enoch Fearey, was a stonemason and plasterer by trade. He immigrated with most of his family to the United States in 1858. He was very fond of his new home country. As a staunch proponent of the right to freedom for all, he admired Abraham Lincoln and supported the newly formed Republican Party (Fearey, 2022).

Catherine Fearey met her future husband, Kazimierz Karpiński, while he was in exile. They married in 1856 in Northampton. Karpiński had fled the Congress Kingdom in 1849 to avoid repressions from the Russian authorities. When abroad, he joined the Polish Democratic Society, a patriotic and political organization supporting the fight for Polish independence and the implementation of a more democratic political system in the country. After he fled, the Russian authorities had sentenced him to confiscation of property and banned from returning to the country (*Dziennik praw*, 1853). When he was granted an amnesty a few years later, around 1859, Karpiński returned to his native land with his new family. However, he did not escape punishment and was briefly imprisoned in the Zamość fortress, as was reported between the lines on the birth certificate of his first daughter, Maria. These facts from Karpińska-Woyczyńska family history have been entirely unknown until very recently. Even Karpińska-Woyczyńska did not mention her mother's nationality in her article "Contribution to the Analysis of 'Senseless' Words in Dreams," which describes some of her childhood experiences (Karpińska, 1914a), despite the fact that it must have affected her and her siblings' sense of identity. In any case, it was not accidental that Karpińska-Woyczyńska knew English well. Perhaps due to her multicultural roots, she was an open-minded person, respectful of differences, maintaining professional and personal contacts with representatives of many nationalities, religions, and political factions.

Karpińska-Woyczyńska spent her childhood with her older siblings: brother, Józef, future physician, and sister, Aniela (later Jabłczyńska), who worked as a teacher after graduating from a high school (*Gymnasium*) and married a well-known Polish chemist and professor at the University of Warsaw, Kazimierz Jabłczyński.

Little is known about the atmosphere of her family home. In an article "Contribution to the Analysis of 'Senseless' Words in Dreams," written at age of 42, Karpińska-Woyczyńska described her "complex of sacrifice and resignation" developed in childhood, which made her "invent rivals for herself, pull herself down to the last place, and let someone else take the first position" (Karpińska, 1914a, p. 167). She was unconsciously afraid of competing and resigned from it, "in order to receive recognition and to reassure herself that she was acting in a noble way" (p. 168). In the course of a personal analysis, she uncovered the source of her complex in her relationship with her father and her older sister, Aniela. She then finally understood its persistent ramifications for her professional and emotional life. She wrote:

> I was the youngest in the family. My sister [Aniela], as the older one, had precedence in receiving treats and gifts. She was always allowed to choose first and I only got what was left. I certainly did not like it, I felt left out and hurt, but never had the courage to disagree with my father's will. [. . .] [I]n the emotional dependency on my father, I was second in line to receive from him only the feelings he had left after giving them to my older sister.
>
> (p. 167)

Ludwika Karpińska-Woyczyńska most probably received her early education at home, typical for Polish children from middle-class families. After the family moved to Warsaw around 1886, she attended the Second Women's High School there. She graduated with a gold medal in June 1891 (Karpińska, 1910). A year earlier, her father died after a long illness (*Kurier Warszawski*, 1890). Since he was the sole family breadwinner, his death must have worsened the family financial situation considerably. After graduation, due to limited job opportunities for women, who could only work as teachers or clerks, Karpińska-Woyczyńska became a private tutor. She did not enjoy her job and called it a "hard duty." She felt that the families that employed her "undervalued her" and treated her "as an automaton to carrying out orders at" (Karpińska, 1914a, pp. 165–166).

Karpińska-Woyczyńska had much greater ambitions. She wanted to study at the university but that was impossible for women at that time in the Russian Empire, including Russian Poland. Women who craved knowledge had to travel abroad and audit classes or, less frequently, enroll as full-time students. However, in 1885, an underground university for women, the Flying University (Pl. *Uniwersytet Latający*) opened in Warsaw. It operated illegally without providing a formal graduation certificate. Karpińska-Woyczyńska wrote about this stage of her life: "I gave lessons and periodically audited lectures [at the Flying University] on chemistry, geology, mineralogy, botany, psychology, logic, the theory of knowledge, and the history of philosophy" (Karpińska, 1910, p. 89). Her choice of lectures indicates that she was interested in natural sciences, philosophy, and psychology. (At the end of the nineteenth century, psychology started to separate itself from philosophy as an independent academic field.) Her first psychology professor was Adam Mahrburg, an excellent lecturer. Mahrburg had studied with Wilhelm Wundt in Leipzig and became an ardent advocate for experimental psychology. The formative influence of Mahrburg's views on Karpińska-Woyczyńska's work can be clearly seen in her unwavering interest in the field (Karpińska, 1910).

Studies in Berlin (1897–1899)

In April 1897, Karpińska-Woyczyńska was able to start pursuing her dreams of university education. She moved to Berlin and audited classes in philosophy and natural sciences at the university (now Humboldt University of Berlin). At the same time, she was working in a psychological laboratory at the university. Experimental psychology had always been her main interest (Karpińska, 1910). She remained active in Warsaw's philosophical and psychological milieu. For example, she collaborated with the first Polish philosophical journal established in 1897, *Przegląd Filozoficzny*, from its inception. Unfortunately, she was forced to put her studies on hold and return to Warsaw in 1899 for financial reasons. This decision might have also been connected with the sudden illness and death of her mother, Catherine, in October 1899 (*Kurier Warszawski*, 1899).

Warsaw (1899–1907)

In the period of 1901–1907, she worked as a teacher in two Warsaw private boarding schools, of Konstancja Swołyńska and of Matylda Karwowska. Their education level corresponded with that of the girls' state high school but did not provide the same formal qualifications. However, private boarding schools were the only educational institutions that employed Polish Roman Catholic female teachers, like Karpińska-Woyczyńska. State schools preferred to employ male teachers, ideally Russian Orthodox. She also translated Richard Avenarius's *On Scientific Philosophy* into Polish (with her sister, Aniela) (Avenarius, 1902) and Ferdynand Tönnies's *Thomas Hobbes: His Life and Science* (Tönnies, 1903) for the Przegląd Filozoficzny Publishing House.

Around that time, she joined the illegal Polish Socialist Party (PPS), thus opening a chapter of active involvement in political and patriotic activity. The PPS program was founded on democratic and socialist values. In addition to regaining Polish independence and introducing a democratic form of government, both personally important to Karpińska-Woyczyńska, it included, *inter alia*:

> Equal rights to all nations incorporated into the Republic of Poland as a voluntary federation; equality of all citizens of all sexes, races, nationalities, and religions; unrestrained freedom of speech, publishing, and gathering; free, compulsory, universal education; [. . .] equal pay for women and men for equal work.
>
> (Program paryski PPS, 1892)

Knowing her later statements and decisions, we can assume that the program largely overlapped with her personal views. Her democratic and socials affiliations were deeply rooted in the tradition of her family, on both the father's and mother's sides. The first manifestation of Karpińska-Woyczyńska's political involvement was her participation in a 1905 school strike in Warsaw, in protest of the increasing russification of Polish schools (Miąso, 2005). The russification policy included a prohibition of using the Polish language in schools, hindered access to education for children from national minorities or from lower social classes, and filling state schools with Russian teachers. The strike demands included the use of Polish language in Polish schools in education and administration, abolishment of the police invigilation of students and teachers at schools, and public control over education. The protesters argued for removal of the denominational, national, and social restrictions in hiring teachers and admitting students. Last but not least, they demanded voidance of discrimination based on sex and gender, giving women rights equal to men to enroll in university (Miąso, 2005). This strongly suggests that the ideals of equal access to education, improvement of the situation of non-Russian teachers in the labor force, and raising the quality of education were particularly important to Karpińska-Woyczyńska.

Studying in Zurich and at the Burghölzli Clinic (1907–1909)

In 1907, Karpińska-Woyczyńska was finally able to resume her interrupted education. She went on to study psychology at the University of Zurich for two years. She summarized: "My studies included the same subjects as in Berlin. Additionally, I audited lectures on anthropology, psychiatry, psychopathology, and psychotherapy of hysteria" (Karpińska, 1910, p. 89). She learned psychoanalytic theory from Carl Gustav Jung's psychiatry lectures at the Burghölzli Psychiatric University Hospital in Zurich. Her immediate enormous enthusiasm for psychoanalysis stemmed from her belief that "the analytical method presents a great analogy to the method of experimental psychology" (Karpińska, 1913a, p. 509). She found herself in Zurich at a very significant time—a year before Jung initiated a lively exchange of letters with Freud. At the Burghölzli, headed by the Swiss psychiatrist Eugen Bleuler, the climate was exceptionally favorable toward psychoanalysis. Freud noted the significance of the Burghölzli Clinic:

> Nowhere else did such a compact little group of adherents exist, or could a public clinic be placed at the service of psychoanalytic researches, or was there a clinical teacher who included psychoanalytic theories as an integral part of his psychiatric course. [. . .] The only opportunity of learning the new art and working at it in practice lay there.
> (Freud, 1955/1900, p. 303)

The Burghölzli was also known for its association experiments. They were carried out in the psychological laboratory under Jung's supervision. Karpińska-Woyczyńska was one of many students who joined the research team. She reported later on this experience in several lectures and in an article, "Experimental Research Into Association of Ideas" (Karpińska, 1912).

During her studies in Zurich, she was still fascinated by the classical experimental psychology, as evidenced by the topic of her PhD dissertation, *Experimental Contributions to the Analysis of Depth Perception*, written under the supervision of a German psychologist, Friedrich Schumann. Karpińska-Woyczyńska must have been a student with considerable knowledge and skills, as she passed her doctoral examination *magna cum laude* on June 12, 1909 (Karpińska, 1910). Her PhD thesis was published the next year (Karpińska, 1910).

Polish and International Psychoanalysis: Zurich, Vienna, Warsaw, Zakopane (1909–1914)

The period after graduation was marked by uncertainty. Karpińska-Woyczyńska hesitated about what career path to choose and kept moving between cities. Despite writing "after I passed my doctoral examination, I lived for some time near Zurich, on the right bank of the lake" (Karpińska, 1913b, p. 311), she also visited Geneva, Warsaw, Vienna, and Milan. The information about her dilemmas of this period can be gleaned from her own publications in which she analyzed her intrapsychic experiences. She described her state as "a tormenting feeling of uncertainty and doubt" (p. 311) and interpreted her symptoms as follows:

> I decided to stick to my chosen path and continue walking in the direction I had selected. But my emotional state did not confirm my decision at all: was I supposed to do this, or should I choose differently? I seriously doubted if the path I had chosen and followed was the right one.
> (p. 312)

We may only speculate what was the alternative path she refers to because of only scarce information she left behind and on the basis of her later decisions. The most likely difficulties she had struggled with seem to be in furthering a professional career and building relationships with men.

There are many indications that Karpińska-Woyczyńska tried to be involved in the development of the international and Polish psychoanalytic movement. She was the only woman to actively participate in a debate on psychoanalysis set off during the First Congress of Polish Neurologists, Psychiatrists and Psychologists in Warsaw in October 1909. It was initiated by Ludwig Jekels's lecture, "Treatment of Psychoneuroses Using Freud's Psychoanalytic Method, and Casuistry" (Jekels, 1910). In 1909 Jekels, the first Polish psychoanalyst and the first translator of Sigmund Freud's works into Polish, began his three-year mission to promote psychoanalysis in Poland (Dembińska and Rutkowski, 2020a, 2020b) At the Congress, she stressed the advantage of psychoanalysis over other techniques, asserting, "Freud's psychoanalytic method reaches the deepest [layers of the psyche] as it explains the origins of pathological phenomena and their interrelation and, from the therapeutic stance, it brings about the most considerable change in a patient" (p. 627). She also underlined the importance of Jung's association experiments in confirming the validity of psychoanalytic theories. Later, on the same day, Karpińska-Woyczyńska, Jekels, Witold Łuniewski, Czesław Sycianko, Kazimierz Kempiński, Witold Chodźko, and Karol Rychliński posted two telegrams, one to Freud, the second to Jung (Chodźko et al., 1909), identifying themselves as the "Polish Freudians." The following years proved that, of the seven signatories, only Karpińska-Woyczyńska and Jekels actually promoted psychoanalysis. The telegram must have been important to Freud as he commented on it in a letter to Jung:

> A few days ago I received from the First Congress of Polish Neurologists a telegram of homage signed, "after violent debate," by seven illegible and unpronounceable Poles. The only one of them known to me is Dr. Jekels; Frau Dr. Karpinska, I hear, studied with you. I have never heard of the five others.
>
> (p. 253)

On Jung's recommendation, Karpińska-Woyczyńska contacted Jekels after the Congress, at the end of 1909 (Freud and Jung, 1974, p. 264). We don't know why she initiated the contact. Most likely, she wanted to start psychoanalytic training or personal analysis with him. She actually did enter personal analysis around this time, with an unidentified German analyst not familiar with the Polish language. This would exclude Jekels as her analyst. We know very little about the process, for example the length of the analysis.

Karpińska-Woyczyńska and Jekels both attended four sessions of the Vienna Psychoanalytic Society (VPS) as guests at the end of 1909 and the beginning of 1910 (Nunberg and Federn, 1967, pp. 353–403). Thus, she was the very first woman to attend the Wednesday evening meetings. She actively participated in discussions and pointed out that the members of the VPS were not very familiar with philosophical theories. Her comments presumably caused Freud to call her "the Polish lady philosopher" (Freud and Ferenczi, 1994, p. 530). She attended her final meeting on January 19, 1910 (and so did Jekels), but her interest in psychoanalysis certainly did not subside. Her relationship with Jekels, however, did sour. This was possibly caused by personal difficulties they both endured, including the suicide of Jekels's wife on January 21, 1910 (Dembińska and Rutkowski, 2020a), and Karpińska-Woyczyńska's turbulent relationship with a mysterious man, Mr. K. (Karpińska, 1914a, pp. 165–168).

Karpińska-Woyczyńska dropped many clues about her love life in her article "Contribution to the Analysis of 'Senseless' Words in Dreams." Following her return to Warsaw in March 1910, she was "torn by contradicting feelings" concerning her relationship with Mr. K. She was wondering, among other things, "whether to go to him to support him, or better not to see him anymore," which led her to extreme emotional instability (p. 166). Soon after, she met Mr. C. and the two started writing to each other. However, this new relationship was also pervaded with dilemmas and triggered her aforementioned resignation complex. In the course of personal analysis with a not yet identified psychoanalyst, she successfully resolved her situation (pp. 164–170). This mysterious analyst might have been Sigmund Freud, but regrettably this claim cannot be corroborated at this time (Dembińska and Rutkowski, 2021). Karpińska-Woyczyńska reached a conclusion that "she does not want to give up anymore" (Karpińska, 1914a, p. 169) and decided to have a relationship with Mr. C., who later became her husband, Dr. Marcin Woyczyński. Thanks to her decision to publish her analysis of one of her dreams, we now have insight into her complex internal life, her desires and dilemmas, beyond her impressive scientific and patriotic activity (Dembińska and Rutkowski, 2018).

When deciding to return to Warsaw after university graduation in March 1910, Karpińska-Woyczyńska must have been aware of the hopeless situation on the labor market. At the beginning of the twentieth century, research centers in Warsaw and other Polish cities generally did not employ psychologists. Scarce job opportunities were offered to men. In early 1910, the editor-in-chief of the Polish philosophical review *Przegląd Filozoficzny*, Władysław Weryho, described the dramatic situation as follows:

> If they stay in the country, respectable psychologists, such as Mr. Abramowski, Mr. Segał, and Miss Stefanowska, will be doomed to unemployment. Those who did stay, such as Mr. Mahrburg and Mr. Dawid were forced to turn to pedagogical activity, although they had certainly preferred creative academic work.
>
> (Kosiakiewicz, 1910, p. 15)

In the aftermath of the 1909 First Congress of Polish Neurologists, Psychiatrists and Psychologists, three scientific societies—Polish Psychological Association (PPA), Polish Child Study Association, and Neurological Section of the Warsaw Medical Society—adopted a resolution to establish a much-needed psychological laboratory in Warsaw. Karpińska-Woyczyńska, member of the PPA since the end of 1909, was selected to help with setting up the new organization, with Weryho and Jakub Segał. The laboratory was launched at the end of 1910, with Edward Abramowski as its head. In the beginning of 1911, Karpińska-Woyczyńska wrote an enthusiastic review of his article: "I personally welcome the author's work with great joy, as it is based on Freud's concepts, still not widely known in Poland. With time, they will become extremely fertile in various areas of normal psychology [i.e., of healthy people]" (Karpińska, 1911, p. 117).

Despite assisting in establishing the psychological laboratory, she did not participate in its research projects. In January 1911 she relocated to the health resort of Zakopane at the foot of Tatra Mountains in the region of Galicia, then under the Austrian rule. Her decision was likely informed by the progressing relationship with Marcin Woyczyński, who lived in Zakopane with his first wife, Maria, and their adopted son, Benedykt, since 1900 (later a famous philosopher). Woyczyński was a graduate of the Military Medical Academy in St. Petersburg. He ran a chemical and bacteriological laboratory in Zakopane. Since 1910 he also had a private medical practice in pulmonology (Lewicki et al., 1912). He and Karpińska-Woyczyńska shared political views. He was a long-time PPS activist and a close friend of Józef Piłsudski. Woyczyński probably moved from Congress Kingdom to the more liberal Austrian Galicia to avoid arrest for patriotic pro-Polish activities. Zakopane of the beginning of the twentieth century was an exceptional place. First, it was a well-known mountain resort at the forefront of the fight against tuberculosis. Second, it was the meeting place for the most prominent Polish artists and scientists, dubbed the "Polish Athens." Finally, it was the "Polish Piedmont" where conspiratorial activities took place and political structures were created with the goal of restoring Polish independence.

The exact date of the Karpińska-Woyczyńska and Woyczyński's wedding is yet to be determined. It must have taken place sometime between 1911 and 1913, since the first documented use of her new surname, Woyczyńska, was in November 1913 (*Czas*, 1913).

There is no doubt that immediately after moving to Zakopane at the beginning of 1911, Karpińska-Woyczyńska found herself at one of the intellectual and conspiratorial centers of Poland. There she wrote her most substantial psychoanalytic works, including "On the Psychological Foundations of Freudism" first published in the Polish philosophical review *Przegląd Filozoficzny* (Karpińska, 1913a), and then in the International Psychoanalytical Association's *Internationale Zeitschrift für ärtzliche Psychoanalyse* in 1914 (Karpińska, 1914b). It was the first scientific psychoanalytically oriented article that wasn't simply a critique of Freud, published in a leading Polish journal on philosophy and psychology. In an excited exchange between Freud and Sándor Ferenczi preceding its publication, the latter noted that the paper "is very good" (Freud and Ferenczi, 1994, p. 532). Ernest Jones identified it as the first recognition of similarities between the ideas of Freud and German philosopher Johann Friedrich Herbart (Jones, 1972). This was significant because Karpińska-Woyczyńska embedded Freud's theories in the philosophical tradition.

In that period, she also published two aforementioned papers referring to her own intrapsychic experiences: "Contribution to the Psychopathology of Everyday Life" (Karpińska, 1913b) and "Contribution to the Analysis of 'Senseless' Words in Dreams" (Karpińska, 1914a), both in psychoanalytic journals. Freud quoted the 1914 paper in the revised edition of his *Interpretation of Dreams* from 1919 (Freud, 1957/1914). Karpińska-Woyczyńska's innovative idea of Herbart as predecessor of Freud made her relatively well remembered by mainstream psychoanalysts. However, her Polish nationality was forgotten with time. One reason for that was that she mostly published in German and signed her work with a non-Polish version of her name: Luise von Karpinska. Second, scientists rarely recognized her Polish nationality in their publications, as was the case of many Polish psychoanalysts born in the partitioned Poland and educated in German-speaking lands (cf. Magnone, 2016, 2023).

In 1911 Kraków (then Germ. Krakau), just 70 miles from Zakopane, became the center of the Polish school of psychoanalysis. The Neurological-Psychiatric Clinic of the Jagiellonian University in Kraków was the only Polish university clinic favorable to psychoanalysis (Dembińska and Rutkowski, 2021). It was headed, from its inception in 1905, by Professor Jan Piltz, an internationally known psychiatrist and neurologist educated at leading Swiss clinics. His professional contacts with Swiss psychiatrists, such as Eugen Bleuler, enabled his employees to gain clinical experience at the Burghölzli Clinic. As a result of having direct contact with psychoanalytical practice, after returning to Kraków, Piltz's associates started applying psychoanalysis in treatment. In 1911, two enthusiasts of psychoanalysis educated in Zurich worked at the Kraków clinic: Dr. Stefan Borowiecki and Dr. Herman Nunberg. Another follower of psychoanalysis, Dr. Karol de Beaurain, opened a private practice in 1911 in Zakopane, where he treated several patients using psychoanalysis, including the famous Polish painter, writer, and philosopher Stanisław Ignacy Witkiewicz, known as Witkacy. At the same time, Jekels began to conduct his "apostolic" activity for psychoanalysis in Kraków (Dembińska and Rutkowski, 2021).

Karpińska-Woyczyńska cooperated with the Neurological-Psychiatric Clinic. Unfortunately, inaccessibility of relevant historical materials prevents us from determining the nature of her collaboration with Kraków psychoanalysts. We know that in July 1911 she participated in the Eleventh Congress of Polish Physicians and Naturalists, where she may have listened to Jekels's lecture on transference. In 1912, she was invited to join a meeting of the Neurological-Psychiatric Clinic to share her experiences from her participation in Jung's association experiments. Her extensive lecture was published in Polish Medical Review, *Przegląd Lekarski* (Karpińska, 1912). In December 1912 she participated in the most important conference of the Polish psychoanalytic movement before the First World War, the Second Congress of Polish Neurologists, Psychiatrists and Psychologists in Kraków. Thanks to Jekels's efforts, one session was dedicated entirely to psychoanalysis. Almost every Polish psychoanalyst delivered a presentation: Borowiecki, Jekels, Nunberg, de Beaurain, Bronisław Bandrowski, Wacław Radecki, Jan Nelken, and Karpińska-Woyczyńska, as the only woman (Bandrowski, 1913). Her lecture examined the psychological foundations of Freudism. In her second lecture given during the session on psychoelectric phenomena, she discussed Jung's association research.

Her undisputed successes notwithstanding, Karpińska-Woyczyńska continued to reproach herself for not working hard enough. As early as in 1910, she planned to translate Freud's *Interpretation of Dreams* into Polish or at least write an article presenting Freud's ideas on dreams, but she failed to execute her plans. She described her inner conflict associated with work ambitions and rivalry, as follows:

> A few months ago [. . .], I heard that my colleague [Polish-born Franciszka Baumgarten] will present a lecture on the exact same subject to a psychological society. This news affected me, because as a result, I reproached myself for being negligent, not for the first time, and allowing someone to outshine me.
>
> (Karpińska, 1913b, p. 309)

The described situation indicates that there was a fierce competition between Polish women psychoanalysts. Contrary to Karpińska-Woyczyńska's belief that she was lagging behind, she must have been admired (or even envied) for her successes. When we look at the number of scientific publications on psychoanalysis, her contribution can only be compared with that of Jekels.

A dream of another Polish psychoanalyst, Eugenia Sokolnicka, confirms the competitive environment (about Sokolnicka see Chapter 11 of this book). In June 1920 she described the following dream to her analyst, Sándor Ferenczi: Karpińska-Woyczyńska is lying on the divan in Sokolnicka's room. The scenery looks as if the former had organized a party at Sokolnicka's place, and accessed her alcohol without permission (Freud and Ferenczi, 2000, p. 27). After returning to her room, Sokolnicka starts protesting against this outright injustice. Karpińska-Woyczyńska only smiles, as if stealing the alcohol was a great joke. Although Ferenczi's interpretation ignores the aspect of rivalry between the two women, the dream is a direct manifestation of the unconscious belief that Karpińska-Woyczyńska had robbed Sokolnicka of something important, most likely the precedence in joining the psychoanalytic circle. In fact, Karpińska-Woyczyńska studied with Jung before Sokolnicka. She was also the first woman to participate in the meetings of the Vienna Psychoanalytical Society and the first Polish woman to be published in major psychoanalytical journals.

In 1914, Karpińska-Woyczyńska published her last psychoanalytic article, "On Psychoanalysis," in the Polish philosophical journal *Ruch Filozoficzny*. She offered an overview of the developments in contemporary international psychoanalysis (Karpińska, 1914c). About the situation in Poland, she wrote: despite the high number of publications, "as yet they have not provided a clear explanation of all of Freud's views, or of the overlapping of psychoanalysis and humanities, or of the frictions within the psychoanalytic movement" (p. 35). She also made an observation that "the more the opponents of psychoanalysis explore the field without reservations, the more their approach changes" (p. 38). Her assessment proved very accurate during the interwar period when many Polish physicians, critical or indifferent to psychoanalysis in the past, joined the circle of its followers.

World War I (1914–1920)

The outbreak of the First World War interrupted Karpińska-Woyczyńska's scientific work. She actively joined the fight for Poland's independence. In October 1914, she enlisted for Piłsudski's Polish Legions as a nurse, alongside her husband who had been called into service as a military doctor. During the Battle of Lemberg in 1918–1919, she defended the city with the Fifth Legionary Infantry Regiment (Więckowska, 1937). After completing

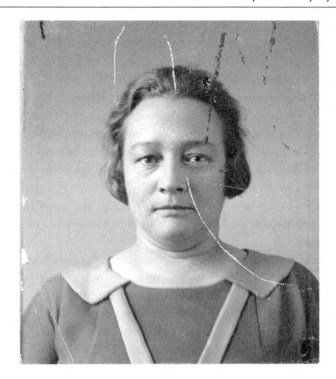

Figure 7.2 Ludwika Karpińska-Woyczyńska, personal file at the Municipal Psychological Laboratory in Łódź.
Copyright: Łódź State Archive (Archiwum Państwowe w Łodzi).

her military service in March 1920, she was awarded the Cross of Valor (Pl. *Krzyż Walecznych*), a Polish military decoration introduced in 1920 and awarded to individuals who demonstrated valor and courage on the battlefield. A few years later she received the Cross of Independence (Pl. *Krzyż Niepodległości*). In the interwar period, it was the second highest Polish military decoration awarded to individuals who had actively fought for the Polish independence. After 1918, in the independent country, Karpińska-Woyczyńska minimized her political involvement and dedicated almost all of her efforts to psychological research.

Interwar Activities (1920–1937)

The reborn Polish state was faced with many urgent issues. Highly educated individuals typically played an important role in the rebuilding process of the country. They prioritized the public good at the expense of their personal and professional ambitions. This was also the case of Karpińska-Woyczyńska, who was named the head of the Municipal Psychological Laboratory in Łódź in May 1920 (Więckowska, 1937). From that time onwards she devoted most of her time to psychological diagnosis of children and adolescents for educational purposes. She put in an enormous amount of work into creating and implementing new standards for psychotechnical testing of students. At that time psychotechnical testing (or psychotechnics)—practical application of psychological tests to predict the future performance of a student or job applicant—was developing dynamically. This time-consuming job was, most likely, the most important factor informing her decision to discontinue psychoanalytic work during the interwar period.

She started by researching intelligence using the Binet-Simon test that aimed to "isolate mentally disabled children from municipal elementary schools" and transfer them to a school for children with special needs, established in Łódź in 1919 as the first Polish institution of the kind (Karpińska-Woyczyńska, 1921, p. 1). While relying on psychological tests, she collaborated directly with elementary school teachers and special needs teachers and organized meetings. The objective of these so-called conferences was to prevent "children from being automatically qualified for a special school based solely on their results of the IQ test" (Karpińska-Woyczyńska, 1923b, p. 71). She pointed out, "progress does not depend on the intellect alone, while slow progress could not be 'blamed' just on the pupil or the school" (Karpińska-Woyczyńska, 1921, p. 24). She adopted a broader social perspective when analyzing the reasons behind some children's low performance at school:

> Sick or sickly, often hereditarily burdened, living in a dark and damp shack [...], malnourished, [...] beaten at home and exploited for various household chores, or left unsupervised and exposed to street life, dirty, scared, and lacking self-confidence, a child is not capable of learning in a typical way.
>
> (pp. 20–21)

She attributed the responsibility for the situation to "current social conditions that hinder the progress of an otherwise healthy child," especially to the six-years-long First World War (p. 20). The next year, she expanded her research on intelligence to other groups of children, such as preschoolers, children with hearing impairment or deaf, epilepsy, stuttering, and antisocial behavior (Karpińska-Woyczyńska, 1922).

In 1923, Karpińska-Woyczyńska was the first person in Poland who employed psychological techniques to screen prospective students for secondary schools in Łódź (Więckowska, 1937). Her great, unfortunately unrealized, dream was to open a career counseling center (Karpińska-Woyczyńska, 1925). In the interwar period, she maintained regular contact with psychotechnical centers abroad and attended several domestic and international psychotechnical congresses (Karpińska-Woyczyńska, 1923a). Between 1921 and 1930, she published a series of articles on child intelligence studies and the activities of the Municipal Psychological Laboratory in Łódź. One of her most significant scientific achievements was a study of the stability of IQ. It led to the conclusion that, generally speaking, people have a stable IQ (Karpińska-Woyczyńska, 1929).

She also contributed considerably to the establishment of the Polish Psychotechnical Society and was a member of the first Editorial Committee of the journal *Psychotechnika* [Psychotechnics], published since 1927. In 1928, when a branch of the Free Polish University of Warsaw opened in Łódź, she was appointed the first associate professor of applied psychology and the head of the Psychotechnics Department at the Faculty of Pedagogy (Zaniewicki, 1930). In addition to her academic work, she regularly gave presentations on general psychology, psychoanalysis, and psychotechnics to various professional groups, usually teachers and probation officers (Więckowska, 1937).

A Roman Catholic throughout her life, Karpińska-Woyczyńska was truly a woman of science. She believed, "regardless of personal religious beliefs, [scientists] must adhere to the principle of excluding spiritual issues from science" (Karpińska, 1909, p. 548).

Unfortunately, in September 1930, Karpińska-Woyczyńska's health suddenly deteriorated and she had to resign from her position at the Municipal Psychological Laboratory in Łódź. According to the medical records from 1930, she was diagnosed with diabetes and heart disease, namely myocardial degeneration (Karpińska-Woyczyńska personal files). Her laboratory associate and successor, Maria Więckowska, evaluated Karpińska-Woyczyńska's work as follows: thanks to her "profound and extensive knowledge [. . .], her arduous work of ten years [. . .] the quality of work at the laboratory was equivalent to other European institutes" (Więckowska, 1931, p. 8). Więckowska described her former supervisor as "extremely meticulous and diligent at work," very modest, depreciating her own qualities and merits, warm and helpful, kind to her assistants, guided by the principle "nothing for herself, everything for others" (Więckowska, 1937, p. 174).

Despite withdrawing from laboratory work, Karpińska-Woyczyńska did not abandon her scientific and community activities. She continued to lecture at the Free Polish University until 1932. In 1931 she participated in the International Psychotechnical Congress in Moscow and, in 1934, in the First Polish Conference of Psychologists Working in the Field of Education. In October 1936 she was elected to the board of the Vilnus Society for the Protection of Children.

In lieu of conclusion, one more episode from Karpińska-Woyczyńska's life should be noted. In May 1926, Józef Piłsudski carried out a military coup and seized power in Poland, overthrowing the democratically elected government. This initiated the period of authoritarian rule of the "Sanation" movement (Pl. *Sanacja*) led by Piłsudski. It was marked by brutal political persecution of its opponents and, *de facto*, ended the period of parliamentary democracy in the reborn Poland. In 1928, Karpińska-Woyczyńska's husband, Woyczyński, took up the position of Piłsudski's personal physician. Thus, she found herself in close proximity to the ruling camp. In this new situation, she tried to continue leading her rich scientific and social life that reached well beyond the "Sanation" circles. She seemed to have been entirely unaware of exposing her husband and herself to political persecution, later called "the Woyczyńskis scandal" (Piasecki, 2015, p. 416). In April 1935, a month before his death, Piłsudski reported to his closest associates that "new, strange, foreign-looking [Russian] people visit Mrs. Woyczyńska" (Składkowski, 2008, p. 32). As a result, she was arrested and interrogated. Piłsudski's people attempted to "uncover her contacts with domestic, foreign, and especially Russian communists" (p. 37). Her husband was forced to resign from the position of Piłsudski's physician.

The investigators were most suspicious of Karpińska-Woyczyńska's USSR-sponsored trip to Moscow in 1931 to attend the Psychotechnical Congress. This may seem surprising but, in fact, the Soviet Union paid for all foreign psychotechnicians to come to the congress (Baley, 1931). When reproached by the interrogators for accepting Soviet money, she replied that she was not involved in politics but in psychology (Składkowski, 2008). The City of Warsaw Police Commander, Marian Kozielewski, later claimed, "Karpińska brought problems upon [her husband] Woyczyński because of her leftist-suffragist nature" (Piasecki, 2015, p. 416). It is also not surprising that, in the opinion of "Sanation's" circle, she "definitely [had] too big of an ego for a wife of Piłsudski's follower" (Piasecki, 2015, p. 416). Indeed, the statements she made during the interrogation were truly astonishing for someone married to Piłsudski's personal doctor. They clearly prove that she was very critical towards "Sanation's" nationalistic authoritarian policies. She commented on the political situation of the period: "We have deviated so much from our dream Poland, where everyone was supposed to be free" (Składkowski, 2008, p. 34).

After several weeks of interrogation, she was released from prison due to the lack of evidence of anti-state activity. However, the damage had already been done. Rumors of her being an alleged Russian spy circulate to this day.

Karpińska-Woyczyńska died on January 30, 1937, in Warsaw from complications triggered by influenza (*Dziennik Polski*, 1937). Many Polish newspapers published short death notices reminding readers of her greatest achievements. World War II and the political turmoil that followed cast a shadow on her accomplishments, causing them to fall into oblivion. There are a few references to Karpińska-Woyczyńska's work in the field of psychotechnics in Polish psychology textbooks, but very little has been written in Poland about her contributions to the development of psychoanalytical theory and practice. This could be blamed on "the dark period of the 1950s that burdened psychoanalysis [in Poland] with the label of imperialist and bourgeois ideology" (Pawlak and Sokolik, 1992, p. 84). Her own decisions also contributed to the situation. Her resignation complex often led her to allow others to replace her. As a result, other Polish woman psychoanalysts who started their psychoanalytic training after Karpińska-Woyczyńska are better remembered by the Polish psychoanalytic community. One example is Eugenia Sokolnicka, who is still largely forgotten. Fortunately, most non-Polish publications on the birth and development of psychoanalysis reference Karpińska-Woyczyńska's work, "On the Psychological Foundations of Freudism" from 1914, the work that should have secured her a position in the history of psychoanalysis (Burgoyne and Leader, 2009; Casini, 2003; Giampieri-Deutsch, 2019; Jones, 1972; Roudinesco and Plon, 2004; Sarup, 1978).

Archival Materials

Birth certificate of Catherine Fearey (1835). Registers of Births, Marriages and Deaths surrendered to the Non-parochial Registers Commissions of 1837 and 1857: Northampton, College Street, Northamptonshire, Denomination: Baptist: Births (1786–1837). Ref. RG 4/902. The National Archive of UK.

Birth certificate of Ludwika Karpińska (1873). Civil registry of St. Bartholomew Roman Catholic parish in Plock. Ref. 50/155/0/—/93. Plock State Archive.

Birth certificate of Maria Karpińska (1859). Civil registry of the Catholic parish of Strzegowo. Ref. 0631/D.

Marriage certificate of Catherine Fearey and Casimer Karpinski (1856). Ref. 3B/202. England and Wales marriages Registration Index, 1837–2005. quarter 4, vol. 3B, p. 202, Northampton, Northamptonshire, England, General Register Office, Southport, England.

Karpińska-Woyczyńska Ludwika the head of the Municipal Psychological Laboratory—Personal Files (1920–1937). Ref. 39/221/0/4.2/64638. Lodz State Archive.

Chodźko W. et al. (Oct. 12, 1909). Telegram to Carl Gustav Jung from psychiatrists in Warsaw, Poland. Box 2, C. G. Jung Papers 1909–1955. Manuscript Division, Library of Congress, Washington D.C.

Reference List

Avenarius, R. (1902). *W sprawie filozofii naukowej*. L. Karpińska & A. Karpińska (Trans.). Warszawa: Wydawnictwo Przeglądu Filozoficznego.

Baley, S. (1931). Sprawozdanie z VII—go Kongresu Psychotechnicznego w Moskwie. *Polskie Archiwum Psychologii*, 4(3), 209–214.

Bandrowski, B. (1913). Psychologia na II. Zjeździe Neurologów, Psychiatrów i Psychologów Polskich. *Ruch Filozoficzny*, 3(2), 27–31.

Burgoyne, B. and Leader, D. (2009). A Problem of Scientific Influence. *Symptom*, 10, 1–8.

Casini, P. (2003). James and Freud on Psychical Determinism. In V. Benci, P. Cerrai, P. Freguglia, G. Israel and C. Pellegrini (Eds.), *Determinism, Holism and Complexity* (pp. 313–325). Boston, MA: Springer.

Czas. (1913). 64(508), 1.

Dembińska, E. and Rutkowski, K. (2016). Letter to the Editor. When and Where Was Ludwika Karpińska-Woyczyńska Born? *Psychiatria Polska*, 50(4), 891–893.

Dembińska, E. and Rutkowski, K. (2018). Ludwika Karpińska, "Polish Lady Philosopher"—A Forgotten Forerunner of Polish Psychoanalysis. *Psychiatria Polska*, 52(4), 753–765.

Dembińska, E. and Rutkowski, K. (2020a). The Reception of Dr Ludwik Jekels' "Apostolic Activity" to Promote Psychoanalysis in Poland Before the Outbreak of World War I. Part 1. *Psychiatria Polska*, 54(6), 1209–1230.

Dembińska, E. and Rutkowski, K. (2020b). The Reception of Dr Ludwik Jekels' "Apostolic Activity" to Promote Psychoanalysis in Poland Before the Outbreak of World War I. Part 2. *Psychiatria Polska*, 54(6), 1231–1254.

Dembińska, E. and Rutkowski, K. (2021). The Beginnings of Psychoanalysis in Poland Before the First World War. *Psychoanalysis and History*, 23(3), 325–350.
Dziennik Polski (1937). 3(33), 2.
Dziennik Praw (1853). 46(141), 146–151.
Fearey, E. (2022). *Civil War Poems*. C. Melnick (Ed.). Grand Junction, CO: Broken Yoke Publishing.
Freud, S. (1955). The Interpretation of Dreams. J. Strachey (Trans.). In J. Strachey (Ed.), *SE, Vol. IV: The Interpretation of Dreams (First Part)*. New York: Basic Books (Orig. publ. 1900).
Freud, S. (1957). On the History of the Psycho-analytic Movement. J. Strachey (Trans.). In J. Strachey (Ed.), *SE, Vol. XIV: On the History of the Psycho-analytic Movement, Papers on Metapsychology and Other Works* (pp. 1–66). London: Hogarth Press (Orig. publ. 1914).
Freud, S. and Ferenczi, S. (1994). *The Correspondence of Sigmund Freud and Sándor Ferenczi, Vol. I: 1908–1914*. E. Barbant, E. Falzeder and P. Giampieri-Deutsch (Eds.). Cambridge, MA: The Belknap Press.
Freud, S. and Ferenczi, S. (2000). *The Correspondence of Sigmund Freud and Sándor Ferenczi, Vol. III: 1920–1933*. E. Barbant and E. Falzeder (Eds.). Cambridge, MA: The Belknap Press.
Freud, S. and Jung, C. G. (1974). *The Freud/Jung Letters*. W. McGuire (Ed.). Princeton, NJ: Princeton UP.
Giampieri-Deutsch, P. (2019). Ernst Mach und Sigmund Freud: Fortsetzung der Philosphie mit anderen Mitteln? In F. Stadler (Ed.), *Ernst Mach—Zu Leben, Werk und Wirkung. Band 29* (pp. 45–73). Cham: Veröffentlichungen des Instituts Wiener Kreis, Springer Nature Switzerland.
Jekels, L. (1910). Leczenie psychoneuroz za pomocą metody psychoanalitycznej Freuda, tudzież kazuistyka. In A. Ciągliński et al. (Eds.), *Prace I-go Zjazdu Neurologów, Psychiatrów i Psychologów Polskich* (pp. 613–628). Warszawa: Wende i sp.
Jones, E. (1972). *Sigmund Freud Life and Work, Vol. I: The Young Freud 1856–1900*. London: Hogarth Press.
Karpińska, L. (1909). IV-ty Międzynarodowy Kongres Psychologiczny. *Przegląd Filozoficzny*, 12(4), 545–553.
Karpińska-Woyczyńska, L. (1910). *Experimentelle Beiträge zur Analyse der Tiefenwahrnehmung*. Leipzig: J.A. Barth.
Karpińska-Woyczyńska, L. (1911). Krytyka i sprawozdania. E. Abramowski. Dissociation et transformation du subconscient normal. *Przegląd Filozoficzny*, 14(1), 113–117.
Karpińska-Woyczyńska, L. (1912). Badania doświadczalne nad kojarzeniem wyobrażeń. *Przegląd Lekarski*, 51(43, 44, 45, 46, 47), 603–604, 617–619, 635–637, 647–649, 677–679.
Karpińska-Woyczyńska, L. (1913a). Psychologiczne podstawy freudyzmu. *Przegląd Filozoficzny*, 16(4), 508–526.
Karpińska-Woyczyńska, L. (1913b). Beiträge zur Psychopathologie des Alltagslebens. *Zentralblatt für Psychoanalyse und Psychotherapie*, 3(6–7), 309–312.

Karpińska-Woyczyńska, L. (1914a). Ein Beitrag zur Analyse "sinnloser" Worte im Träume. *Internationale Zeitschrift für ärztliche Psychoanalyse*, 2(2), 164–170.

Karpińska-Woyczyńska, L. (1914b). Über die psychologischen Grundlagen des Freudismus. *Internationale Zeitschrift für ärtzliche Psychoanalyse*, 2(4), 305–326.

Karpińska-Woyczyńska, L. (1914c). O psychoanalizie. *Ruch Filozoficzny*, 4(2), 33–38.

Karpińska-Woyczyńska, L. (1921). *Badanie dzieci umysłowo niedorozwiniętych ze szkół powszechnych miasta Łodzi*. Warszawa: Drukarnia Rolnicza.

Karpińska-Woyczyńska, L. (1922). Miejska Pracownia Psychologiczna w Łodzi. *Ruch Pedagogiczny*, 9(1–2), 31–35.

Karpińska-Woyczyńska, L. (1923a). Dobór dzieci uzdolnionych i próby zdolności zawodowej młodzieży w Berlinie i Hamburgu. *Ruch Pedagogiczny*, 10(1–3), 18–35.

Karpińska-Woyczyńska, L. (1923b). Rola psychologii w doborze dzieci umysłowo upośledzonych do szkół pomocniczych. *Ruch Pedagogiczny*, 10(4–6), 65–75.

Karpińska-Woyczyńska, L. (1925). Znaczenie ekonomiczne i społeczne poradnictwa zawodowego. *Przegląd Włókienniczy*, 4(4–5), 32–34.

Karpińska-Woyczyńska, L. (1929). Sprawozdanie z działalności w r. 1928—Miejska Pracownia Psychologiczna. *Dziennik Zarządu m. Łodzi*, 11(41), 742–750.

Kosiakiewicz, W. (1910). Pracownia psychologiczna w Warszawie. *Świat*, 5(5), 14–15.

Kurier Warszawski. (1890). 70(7), 4.

Kurier Warszawski. (1899). 79(293), 8.

Lewicki, S. A., Orłowicz, M. and Praschil, T. (1912). *Przewodnik po zdrojowiskach i miejscowościach klimatycznych Galicji*. Lwów: Krajowy Związek Zdrojowisk i Uzdrowisk.

Magnone, L. (2016). *Emisariusze Freuda. Transfer psychoanalizy do polskich sfer inteligenckich przed drugą wojną światową*. Kraków: Universitas.

Magnone, L. (2023). *Freud's Emissaries: The Transfer of Psychoanalysis Through the Polish Intelligentsia to Europe 1900–1939*. T. Bhambry (Trans.). Lausanne: Sdvig Press.

Miąso, J. (2005). Walka narodowa o polską szkołę w Królestwie Polskim w latach 1905–1907. *Rozprawy z Dziejów Oświaty*, 44, 75–103.

Nunberg, H. and Federn, E. (Eds.) (1967). *Minutes of the Vienna Psychoanalytic Society, Vol. II: 1908–1910*. New York: International UP.

Pawlak, K. and Sokolik, Z. (1992). Historia psychoanalizy w Polsce. *Nowiny Psychologiczne*, 4(2), 83–88.

Piasecki, W. (2015). *Jan Karski. Jedno życie. Kompletna historia. Vol. I*. Kraków: Insignis.

Program paryski PPS (1892). *Paris Program of PPS (1892)*. Online at https://ppspl.eu/partia/historia/program-paryski/. Accessed July 14, 2022.

Roudinesco, E. and Plon, M. (2004). *Wörterbuch der Psychoanalyse. Namen, Länder, Werke, Begriffe*. Wien: Springer.

Sarup, G. (1978). Historical Antecedents of Psychology: The Recurrent Issue of Old Wine in New Bottles. *American Psychologist*, 33(5), 478–485.
Składkowski, S. (2008). Tajemnica rodzinna lekarza przybocznego marszałka. Ostatni rozkaz Józefa Piłsudskiego. In S. Nowinowski (Ed.), *Pęk kluczy* (pp. 31–38). Łomianki: LTW.
Tönnies, F. (1903). *Tomasz Hobbes: życie jego i nauka*. L. Karpińska (Trans.). Warszawa: Wydawnictwo Przeglądu Filozoficznego.
Weryho, W. (1908). Dziesięciolecie "Przeglądu Filozoficznego". *Przegląd Filozoficzny*, 11(1–2), I–XX.
Więckowska, M. (1931). *Sprawozdanie z działalności Miejskiej Pracowni Psychologicznej i Poradni Zawodowej w Łodzi*. Łódź: Towarzystwo "Patronat nad Młodzieżą Rzemieślniczą i Przemysłową" w Łodzi.
Więckowska, M. (1937). Dr Ludwika Karpińska-Woyczyńska. Wspomnienie pośmiertne. *Polskie Archiwum Psychologii*, 9(3), 170–174.
Zaniewicki, Z. (1930). *Szkoły Wyższe Rzeczypospolitej Polskiej*. Warszawa: Wydawnictwo Kasy im. J. Mianowskiego.

Chapter 8

Nic Waal

Speaking in Tongues

Håvard Friis Nilsen

A charismatic representative of the new and mysterious psychoanalytic profession, Nic Waal embodied an image of a modern progressive woman: she combined intelligence and a university degree in medicine with progressive cultural and political views (also on sex and gender issues) and had a seductive personality, bobbed hair, and a short nickname. Drawn to psychoanalysis during her medical studies, she pursued analytic training in Berlin immediately after graduation to become one of Norway's first psychoanalysts and members of the International Psychoanalytical Association (IPA) (Nilsen, 2005, 2016). She became a well-known public speaker on social and health policies and a pioneer of child psychiatry (Lange, 2002); the institute for child psychiatry she founded is still thriving today in Oslo. She deserves recognition also for her active, courageous role during the German occupation of Norway in 1940–1945. As a member of resistance groups and networks that arranged escape routes to Sweden, she played a central role in the successful rescue operation of a Jewish children foster home in 1942.

Childhood and Early Years

Nic Waal was born in Kristiania (now Oslo, Norway) as Caroline Schweigaard Nicolaysen on January 1, 1905, as the youngest of four siblings in a middle-class family with two servants and a maid. Her father, Vilhelm Bernhoft Nicolaysen (1866–1929), was a captain, later major in the Norwegian army. Educated as an engineer, he came from a family of officers and businessmen with connections to families of fine pedigree, and he was politically conservative and practiced horse riding and ski jumping, typical élite sports at the time. Nic's mother, Anna (née Horn, 1872–1933), belonged to a renowned family; her father Hassa Horn (1837–1921) was

DOI: 10.4324/9781003455844-12

This chapter has been made available under a CC-BY-NC-ND 4.0 license.

the mayor of Kristiania. Trained as a teacher, Anna was well read and knew the classics as well as the latest progressive ideas of women's emancipation. She played the piano and loved to play four-handed with her sister, or gather chamber musicians in the home. Her teacher training was not put to practice, however, as she had to stay at home and care for the family, especially after her husband fell ill. This was a source of great bitterness, and she instilled in Nic a firm wish to have a professional training that led to a secure position.

Although living in an affluent area on the ground floor of a villa on Fearnleys gate, the Nicolaysen family wasn't wealthy, and the economic hardships troubled Nic's father, who was prone to mood swings and outbursts of temper. These later worsened into depressions and at least one psychotic episode, and in later years, he was hospitalized with depression for long periods of time (Waal, 1991, p. 15).

An Independent Woman

Nic was born in the year of Norway's independence, as the asymmetric union between Norway and Sweden was dissolved in 1905. Certainly, independence was one of Nic's personality traits from early childhood on. The bourgeois family background stood in stark contrast to her father's illness and mental problems, a tension which perhaps fostered the rebellious streak in Nic. A typical *flapper* in the 1920s, she wore her hair short, loved jazz, and explored Europe on her own during summer holidays. Nic was independent in so many ways: intellectually, financially, politically, and sexually. She demonstrated a woman's freedom to read, to study, to become an MD, to engage in socialist groups, and to have as many lovers as she wished. Late in life, she looked back on her childhood and noted that when she was growing up sexual education was nonexistent for girls:

> [W]hen I was 12, everything concerning sexuality was taboo. I read the dictionary and Mary Stopes [British paleobotanist and women's rights activist] at night, by the candlelight. My mother did not explain the mysteries of menstruation to me, so when I got it, I thought I had caught some terrible and shameful disease; something to do with uncleanliness. At the same time, she *did* tell me that women did not have sexual feelings, but had to succumb to their husbands in conjugal duty. I thought it was dreadful, but Mary Stopes, who among other things stated that a

marriage was most happy when a couple was connected both physically and mentally, eased my heart.

(Waal, 1959, original emphasis)

Sometimes described as "strikingly beautiful," a student friend added that when he met her again, he felt she wasn't actually all that pretty. However, "she had an irresistible charm, and when she laughed, her rays hit. She had a particularly intense girlish charisma, erotic and enticing" (Bull, 1988, p. 31). A later friend commented, "everybody was fascinated with Nic. And she didn't always make it easy for other women in the group" (personal communication from Sigrid Braatøy, 2002). Throughout her life, she would assert herself, take leadership, or assume roles of responsibility within groups. Often, she would find herself competing with men. After graduating from college in 1923, Nic started studying medicine, still at the time an education overwhelmingly dominated by men.

On her lone trip to Paris in 1926, she met Sigurd Hoel (1889–1960), an editor and writer 14 years her senior, whose book, *Conrad*, she has just read. They connected instantly and became lovers. Hoel knew many of the most exciting artists and intellectuals in the city, including young Ernest Hemingway, ten years Hoel's junior. Both Nic and Hoel loved Hemingway's first novel, *The Sun Also Rises*, which had just appeared in 1926. As an editor at Norway's largest publishing house, Gyldendal, Hoel secured the first Norwegian translation of the novel and, in fact, its first translation into another language. Sigurd and Nic adored the novel because Hemingway described in it the "lost generation" that, sickened after the First World War with the older generation's hypocrisy, discarded all traditional values while exploring sexuality and gender roles in Paris. The book's female protagonist, aristocrat Lady Ashley, who only went by the nickname "Duff," may have inspired Caroline Schweigaard Nicolaysen to change her name to "Nic."

Hoel proposed to Nic within a year and they decided to marry. Still, she was openly ambivalent about the institution of marriage. She reflected on the reasons behind her ambivalence later in life:

I had a glowing conviction that women's liberation was not only about intellectual emancipation the way my mother saw it, but also about women's right to feel emotions with their bodies and to determine their own destinies in love. I felt this long before I had any experience. But my mother and father were not happy. When I was little, I did not want to marry, and I had a very strong opinion about that.

(Waal, 1959)

The year Nic and Hoel got married, he published his breakthrough novel, *Sinners in Summertime* (Norw. *Syndere i sommersol*), portraying his wife as the main character, Evelyn, among a group of friends enjoying a summer holiday on an island in the Oslo fiord (Hoel, 1927). While discussing Freud and how he stripped the previous generation of its credibility, the group declared themselves liberated from conventional morals and ready for the future. They were armed with "Freudian gunpowder," as Hoel put it, many years later:

In those days, before the Moscow purges, radicalism was still untainted. But gradually, Freud superseded Marx as the radical of the day. We read Marx, although with certain reservations. Aside from the fact that the man was surrounded by an impenetrable beard, and writing in an equally impenetrable German, far worse was the fact we discovered, that he had not read Freud! As he had been dead for ten years before Freud published his first writings, he did have a sort of an excuse, but it nevertheless seemed like a major defect. It was like a revolutionary writing before the invention of gunpowder. We, however, were armed with bullets and cartridges in every pocket!

(Hoel, 1954, p. 4)

Nic was portrayed as a woman who upsets the stability and harmony of the group when she arrives; the men were transfixed by her strong personality, while the women became jealous. As the book sparked controversy on publication, it quickly became a bestseller. It has been reprinted in countless editions and adapted for two movies. Hoel would portray Nic again in the novel *A Day in October* (Hoel, 1931), where her emotional instability formed part of the narrative. From the early 1930s, Hoel and Nic were both public figures, spearheading psychoanalysis in Norway both as a new method of treatment and as a literary tool. As a married couple, Sigurd and Nic embodied the psychoanalytic unity of medicine and literature, the creative field and new commonality between medical doctors and writers of fiction, that appeared in every country where psychoanalysis gained ground.

Nic in Analysis With Harald Schjelderup

Devoted to Freud and psychoanalysis, Sigurd and Nic discussed their differences, their marriage, their sexuality, and their love through a Freudian lens. Their letters from 1927 until the mid-1930s are filled with psychoanalytic references and information about their respective mood swings and depressions. Shortly after their wedding, when she was still a medical student, Nic entered a psychoanalytic therapy with Professor Harald Schjelderup from the University of Oslo. He was a professor of psychology and Norway's first psychoanalyst, trained by Eduard Hitschmann in Vienna and Oskar Pfister in Zurich. Nic was his very first psychoanalytic patient.

Despite her many talents, impressive achievements, and general popularity, Nic was suffering from what she called "a sense of 'soul cleavage,' depression, anxiety and various somatic symptoms" (Schjelderup, 1930, p. 126). Sometimes, often around noon, she would feel overwhelmed by an irresistible urge to utter childish sounds. She did not know the origin of the sounds, but she was certain that they had a meaning, without knowing its exact nature. The feeling would overcome her in a very peculiar way, difficult to describe. Although not religious, Nic described it as "containing the Spirit." She could easily understand the religious belief of "holding God within oneself." She would remain fully conscious during the fit. Still, she was unable to invoke the condition at will or replicate the sounds. During a seizure, she would feel like a child. She would lose the ability to speak adult language and the awareness of the adult world. "I am not the one speaking, it is something living deep inside me—it is as if I cannot comprehend the world" (Schjelderup, 1930, p. 126).

The seizure happened once during her analysis with Schjelderup, in the phase of transference. Schjelderup described Nic as extremely intelligent. He proceeded to outline the peculiar phenomenon of Nic speaking in tongues. Coming from a clerical family, this symptom had a particular appeal to him, as it was usually associated with religious ecstasy experienced in sects, ever since St. Paul's first descriptions of such occurrences in the Bible. It also provided him with a case that allowed him to build upon psychoanalytic work of his analyst, Oskar Pfister. Pfister interpreted the phenomenon of speaking in tongues in an article on the psychological deciphering of religious glossolalia and automatic cryptography from 1912. He claimed that the organizing principle behind the phenomenon was similar to that found in dreams and neuroses: a complex of painful experiences and memories were hidden under and given form by seemingly meaningless syllables and phonetic expressions (Pfister, 1912, p. 781; cf. Kienast, 1974). Schjelderup's case study of Nic offered further empirical material, as well as a rare case of non-religious tongue-speaking.

Nic provided the material for interpretation during analysis when she managed to write down syllables during one of her fits:

Bosche, bosche, maino
Veine bine momo
Lana-lana meina,
Bischta-butta. Taina!
Dutta-kaaaaada!
Vista mysse!!
Moi-moi, usta, byyy
Na veidane loo
Buschta, bitta
Mainanano buta.
Buuuu la muosta
Veinana. Mi!

Schjelderup encouraged Nic to make free associations between the lines. As a result, it suddenly appeared that to her that the syllables were bursting with emotional content. By repeating the sounds and having the analyst repeating them as well, she gradually accessed childhood memories associated with emotions embedded in the sounds.

Bosche, bosche, maino: (First strong anxiety). "It is so dark. O and sch tell me I am alone. No one can hear me. B means me, they called me Bitteba when I was little. It means that something has gone away as in 'gone, gone', when one is hiding [*Borte, borte=Norwegian 'gone, gone'*]. Sch means quiet, like in hush."

Maino: (First deep despair, crying). "It is a connection of ai and o-m is me-ai is sorrow. In the Russian theatre in Paris, they always said ai, ai when they were sad—there is something sad, slow and weeping over 'ai'—like in 'poor little me' is reduced to 'ai. 'No' means thumb sucking, comfort—I see a thumb-mother, mother, I hear someone say 'mo' and put a finger in my mouth: it is nice." [. . .]

Taina: "Taina means: I long terribly for you. T=you, ai=so sad! The whole word expresses longing. Na= 'now have', 'now have you'."

Dutta kaaaada: "It means something terrible—kada: very cold and empty and so painful one must die.—I can't bear it. You are gone, won't come back!" Cold—dada—the cruel nanny.—Then it means that you or God or somebody else must take the cold nanny away. Dutta means you take.

Vista mysse: "Mysse alone is a name for myself. Me kiss, me being kissed; when I say Mysse-myss, I come running and want to hug and be hugged, which is a caressing and warm feeling." But Vista means that I want to be bad (Vi = vil (want), s = slem (bad), ta = take) against something, break something. Vista mysse together means that I pretend to be nice, but want to be bad.

Nic mentions a Parisian Russian theatre in her associations. Some of the words were indeed Russian—but neither Nic nor Schjelderup had noticed. "Bosche, bosche" is "God, oh God" in an old Russian prayer, and "taina" stands for "secret." As Nic associated freely within the tongue-speaking, hidden meanings were uncovered and childhood memories came back. Her analysis with Schjelderup demonstrated that Freud's method of free association worked not only in the case of dreams, but also in the analysis of other emotionally charged forms of expression. In Schjelderup's view, the meaningless syllables were an example of Freud's concept of condensation—how layers of emotional content could be condensed into one expression, whether a dream or in this case a sound. In Nic's case, emotional content and several words from child's vocabulary not yet mastered by it, were condensed and compressed into simple sounds. Furthermore, Schjelderup believed that the sounds were not reconstructions of an adult but a result of a genuine regression to an infantile stage in language development, accompanied by a re-enactment of the emotional experiences of a one- or two-year-old (Schjelderup, 1930, p. 126). The re-enactment of her childhood emotions led to a further exploration and working-through of her forgotten past.

Schjelderup proceeded to outline Nic's family situation and early traumatic experiences as they came up during analysis: Nic was the youngest of four siblings; she had a brother and two sisters. At the time of her birth, her parents' relationship was not in a good condition. When she was two or three, her father suffered "a nervous breakdown" (Schjelderup, 1930, p. 15). He was overworked, insomniac, plagued with anxiety, and so distressed that he struggled to write his own name. He was short-tempered and exploded with rage regularly. As Nic was a very emotional child, she became hypersensitive to her father's mood swings.

The owner of the apartment they lived in was a strict old man with a cruel appearance. Nic remembered that she turned him into an object of resentment. One day, when she was about four or five, she dropped a cricket bat from the window with the intention of hitting him. She missed and was given a scolding by her mother (Schjelderup and Schjelderup, 1972, p. 16). Working through the memory of this incident revealed her ambivalence towards her father who had merged with the landlord in an unconscious fantasy. Nic uncovered feelings of guilt and murderous impulses. Schjelderup interpreted the ambivalence towards her father as the root of her identity problems in adulthood. Her childhood recollections also included a memory of sexual abuse and possible rape by a young man in the neighborhood, over 16 years her senior. Schjelderup believed that the memory of the sexual abuse was real.

> I feel unwell . . . I thought of something . . . I am terribly nervous . . . it is so uncertain—I was thinking of the two street boys, especially Albert— with his big, red face, blond—just like the one that turned up on the balcony—I tried to brush it aside, but instead had a feeling—something appears, it comes, I feel I must hit and scream and push it away . . . and I realized something I had not thought of before, sometimes when I hear you [the analyst] take a breath, I feel a shock, I am confused by anxiety and feel like hitting.

When asked about the feeling that gripped her, she responded:

> It is definitely localized, I am helpless against it, and I do not understand what it is—I cannot see anything—something is huge and very warm. It touches my genitals . . . because I *now* know what a penis is, I think of the glans penis, but I feel it is the adult's interpretation . . . It is dark, therefore I cannot see anything.
> (Schjelderup and Schjelderup, 1972, pp. 18–19, original emphasis)

In the case study based on Nic's analysis, Schjelderup diagnosed her as a narcissist with the tendency to return to an infantile stage when the life was too harsh. Nic's self-love was connected with her strong sense of oneness with the world, with all living beings. Her religious feelings resembled pantheism, with no clear boundary between her and God's universe.

While Nic was in analysis, her husband, Sigurd, was not pleased with their marriage and felt that Schjelderup developed a counter-transference and infatuation with Nic. It does seem that many men who knew her had a period of infatuation. "Even Schjelderup loves Nic," Sigurd complained (Waal, 1991, p. 72). He also felt that the analysis transgressed the confidential space of their marriage: Nic was sharing her innermost secrets with one more person. He wrote to her about this problem for years:

> [Y]ou tried to confide in me too, once in a while—but I have probably closed myself up, or been inept in the situation, or was hurt and hateful—and then you had an infantile condition caused by your analysis, and then reacted to my mistakes or my rejections of you or whatever, like you reacted to your father and your mother when you were little and did not get the understanding you needed. In other words, you closed yourself up. And Schjelderup, who should have tried to prevent this, was himself infatuated with you, and argued that I was unreasonable—which maybe I have been, I analyze all this from abstract concepts—and then, you stopped confiding in me. And when the trust was gone, there were actions, you were afraid of telling me about—because you feared the consequences of sharing them with me.
>
> (Hoel, 1931)

This is one of several letters from Sigurd discussing how the trust had deteriorated between them, and it would be a recurrent theme over the next few years. Nic's response was that Sigurd kept aloof by a shield of superficial irony and politeness, throwing her into ruminations bordering on obsession. Their letters reflect ebbs and flows of depression and love, and Nic's love letters would typically end with syllables from her secret language, with love associations. She often signed her letters with signatures that originated from her speaking in tongues: *Moi-Moi* (I am happy), *Vista Mysse and Mysse-myss* (I want to be kissed).

Becoming a Psychoanalyst

Nic claimed the analysis with Schjelderup changed her life and probably even saved it. She decided to specialize in psychiatry and practice psychoanalysis. Before she took her medical degree in the fall of 1930, as the only woman in her class, she received a three-month-long internship at the Paris Clinique Charcot in 1928, accompanied by a stipend. The year she qualified as a doctor, she moved to Berlin to study psychology at the university under Wolfgang Kohler, and psychoanalysis at the Berlin Training Institute. Her training analysts were Salomea Kempner and Otto Fenichel. In 1930–1931 Berlin was like a keg of gunpowder about to explode. On the one hand, the Nazis were marching in the streets, the Communists were demonstrating, and the political tensions were increasing. On the other hand, it was a cultural melting pot bursting with creative energy: cabarets, cafés, clubs, music, artists, writers, Marlene Dietrich, Bertolt Brecht, Klaus Mann. Nic got to experience a culture that was eradicated just a few years later.

She studied at university, underwent analysis, and went to lectures and seminars at the Berlin Institute until 1933. On July 4, 1933, she was elected to be a member of the German Psychoanalytic Society (DPG) based on her lecture "On Fire-Extinguishing and Homosexuality" (Boehm, 1933, p. 520). After Hitler's coming to power in 1933, Otto Fenichel relocated with his family to Oslo, and Wilhelm Reich relocated to Denmark. While she went in analysis with Fenichel, her husband Sigurd began an analysis with Reich. She later described how Fenichel's voice would grow shrill when she mentioned Reich's name during analytic hours (Waal, 1958). Fenichel and Reich who had been close friends since 1920 fell out after the Luzern conference in 1934, where Reich was expelled. Reich felt Fenichel had kept low and not come to his defense, in order to remain loyal with Anna Freud, Ernest Jones, and the IPA, while Fenichel for his part thought Reich was too confrontational and egocentric. Gradually, the Norwegian analysts including Nic sided with Reich. She found Reich's *Character Analysis* to be an excellent tool for understanding psychoanalytic technique, went in training analysis also with him, and became a close friend of his during the five years he spent in Norway (until 1939).

In April 1934 Fenichel started sending out his secret circular letters (*Rundbriefe*) from Oslo to selected analysts who reacted against the worrisome tendencies in the German society. The circular letter arose from Professor Harald Schjelderup's Easter conference gathering psychoanalysts from Germany and the Nordic and Scandinavian countries at the University of Oslo. Fenichel had a large network of analysts grown out of his Berlin "seminars for naughty children" (Germ. *Kinderseminar*), that he led from 1924 until his emigration in 1933, and it came to good use now in this form of intellectual and political underground resistance. Most of the recipients later destroyed their copies of the letters, as they were considered dangerous to their lives if they still lived in Germany, but Nic kept all of hers. The recipients of the first circular letter in April 1934 included Nic, Edith Jacobssohn (later Jacobson), Wilhelm and Annie Reich, Georg Gerö, Erich Fromm, Frances Deri, Käthe Misch, Vera Schmidt, and Sabina Spielrein (Reichmayr and Mühlleitner, 1998, p. 66). Fenichel asked for feedback on the circular letter and how the recipients saw their own roles and possible contributions to it, as well as suggestions for more recipients. In the second circular letter, also from April 1934, Fenichel noted that their Russian colleagues Jakob Kogan, Vera Schmidt, and Spielrein had no need to work actively in a left-wing opposition themselves and had little interest in the organizational rifts within the IPA branch societies, so Fenichel suggested to continue to keep them informed but regard them as part of the wider group rather than the core (cf. Reichmayr and Mühlleitner, 1998, p. 78).

Figure 8.1 Psychoanalysts in Soviet Russia. Back row, from left to right: Sabina Spielrein (most probably) and Wilhelm Reich. Front row, from left to right: Vera Schmidt, Annie Reich, unknown, Moscow, 1929.

Copyright: A. A. Brill Library & Archive. New York Psychoanalytic Society & Institute.

In the next letter, Fenichel proposed defining the group by three "outer circles." The first one consisted of "colleagues who are to be informed of all-important matters, and only temporarily not informed about the nature of [the] cooperation, as a precaution, and who do not take on any obligations" (p. 83). This included Fromm, Spielrein, Schmidt, Misch, and Barbara Lantos, among others. The second group, "the true sympathizers," included, i.e., Lotte Liebeck, Harald Schjelderup, Anny Angel (later Rosenberg Katan), and Werner Kemper. The inclusion of Kemper, who later took up a leading position at the so-called Göring Institute in Berlin, may seem puzzling, but he was an analysand of Wilhelm Reich and at this point considered part of the wider group (Nilsen, 2022). The final group, "those who are likely to become sympathizers soon," included Sàndor Rado, Ola Raknes, and Steff Bornstein, among others (p. 83).

Fenichel's circular letters addressed current political events, the affairs of the psychoanalytic movement, and theoretical developments. Thanks to his encyclopedic knowledge of psychoanalytic literature, Fenichel was able to discuss the ideas of Melanie Klein as easily as Sabina Spielrein's paper on children's drawings made with eyes open and closed (Spielrein, 2019/1931). Fenichel and Wilhelm Reich may have met Spielrein in 1929 during their visit to Soviet Russia, if not earlier. They stayed in Moscow with Vera Schmidt and her family, and as Fenichel mentioned Spielrein and Schmidt together as "their Russian colleagues," it may indicate that Spielrein met them in Moscow at this time.

Nic was one of the recipients of the circular letters from the start, and her collection actually formed part of the basis for their later publication in 1998 (Reichmayr and Mühlleitner, 1998). In the second letter, Fenichel states that the "organization" that forms the core of the circular letters consists of the five IPA members in the group, namely Fenichel, Gerö, Nic, Edith Jacobssohn, and Wilhelm Reich (Reichmayr and Mühlleitner, 1998, p. 78).

For many years, from 1924 when she first became a member of the Labor Party, Nic was also politically involved with a Marxist student group Towards Dawn (Norw. *Mot Dag*). Led by Erling Falk, a charismatic businessman who had worked in the US and learned organizational work from Bill Haywood at the International Workers of the World (IWW), Mot Dag soon counted an impressive group of intellectual and highly educated members. The group was predominantly male; Nic was an exception there too. Sigurd Hoel was the editor of the group's periodical for a few years, and

Fenichel was connected to the group and gave lectures on psychoanalytic and political themes for them when he lived in Norway between 1933 and 1935. After he left for Prague in 1935, his residence permit was not renewed.

Nic, Ernest Jones, and the Arrest of Edith Jacobssohn

In 1935, Nic traveled to England on a fellowship to work at the British Institute for Psycho-Analysis. Soon after her arrival, Ernest Jones informed her that the Gestapo had arrested her friend, Edith Jacobssohn, in Germany, on October 24, 1935. Jacobssohn was a member of the Berlin Society as one of Fenichel's analysands and also a close friend of Wilhelm Reich. She was involved with the political group the New Beginning (Germ. *Neu Beginnen*), which was the background for her arrest. She was charged with high treason and was facing torture and long and harsh imprisonment. Four days after the arrest, Wilhelm Reich wrote to Nic about this urgent matter. He explained that the Gestapo first arrested one of Jacobssohn's leftist patients. The patient later committed suicide. Reich also informed Nic that he had sent the Danish writer Ellen Siersted, mutual friend from Copenhagen, to Berlin to help Jacobssohn obtain legal assistance. He urged Nic to get in touch with as many prominent public figures in England as possible:

> Please refer to me and get in touch with [Bronisław] Malinowski, [Henry] Havelock Ellis, [Max] Hodann, [Alexander Sutherland] Neill, [Bertrand] Russell, Stella Browne, Mrs. Jameson (friend of Trygve Braatoy), and [Julian] Huxley. [. . .] The main thing is to have everything ready in case we see that Gestapo will not release Edith. Then we can intervene through the press. Please omit Jones and the IPA. Edith should not be associated with psychoanalysis.
>
> (Reich, 1935)

Meanwhile, Schjelderup contacted the German authorities to speak on Jacobssohn's behalf. Schjelderup was one of very few professors among the analysts, and since Nazi ideology idealized all things Nordic, support from a protestant Norwegian professor could perhaps carry some weight. His intervention especially upset Felix Boehm (1881–1958), the newly installed president of the German Psychoanalytic Society and director of the Berlin Training Institute. Boehm felt that by revealing the connection between Jacobssohn and psychoanalysis to the authorities, Schjelderup endangered psychoanalytic institutions in Germany. Nic informed Boehm that the Gestapo already knew, as they had found Jacobsohn's patient lists (Hoel [Waal], 1935c). In the years to come, Boehm became an increasingly controversial central figure of the "Aryanized" Berlin Institute of Psychoanalysis, fully supporting Nazism, but at this point, he had not yet shown his true colors.

Nic informed Reich that only Neill, Stella Browne, and Dora Russell were very optimistic. Dora's husband, Bertrand Russell, was pretty discouraging. The remaining intellectuals she had contacted were vague and fearful of political engagement (Hoel [Waal], 1935c). On October 30 Ernest Jones scribbled a brief note to Anna Freud; he communicated with her regularly regarding the issues of emigration:

> Edith Jacobson has been arrested in Berlin and is thought to be in danger of her life. She has Left sympathies and was analyzing a Communist whom the Nazis captured and killed recently. Perhaps they wanted to get further information out of her, which she refused to give. The question is whether she would be in a safer position if it were known in Germany that people in other countries are concerned with her welfare and are—so to speak—watching what is happening. If you think anything could be done and what Instanz [sic] should be approached in this case, please communicate with me as soon as possible. It happened a few days ago.
>
> (Jones, 1935a)

On Jones's suggestion, Nic volunteered to travel to Germany to investigate. In a letter to Anna Freud, Jones stated that he had interviewed four candidates for this "Scarlet Pimpernel Adventure" before selecting Nic. (The Scarlet Pimpernel was a famous book series at the time about an undercover agent working to rescue victims of the French Revolution in France.) "I should of course like to go myself," added Jones "but there are several reasons against it at the moment. I am not sure that I should be quite safe in Germany, for I have probably compromised myself with the Nazis through a good many contacts" (Jones, 1935b). Nic, a close friend of Marxist analysts: Wilhelm Reich, Otto Fenichel, and Edith Jacobssohn herself, was most probably in much greater danger than he was, but this evidently did not occur to Jones.

Jacobssohn's arrest was the first direct attack of the Nazi regime on a psychoanalyst. The IPA leadership, in particular Ernest Jones and Anna Freud,

Figure 8.2 Nic Waal at the time of her Berlin assignment from Ernest Jones, 1935.
Reproduced with permission of Håvard Friis Nilsen.

worried about the future of psychoanalysis in Germany. According to him, some of the members proposed to dissolve the Society, but the IPA decided against it. Others, including Boehm, wanted to sever the link with the IPA, to minimize its characteristic as the "Jewish Science." The IPA decided against that too. In October 1935, Jones stated bluntly: "there was no way of saving the Jewish members of the Society, who have had to resign and will presumably emigrate" (Jones, 1935a). With reference to the German Psychoanalytic Society, Jones described the situation in November 1935 as "chronically precarious, threats and warnings against [the members] and Psycho-Analysis accumulate as time goes by" (Jones, 1935c).

Jones was quite open about his views on the future of his Jewish colleagues in Germany. In the already quoted letter to Anna Freud on Jacobssohn's case he stated:

> I shall not be surprised at news that all Jews have to resign from the Berlin Society. Deplorable as it would be, I should still say that I prefer

Psycho-Analysis to be practiced by Gentiles in Germany than not at all, and I hope you agree with this. Naturally, we should at once make them all direct members of the IPV. An Austrian, who has just arrived in London from Berlin says that 20 Austrian Social Democrats were arrested there in connection with just the same affair as E.J's [Edith Jacobssohn's]. He expressed the hope that enough of them would confess to make it unnecessary to torture her.

(Jones, 1935b)

Max Eitingon, the founder and benefactor of the Berlin Institute, had to resign as the director of the Institute and president of the IPA in 1933. Felix Boehm was selected as a non-Jewish analyst to replace him as director of the Institute. Similarly, gentile Carl Müller-Braunschweig was appointed president of the committee of the German Psychoanalytic Society in 1933. The two were elected on November 18, 1933, and from then on, they gradually adapted psychoanalysis to the prevailing ideology of the Hitler regime. Müller-Braunschweig wrote to Wilhelm Reich in 1934, asking him to understand the necessity of removing his name from the list of members. Not long after Nic visited them, in December 1935, the few remaining Jewish members were forced to resign from the German society of psychoanalysis.

Nic traveled to Prague, Vienna, and Berlin to meet with Anna Freud, Felix Boehm, and Werner Kemper. Kemper (1899–1975) was another central figure of the "Aryanized" Berlin Institute of Psychoanalysis, soon to be renamed the German Institute for Psychological Research and Psychotherapy (the so-called Göring Institute) (Cocks, 1997). Kemper was an analysand of Wilhelm Reich and a friend of Fenichel and many of the Norwegians. He maintained contact with them, also during the Göring Institute period (Nilsen, 2022, pp. 306–307). Nic's close friend, Astri Brun, stayed in Berlin during the war. She and her husband, Theo Ortner, were neighbors and friends of Werner Kemper and his wife throughout the war (Nilsen, 2016, p. 128). After the war, Reich wrote to Kemper and sent several food parcels, and a parcel of books via Willy Brandt, later chancellor of the Federal Republic of Germany (Higgins, 2012, p. 5). During one of her travels in connection with Jacobssohn's case, Nic found herself in Paris, where she met the analyst René Spitz. He put her in touch with one of the foremost German barristers living in Paris at the time. Using his extensive contacts in Germany, he had successfully intervened in similar cases in the past (Spitz, 1935). Nic traveled from Paris to Berlin. In a letter to Sigurd Hoel from this trip (written while still in Berlin or later), Nic painted a vivid description of Berlin transformed completely under the dictatorship:

> Berlin was awful. I am still absolutely nauseated and distressed. It still sends shivers down my spine, and I feel totally sick and depressed. It is incomparably much worse than a year ago. Such barbarism is allowed to prevail day by day, without people around the world rising up against it in a wild angry scream. It was a dreadful experience, trying to stay calm, I mean. Upon seeing a melancholic Jewish face, on an extremely rare occasion, I felt like bursting into tears, calling out: "Here's a friend!" But no such thing was possible. If I tried to look at them and smile, they blushed and averted their eyes. Even on a full bus no one sat next to a Jew. And [Julius] Streicher's magazine [*Der Stürmer*, an instrument of mass propaganda for the NSDAP] was pasted on bright red news posts on all of the grand boulevards. In the suburbs, a Jew cannot walk into an ordinary shop. Of course, my suitcase was opened and searched at the hotel, and a telegram from London requesting my return was delayed by 24 hours. The hotel porter blushed in distress when I made a fuss about it. And yet, I do not think we can even imagine how it affects them (Boehm and Kemper). They are stricken with panic and despair, have no faith in the pressure from abroad, on the contrary: they believe it will lead to more terror. Now I have to finish. To run to Käthe Misch [psychoanalyst] with the latest news. I'll tell you more about Edith later. They haven't found anything. I am so infected by all this secrecy that I hardly dare to put facts down on paper—with mail and phone censorship! But my mission went well. Your Moi-Moi.
> (Hoel [Waal], 1935b)

At the bottom of the page, as if she just couldn't get the haunting memories of Berlin from her head, Nic added: "The uncanniest thing about Germany is that the youth is completely ignorant of the past. They believe in the propaganda! I could give you some horrific examples. And the terror makes the older people confused and irrational in their struggle" (Hoel [Waal], 1935b).

In her reference to Boehm and Kemper, Nic describes two former colleagues in a situation of terror, with no hope for change in the foreseeable future. She does not condemn them or insinuate opportunism or ill will. She simply sees them as frightened people who have lost hope. Nic's visit to Boehm and Kemper takes place in a transitional phase, where no one can really foresee the future or how long the dictatorship would go on or how far it would go. Nic is understanding of Boehm and Kemper's situation, but already at this point, she sees that Boehm is adaptive and prone to accommodate the Nazis.

After returning to Oslo, Nic described her trip in a letter to Ernest Jones. She expressed criticism of Anna Freud's wish to isolate psychoanalysis from politics at all cost. According to Nic, Anna Freud had said to her, "analysis had to go before all things" (Hoel [Waal], 1935a). She found Jacobssohn careless for jeopardizing analysis with her political activities. Two years earlier, Anna Freud made the same accusation against Wilhelm Reich in a letter to Jones. Nic, however, disagreed. As she wrote to Jones, she regarded Anna's views as overly simplistic:

> When we now have to see in what terrible way Boehm has to conceal so many of the scientific facts, and that they are forced by the German government in reality, not only formally, to be in accordance with the German theories, then I think it is an illusion that they can keep the analytical science pure.
>
> (Hoel [Waal], 1935a/1936)

Nic argued that the international psychoanalytic community should consider not only the difficulties endured by the colleagues who had remained in Germany and support the efforts of the German and perhaps later the Austrian resistance movements. In a letter to Wilhelm Reich, in November of 1935 she described the "disheartening" situation in Berlin and revealed that she had had the impression that Werner Kemper, previously regarded as part of the group centered around Fenichel and Reich, was being strongly influenced by the more "adaptive" Felix Boehm (Hoel [Waal], 1935c). The year 1936 would see psychoanalytic society incorporated into the so-called Göring Institute under Matthias Heinrich Göring (Cocks, 1997). The German Society was finally dissolved in November 1938. Nic's instincts were correct; Boehm joined the Nazis and contributed to expelling Jewish colleagues. Unfortunately, she was also correct in worrying that Kemper would follow Boehm's route.

Resistance During World War II

Until 1939, Nic worked full-time as a psychoanalyst in a private practice in Oslo. In 1939 she joined the Gaustad Clinic for psychiatric patients as an assistant and a substitute doctor. She kept that position until 1947.

After the German invasion of Norway in 1940, Nic was recruited by the secret intelligence organization, XU (X for "unknown," U for "undercover"). It worked on behalf of the Allied powers in occupied Norway. Her courage and commitment to the resistance cause were the prevailing traits in the war years. She wrote a confidential pamphlet for intelligence agents containing medical advice on how to fake major illnesses. For example: how to receive approval of sick leave from employers during a mission or during the period of recuperation. There is also proof strongly suggesting that she organized and participated in a successful bank robbery during the war to finance the resistance movement. With her second husband, Wessel, she organized escapes to Sweden for many members of the resistance movement in Norway as well as for Norwegian Jews. This eventually led to Nic's and Wessel's imprisonment twice. She was held captive at the police headquarters at Møllergata 19 and at Grini, the local concentration camp. While Grini was not a death camp, many arbitrary executions took place there. She later wrote about her imprisonment:

> When I was interred at Grini during the occupation, the most painful part of it was that I did not know where my children were or how they were doing—they were then two and four. I was ridden by doubts then and also earlier, about whether a mother had the right to take part in illegal activities, and to risk her own life and the lives of her children. It cost me a lot to adopt the position that children could not be happy in a Gestapo-world, and that it was every mother's duty to stand with all who fought to save the world from terror and torture. I thought that our battle would lead to a better world, even if we ourselves would perish. Today my children have grown up, and will send [their] children into a world that is worse than when I was nine at the outbreak of the First World War, and also worse than when I was a mother at the outbreak of the Second.
>
> (Waal, 1959)

Nic's most memorable contribution to the war efforts was the part she played in the rescue of the Jewish children's home in 1942 (Levin, 2009). Fourteen Jewish children between the ages of seven and 14 came to Oslo from Vienna in 1938 to escape the Nazis. After the German occupation of Norway in 1940, the children were not safe. On November 26, 1942, an anonymous phone call was made to the children's home warning that the children will be arrested and deported the next day. Children were awakened

Figure 8.3 Nic Waal, during the Second World War.
Reproduced with permission of Helge Waal.

and asked to quietly get dressed in the middle of the night. They were told to carry their boots in their hands and tip-toe down the stairs, because the lady living on the ground floor was a known Nazi sympathizer. Nic was waiting outside in a car. As a medical doctor, she had the right to order gasoline for house calls, otherwise strictly rationed. Nic made two trips to her friend Gerda Tanberg's house, each with seven children crammed into her car. All 14 children were put to bed on the ground floor in Gerda's house. When Nic was driving back to the children's home after the first trip, she was signaled by the police. She kept her calm, stopped the car, and showed her medical credentials. She was allowed to drive away, and then collected the rest of the children.

Within the fortnight, the children were transported near the Swedish border. They crossed the border at night, on foot with the director of the children's home, Nina Hasvoll, a psychoanalyst trained in Berlin under Adelheid Fuchs (Nilsen, 2022, p. 414). They were accompanied by two more psychoanalysts, Stefi Pedersen (1908–1980), who came to Oslo from Berlin with her analyst, Otto Fenichel, in 1933, and Lotte Bernstein (formerly Liebeck) who fled to Oslo with the help of Werner Kemper and invited by Wilhelm Reich in 1935. They built a fire and sat down with all the children on some cut-down trees. The children's little rucksacks were rather void of food after the long walk. When Stefi opened one of them to see how much was left, she found among old paper scraps, breadcrumbs, and a little silver star to hang on a Christmas tree. Surprised, she held it up. The boy who owned the rucksack looked embarrassed. But in one rucksack after the other, more pieces of Christmas decorations were found; cardboard stars and bells covered with glittering silvery powder that the children had brought with them when they realized they would not return to this house. The children had all wanted to keep something shining and bright, representing joy and hope. The decorations on the Christmas tree in the children's home had provided those objects of hope. Otherwise, their only possessions were the clothes they walked in. Nic, Nina, Stefi, and Lotte were all honored by Yad Vashem as the Righteous Among the Nations in Israel in 2006. Several of the children were present at the ceremony.

Figure 8.4 Nic Waal, late 1940s.
Reproduced with permission of Helge Waal.

Postwar Years

After the war, Nic Waal played a central role in establishing child psychiatry as a discipline and research area. Waal's contributions overlapped chronologically with the work of Anna Freud and Melanie Klein in Britain. She was inspired by their work and built professional ties between her own clinic and the Tavistock Child Guidance Clinic in Britain and the Menninger Clinic in Topeka. She never disguised, however, that her main inspiration was Wilhelm Reich, a fact that probably contributed to many professional struggles and that she was often kept on the sidelines for positions in Oslo. In a letter to Reich from 1957 that reached him shortly before his death, she connected her affiliation with Reich with the marginalization:

> You have been my most important teacher in my entire life, helping me to become honest and strong and vital. I will never forget it. Although I had to go my own way—to become as good as possible for the mankind and in my own pace—I feel that I never had to compromise in any disloyal way. Because I named you the creator of my ideas and technique, I had quite considerable difficulties for a long time. I lost positions, was slandered against and . . . ostracized, but you [taught] me that doing something truthfully and sticking to it was the only way of staying alive.
> (Waal, 1957)

She interned at the Menninger Clinic in Topeka in 1947–1948 and published a case study of an anxiety neurosis in a small child (Waal, 1948). Her colleagues were reportedly mildly shocked at her habit of frequenting "bars and nightclubs for Black people" (personal communication from Sigrid Braatøy, 2002). Apparently, they were not as attuned to jazz music and the great jazz culture explosion of the 1950s as Nic, who brought home a stack of Charlie Parker vinyl records.

Despite the sidelining, in 1946 she was appointed the director of the Mental-Hygienic Polyclinic for children in Oslo. She headed it until 1954, when she became the vice chair of the International Association for Child Psychiatry. She gave an important lecture at the Institute for Child Psychiatry in Toronto in 1954 about her treatment of an autistic child, which was later published in a volume focusing on the emotional problems of children under six (Waal, 1956).

She focused all of her energy on developing her own institute, Nic Waal's Institute for Child Psychiatry, built gradually from a core of close colleagues working as a team in child care and psychiatry. The institute was opened in 1953 and is still in operation as part of Lovisenberg Hospital in Oslo. At her clinic, with two of her colleagues, Nic developed a diagnostic tool called "Nic Waal's method for somatic psycho-diagnostics" (Waal et al., 1957). Inspired by Reich, she explored muscular tensions and rigidities in a systematic way, in addition to listening to her patients' life stories (Waal et al., 1956). She remained adamant that medical doctors needed to retain a social perspective and accept that some seemingly mental problems were a result of poverty and frustrating life conditions.

The war had taken a toll on her. Her nerves were frail, and she struggled with an alcohol addiction. She remarried once more, but her third

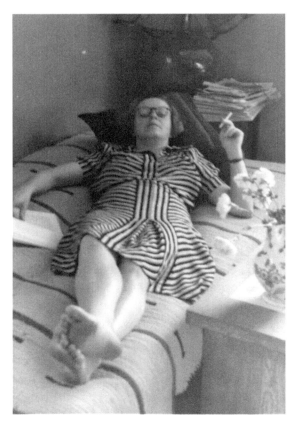

Figure 8.5 Nic Waal, a modern woman: intelligent, independent, reading, loving, and smoking.

Copyright: National Library of Norway, public domain.

Figure 8.6 Nic Waal reading to her children, Helge and Berit, ca. 1944.
Copyright: Wilhelm Reich Archives.

husband, Alex Helju, drowned in a boating accident in 1954. There were three people in the boat and only Nic survived—and just barely. When the boat capsized in a storm, Nic held onto it for hours while watching the two men disappear in the dark. Her colleagues, Carl Martin Borgen and Fiffi Piene, recounted that despite her problems, she successfully headed the institute. She was generally regarded as an unrivalled expert in diagnosing psychiatric disorders, with an almost uncanny sense of other people's psychological constitutions (personal communication from Carl Martin Borgen, 2005).

Nic Waal died of a heart attack in 1960. She was only 55 years old. On the 100th anniversary of her birth, Norway issued a postal stamp with her portrait. Her son, Helge Waal, is a psychiatrist specializing in addiction problems. Nic's daughter, Berit Waal, also followed in her mother's footsteps and became a psychologist. Nic Waal is remembered in Norway as a courageous resistance fighter, one of the first women physicians, and a pioneer of psychoanalysis and child psychiatry.

Archival Materials

Jones, E. (1935a). Letter to Anna Freud from Oct. 30, 1935. Archives of the British Psycho-Analytic Society, Folder G07/BC/F01/11.
Jones, E. (1935b). Letter to Anna Freud from Nov. 11, 1935. Archives of the British Psycho-Analytic Society, Folder G07/BC/F01/15.
Jones, E. (1935c). Letter to Princess Marie Bonaparte from Dec. 4, 1935. Archives of the British Psycho-Analytic Society, Folder G07/BC/F02/01.
Hoel, Sigurd (1931) Letter to Nic Hoel, 15. 8. 1931. Nic Waal Private Papers. Courtesy of Helge Waal.
Hoel [Waal], N. (1935a). Letter to Ernest Jones from Jan. 4, 1935. Archives of the British Psycho-Analytic Society. [Correct date: 1936].
Hoel [Waal], N. (1935b). Letter to Sigurd Hoel from Nov. 14, 1935. The National Library, Manuscript Division, Oslo, Ms. Folder "Sigurd Hoel Papers."
Hoel [Waal], N. (1935c). Letter to Wilhelm Reich from Nov. 17, 1935. WRIT-Archives, Ms. Folder C: Correspondence: Nic Hoel [Waal].
Reich, W. (1935). Letter to Nic Hoel from Oct. 28, 1935. WRIT-Archives, Ms. Folder C: Correspondence: Nic Hoel [Waal].
Spitz, R. (1935). Letter to Ernest Jones from Dec. 7, 1935. Archives of the British Psycho-Analytic Society. MS. fol. BPS—G/07/BC/F02/03.
Waal, N. (1957). Letter to Wilhelm Reich from Jan. 25, 1957. Archives of the Wilhelm Reich Infant Trust, Ms. Folder C: Correspondence.

Reference List

Boehm, F. (1933). German Psycho-Analytical Society. *Bulletin of the International Psychoanalytic Association*, 14, 520.
Bull, T. (1988). *For å si det som det var*. Oslo: J.W. Cappelens forlag.
Cocks, G. (1997). *Psychotherapy in the Third Reich: The Göring Institute*, 2nd ed. New Brunswick: Transaction Publishers.
Higgins, M. B. (Ed.) (2012). *Where's the Truth? Wilhelm Reich Letters and Journals 1948–1957*. New York: Farrar, Straus & Giroux.
Hoel, S. (1927). *Syndere i sommersol*. Oslo: Gyldendal Norsk Forlag.
Hoel, S. (1931). *En dag i oktober*. Oslo: Gyldendal Norsk Forlag.
Hoel, S. (1954). Introduction. In T. Braatøy (Ed.), *Livets cirkel. En psykoanalytisk tolkning av Knut Hamsuns forfatterskap* (pp. 3–7). Oslo: Cappelen forlag.
Kienast, H. W. (1974). The Significance of Oskar Pfister's In-Depth Pastoral Care. *Journal of Religion and Health*, 13(2), 83–95.
Lange, J. (2002). Nic Waal—norsk barnepsykiatris mor. *TNLF*, 122, 296–297.
Levin, I. (2009). Det jødiske barnehjemmet og Nic Waal. *Tidsskrift for norsk psykologforening*, 46(1), 76–80.
Nilsen, H. F. (2005). Nic Waal. In K. Helle and J. G. Arntzen (Eds.), *Norsk Biografisk Leksikon: Vol. X* (pp. 72–74). Oslo: Kunnskapsforlaget.
Nilsen, H. F. (2016). *Resistance in Therapy and War. Psychoanalysis in Norway 1920–45*. Oslo: University of Oslo.

Nilsen, H. F. (2022). *Du må ikke sove: Wilhelm Reich og psykoanalysen i Norge*. Oslo: Aschehoug forlag.

Pfister, O. (1912). Die psychologische Entratselung der religiosen Glossolalie und der automatischen Kryptografie. *Jahrbuch für psychoanalytische Forschungen*, 3, 781.

Reichmayr, J. and Mühlleitner, E. (Eds.) (1998). *Otto Fenichel: 119 Rundbriefe (1934–1945)*. Frankfurt am Main: Strömfeld Verlag.

Schjelderup, H. K. (1930). Psykologisk analyse av et tilfælde av tungetale. In G. Aspelin and E. Akesson (Eds.), *Studier Tillägnade Efraim Liljequist* (pp. 123–149). Lund: Skanska Centraltryckeriet.

Schjelderup, H. K. and Schjelderup, K. (1972). *Religion og psykologu. En studie over tre religiøse opplevelsestyper*. Oslo: J. W. Cappelen forlag.

Uber drei Haupttypen der religiosen Erlebnisformen. Berlin: Walter de Gruyter.

Spielrein, S. (2019). Children's Drawings with Eyes Open and Closed. In P. Cooper-White and F. Kelcourse (Eds.), *Sabina Spielrein and the Beginnings of Psychoanalysis: Image, Thought, and Language* (pp. 330–366). London and New York: Routledge (Orig. publ. 1931).

Waal, H. (1991). *Nic Waal. Det urolige hjerte*. Oslo: Pax Forlag.

Waal, N. (1948). A Case of Anxiety-Neurosis in a Small Child. *Bulletin of the Menninger Clinic*. Kansas, 22, 143–151.

Waal, N. (1956). A Special Technique of Psychotherapy with an Autistic Child. In G. Chaplan (Ed.), *Emotional Problems of Early Childhood* (pp. 431–451). New York: Basic Books.

Waal, N. (1958). On Wilhelm Reich. In P. Ritter (Ed.), *Wilhelm Reich. A Memorial Volume*. Nottingham: Ritter Press.

Waal, N. (1959). *Hva jeg mente og hva jeg mener*. Norwegian Broadcasting Corporation (NRK) Radio. [Lecture].

Waal, N., Christiansen, B. and Killingmo, B. (1956). *Personlighetsdiagnostikk med henblikk på strukturbeskrivelse. Utkast til begrepssystem*. Oslo: Nic Waals Institutt.

Waal, N., Grieg, A. and Rasmussen, M. (1957). *Nic Waals metode for somatisk psykodiagnostikk. Beskrivelse av undersøkelsesmetoden og utkast til et begrepssystem*. Oslo: Nic Waals Institutt.

Chapter 9

Barbara Low
"The Little Bit of Pioneering" or the Beginnings of British Psychoanalysis

Richard Theisen Simanke

A few months before her death, on September 11, 1955, the psychoanalyst Barbara Low wrote in one of her letters to an American scholar, Edward Nehls, that, concerning the development of British psychoanalysis, she "was in no way a pioneer." However, she also acknowledged the fact of being among the "six or seven doctors" who founded the British Psychoanalytical Society (BPS) and "the only woman" as well as, for a long time, "the only Jew" amongst the group. She proceeded: "The little bit of 'Pioneering' I did was to write the first small Text-Book on P.A. (*P.A., a Brief Outline of the Freudian Theory*) which had a good deal of success, + Freud approved of it" (Greer, 2014, p. 191).

It is interesting how Low managed to disavow and reaffirm her crucial role in the early development of British psychoanalysis in the same passage. Greer (2014) comments on her tendency to dismiss herself and her accomplishments, both in general terms and, more specifically, in her correspondence with Nehls. She speculates that this aspect of Low's character may be explained "whether on account of her being a Jew or perhaps as a hangover from her childhood" (p. 85). Be that as it may, she *was* truly and without a doubt a pioneer, despite her own disclaiming words: she had been involved with psychoanalysis even before she participated in the founding of the British Psychoanalytical Society in 1919. Indeed, to be among the few founding members of the BPS and to have authored a successful introductory textbook worthy of Freud's approval are no small accomplishments. Besides her reluctantly accepted pioneering role, she was an active member of the BPS for more than 30 years. She acted as a librarian of the Institute of Psychoanalysis, lectured extensively, reviewed and translated psychoanalytic works, argued emphatically for the social functions of psychoanalysis, and wrote about many different topics, especially on

DOI: 10.4324/9781003455844-13

the psychoanalytic contributions to education. Now however, her name is almost exclusively associated in the history of psychoanalysis with the term and concept of the Nirvana principle, first proposed in her textbook and adopted by Freud. In fact, she mentioned the Nirvana principle only once in all of her writings, but Freud made it widely known. This circumstance has undoubtedly contributed to keeping all her other activities in the shadows (cf. Caropreso and Simanke, 2022). The objective of this chapter is to shed some new light on Barbara Low's life and career, by presenting the main aspects of her contributions to psychoanalytic institutions, theory, and practice.

Low's career was, in many ways, typical of the early pioneers of British psychoanalysis. A better knowledge of the early psychoanalytic developments in the UK will provide a more comprehensive understanding of Low's life. She was a typical representative of the group of women who became attracted to psychoanalysis in the early days of its dissemination in Britain: an emancipated intellectual, with an academic education, politically active, and interested in the scientific and literary avant-garde of her time.

The first part of this chapter provides some basic biographic information mapping Low's path toward psychoanalysis. Next, her psychoanalytic career will be presented and discussed in this chapter along three lines of inquiry. The first is her involvement with the BPS, with a special attention to her participation in the Freud-Klein controversies of the 1940s. The second topic is her interest in literature and its relationship with psychoanalysis. The third, her sense of concern with the social functions of applied psychoanalysis, especially its contributions to education, and with the dissemination of psychoanalytic knowledge. The chapter will conclude with a synthesis of Low's contributions to psychoanalysis.

From the Classroom to the Couch

Barbara Low was born Alice Leonora Low on July 29, 1874, in London. She was known as "Barbara." Her birth year was widely believed to be 1877 (Franklin, 1956; Yorke, 2005b) until Julie Greer (2014) found her original birth certificate. Her father was Jewish Hungarian businessman Maximilian Low (1830–1900), and her mother, Therese Low (1836–1887, née Schacherl), was a daughter of an Austrian rabbi. Her father joined the Opposition Party, a nationalist Hungarian party led by Lajos Kossuth, and supported Kossuth's brief presidency during the Hungarian Civic Revolution (1848–1849). After the failed revolution, Maximilian immigrated to London where he successfully established himself as a merchant and trader. Therese joined him in 1855. The Lows had 11 children, born between 1855 and 1876. Barbara was the second youngest.

Maximilian Low's commercial success did not last long. In 1878, when Barbara was only four years old, a series of bad financial decisions led to the loss of the family's fortune and properties. Maximilian's emotional instability may have precluded him from recovering the losses. As a result, the family began to disperse, with the older brothers leaving home to find work and make a living. Then, Therese Low's death in 1887 left the older sisters in charge of the younger ones (Chapman-Huston, 1936).

Despite the financial hardships and all other adversity, the family managed to provide an excellent education to each of the 11 children. Most of the Low siblings were notably well accomplished in all walks of life. Barbara's older brothers, Sidney James Mark Low and Alfred Maurice Low, both were distinguished journalists and historians. They were knighted in 1918 and 1922, respectively (Rubinstein et al., 2011). Her older sisters, Frances Helena Low and Florence Blanche Low, were also journalists. The latter was a school headmistress as well. Another sister, Edith Clara Low, who later married the psychoanalyst Montague David Eder, was a teacher and a writer. Four more of her siblings were scholars and educators, according to the family history.

Like all her siblings, Barbara Low also received a first-class progressive education. She attended an excellent girls' school named after the pioneer of the British girls' education, Francis Mary Buss School, and later took her academic degree at the University College London, likely in English language or literature. Afterwards, she qualified as a teacher at the Maria Grey Training College, the first teacher training college for women in Great Britain, also named after another British pioneer in women's education. After teaching for some time at a few girls' schools, Low worked at the Hackney Downs Boys' School during the First World War. After the war, she lectured in education, history, English language, and literature at the London County Council Training College for Teachers in Fulham where she was highly valued (Greer, 2014; Yorke, 2005b; Franklin, 1956).

The final years of her teaching career overlapped with the beginnings of her involvement with psychoanalysis. She had her first contact with Freud's ideas through a Jewish Lithuanian physician and Zionist leader, Montague

David Eder, who married her sister, Edith, in 1909. At that time, Eder was already turning his professional and scientific interests towards psychoanalysis. The shift was sped up by the turmoil surrounding his divorce from his previous wife, who ended up committing suicide. His relationship with Edith, then also married, was burdened and stressful at first. Hence, they both began an analysis: Eder with Ernest Jones, Edith with Carl Jung (Thomson, 2011; Paskauskas, 1998, p. 197). On September 30, 1911, Eder gave the very first address on Freudian psychoanalysis before a medical society in England (Eder, 1911; Jones, 1912). Eder was largely responsible for Low's commitment to psychoanalysis. Additionally, they shared a common interest in politics and literature and friendship with D. H. Lawrence, among other things. Besides the family ties, the fact of being the only two Jews in the British psychoanalytic movement before the arrival of the Continental émigrés most likely contributed to their close relationship.

Low became involved with psychoanalysis in the early 1910s. According to Kuhn (2017), in January 1913 both Barbara and her sister, Edith, attended a meeting of the recently created Psycho-Medical Society, which succeeded the earlier Medical Society for the Study of Suggestive Therapeutics. During this meeting, Sándor Ferenczi's 1912 paper, "The Psychoanalysis of Suggestion and Hypnosis," was discussed. Many other women who were soon to play significant roles in the early stages of development of British psychoanalysis were also present, such as Constance Long, Jessy Murray, and Joan Riviere.

During his time in North America (1908–1912), Ernest Jones worked toward organizing a national psychoanalytic society and fostering psychoanalytic thought there. The American Psychoanalytic Association (APsA) was officially established on May 9, 1911, in Baltimore, with James Jackson Putnam as its president and Jones as the secretary (Maddox, 2006), as the second society in the US, after the New York Psychoanalytic Society (NYPS). After his return to England in the middle of 1912, Jones almost immediately started to plan for a psychoanalytic association to be formed in London. However, his return coincided with the growing estrangement between Freud and Jung. The rift had been widening and was about to reach a point of no return. On the personal level, Jones was more than glad to replace Jung as Freud's second-in-command. On the other hand, however, the London Psychoanalytical Society (LPS), founded on October 30, 1913, was born with an innate internal division that accounts for its brief existence, at least partially. Jones was the first president of LPS, Eder was first secretary, and Douglas Bryan was vice president. In his "The Organizing of Psychoanalysis in Britain" Hinshelwood included two women, Barbara and Edith (Hinshelwood, 1998, p. 90).

The London Psychoanalytical Society, weakened by constant conflicts often caused by the growing opposition between Jungian and Freudian factions (Hinshelwood, 1998), was dissolved in 1919. It was replaced by the British Psychoanalytical Society (BPS), now freed from the dissident elements (Robinson, 2011). Barbara Low was the only woman and the only Jew among its founding members, as she proudly recalled in the final year of her life (Greer, 2014, p. 191). Eder—one of the Jungian troublemakers—was away, preoccupied with his Zionist activities, and would not return to London until 1922 (Thomson, 2011). Most members of BPAS had a Christian background, often with an agnostic orientation and predominantly humanist concerns (King, 1991a). As merciless as the purge was, the effects of it were positive since the new association was developing fast and growing strong right from its inception. Created on February 20, 1919, BPAS held its first scientific meeting in May. Barbara Low gave a paper during the second meeting, on June 12, 1919: a methodological report on "Note-Taking and Reporting of Psychoanalytic Cases" that emphasized "the British preoccupation with the immediacy of the clinical situation" (Kohon, 2018, p. 28).

Low would not remain the only woman in the British Psychoanalytical Society for long. Hinshelwood (1998) reports that in the Society's first year of existence (1919), five out of the 27 members were women. Four years later, in 1923, the number of women increased to 17 out of 54. Thus, BPAS had the highest proportion of female members out of all societies affiliated with the International Psychoanalytical Association (IPA). There are multiple reasons behind this exceptional situation. First, women from families belonging to the economic and intellectual elites became acquainted with Freud's ideas to some extent via artistic and literary circles where psychoanalysis became fashionable even before the First World War and the beginnings of the British psychoanalytic movement. As Sally Alexander put it, one of the main reasons psychoanalysis flourished on the British soil was "the interest of emancipated women" (Alexander, 1998, p. 137). Second, during World War I, many British women started working professionally, outside home (Alexander, 1998). When the war was over, the trend, supported by the emancipatory movements, continued. Some women sought higher education and training allowing them to have a professional career. Approximately half of the first-generation British women analysts had previously worked at the Medical-Psychological Clinic founded in 1913 by medical doctor and suffragette Jessie Murray and co-principal of a high-class liberal private school, Fir Grove House Ladies' School, Julia Turner (cf. Valentine, 2009; Raitt, 2004).

The Medical-Psychological Clinic offered low-cost mental-health services to a broad clientele. Its employees received eclectic clinical training based on a number of schools, including psychoanalysis. The number of staff, including women, increased during the First World War when the number of patients seeking treatment for shellshock and other nervous diseases increased understandably.

Ernest Jones reportedly favored women analysts out of personal sympathy and because promoting women facilitated his project of advancing British psychoanalysis to the forefront of the international psychoanalytical movement. Finally, in the 1920s, the new frontiers of psychoanalytic knowledge and practice laid in fields of child analysis, preoedipal development, and feminine sexuality—themes that preoccupied early women analysts (Thomson, 2011).

Figure 9.1 Possibly the only existing photograph of Barbara Low, Congress of the Psychoanalytic Society in Lucerne, 1934.

Photography by Tim Nahum Gidal. Copyright: The Israel Museum, Jerusalem.

The considerable contributions of women to early British psychoanalysis comprised participation and formulating new theories. Meisel and Kendrick remarked that in the 1920s, "what intellectual spark there was [at the BPAS] seems often to have come from the women" (1985, p. 43). These women included Barbara Low, Ella Sharpe, Mary Chadwick, Sylvia Paine, and Marjorie Franklin.

Dissemination of Knowledge and the Nirvana-Principe

From the historical viewpoint, dissemination of knowledge was Low's most successful accomplishment—she is remembered today almost solely for her introductory book, *Psychoanalysis: A Brief Account of the Freudian Theory* from 1920, where she first presented her Nirvana principle concept. It was the first textbook on psychoanalysis by a British author. A journalist, M. K. Bradby, published her textbook *Psychoanalysis and Its Place in Life* the previous year but it was mainly dedicated to Jung (Bradby, 1919; cf. Bair, 2004). Readers could still resort to two more English-language books by American authors: Wilfrid Lay's *Man's Unconscious Conflict* (1917), admittedly a "popular" presentation of psychoanalytic ideas, and a short introductory account, *What Is Psychoanalysis?*, written in a practical Q&A format by one of the first American psychoanalysts, Isadore Henry Coriat (1919). In his Preface to Low's book, *Psychoanalysis: A Brief Account of the Freudian Theory*, Jones wrote that it was not the first attempt at a clear and rigorous account of Freud's views, likely having these predecessors in mind. He did however regard Low to be better prepared for this task than the previous authors. According to Richards (2000), all the other introductory books were published after Low's.

Low's *Psychoanalysis: A Brief Account of the Freudian Theory* was arguably one of the most successful psychoanalytic textbooks. The second edition of the book from April 1920 was scheduled already in October. It was followed by a reprint in March 1921 and a revised edition in February 1923. The book was widely reviewed, most often favorably. It became influential, especially in the field of application of psychoanalysis to education and criminology (the book's last chapter is dedicated to educational and other social impacts of psychoanalysis). For example, author of many popular books on crime and criminals John Cuthbert Goodwin relied heavily on Low's book for psychoanalytic insight (Richards, 2000).

The book's popularity and influence stemmed from its introductory character and applied approach. It was not connected to the fact that Low proposed in it the idea of a Nirvana principle, later attached to Low's name due to Freud's acknowledgement and adoption of the idea. The book reflected Low's deep engagement in popularizing psychoanalysis and its social applications, as well as her being a devotee to the psychoanalytic cause, stimulated by a relentless, as John Bowlby called it, "missionary zeal" (Kahr, 2012, p. 38).

In her letter to Nehls from February 16, 1954, Low admitted to finding writing too tricky, "except reviewing" (Greer, 2014, p. 186). She was indeed a prolific reviewer of books and papers on psychoanalysis and other related topics. She published about 40 reviews in psychoanalytic journals alone and many more in the general press. As a reviewer, she contributed to the dissemination of psychoanalytic knowledge. She offered summaries of most recent publications to the growing general readership interested in psychoanalysis.

Low and the Freud-Klein Debate

Like many other members of the newly founded British Psychanalytic Society, Low traveled abroad to undertake a personal analysis in the early 1920s. She chose to have hers with Hans Sachs in Berlin, as did Sylvia Payne and Ella Sharpe. She later had another training analysis with Jones (King, 1991a). After becoming a full member of BPAS and a practicing psychoanalyst, she became even more committed to the movement. Throughout her career, Low actively participated in the meetings of BPAS and debates. Late in life, John Bowlby remembered her as someone who "frequently spoke at meetings, sometimes for rather too long," while avoiding personal attacks and always having "the interests of psychoanalysis at heart" with a somewhat "missionary zeal" (Kahr, 2012, p. 38). She held many different positions of responsibility. In 1924, a few years after the creation of the BPAS, Jones founded the Institute of Psychoanalysis following the example of the Berlin Institute, as a legal institution integrating clinical practice, training, publishing, and research. It absorbed the International Psychoanalytic Press along with its recently established partnership with Leonard and Virginia Woolf's Hogarth Press to publish Freud's works in English (Maddox, 2006). For years, Low acted as the Institute's librarian—a crucial role considering its editorial, archival, and research functions (Franklin, 1956).

Years later, in 1938, Barbara Low joined the first directorial board of the Imago Publishing Company, along with a modernist writer and publisher, John Rodker, and Freud's son, Martin Freud (Yorke, 2005a). The new publishing house was created shortly after Freud's arrival in London, in June 1938, in response to the loss of German psychoanalytic journals and the publishing house, *Internationale Psychoanalytische Verlag*, under the Nazi regime. It was founded by Rodker and undertook the lengthy project of publishing Freud's *Collected Works* beginning in the 1940s, and other vital writings, such as the Freud-Fliess correspondence in 1950. Barbara Low also led the London hospitality committee formed in March 1939 for the "Colleagues from Austria" (Maddox, 2006).

In a letter from February 16, 1954, to Edward Nehls, Low claimed, "about the only thing I've ever been able to do successfully is Lecturing" (Greer, 2014, p. 186). She was an experienced lecturer even before she became an analyst, was part of the Public Lectures Committee, and enjoyed lecturing to a broader audience (King, 1991b). In fact, many of Low's lectures did not go unnoticed and had significant consequences. For example, on May 4, 1927, Low presented to BPAS members a long and detailed review of Anna Freud's recently published book, *Introduction to the Technique of the Analysis of Children* (1927). This was after Kleinian ideas had already begun spreading in England, Melanie Klein had moved to London, and Anna Freud had given a paper in Berlin on March 19, 1927, criticizing Melanie Klein. The review was indicative of the growing influence of Kleinian views within British psychoanalysis. In his letter to Freud from September 30, 1927, Jones remarked that Low's review was excellent, comprehensive, and practically an English translation of the German text (Paskauskas, 1998, p. 724). The review actually triggered the so-called Freud-Klein debate and led to the crucial *Symposium on Child-Analysis*. Still, while the critical contributions by Melanie Klein, Joan Riviere, Nina Searle, Ella Sharpe, Edward Glover, and Jones to the debates that followed, on May 4 and 18, were later published in the *International Journal of Psychoanalysis*, Low's review that set them in motion was not included (Maddox, 2006; King, 1983; Kohon, 2018). As the debates kept gaining momentum, Low joined Melanie Klein and Nina Searle in February 1929 in a special committee to discuss the training of child analysts.

The tensions continued for another decade to eventually explode in the early 1940s, after Freud's death, in the form of the so-called Freud-Klein controversies (King, 1983; King and Steiner, 1991), also sparked by Low's paper. On November 5, 1941, she spoke before the Society about "The Psychoanalytic Society and the Public." After her talk, heated debates went on for two more Scientific Meetings.

Discussion of Low's participation in the Freud-Klein controversies deserves a separate chapter. Here, I will only highlight some episodes to indicate her central role in that momentous series of events, following the book *The Freud-Klein Controversies* edited by Pearl King and Riccardo Steiner (1991). By then, Low was "one of the oldest members of the first generation of British psychoanalysts" (Steiner, 1991, p. 178), at the Society for more than 20 years. She was, in every respect, regarded as a veteran by her peers. The controversies took place during the Second World War, while many other senior members of the British Psychanalytic Society were away from London, either in military medical service or in the countryside, especially after the traumatic experiences of the bombing campaign, the Blitz (September 1940–May 1941). Under these circumstances, the debates were often led by the junior members. According to King, Low took the more conservative, Freudian side, against the Kleinian group (King, 1987). Many of her longstanding theoretical and practical ideas, such as the contribution of psychoanalysis to education, inclined her to agree with the views maintained by Anna Freud and her followers. Kohon, however, included Low in the Middle (or Independent) Group (Kohon, 2018; cf. Caropreso and Simanke, 2022).

During the third debate, on December 17, 1941, another senior member, John Rickman, who was, like Low, very concerned with the social responsibilities of psychoanalysis, lost his temper and violently accused the British Psychanalytic Society's officers and directors of being disrespectful to the public, inconsiderate of other professional categories, and ignorant of the broader community's interests and needs. As a result, Low and three other members signed a letter to the Council demanding an extraordinary Business Meeting to discuss BPAS modus operandi. It became the first of five meetings held between February and June 1942 that constituted the first phase of the Freud-Klein controversies. In the first of these meetings, Low gave another paper, in which she elaborated on her previously presented views and gave more arguments pro and contra. The core of her argument was that the difficulties in dealing with the public arose from BPAS's internal divisions resulting from scientific differences. During the second Business Meeting in March, she argued for creating a subcommittee to settle these scientific differences. The discussion of her proposal led BPAS to elect a five-member committee to inquire into the issues concerning tenure of office and multiple official positions during the Annual General Meeting held on July 29. Barbara Low was elected to sit on the committee, alongside Anna Freud, Edward Glover, Sylvia Paine, and Adrian Stephen, via in-person and postal secret vote. She often proposed voting on resolutions on topics related to her main concerns, such as the BPAS's public relations, and later supported creating a special Educational Section (Extended Annual Meeting, November 3, 1943). Low remained one of the most committed participants of the debates on the subject of the Freud-Klein controversies until 1944, when Glover resigned.

Psychoanalysis and Literature

In the 1920s, psychoanalysis in Britain was intertwined with literature, including the English classics, as well as the avant-garde and modernist trends. The intersection between psychoanalysis and literature was not new. It was initiated by Freud's remarks on the oedipal roots of Hamlet's hesitation in his *Interpretation of Dreams*. In the next two decades Freud contributed a series of literary studies. Ernest Jones was among the first psychoanalysts to follow Freud in the exploration of the interface. His "A Psychoanalytic Study of Hamlet" from the collection *Essays on Applied Psychoanalysis* (Jones, 1923/1910) was an extended revised version of his earlier papers published in English and German in 1910. In the mid-1920s, Virginia Woolf stated, "if you read Freud, you know in ten minutes some facts [. . .] which our parents could not have guessed for themselves" (Forrester and Cameron, 2017, p. 511), thus positioning Freud as one of the icons of the British modernism.

In this respect, Barbara Low's career is typical for British psychoanalysts of her time. As seen earlier, she was academically educated and taught English language and literature, education, and history at the Fulham Training College for Teachers before becoming a psychoanalyst. It seemed that Sigmund Freud himself knew Barbara Low as an expert in English literature. In a four-page note she sent Kurt Eissler on June 28, 1954, in lieu of an interview, she was said to have met Freud for the first time in Berlin during the IPA Congress in 1922. According to her, they "talked almost entirely of books and authors," and Freud "was interested that H. G. Wells and Shaw were friends of [her] family and [her]self" (Low, n.d.; cf. Silva, 2019). Indeed, Wells was a friend of Barbara's brother Walther Low (Rubinstein et al., 2011), while her sister, Edith, had had a brief affair with Wells before she married Eder (Maddox, 1994). Low also knew Wells and Bernard Shaw from the left-wing intellectual Fabian Society to which they all belonged. She briefly met Freud on other occasions: at the Hague and Innsbruck IPA conferences and when she visited him with Edith on June 9, 1938, just days after he arrived in London, but this was the closest contact she had with him (Greer, 2014, p. 78).

Low's excellent English and German language skills put her in a position to translate psychoanalytic writings. She prepared an English translation of Hermine Hugh-Hellmuth's text. Then, she translated two books by Anna Freud, *Introduction of Psychoanalysis for Teachers* (1931) and *Psychoanalysis for Teachers and Parents: Introductory Lectures* (1935), as well as works by other psychoanalytic authors, such as Oskar Pfister (1922). She also often proofread and revised other people's translations, as noted by Jones in his letters to Freud (Paskauskas, 1998, pp. 489, 552–553). More notably, Low collaborated on the translation of Sigmund Freud's case study of homosexuality in a woman, dedicated to the young Margarethe Csonka (Freud, 1920). According to Graham Richards, these early English translations of psychoanalytic works, including Freud's, were creating an "anglophone psychoanalytic language [that] very rapidly came to possess a distinctive, readily identifiable, technical character." He credited Jones, James and Alix Strachey, and Barbara Low for this achievement (Richards, 2000, p. 185). Forrester and Cameron also included Low in the select group of "reliable translators and proofreaders," alongside Joan Riviere, John Flügel, William Stoddart, and Caroline Hubback (Forrester and Cameron, 2017, p. 533).

The most significant intersection between psychoanalysis and literature in Low's life was her friendship with the novelist D. H. Lawrence and his wife, Frieda. Barbara met Lawrence through her brother-in-law, David Eder, who, in turn, was introduced to him by her niece Ivy. Ivy had spent six weeks with him and Frieda as a guest in their Italy home at the Fiascherino beach near La Spezia during the summer of 1914 after having written to Lawrence through his publishers and received an unexpected invitation. Lawrence's friendships with Barbara and Eder were to last much longer than Ivy's early admiration for him. Lawrence and Eder had much in common, including a shared enthusiasm for the Utopian project for a community of writers. As Maddox puts it, "the Eders [David and Edith] were the epitome of progressivism," and Lawrence would visit them frequently in their Hampstead

Garden home, "a community in its own right," and "a center for socialists, feminists, psychoanalysts, and Zionists" (1994, p. 196).

Both Eder and Barbara essentially introduced Lawrence to psychoanalysis; however, he must have had previous contact with psychoanalytic ideas through his wife, Frieda, a close friend of Otto Gross. Some of his early novels already show signs of this influence, for example, *Sons and Lovers*, enthusiastically called "a book about the Oedipus complex" by Ivy Low (Maddox, 2006, p. 123, 1994, p. 182). According to Barbara Low, Lawrence began to read psychoanalytic writings around 1916 after she, Eder, and Edith had initiated him into psychoanalysis. They later lent him Carl Jung's *Symbols of Transformation* (Delavenay, 1989). Afterward, Lawrence would incorporate psychoanalytic elements into his novels. Sometimes in a satirical way, as in the case of "the Russian" character, Libidnikov, in *Women in Love* (1920), a likely combination of Ivy's husband's name, Maxim Litvinov, and the term "libido" (Brown, 2019). He also wrote two critical essays, "The Psychoanalysis and the Unconscious" and the "Fantasia of the Unconscious," initially intended as a response to the criticism of *Sons and Lovers* by the psychoanalytic community. English writer and journalist Douglas Goldring remarked,

> [Samuel S.] Koteliansky and Barbara Low were among Lawrence's closest friends. [. . .] Lawrence's association with them lasted so long that a considerable correspondence must have resulted from it [. . .]. Lawrence's Psycho-Analytical studies were, I believe, largely directed and encouraged by Miss Low, whom I suspect of a considerable share in his *Psychoanalysis and the Unconscious*.
> (Nehls, 1957, p. 491; cf. Greer, 2014, p. 79)

Psychoanalysis and Education

The Berlin Psychoanalytic Polyclinic was created by Max Eitingon, Karl Abraham, and Ernst Simmel in 1920 to provide training opportunities for new analysts and affordable treatment for low-income patients. Possibly, during her stay in Berlin for an analysis with Hans Sachs, Barbara Low might have familiarized herself with it. In 1920, she argued emphatically for the creation of a similar institution. It was established four years later, in January 1924, as the Institute of Psychoanalysis (Robinson, 2011; Glover, 1966). Her involvement in setting up the Institute reflects her concerns with the social role of psychoanalysis and explains many aspects of her career and the reasons for dedicating her life to psychoanalytic work.

Her emphasis on the role and significance of the Institute explains the character of her involvement better, including her official positions at the Institute, at the library and the Public Lectures Committee, as well as her views expressed during the Freud-Klein controversies, such as her paper responsible for triggering the debates. Her published works can also be understood from this perspective. They predominantly deal with applied psychoanalysis, especially the socially informed question of its contributions to education. She was also devoted to the dissemination of psychoanalytic knowledge, including in her textbook on psychoanalysis, *Psychoanalysis: A Brief Account of the Freudian Theory*, that became her best well-known work and intense and constant reviewing activity.

The issue of applying Freud's ideas in education has been on the agenda of British psychoanalysis for a while, including Jones's two chapters from 1910 and 1912 later included in his *Papers on Psychoanalysis* (Jones, 1913a/1910, 1913b/1910). It is not surprising that, as a former teacher, Low devoted some of her earliest publications to the subject, in the 1920s. In October and November 1923, Jones, Low, and other British analysts delivered lectures in applied psychoanalysis "under the auspices of the Sociological Society." They covered a number of diverse, interdisciplinary topics: "The Relationship of Psychoanalysis to Sociology" (Jones), "Man and the Individual" (James Glover), "The Family" (John Flügel), and "Vocation" (Ella Sharpe). Predictably, Eder spoke about "Politics" and Low about "Education." The lectures were published the following year in a collection under Jones's editorship (Jones, 1924) (Richards, 2000). It appears that Low valued the publication highly, as she referred to it frequently in her later writings, such as on the front page of her most important book on psychoanalysis and education.

In 1928 Low published arguably one of the most thorough and systematic examinations of potential psychoanalytic contributions to education, *The Unconscious in Action* (in England, 1928b) and *Psychoanalysis and Education* (in the USA, 1928). She recognized Jones's "Psychoanalysis and Education" (Jones, 1913a/1910) as a landmark publication on the subject. In the context of education, she saw psychoanalysts as consultants to educators advising them on psychological matters. Teachers would turn to them when confronted with behavioral and emotional issues hindering their students' learning abilities, as they do with medical doctors with physical health issues. Additionally, psychoanalysts can also help teachers increase their psychological knowledge and understanding of their students' way of thinking, especially with regards to sexuality. Finally, Low advanced some psychoanalytically informed hypotheses on the psychology of learning, centered on the concept of sublimation. Thus, she paved the way for a more cognitive approach in psychoanalysis and a critical evaluation of some of the leading educational trends of the early twentieth century.

Despite the resistance to applying psychoanalysis to education, identified by Low in her paper from 1929, her book from 1928 was very well received. It was favorably, yet cautiously, prefaced by Sir Thomas Percy Nunn, one of the most renowned British educators of the first half of the twentieth century. Reviewers usually praised Low's objectivity and clarity in presenting key psychoanalytic concepts to a non-expert public (Newell, 1931). They also valued her advice to psychoanalysts not to impinge on the responsibilities of educators. Some reviewers regarded Low's approach to education as cutting edge and as filling "a definite gap in educational literature" (Flower, 1928, p. 477). It had some impact on analysts who discussed the crossover of psychoanalysis and education following Low's publication (Searl, 1932) but later fell into almost complete oblivion. The book is inexplicably absent from Low's publications listed at the end of Marjorie Franklin's obituary of Low (1956), and there is a mistake in the title in the otherwise excellent online biographical lexicon of women psychoanalysis, *Psychoanalytikerinnen: Biografisches Lexikon* (Nölleke, 2007–2023).

Conclusion

Much more could be said about Barbara Low's career and professional accomplishments. Her contributions to promoting psychoanalysis and disseminating knowledge was not restricted to reviews in psychoanalytic journals. She was a frequent contributor to the *Times Educational Supplement* (Richards, 2000) and author of nonprofessional publications (Franklin, 1956).

Low's political views reflected her social concerns. She was a member of the Labor Party and the Fabian Society. When a group of psychoanalysts—Marjorie Franklin, Edward Glover, Grace Pailthorpe, and Melitta Schmideberg—founded the Institute for the Scientific Treatment of Delinquency (ISTD) in 1931 (now the Centre for Crime and Justice Studies, cf. Nölleke, 2007–2023), Low started an intensive collaboration with it, as both a lecturer and an analyst, that she continued until her death. According to Franklin, she participated in a conference held at ISTD in the final year of her life, despite being physically debilitated (1956, p. 473).

Low's contributions to the psychoanalytic theory were significant. She introduced a new concept, the Nirvana principle, in her 1920 textbook. Freud's reception and acceptance of it underwent a particular development that brought him closer to Low's original view. Freud took up not only the term, but also Low's concept itself (Caropreso and Simanke, 2022). In another one of her writings, "The Psychological Compensations of the Analyst" from 1935, Low made an early attempt at theorizing countertransference and distinguishing it from other phenomena experienced by analysts in their work with patients.

All in all, it is surprising how little attention Barbara Low has received in the history of psychoanalysis and that only her contribution to the Nirvana principle has been viewed as worth mentioning. Except for Franklin's obituary and a few short entries in reference works, the only article dedicated to her, as of today, has been written by Marcus Vinicius Silva (2019). It is an introductory account in Portuguese, published in a Brazilian nonacademic magazine and mainly focused on the Nirvana principle. When writing this paper, I had to gather information about Low's life and work from several works on other topics. A number of small biographical mistakes concerning her family also adds to this disregard (Yorke, 2005b; Franklin, 1956; Jewish Virtual Library).

Archival Materials

Low, B. (n.d.). Note to Kurt Eissler from June 28, 1954. In *Sigmund Freud Papers: Interviews and Recollections, 1914–1998. Set A, 1914–1998; Recollections.* Library of Congress. Online at www.loc.gov/item/mss3999001651. Accessed August 15, 2022.

Reference List

Alexander, S. (1998). Psychoanalysis in Britain in the Early Twentieth Century: An Introductory Note. *History Workshop Journal*, 45, 135–143.
Bair, D. (2004). *Jung: uma biografia*. São Paulo: Editora Globo.
Bradby, M. K. (1919). *Psychoanalysis and Its Place in Life*. London: Henry Frowde, Hodder & Stoughton.
Brown, C. (2019). "The Young Russian:" Lawrence, Libidnikov and London's Russians in the First World War. *Journal of D. H. Lawrence Studies*, 5(2), 103–123.

Caropreso, F. and Simanke, R. T. (2022). Barbara Low and Sabina Spielrein: Misrepresentations of their Work in the History of Psychoanalysis. *American Imago*, 79(2), 169–195.

Chapman-Huston, D. (1936). *The Lost Historian: A Memoir of Sir Sidney Low*. London: John Murray.

Coriat, I. H. (1919). *What Is Psychoanalysis?* New York: Moffat, Yard & Co.

Delavenay, E. (1989). Early Approaches to D. H. Lawrence: Records of Meetings with Frieda Lawrence, Havelock Ellis, Barbara Low, Ada Lawrence-Clark, and William Hopkin. *The D. H. Lawrence Review*, 21(3), 313–322.

Eder, M. D. (1911). A Case of Obsession and Hysteria Treated by the Freud Psychoanalytic Method. *British Medical Journal*, 750–751.

Flower, G. C. (1928). "The Unconscious in Action. Its Influence Upon Education." By Barbara Low. With a Foreword by T. Percy Nunn, M.A., D.Sc., D. Litt (University of London Press, 1928, p. 226). *International Journal of Psychoanalysis*, 9, 477–480.

Forrester, J. and Cameron, L. (2017). *Freud in Cambridge*. Cambridge: Cambridge UP.

Franklin, M. (1956). Barbara Low. *International Journal of Psychoanalysis*, 37, 473–474.

Freud, A. (1931). *Introduction of Psychoanalysis for Teachers*. B. Low (Trans.). London: Allen & Unwin.

Freud, A. (1935). *Psychoanalysis for Teachers and Parents: Introductory Lectures*. B. Low (Trans.). New York: Emerson Books.

Freud, S. (1920). The Psychogenesis of a Case of Homosexuality in a Woman. B. Low and R. Gabler (Trans.). *International Journal of Psychoanalysis*, 1, 125–149.

Glover, E. (1966). Psychoanalysis in England. In F. Alexander, S. Eisenstein and M. Grotjahn (Eds.), *Psychoanalytic Pioneers* (pp. 534–545). New York: Basic Books.

Greer, J. A. (2014). *Learning from Linked Lives: Narrativizing the Individual and Group Biographies of the Guests at the 25th Jubilee Dinner of the British Psychoanalytical Society at the Savoy, London, on 8th March 1939*. Southampton: University of Southampton [Unpublished doctoral dissertation].

Hinshelwood, R. D. (1998). The Organizing of Psychoanalysis in Britain. *Psychoanalysis and History*, 1(1), 87–102.

Jones, E. (1912). M. D. Eder, A Case of Obsession and Hysteria Treated by the Freud Psychoanalytic Method. Brit. Med. Journ., Sept 30, 1911, p. 750. *Zentralblatt für Psychoanalyse*, 2, 355.

Jones, E. (1913a). Psychoanalysis and Education. In E. Jones (Ed.), *Papers on Psychoanalysis* (pp. 393–415). London: Baillière, Tindall & Cox (Orig. publ. 1910).

Jones, E. (1913b). The Value of Sublimation Processes in Education and Re-education. In E. Jones (Ed.), *Papers on Psychoanalysis* (pp. 416–432). London: Baillière, Tindall & Cox (Orig. publ. 1910).

Jones, E. (1923). A Psychoanalytic Study of Hamlet. In E. Jones (Ed.), *Essays on Applied Psychoanalysis* (pp. 1–98). London and Vienna: The International Psycho-Analytical Press (Orig. publ. 1910).

Jones, E. (Ed.) (1924). *Social Aspects of Psychoanalysis*. London: William & Norgate.

Kahr, B. (2012). Reminiscences by John Bowlby: Portraits of Colleagues. *Attachment*, 6(1), 27–49.

King, P. (1983). The Life and Work of Melanie Klein in the British Psychoanalytic Society. *International Journal of Psychoanalysis*, 64(3), 251–260.

King, P. (1987). Review of *The British School of Psychoanalysis: The Independent Tradition*. Edited by Gregorio Kohon. *International Journal of Psychoanalysis*, 68, 553–554.

King, P. (1991a). Background and Development of the Freud-Klein Controversies in the British Psycho-Analytical Society. In P. King and R. Steiner (Eds.), *The Freud-Klein Controversies, 1941–45* (pp. 7–27). London: Routledge.

King, P. (1991b). Biographical Notes on the Main Participants in the Freud-Klein Controversies in the British Psycho-Analytical Society, 1941–45. In P. King and R. Steiner (Eds.), *The Freud-Klein Controversies, 1941–45* (pp. ix–xxi). London: Routledge.

King, P. and Steiner, R. (1991). *The Freud-Klein Controversies, 1941–45*. London: Routledge.

Kohon, G. (2018). Notes on the History of the Psychoanalytic Movement in Britain. In G. Kohon (Ed.), *British Psychoanalysis: New Perspectives in the Independent Tradition* (pp. 25–49). London and New York: Routledge.

Kuhn, P. (2017). *Psychoanalysis in Britain, 1893–1913: Histories and Historiography*. London: Lexington Books.

Lay, W. (1917). *Man's Unconscious Conflict*. New York: Dodd & Mead.

Low, B. (1923). *Psychoanalysis: A Brief Account of the Freudian Theory*. London: George Allen & Unwin Ltd. (Orig. publ. 1920).

Low, B. (1928a). *Psychoanalysis and Education*. New York: Harcourt, Brace & Co.

Low, B. (1928b). *The Unconscious in Action: Its Influence upon Education*. London: University of London Press.

Low, B. (1929). A Note on the Influence of Psychoanalysis Upon English Education During the Last Eighteen Years. *International Journal of Psychoanalysis*, 10, 314–320.

Low, B. (1935). The Psychological Compensations of the Analyst. *International Journal of Psychoanalysis*, 16, 1–8.

Maddox, B. (1994). *D. H. Lawrence: The Story of a Marriage*. New York: Simon & Schuster.

Maddox, B. (2006). *Freud's Wizard: Ernest Jones and the Transformation of Psychoanalysis*. Cambridge, MA: Da Capo Press.

Meisel, P. and Kendrick, W. (1985). Introduction. In P. Meisel and W. Kendrick (Eds.), *Bloomsbury/Freud: The Letters of James and Alix Strachey, 1924–1925* (pp. 1–50). New York: Basic Books.

Nehls, E. (1957). *D. H. Lawrence: A Composite Biography, Vol. 1: 1885–1919*. Madison, WI: The University of Wisconsin Press.

Newell, H. W. (1931). "Psychoanalysis and Education." By Barbara Low. New York: Harcourt, Brace & Co., 1928, p. 224. *Social Service Review*, 5(3), 506–508.

Nölleke, B. (2007–2023). *Psychoanalytikerinnen. Biografisches Lexikon*. Online at www.psychoanalytikerinnen.de/. Accessed Dec. 26, 2022.

Paskauskas, A. R. (Ed.) (1998). *Correspondance Complète: Sigmund Freud-Ernest Jones (1908–1939)* [Complete Letters: Sigmund Freud-Ernest Jones, 1908–1939]. Paris: Presses Universitaires de France.

Pfister, O. (1922). *Expressionism in Art: Its Psychological and Biological Basis.* B. Low and M. A. Müge (Trans.). London: Kegan, Paul, Trench, Trübner & Co.

Raitt, S. (2004). Early British Psychoanalysis and the Medical-Psychological Clinic. *History Workshop Journal*, 58, 63–85.

Richards, G. (2000). Britain on the Couch: The Popularization of Psychoanalysis in Britain, 1918–1940. *Science in Context*, 13(2), 183–230.

Robinson, K. (2011). A Brief History of the British Psychoanalytic Society. In P. Loewenberg & N. L. Thompson (Eds.), *100 Years of the IPA: The Centenary History of the International Psychoanalytic Society* (pp. 196–230). London: Routledge.

Rubinstein, W. D., Jolles, M. A. and Rubinstein, H. L. (Eds.) (2011). *The Palgrave Dictionary of Anglo-Jewish History*. London: Palgrave Macmillan.

Searl, M. N. (1932). Some Contrasted Aspects of Psychoanalysis and Education. *British Journal of Educational Psychology*, 2(3), 276–296.

Silva, M. V. N. (2019). Barbara Low e o princípio de Nirvana. *Lacuna*, 7, 7. Online at https://revistalacuna.com/2019/08/07/n-7-7/. Accessed Aug. 16, 2021.

Steiner, R. (1991). Background to the Scientific Controversies. In P. King and R. Steiner (Eds.), *The Freud-Klein Controversies, 1941–45* (pp. 171–198). London: Routledge.

Thomson, M. (2011). "The Solution of His Own Enigma": Connecting the Life of Montague David Eder (1865–1936), Socialist, Psychoanalyst, Zionist, and Modern Saint. *Medical History*, 55(1), 61–84.

Valentine, E. R. (2009). "A Brilliant and Many-Sided Personality": Jessie Margaret Murray, the Founder of the Medical-Psychological Clinic. *Journal of the History of the Behavioral Sciences*, 45(2), 145–161.

Yorke, C. (2005a). Imago Publishing Company. In A. Mijolla (Ed.), *International Dictionary of Psychoanalysis, Vol. II* (pp. 801–802). Detroit: Thomson Gale.

Yorke, C. (2005b). Low, Barbara (1877–1955). In A. Mijolla (Ed.), *International Dictionary of Psychoanalysis, Vol. II* (pp. 996–997). Detroit: Thomson Gale.

Websites

The Centre for Crime and Justice Studies. Online at www.crimeandjustice.org.uk/about/history. Accessed Dec. 26, 2022.

Jewish Virtual Library. Online at https://www.jewishvirtuallibrary.org/low. Accessed Dec. 26, 2022.

Chapter 10

Vilma Kovács and the Community of the Budapest School of Psychoanalysis

Anna Borgos

Introduction: The First Hungarian Women Analysts

The new science of psychoanalysis and women saw a mutually open and fruitful interaction in early twentieth-century Hungary. On the one hand, the not yet consolidated theory and profession needed female followers and contributors. On the other, women perceived psychoanalysis as an exciting and, at the same time, accessible field. In Hungary the proportion of women analysts was the highest in Europe in the late 1930s, reaching 48 percent in 1937 (cf. Giefer, 2007).

Social and political factors strongly influenced individual life stories and the psychoanalytic profession itself by providing opportunities and setting limitations for prospective and practicing women analysts. In the twentieth century, the status of being a Jew, a woman, and a psychoanalyst was changing and it was often exposed to persecution in the region. Therefore, the careers of the first female analysts in Hungary are intertwined with the history of assimilation, emigration, and cultural transformations. While at the turn of the twentieth century, the status of being a woman was a greater obstacle to a scholarly career than being a Jew, from the 1920s–1930s onward, it was the latter that increasingly served as a basis for exclusion (cf. Borgos, 2021b). From the 1950s until the mid-1970s, psychoanalysis itself became repressed in Hungary. However, the active presence of women in psychoanalysis in Hungary in high numbers was due to the fact that most of them could finish their studies by September 1920, before the introduction of the *numerus clausus*. This law limited the proportion of all minority nationalities among university students to 6 percent. The law was clearly aimed at restricting the number of Jewish students. They were the only group that suffered from the implementation of the law, as their proportion at the university in the 1910s was approximately at 15 percent in the

1910s in Hungary. Openness to non-medical or lay analysts in Budapest also facilitated the involvement of women. This was especially important after the Medical Faculty of the Budapest University applied a *numerus nullus* (a total ban) for women in the 1920–1926 period.

In the Hungarian psychoanalytic movement, the ratio of Jews among women analysts was even higher than among men. Actually, before World War II, with just one exception, all female members of the Hungarian Psychoanalytical Society were Jewish. The situation was similar in most branches of science and in higher education as a whole, at least before 1920. According to social historian Victor Karády, while Christian families were more attached to traditional family and gender roles, assimilated middle-class Jewish families were increasingly opening up to modern female roles, especially with reference to women's education. Social mobility was a possibility, an opportunity, but also a pressure for them. The education for daughters was increasingly considered a cultural, family, and marriage "capital," or in fact an alternative to marriage (Karády, 1994).

The activity of most Hungarian women analysts in the 1920s and the 1930s was predominantly linked with the issues of the early mother-infant relationship, child analysis, and education. This was the case of Alice Bálint, Lillián Rotter, Alice Hermann, Kata Lévy, Klára Lázár, Margit Dubovitz, Erzsébet Kardos, and Lucy Liebermann. This tendency reflects the place of women in the Hungarian society of the period. At the same time, these fields and subject matters were central to and constitutive for psychoanalysis, especially the so-called Budapest School, hence they cannot be regarded as specifically "feminine." (The "Budapest School of psychoanalysis" refers to the special interest of the Hungarian group of analysts headed by Sándor Ferenczi, including intersubjectivity, trauma, early mother-infant relationship, and interdisciplinarity.) On the other hand, women analysts often approached these issues from a unique viewpoint, "from within."

With the opening of the Budapest Psychoanalytic Polyclinic in 1931, child analysis and education became some of the key focuses: the Hungarian Psychoanalytical Society's informative and counselling activity broadened and solidified. These developments might have also attracted more women analysts who, in turn, contributed to further improvements. Through their therapeutic, educational, and organizing work women were also important disseminators of psychoanalytic knowledge.

That said, Hungarian women analysts were engaged in other areas as well, often as pioneers, such as the psychoanalytic technique and training

(Vilma Kovács), psychoanalytic ethnography (Alice Bálint), Buddhism (Edit Gyömrői), and the therapy of schizophrenia (Lilly Hajdu).

The life and oeuvre of female analysts in prewar and interwar Europe are still much less known than that of their male counterparts. The work of female analysts was erased to a higher degree and is more difficult to research also because, for many far-reaching reasons, they did not publish a lot (with a few important exceptions). At the same time, their important work as therapists, teachers, and organizers has remained largely invisible. They led interesting and often turbulent and tragic lives, which share several common features and are of professional and social relevance. I will start by introducing a number of pioneering Hungarian women psychoanalysts in a nutshell. Then, I will give a detailed presentation of the life and oeuvre of Vilma Kovács, one of the earliest Hungarian female analysts.

Lilly Hajdu (1891–1960)

Figure 10.1 Lilly Hajdu, Budapest Medical Chamber ID, ca. 1930.
Reproduced with permission of Judit Luif.

Hajdu's biography is an especially tragic emblem of how politics and psychoanalysis were interlocked in twentieth-century Hungary. She was born in Miskolc to a lower-middle class, deeply assimilated Jewish family, as a third child. She graduated from the Medical Faculty of the Budapest University in 1914 as one of the first female students. During the 1910s, she was a member of the Galileo Circle (Hun. *Galilei Kör*), an influential, freethinker students' society in Budapest. After the First World War, she was named the director of the Frim Institute for people with intellectual disabilities. Together with her husband, physician Miklós Gimes, she transformed it into an institute for nervous children (Schiess, 1999). In 1927 she started her training analysis with Vilma Kovács. Shortly thereafter she opened her own analytical practice. It became a source of professional recognition and stable livelihood. Her analytic work focused on the psychoanalytic treatment of schizophrenia (Hajdu-Gimes, 1940). Her husband, then training to be an analyst, was deported to the Leitmeritz concentration camp during the Second World War where he died. Lilly Hajdu survived the Holocaust by hiding in Budapest (Kende, 2003).

After the war, in 1947, she became the president of the Hungarian Psychoanalytical Society. She held that position until the forced dissolution of the Society in 1949, after the communist takeover, when the status of psychoanalysis and psychology as a whole received the (Stalinist) label of "bourgeois pseudo-science." In the 1950s, she worked in the National Institute of Neurology and Mental Disorders, including as its director for three years. Due to her position, she was forced to participate in the mandatory "Pavlovization" of psychology and psychiatry. She did, however, try to retain her psychoanalytic identity. Unfortunately, at the time of the professional and institutional peak of her career, the official scientific approach was very far from her own interests and intellectual/professional background.

Her son, Miklós Gimes Jr., became one of ideological leaders of the failed Hungarian Revolution of 1956. Its claims included the withdrawal of occupying Soviet troops, free elections, and the freedom of speech and press. As the tertiary accused in the Imre Nagy trial (with the former prime minister, Imre Nagy, and the minister of national defense, Pál Maléter), he was executed in 1958 (Révész, 1999; Schiess, 1999). Hajdu's daughter, Judit Gimes, immigrated to Switzerland in 1956. Hajdu wanted to join her, but the government refused her a passport. When her passport request was rejected for the third time in 1960, Hajdu took her own life.

Edit Gyömrői (1896–1987)

Gyömrői Edit Ceylon szigetén 1940-ben
A Magyar Hírek felvétele (PIM)

Figure 10.2 Edit Gyömrői, Ceylon, 1940.
Photograph by Magyar Hírek, *Hungarian News*. Copyright: Petőfi Literary Museum.

In the course of her life, Edit Gyömrői had many names, places of residence, and professions. She was born into an assimilated Jewish family belonging to Budapest's middle class. Her father, Márk Gelb, was a furniture manufacturer, and her mother was Ilona Pfeifer. In 1899 they changed the family name to Gyömrői. Edit became interested in psychoanalysis through her uncle, István Hollós—an important early psychoanalyst and psychiatrist of the Budapest School. At the age of 18, she married a chemical engineer, Ervin Rényi. They had a son and divorced four years later. After the fall of the Hungarian Soviet Republic (a short-lived communist state that existed from March 21, 1919, to August 1, 1919), she immigrated to Vienna. In 1923 she moved to Berlin with her second husband, journalist László Tölgy (né Glück), and worked as a costume designer at the Neumann Produktion film studio. After a psychotherapy and training analysis with Otto Fenichel, she opened her own practice. Her closest circle of colleagues included Marxist analysts, such as Fenichel, Annie and Wilhelm Reich, Edith Jacobson, and Siegfried Bernfeld. She was also part of the leftist so-called Child Seminar (Germ. *Kinderseminar*) organized by Fenichel outside the Berlin Institute (Ludwig-Körner, 1999; Fenichel, 1998). She left Germany for Prague in 1933 after Hitler came to power. In 1934, she returned to Budapest, where she held seminars for mothers and educators at the Polyclinic and worked as an analyst (e.g., with the poet, Attila József).

She migrated to Ceylon in 1938 with her third husband, journalist László Ujvári. Her son stayed in Hungary where he was drafted into the labor service (forced labor of Hungarian-Jewish men during the Second World War). It wasn't until after the war that Gyömrői found out about his death of typhoid in 1943. She then also learned that her younger sister died in a concentration camp. In Ceylon, she started lecturing and teaching seminars on psychoanalysis but found it difficult to cope with the cultural and institutional differences (cf. Fenichel, 1998; Gyömrői and Rickman, n.d.). In an attempt to adapt to the local culture, she started studying Buddhist philosophy and religious history at the University of Colombo, learned the Pali language. In 1944 she defended her doctoral dissertation, *The Role of the Miracle in Early Pali Literature* (Ludowyk-Gyömrői, 1944). She founded a weaving school for rural women. She also became involved in local leftist and women's politics, as an active member of the women's section of the (Trotskyst) Lanka Sama Samaja Party (LSSP). In 1947, she took part in the foundation of the first autonomous Ceylon women's association, the United Women's Front (EKP—Eksath Kantha Peramuna) (Jayawardena, 1995).

In Ceylon she met her fourth husband, Evelyn Frederick Charles Ludowyk, a Shakespearean scholar and head of the English Department at the University of Colombo. In 1956, the couple moved to London. Gyömrői joined the staff of the Hampstead Clinic and the Anna Freud's circle. She run a private practice until the age of 80. Her best-known paper is the "Analysis of a Young Concentration Camp Victim" (Ludowyk-Gyömrői, 1963), one of the first papers on the subject. The patient survived the concentration camp at the age of five and came to Gyömrői at the age of 17. Gyömrői's German-language autobiographical novel, *Gegen den Strom* (Against the

Current), written around 1945, was published in German in 2014 and in Hungarian in 2015 (as *Szemben az árral*).

Alice Bálint (née Székely-Kovács) (1898–1939)

Figure 10.3 Alice Bálint, passport photograph, 1927.
Reproduced with permission of Judith Dupont.

Alice Bálint was the daughter of Vilma Kovács. During her short life of only 41 years, she carried on rich theoretical, therapeutic, and educational activities (Dupont, 2015, pp. 265–269; Borgos, 2019, pp. 28–29, 2021a, pp. 95–100). Using a contemporary term: she had interdisciplinary interests. Besides psychoanalysis, she was engaged in the equally new science of ethnology and cultural anthropology. Her new approach to the mother-infant relationship made her a forerunner of the object relations theory.

Bálint studied a variety of disciplines in many different departments: mathematics in Budapest (1916–1919), law in Vienna (1920), and ethnology in Berlin (1921–1923). After her marriage to Mihály Bálint in 1921, the couple moved to Berlin where Alice Bálint worked at the Ethnological Museum. The following year they both entered analysis with Hanns Sachs. Dissatisfied with his overly theoretical sessions, they returned to Budapest in 1924 to finish the analysis with Sándor Ferenczi. Their son, János, was born in 1925. Alice Bálint continued to see psychoanalytic patients, held courses in psychoanalytically oriented child psychology for educators and parents, presented at congresses, and published regularly in international psychoanalytic journals, *Internationale Zeitschrift für Psychoanalyse*, *Imago*, and *Zeitschrift für Psychoanalytische Pädagogik*, as well as Hungarian pedagogical journals, *Gyermeknevelés* (Child Rearing) and *A Jövő Útjain* (On the Paths of the Future). (A complete edition of her writings was published in the French psychoanalytic journal, *Le Coq-Héron* (Bálint, 1997, 1998.)

She (like her husband) saw the mother-infant relationship as a primary object relation in which the infant also actively participates (e.g., Bálint, 1949). Her book, *A gyermekszoba pszichológiája*, was translated into German, French, Spanish, and English (as *The Psycho-Analysis of the Nursery*, Bálint, 1953/1931). She made important contributions to education by writing about a number of taboo topics, such as onanism and sex education (Bálint, 1990/1941).

In 1939 the political situation forced the Bálints to flee Hungary. They found refuge in Manchester, but Alice Bálint died only a few months later, in August 1939, due to a ruptured aneurysm.

Vilma Kovács (1879–1940)

"She did everything a woman was not allowed to do in her time: she divorced, had a profession and income, smoked and even learned to drive"—as Judith Dupont, psychoanalyst and granddaughter of Vilma Kovács, characterized her (Dupont, 2015, p. 261).[1] Kovács, one of the first Hungarian women psychoanalysts, traveled a long way in the course of her life, both socially and professionally. From difficult family circumstances, through a therapy with Ferenczi, she became an influential contributor to the early development of Hungarian psychoanalysis, one of Ferenczi's closest colleagues, and the manager of his legacy.

Vilma Kovács (née Prosznitz) was born in 1879 in the town of Szeged in southern Hungary to a Jewish family. Her ancestors had emigrated from Spain to Vienna and then to Hungary (Dupont, 2015). She was the youngest of three daughters. Her father, Simon Prosznitz, was a wholesaler, and her mother was Berta Freund. Her uncle, Moritz Benedikt, was the editor of the prestigious liberal Viennese political daily, *Neue Freie Presse* (New Free Press). Later his son, Ernst Martin Benedikt, became the newspaper's editor in chief. Her great-great-grandfather Marcus Benedict (or Mordecai Benet) was the chief rabbi of Moravia and well-known throughout Europe (Ginzberg, 1901–1906).

Vilma was six years old when she lost her father and her family plunged into financial difficulties. At the age of 18, she was married to an engineer, Zsigmond Székely, 15 years her senior. By the age of 22, she already had three children. The birth of the children put a considerable strain on her body; she contracted tuberculosis and went to be cured in a sanatorium in the Tatra Mountains. There she became friendly with the architect Frigyes Kovács, they fell in love, and he asked her to marry him (the wedding took place in 1908). As Zsigmond Székely refused to give her a divorce, it was

Figure 10.4 Vilma Kovács, ca. 1910.
Reproduced with permission of Judith Dupont.

decided in the course of divorce proceedings that the situation was Vilma's fault. As a result, the court ordered the children to stay with the father. After the divorce, she was able to meet with them only in secret. Eventually, in 1910, the three children escaped their father to live with Vilma in a villa built by Frigyes Kovács on the western side of the Danube River, in the elegant part of Budapest.

The new family, consisting of Vilma, her three children, and her second husband, were very close, as a result of previous vicissitudes. Their intensive and warm correspondence also reflects the intimate character of the relationships. The family enjoyed a vibrant intellectual life. Regular Sunday guests included painter Róbert Berény, composer Leó Weiner, piano teacher Margit Varró, her student Lajos Kentner, as well as Sándor Ferenczi and his wife, Gizella (Dupont, 2015, p. 27).

Vilma Kovács started her personal analysis with Sándor Ferenczi towards the end of World War I, with symptoms of agoraphobia. The successful therapy developed into a training analysis, and they established a master-student relationship. She opened a private practice as early as in the beginning of the 1920s. Her granddaughter (the daughter of painter Olga Székely-Kovács, also Olga Dormandi) Judith Dupont recalled the interior of Vilma's consulting room from her childhood as follows:

> I remember well my grandmother's consulting room and her bureau, above which there were rows of shelves. At the top, as if on a throne, there was a bust of Freud made by my mother, the only copy of which was lost when my grandparents' house was demolished at the end of the war. At the head of the couch, next to the armchair, a New Zealand batik was hanging on the wall, which [psychoanalyst] Géza Róheim gave to my grandmother, his analyst, when he returned from his long study trip to Australia.
>
> (Dupont, 2015, pp. 28–29)

In 1924 Kovács joined the Hungarian Psychoanalytical Society and became one of Ferenczi's closest colleagues and then friend (cf. Ferenczi and Ferenczi, n.d.). The next year, she was appointed head of the training committee of the Society. In the years that followed, she gave lectures to the association on the following topics: "The Analysis of a Tic Case" (1924), "The Consequences of Active Verbal Intervention and the Narcissistic Regression" (1926), and "A Self-Written Tale of a Child" (1928) (Giefer, 2007). She translated a number of works into Hungarian. These included

Freud's *Beyond the Pleasure Principle* (1923/1920), his *Autobiography* (together with the journalist and editor, Ignotus; Freud, 1936/1925), and Ferenczi's book *Thalassa: A Theory of Genitality* (Ferenczi, 1924), written originally in German.

Throughout her life, she published little (Kovács, 1925, 1926, 1928, 1931, 1933) and focused on organizing, training candidates, and analyzing patients. Ferenczi's mention of Vilma Kovács in one of his letters to Ernest Jones indicates that she was conducting training analyses as early as 1923, on a "philanthropic" basis, before the official opening of the Polyclinic in 1931. Ferenczi wrote: "A (lay) candidate by the name of Mrs. Kovács, translator of the *Beyond the Pleasure Principle*, a wealthy lady, is filling the role of a polyclinic for me; she currently treats five pat[ients] (amongst them two doctors in training), almost for free" (Ferenczi and Jones, 2013, p. 87).

She built a personal and professional network of younger female colleagues and served as an influential role model for them, and certainly for her daughter, Alice Bálint. The list of her analysands indicates a certain "matrilineal" relation: she analyzed and trained Lilly Hajdu, Alice Hermann, and Erzsébet Kardos. She also trained the following male analysts: Géza Róheim, Zsigmond Pfeifer, Endre Almásy, László Révész, Sándor Lóránd, and Lajos Székely. In the 1930s she treated Imre Hermann too, who did not like Vilma Kovács very much, perhaps because his wife, Alice Hermann, adored her a lot (Harmat, 1994, p. 220).

Ferenczi's letters document several episodes from Vilma Kovács's professional work and its reception. In a 1924 letter written to her from Baden-Baden, he wrote about his former patient referred by him to Vilma Kovács. Kovács cured the patient of neurotic symptoms and morphinism in 18 months. Ferenczi believed that the patient might now be suitable for becoming a therapist. He wrote to Vilma: "I think such a successful cure-analysis is at the same time the best training analysis. [. . .] I find it important to write down that this is the first case in which the Berliners [the Berlin Psychoanalytic Polyclinic] (apparently) want to acknowledge Your analyses as equal with theirs" (Ferenczi, September 24, 1924).

In another letter, written during his 1927 trip to New York, he also wrote about her activities with recognition. He reported arguing for lay analysis to the American Psychoanalytic Association using her example:

> The main thing is that I'm impressed by your extraordinary performance; that you are able to maintain a relatively large amount of order, both

outward and inward. [...] I'm glad that in theoretical and practical direction that little (or much?) that you received from me, keeps working—and also independently—in you. [...] I appreciate very, very much what you do relying on yourself, dear Vilma, both within and outside your family. Recently in the American psych[oanalytic] association—defending lay analysis—You were one of my main arguments.

(Ferenczi, Jan. 8, 1927)

Not all of her patients were impressed with her work. The writer Lajos Nagy, who was in analysis with her in 1927, recalled it rather ambivalently in his diaries:

At that time I went for analysis to Mrs. Kovács, by the way. Mrs. Kovács is a sad memory of mine. I liked her and I feel sorry for her. Poor thing. [...] Anyway, it's not my fault that we didn't get anywhere, but hers; she was weak for the analysis.

(Nagy, Dec. 30, 1940)

Figure 10.5 Vilma Kovács, ca. 1930.
Reproduced with permission of Judith Dupont.

Ferenczi valued Vilma Kovács's organizing skills too. In October 1930, in his birthday congratulatory letter from his summer holiday on Capri, he thanked Vilma Kovács for her caring activities: "Last year, in addition to all your personal kindness, you even took care of our house and the Polyclinic. This deserves special thanks and gratitude" (Ferenczi, Oct. 10, 1930).

In July 1931, the psychoanalytic Polyclinic officially opened in Budapest, as the General Neuro- and Mood Disorder Clinic. A psychoanalytic training institute possibly operated out of Ferenczi's private office since the fall of 1929 (Mészáros, 2014, p. 83). The Polyclinic was created to help patients in a bad financial situation; it provided treatment "exclusively for justified poor-fated outpatients" (News archive of the Hungarian Telegraph Office, June 30, 1931). It was at first managed by Ferenczi and, after his death, by Mihály Bálint. In addition to therapeutic work, it also housed a library and hosted lectures, training seminars, and association meetings.

The opening of the Polyclinic took place despite a strong official resistance, thanks to, *inter alia*, Vilma Kovács's intervention. As reported by Ferenczi in his letter to Max Eitingon from May 31, 1931:

> Thanks to the efforts of Dr. [Mihály] Bálint, Frau Kovács, and one of her patients, despite vehement opposition from the State Health Council, permission to establish the polyclinic was finally granted us by the Ministry of Public Welfare. We, totally from our own means, rented a five-room apartment and will set it up in a few weeks, so that I will already be able to report to the Congress the beginning of the therapeutic and instructional activity there.
>
> (Freud and Ferenczi, 2000, p. 411)

The apartment was rented from Vilma's husband, Frigyes Kovács, on the ground floor of the building, at 12 Mészáros street. Judith Dupont described the building and its residents as follows:

> In the Buda building of 12 Mészáros street, which was his [Frigyes Kovács's] own and which he himself built, my parents [Olga Székely-Kovács/Dormandi and Ladislas Dormandi] and I lived on the fifth floor, next to my grandmother's widowed sister, Irén Székely. The Bálints lived on the fourth, my uncle Ferenc on the third, Nóra, one of my father's

sisters and her family on the second and Erzsébet Bér, my grandmother's cousin, on the ground floor. [. . .] On the ground floor there was the psychoanalytic polyclinic [. . .], led by Sándor Ferenczi: most psychoanalysts, including Mihály Bálint and my aunt, Alice, worked there for one or two days a week for free.

(Dupont, 2015, pp. 22–23)

The Polyclinic consisted of a waiting room, three therapy rooms, and a big hall transformed into a meeting room used for both the Society gatherings and the library. The patients (at first mostly children) were referred to the Polyclinic by doctors. The analysts worked for free or for a minimum fee that was affordable to the patients, usually about 5 pengős (an equivalent of 1 US dollar at the time) (Danto, 2005, pp. 233–236). The Polyclinic sustained itself from members' contributions, course fees, and small donations from patients.

In the 1930s, Vilma Kovács started conducting seminars on psychoanalytic technique for psychoanalytic candidates. Technique in psychoanalysis is much more than a narrow methodological issue. According to one of Kovács's students, István Székács-Schönberger, it is about "a deeper understanding of two people's spiritual connection and the resulting activity and changes created in both parties participating in the process" (Székács-Schönberger, 1993, p. 78). The seminars took place in her own villa, on Orvos Street. The choice of location, outside of the Polyclinic, indicated the connection of her upper middle-class hospitality with her professional skills. István Székács-Schönberger recalled the apparent bourgeois milieu the following way: "We sat there in the salon [. . .]; at the beginning of the seminar the liveryman served black coffee. But this [wealth] was not from the analysis, but from her husband's income" (Javorniczky, 1990, p. 46). He described Kovács's seminars as follows:

The point of her seminars was that biweekly someone under training had to report on a patient in an approximately 1.5 hours long presentation. [. . .] Apart from the trainees, these discussions were attended by Alice Bálint (daughter of Vilma Kovács), Zsiga [Zsigmond] Pfeifer [. . .] and Endre Almásy [. . .]. They commented frequently and were able to correct and advise very effectively in order to help with the practical development of the presenting young analyst.

(Hadas, 1995, p. 21)

Székács also recalled the attitude of Vilma Kovács as a therapist and trainer, which was based on equality and support, in accordance with the Ferenczi school and her own views:

> Technically this is about the attitude towards the patient. One must not be boastful. Vilma Kovács, for example, never told the patient that she was *interpreting* something, because interpretation suggests that the analyst intellectually stands beyond the patient. She always said she was *showing* this and that. [. . .] Furthermore I learned from her that one always has to respect the patient and has to relate to them in a gentle, motherly and supportive way. One must not cure violently.
> (Székács-Schönberger, 1993, p. 78, original emphasis)

In April 1933, the minutes of the Hungarian Society acknowledged her successful training of candidates (Giefer, 2007), on Ferenczi's initiative (who died just three weeks later). Vilma Kovács's position within the Hungarian psychoanalytic movement and Ferenczi's appreciation for her work were reflected by the fact that he named her the manager of his archive, now at the Freud Museum in London. After her death it was taken over by Mihály Bálint and, after his death, by Vilma's granddaughter, Judith Dupont.

As already mentioned, scholarly publication was not one of the major fields for Vilma Kovács. She published only five articles during her lifetime, between 1925 and 1935. They came out in German in the *Internationale Zeitschrift für Psychoanalyse* and the *Imago*, and in English in the *International Journal of Psycho-Analysis*. They were published in Hungarian much later, in a posthumous collected volume (Kovács, 1993). These included two case studies: on a tic (Kovács, 1925) and an impotence case (Kovács, 1931). Secondly, theoretical and methodological writings: on the relationship of unconscious fantasies and male sexuality (Kovács, 1926) and on the active technique (Kovács, 1928). Finally, her most important study on training- and control-analysis (Kovács, 1936/1933).

Kovács's studies reveal skillful interpreting skills and a good writing style. However, they mostly stay within the Freudian theoretical framework (castration complex, penis envy, sexual repressions). On the other hand, they demonstrate a therapeutic attitude which, following Ferenczi, applied the active technique with a special attention to the role of countertransference. In a letter from April 25, 1940, to her younger daughter, Olga

Székely-Kovács (or Olga Dormandi), Vilma makes it clear that in her theoretical concepts she was closer to Ferenczi's views than Freud's:

> Freud writes about the *Todestrieb* [death instinct] in *Jenseits des Lustprinzips* [*Beyond the Pleasure Principle*]; he presumes it and proves its existence by the repetition compulsion. Certainly Ferenczi's conception is closer to me and it's also more justifiable clinically than the death instinct. You can get it from the library of the clinic for sure. The *Jenseits* is an unclear book. I translated it so that I might understand it better, but no one understands it. It's a fantasy that Freud allowed himself.
>
> (Kovács, April 25, 1940)

The writings suggest that her viewpoint was not affected by the fact that she was a woman. The exception is her mentioning of the transference of one of her patients: "The fact that I am a lay analyst, moreover a woman, gave him a chance to repeat his [both devaluating and shameful] attitude towards his father and revaluate it during the analysis" (Kovács, 1931, p. 454).

Her main field of interest was the process of analytic training, made mandatory following the decision of the Seventh International Psychoanalytic Congress in Berlin in 1922. She continues to be referred to most frequently in this respect. She organized and described the "Hungarian" training system. Its distinctive feature is that the first few cases of the trainee are supervised by his or her own training analyst, not a separate analyst, and discussed in an analytic setting. In her 1933 paper, Kovács provided an overview of the history of the psychoanalytic training system from its beginnings (the nonformalized readings and association experiments in Zurich in the late 1900s) and introduced the "Hungarian method" of supervision. As she pointed out, a training analysis ends when the candidate acquires a flexibility enabling him or her to treat patients of different personalities and backgrounds in an unbiased way and, generally speaking, to turn from the self to the outside world. According to the Hungarian system, a training analyst is more suitable to be a supervisor (a "control analyst") than a different analyst is, due to his or her deep knowledge of the trainee and the nature of their past relationship. This, of course, implies a different (theoretical and methodological) approach regarding supervision itself. It allows for more space for the candidate's own associations and the work with countertransference, compared to the didactic function and view of supervision (represented most strongly by Edward Bibring).

> In my view, on the other hand, the more correct procedure is for the control-analysis to be conducted throughout by the candidate's own training-analyst; for it may transpire, when the former has begun to treat patients, that the time has not yet come to terminate his own analysis. [. . .] If the candidate continues his own analysis when he begins to analyze patients, the two parallel pieces of work bring to light those sides of his personality which have hitherto received too little attention or none at all, or at least could not manifest themselves in so expressive a fashion. All his good and bad qualities, and also his weaknesses, are revealed: for example, his incapacity for objectivity; his impatience; his vanity; his inability to bear criticism.
>
> (Kovács, 1936, pp. 350–351)

Why was she particularly interested in this issue? I believe that it must have been a personal concern. First of all, it resulted from her own analysis. Second, from the (theoretical and practical) influence of Ferenczi. Finally, more generally, from her experience of connecting professional and personal fields in analytic work, training, and organizing.

The method described by Vilma Kovács has been followed exclusively in Hungary, and not by all analysts. There was little discussion on the Hungarian model among her contemporaries. The 1947 "London Standing Rules" required that the supervisor was distinct from the training analyst, thus practically banning the Budapest model (Bálint, 1948; Soreanu, 2019).

At the end of 1938, amidst the increasingly dangerous political situation, Vilma Kovács moved with her husband to Paris, to join her younger daughter, Olga Székely-Kovács. They found it difficult to make a living in the new city, due to the fact that Frigyes Kovács was unable to restart his career as an architect. Vilma, who spoke good French, reached out to a number of French analysts. Marie Bonaparte offered to provide her with patients, but Frigyes, a middle-class man with traditional views on gender roles, did not want to be supported by his wife. Thus, they returned to Budapest a few months later, at the cusp of the Second World War (Dupont, 2015, p. 32).

In August 1939, her daughter, Alice Bálint, died unexpectedly. This fundamentally shook the course of Vilma's life and further purpose. Her letters from that period paint a picture of her state of mind and everyday life. The letters to her younger daughter, Olga, show not only her grief and the emotional vacuum left by the loss of Alice, but also the elementally close and loving relationship she had with both her daughters. Shortly after Alice's death, she wrote to Olga:

> Now I can see how much better I loved listening to Alice than myself; now I am forced to be smart and put it all together. Otherwise, days of complete emotional emptiness alternate with very bad days, which I still like better than the former.
>
> (Kovács, after August 1939)

In December 21, 1939, she wrote:

> It's hard to endure this Christmas, being so robbed of all the joy. I had to talk about it; I often can't write because I don't want to write about how unhappy I am. But there's nothing else with me. Work goes on, no one else cares, no one who comes here gives me anything. Fri[gyes] is also often sad, the kids too [possibly of Ferenc Székely-Kovács]. And here we sit in this beautiful home where it used to be so good and every memory just hurts, because everything is just a memory and today it's not even a life. One just waits for time to pass and chases the days in the hope that one day something good will happen. People try to be nice to me, but no one can find the magic word which would give me some relief.
>
> (Kovács, Dec. 21, 1939)

Vilma Kovács survived her daughter, Alice Bálint, by a mere nine months. She died on May 15, 1940, from peritonitis. The time gap between their deaths may be interpreted symbolically: she carried her daughter for the final nine months, not in her body, but in her memory. In his letter to his sister-in-law Olga Székely-Kovács from May 21, Mihály Bálint reported on the death of her mother, while anticipating the impending dreadful political events:

> My little Olga, the telegram just arrived that Anyus [Hun. Mommy, Vilma Kovács] died. Last Saturday I got a letter from George [the doctor] where he described the course of the illness and the situation found at the operation and I knew already that a recovery was more or less unlikely. Now you probably know yourself that the inflammation of the

gall bladder started again, that it perforated and became a general peritonitis. For Anyus it is maybe better to have been freed from the coming horrors. And her passionate temperament would not accept the fact that Alice left us. But for us, it will be very painful. The world has become even emptier, and we even poorer.

(Dupont, 2002, p. 363)

In a letter to Mihály Bálint, Anna Freud reacted with shock and disbelief to the news of the death: "Is it really true that Mrs. Kovács is dead? This again seems so incomprehensible and unexpected that I didn't even want to believe it" (Freud, June 2, 1940).

A letter from a frequent guest of the Kovács villa, composer Leó Weiner, to another one-time guest, the noted piano teacher Margit Varró, indicates—through the expressed absence—that the sense of closeness and warmness he used to feel in the villa were created by the female family members:

I see the Kovácses sometimes. Sometimes? Not more frequently, because I always feel there the rigidity I was complaining about formerly. Frici [Frigyes Kovács] is rather "patronizing" than kind; Feri [Ferenc Székely-Kovács] is sarcastic and arrogant. [. . .] Ultimately I never feel good there and I'm always glad to be out of the door. Well, I had a connection only to the three women there, two of whom are unfortunately not alive anymore!

(Berlász, 2005, p. 28)

Alice Hermann, Vilma Kovács's former patient who became her close colleague and friend, gave a memorial lecture on Vilma Kovács to the Hungarian Psychoanalytical Society in 1940 (Hermann, 1946, p. 89). The obituary for the *Internationale Zeitschrift für Psychoanalyse* was written by her analysand and colleague Sigmund Pfeifer. He stressed the most important aspects of her personality and her method of working: freedom from dogmas, empathy, capacity for providing help, and a relationship to reality labelled as "womanly" by Ferenczi.

As the teacher of psychoanalysis, she was never dogmatic, not even when conveying the thoughts and methods of her own teacher, Ferenczi, which she maintained thankfully. She possessed a lot of the quality that Ferenczi called "a womanly sense of reality." [. . .] But her most important area of activity was the analytic work with her patients. Here she could unfold her special abilities to the artistic and careful study of the human soul and use her helpfulness. Her tact, her sense of people, her firm knowledge and courage were present in almost every minute in the society. She willingly passed on her knowledge to her colleagues and disciples.

(Pfeifer, 1941, pp. 376–377)

I agree that her aforementioned skills manifested in her analytic work too. But, as I attempted to show in this chapter, the accomplishments of Vilma Kovács transcended the analytic practice. Coping with the difficult circumstances of her early life, breaking out of a bad relationship, she could unfold her intellectual interest associated with important social skills and motivation/ambition. As a female pioneer of psychoanalysis who actively participated in the formation of the psychoanalytic institutions in Hungary and the dissemination and struggles of the psychoanalytic thought, Vilma Kovács demonstrated the ability and need for autonomy and initiative, while retaining a sense of loyalty to the profession (as a theory, an institution, and a community). Her career represents the productive fusion of traditional and modern women's roles: those of a caregiver and an intellectual. In addition to her work as a therapist and trainer, the function of an institutional supporter, organizer, "networker," and "guardian" were at least as significant. Through all these activities, she was furthering the status of both psychoanalysis and an intellectual woman.[2]

Notes

1 For texts where no English translation exists, such as this one, the quotations were translated by Anna Borgos.
2 An earlier version of this chapter was published in Borgos, 2021a.
    I would like to thank Pál Lányi for the information about Vilma Kovács's ancestors and Judith Dupont for making the correspondence between Vilma Kovács and her two daughters, Olga Székely-Kovács and Alice Bálint, available to me.

Archival Materials

Ferenczi, S. and Ferenczi, G. (1924). Letter to Vilma Kovács, Baden-Baden, Sept. 24. Sándor Ferenczi's Archive, Freud Museum Archives, London.
Ferenczi, S. and Ferenczi, G. (1927). Letter to Vilma Kovács, New York, Jan. 8. Sándor Ferenczi's Archive, Freud Museum Archives, London.
Ferenczi, S. and Ferenczi, G. (1930). Letter to Vilma Kovács, Capri, Oct. 10. Sándor Ferenczi's Archive, Freud Museum Archives, London.

Freud, A. (1940). Letter to Michael Bálint, June 2, British Psychoanalytical Society Archives, London.
Gyömrői, E. and Rickman, J. (n.d.). Correspondence. British Psychoanalytical Society Archives. London, P03—C—A—03.
Javorniczky, I. (1990). Interview with István Székács-Schönberger. Private property of the István Székács-Schönberger estate.
Kovács, V. (n.d.). Letters to Olga Székely-Kovács, after August 1939. Private Papers of Judith Dupont.
Ludowyk-Gyömrői, E. (1944). *The Role of the Miracle in Early Pali Literature*. Archives of the Sándor Ferenczi Society, Budapest.
Nagy, L. (n.d.). The diaries of Lajos Nagy. Petőfi Literary Museum, Collection of Manuscripts.
News archive of the Hungarian Telegraph Office, June 25, 1931.
[Opening the Polyclinic of the Hungarian Psychoanalytical Society . . .] (June 30, 1931). *News Archive of the Hungarian Telegraph Office*. Online at https://archiv1920-1944.mti.hu/. Accessed May 30, 2023.

Reference List

Bálint, A. (1949). Love for the Mother and Mother-Love. *International Journal of Psycho-Analysis*, 30, 251–259.
Bálint, A. (1953). *The Psycho-Analysis of the Nursery*. London: Routledge & Kegan Paul (Orig. publ. 1931).
Bálint, A. (1990). *Anya és gyermek*. Budapest: Párbeszéd (Orig. publ. 1941).
Bálint, A. (1997, 1998). Œuvre complète. *Le Coq-Héron*, 147, 153.
Bálint, M. (1948). On the Psycho-Analytic Training System. *International Journal of Psycho-Analysis*, 29, 163–173.
Berlász, M. (2005). Drága Grétém! Weiner Leó levelei Varró Margithoz 1938–1960. *Muzsika*, 48(8), 25–29.
Borgos, A. (2019). Alice Bálint and Her Diaries: "This Little Fixation Seems to Remain . . .". *Psychoanalysis and History*, 21(1), 23–52.
Borgos, A. (2021a). *Women in the Budapest School of Psychoanalysis: Girls of Tomorrow*. Abingdon and New York: Routledge.
Borgos, A. (2021b). "Put a Stop to the Excessive Influx": The Rhetoric of Restriction Regarding Female and Jewish Students at Budapest University, 1900–1930. *Hungarian Studies Review*, 48(1), 48–78.
Danto, E. A. (2005). *Freud's Free Clinics. Psychoanalysis and Social Justice, 1918–1938*. New York: Columbia UP.
Dupont, J. (Ed.) (2002). Excerpts of the Correspondence of Michael and Alice Balint with Olga, Ladislas, and Judith Dormandi. *American Journal of Psychoanalysis*, 62(4), 361–362.
Dupont, J. (2015). *Au fils du temps . . . Un itinéraire analytique*. Paris: Campagne Premiere.
Fenichel, O. (1998). *119 Rundbriefe, 1934–1945*. J. Reichmayer and E. Mühlleitner (Eds.). Frankfurt am Main and Basel: Stroemfeld Verlag.

Ferenczi, S. (1924). *Katasztrófák a nemi működés fejlődésében*. V. Kovács (Trans.). Budapest: Pantheon.

Ferenczi, S. and Jones, E. (2013). *Letters 1911–1933*. F. Erős, J. Szekacs-Weisz and K. Robinson (Eds.). London: Karnac Books.

Freud, S. (1923). *Túl az örömelven. A halálösztön és az életösztönök*. V. Kovács (Trans.). Budapest: Világirodalom (Orig. publ. 1920).

Freud, S. (1936). *Önéletrajz*. V. Kovács (Trans.). Budapest: Pantheon (Orig. publ. 1925).

Freud, S. and Ferenczi, S. (2000). *The Correspondence of Sigmund Freud and Sándor Ferenczi, Vol. III*. P. T. Hoffer (Trans.). E. Brabant, E. Falzeder and P. Giampieri-Deutsch (Eds.). Cambridge, MA and London: Belknap Press.

Giefer, M. (Ed.) (2007). *Korrespondenzblatt der Internationalen Psychoanalytischen Vereinigung 1910–1941*. Bad Homburg. Online at www.luzifer-amor.de/fileadmin/bilder/Downloads/korrespondenzblatt_1910-1941.pdf. Accessed Nov. 21, 2022.

Ginzberg, L. (1901–1906). Benet, Mordecai B. Abraham (Marcus Benedict). *The Jewish Encyclopedia*. Online at www.jewishencyclopedia.com/articles/2937-benet-mordecai-b-abraham-marcus-benedict. Accessed Dec. 2, 2022.

Gyömrői, E. (2014). *Gegen den Strom*. Berlin: Christiane Ludwig-Körner.

Gyömrői, E. (2015). *Szemben az árral*. János Kis (Trans.). Budapest: Jelenkor.

Hadas, M. (1995). Beszélgetés Dr. Székács Istvánnal. *Replika*, 19–20, 10–41.

Hajdu-Gimes, L. (1940). Contributions to the Etiology of Schizophrenia. *Psychoanalytic Review*, 27(4), 421–438.

Harmat, P. (1994). *Freud, Ferenczi és a magyarországi pszichoanalízis*. Sopron: Bethlen Gábor Publisher.

Hermann, I. (1946). Hungarian Psycho-Analytical Society. *International Journal of Psycho-Analysis*, 27, 87–92 [Report of 1940–1946].

Jayawardena, K. (1995). *The White Woman's Other Burden: Western Women and South Asia During British Rule*. London and New York: Routledge.

Karády, V. (1994). A társadalmi egyenlőtlenségek Magyarországon a nők felsőbb iskoláztatásának korai fázisában. In M. Hadas (Ed.), *Férfiuralom. Írások nőkről, férfiakról, feminizmusról* (pp. 176–195). Budapest: Replika Kör.

Kende, É. (2003). Az én 1944/45-ös krónikám. *Mozgó Világ*, 29(12), 59–75.

Kovács, V. (1925). Analyse eines Falles von "Tic convulsif". *Internationale Zeitschrift für Psychoanalyse*, 11, 318–324.

Kovács, V. (1926). Das Erbe des Fortunatus. *Imago*, 12, 321–327.

Kovács, V. (1928). Beispiele zur aktiven Technik. *Internationale Zeitschrift für Psychoanalyse*, 14, 405–408.

Kovács, V. (1931). Wiederholungstendenz und Charakterbildung. *Internationale Zeitschrift für Psychoanalyse*, 17, 449–463.

Kovács, V. (1936). Training- and Control-Analysis. *International Journal of Psycho-Analysis*, 17, 346–354. (Orig. publ. 1933).

Kovács, V. (1993). *Fortunatus öröksége*. J. Szilágyi (Ed.). Budapest: Párbeszéd.

Ludowyk-Gyömrői, E. (1963). The Analysis of a Young Concentration Camp Victim. *The Psychoanalytic Study of the Child*, 18, 484–510.

Ludwig-Körner, C. (1999). Edit Ludowyk Gyömrői. In C. Ludwig-Körner (Ed.), *Wiederentdeckt—Psychoanalytikerinnen in Berlin* (pp. 119–148). Berlin: Bibliothek der Psychoanalyse, Psychosozial Verlag.

Mészáros, J. (2014). *Ferenczi and Beyond: Exile of the Budapest School and Solidarity in the Psychoanalytic Movement During the Nazi Years*. London: Karnac Books.

Pfeifer, S. (1941). Vilma Kovács. *Internationale Zeitschrift für Psychoanalyse*, 26, 376–377.

Révész, S. (1999). *Egyetlen élet. Gimes Miklós története*. Budapest: 1956 Institute, Sík Kiadó.

Schiess, R. (1999). *Wie das Leben nach dem Fieber. In Zusammenarbeit mit Juca und Gábor Magos-Gimes*. Giessen: Psychosozial Verlag.

Soreanu, R. (2019). Supervision for Our Times: Countertransference and the Rich Legacy of the Budapest School. *American Journal of Psychoanalysis*, 79, 329–351.

Székács-Schönberger, I. (1993). Utószó. In V. Kovács (Ed.), *Fortunatus öröksége* (pp. 77–83). Budapest: Párbeszéd.

Part IV

Beyond the Holocaust

Chapter 11

Eugenia Sokolnicka and Sophie Morgenstern

The Intertwining of Life, Work, and Death

Ursula Prameshuber

I came across the names of two Polish Jewish female pioneers of psychoanalysis, Eugenia Sokolnicka and Sophie Morgenstern, when researching the subject of psychosuiciders. Both women died young, by suicide, and in Paris. I quickly realized that, as many other female pioneers, these two have fallen into oblivion. We can only speculate about their motivations and mindsets. Their contributions to psychoanalysis, especially in the field of child analysis, have been underestimated.

Eugenia Sokolnicka: Childhood, Early Life, and Education

Eugenia Sokolnicka (later also Eugénie) was born Eugenia Kutner on June 14, 1876, in Warsaw into a Jewish family of wealthy intellectuals and patriots (Magnone, 2016, 2023).[1] As argued by Jarosław Groth, "it seems that Eugenia was brought up in a family more likely to identity with repressed Poland than with its Jewish heritage" (2015, p. 61). Her paternal grandfather and uncle had participated in the two major nineteenth-century insurrections against Russian rule in Poland: the November Uprising (1830–1831) and the January Uprising (1863–1864). Her mother, Paulina (née Flejszer), was a quite well-known women's patriotic movement activist, who had been arrested in 1863. She was celebrated with a state funeral in newly independent Poland in 1918 (Geissmann and Geissmann, 1998). Sokolnicka's father, Maurycy Kutner, was a banker.

It is most likely that Sokolnicka received early education at home, from a French governess. Despite completing comprehensive archival research into Sokolnicka's life, Lena Magnone was unable to confirm if Eugenia graduated from a state high school (a *Gymnasium*) or a private boarding school for girls (2016, 2023). She was able to establish that Sokolnicka

DOI: 10.4324/9781003455844-16

relocated to Paris in 1899 or earlier. She studied natural sciences at Sorbonne University and audited the psychology classes of Pierre Janet and Jean-Martin Charcot at Collège de France. In the fall of 1902, she took a bachelor degree in science (Fr. *licence ès sciences*), after completing just two years. Then, she studied bacteriology for three months at the Pasteur Institute (Magnone, 2016, vol. II, p. 10).

From Paris, Sokolnicka most likely relocated to Berlin to join her future husband, Michał Sokolnicki, a Polish historian and diplomat, whom she met in Paris. The couple returned to Poland, where Sokolnicka converted to Catholicism and married Michał in October 1903 in Warsaw (Magnone, 2016, vol. II, p. 10). Sokolnicki went on to become the private secretary to the Polish chief of state, Józef Piłsudzki (Groth, 2015). There is little information available regarding Sokolnicka's time in Poland, other than she most probably worked as a science teacher (Geissmann and Geissmann, 1998, p. 134) and wrote a popular school textbook on zoology, botany, and mineralogy (Sokolnicka, 1906).

No information is available concerning her move back to Berlin, but we do know she lived there in 1904 (Magnone, 2016, 2023). We also know that in May 1910 Sokolnicka traveled to Zurich to undertake psychiatric training at the Burghölzli Clinic (now University Hospital of Zurich) under its director. The period under Bleuler's directorship, 1898–1927, is considered the "golden age" of Burghölzli (Kallivayalil, 2016, p. 226). At first, Bleuler encouraged bringing psychoanalytic teachings into patient treatment. Burghölzli became the first psychiatric clinic to do so (Ellenberger, 1970). In 1907 Bleuler, Ludwig Binswanger, and Édouard Claparède started the Freudian Group of Zurich. Carl Gustav Jung worked at the Burghölzli between 1900 and 1909 (cf. Graf-Nold, 2001). However, in 1910 Bleuler started distancing himself from Freud. He considered his ideas too dogmatic. The following year he resigned from the International Psychoanalytical Association (IPA) (Kallivayalil, 2016, p. 227) and then published *A Criticism of the Freudian Theory* (Bleuler, 1913).

In March 1912, Sokolnicka became a member of the Zurich psychoanalytic group, affiliated with the IPA. The next year, when Freud broke his relationship with Jung, she sided with the former (Magnone, 2016, vol. II, p. 15).

Two Analyses

In 1913 Sokolnicka traveled to Vienna for an analysis with Freud. They started a traditional, six-days-a-week analysis but it only lasted less than three months or 68 hours (May, 2007, p. 166). At that time, Sokolnicka was in the process of separating from her husband. We may only assume that it became the main focus in her short analysis.

The separation from Michał and subsequent settlement impacted Sokolnicka's finances unfavorably. It was her belief that her financial troubles were the reason behind Freud's decision to abruptly discontinue the analysis. This made her deeply dissatisfied with Freud and understandably bitter. Her second analyst, the initiator of the International Psychoanalytical Association (IPA) (est. 1910) and founder of the Hungarian Psychoanalytical Society (est. 1913), Sándor Ferenczi, wrote to Freud, "She came with complaints about you. You had turned her down only because of money matters [. . .] and out of that personal motive you interrupted her almost finished analysis" (Falzeder and Brabant, 2000, p. 23). Freud's replies typically focused on his personal dislike for Sokolnicka. He was very open about it, in his correspondence with Ferenczi and Otto Rank. What's more, Freud clearly disapproved of Ferenczi's acceptance of Sokolnicka. He stated, "you evidently have a weakness for the disagreeable person" (p. 45). Ferenczi explained that his "weakness" for Sokolnicka had to do with her "unusual psychoanalytic talent" (p. 48). However, Freud dismissed Ferenczi's argument and continued to dwell in his dislike:

She has always been repugnant to me, despite undeniable talent. [. . .] I don't consider her a paranoia but a basically disgusting person; she doesn't want to see now that she has become an old woman. In that there is little to be done, and the development of quite crazy [. . .] traits can hardly be impeded.

(p. 29)

The analysis with Ferenczi started in 1920, when Sokolnicka was 36 years old and lasted a year. Jarosław Groth argued that the analysis could be treated as supervision (2015). Sokolnicka suffered from psychological fragility, personality disorders, and strong suicidal tendencies. Ferenczi reported to Freud, "Her suicide threats, which appear in a questionable light through an attempt at poisoning herself and through the infantile suicide attempt known to you (jumping into hot water), command me not to give up the case" (Falzeder and Brabant, 2000, pp. 25–26). Her divorce remained the key issue, also in her therapy with Ferenczi. He reported:

The divorce from her husband was well on its way on her arrival and seems now to be ended. It ended up with a dispute over money [. . .]

in which she got short end of the stick [. . .]. From time to time during the analysis a retrospective (albeit rapidly transitory) regret about her divorce was put into words.

(pp. 23–24)

Ferenczi was a very empathic and dedicated analyst. He deeply appreciated Sokolnicka's intellectual abilities and her analytic talent (Falzeder and Brabant, 2000, p. 48). The therapy, however, was unsuccessful. Most importantly, Ferenczi failed to cure Sokolnicka's suicidal tendencies.

Commitment to Psychoanalysis: Vienna, Munich, Warsaw

In the period between the two analyses, Sokolnicka lived in Vienna, Munich, and Warsaw, studying, seeing patients, and building the psychoanalytic movement. Starting in April 1914, she attended several meetings of the Vienna Psychoanalytic Society (VPS) as a guest. She joined the VPS as its full member in November 1916 (Nunberg and Federn, 1975, p. 340). In 1914 she briefly lived in Munich. Freud welcomed her decision to move there, as he had hoped she would spread the psychoanalytic theory and practice there. One of her Munich analysands was Felix Boehm, the future pro-Hitler president of the German Psychoanalytic Society (DPG) and director of the Berlin Training Institute, later known as the Institute for Psychological Research and Psychotherapy or the Göring Institute.

At the cusp of the First World War or shortly after it started, Sokolnicka moved back to Warsaw where she set up a private practice (Magnone, 2016, 2023). During the war, she was in close contact with Otto Rank, who was stationed in Kraków for two years (cf. Chapter 3 in this book). In his letter to Freud from June 5, 1918, Rank communicated to Freud her successes in building the psychoanalytic movement in Poland, while noting the obstacles:

In Warsaw she's done a lot in a short time. She has interested and recruited many people for psychoanalysis (physicians, teachers, etc.) and organized lectures and courses; she claims some therapeutic successes too. I've seen that in Warsaw she fights against a wall of closed-mindedness and meanness.

(Lieberman and Kramer, 2012, p. 84)

In an earlier letter, from July 7, 1917, Rank reported that Sokolnicka "informed [him that] a psychoanalytic association is just being set up" in Warsaw (Lieberman and Kramer, 2012, p. 72). Her ambitious plan did not come to fruition (possibly impacted by fact that Poland regained independence after World War I). However, the Polish Society for the Development of Psychoanalysis (PTRP) was not founded until 1991, almost a 100 years later, and the Institute of Psychoanalysis and Psychotherapy (IPP) was founded the next year (Groth, 2015).

After moving to Budapest in 1920 for her analysis with Ferenczi, she actively participated in the meetings of the local psychoanalytical society, held in German for her sake. In March 1920, she presented the case of the boy from Minsk to the Budapest society. In September that year she presented a paper, "On the Diagnosis and Symptomatology of the Psycho-Analytical Theory of the Neuroses" (1920), in which she compared a pre-analytical and an analytical diagnosis. In November she gave one more presentation (the details of which remain unknown). In Budapest she also trained at a psychiatric hospital, the Yellow House, where she was praised for her accurate interpretations by Istvan Hollós, a psychoanalyst who worked there (Geissmann and Geissmann, 1998, p. 136).

The Case of a Boy From Minsk

One of Sokolnicka's Warsaw patients, treated in April 1919, was a young boy from Minsk (now in Belarus) who suffered from an obsessive neurosis (Sokolnicka, 1920, 1922). It was one of the very first child analyses in history, predating the work of Anna Freud. The patient was a ten-year-old Polish Jewish boy suffering from severe phobia of being touched. His mother had to dress him and feed him following very strict rituals:

> If anything happened contrary to his compulsion he literally writhed with pain. At such times he would seem to lose consciousness, then he would fall into a rage [. . .] this would end in a fit of convulsive sobbing and he would fall exhausted into a chair.
> (Sokolnicka, 1920, p. 306)

While in his famous case of child analysis of Little Hans, Freud saw the boy only once and conducted his analysis through meetings with the boy's father, who was Freud's patient, Sokolnicka remained in close direct contact with her young patient. Their sessions took place late in the afternoon, due to the time-consuming dressing and feeding rituals, in her home.

> At the beginning of the treatment, I aimed exclusively at overcoming the extremely reserved and difficult character of the boy and his inhibition of thinking, in order to enable me to establish some sort of contact with him. My influence was therefore partly analytical and partly pedagogical, but was based throughout on analytical knowledge.
> (Sokolnicka, 1920, p. 308)

Instead of play therapy, Sokolnicka analyzed the boy's dreams with the help of free associations. Each recounting of a dream was followed by a description of the associations and then by an interpretation. Using classical Freudian analysis, she worked with his oedipal fantasies and castration fears. She also introduced the boy to his sexuality and provided sexual education.

Sokolnicka's approach resembled Ferenczi's active technique (cf. Ferenczi, 2019/1926). In this form of therapy, analyst plays a more active, intervening role than in the classical Freudian analysis. They express their points of view, interpret the events, give commands and forbiddances, and suggest solutions. In fact, in his lecture at the 1920 Sixth Psychoanalytic Conference of the International Psychoanalytical Association in The Hague, Ferenczi discussed his active technique using Sokolnicka's case of the boy from Minsk as an example. What she called "pedagogical" in the preceding quote could be described as active therapy. Ferenczi had also used his active technique in his work with Sokolnicka.

Sokolnicka's treatment of the boy lasted six weeks and was very successful: the severe symptoms went away. Her paper about the case, "The Analysis of a Case of Infantile Obsessional Neurosis," was published in 1920 in *Internationalen Zeitschrift für Psychoanalyse* and then translated into English (Sokolnicka, 1922). It was one of the very first cases of child analysis to be published, preceded only by Freud's case of Little Hans from 1909 (1953/1909) and Hermine Hug-Hellmuth's book on the mental life of children (1919/1913). In the conclusion of her paper, Sokolnicka discussed the reasons behind the boy's quick recovery. She described her work with the boy not as a methodical analysis but "a treatment, which was more due to pedagogic-psychological methods, aided by the insight afforded by psychoanalytical knowledge" (Sokolnicka, 1922, p. 319). She underlined the importance of transference in every psychotherapeutic and pedagogical work, even if used by therapists, physicians, and educators unconsciously and in a non-systematic way. She discussed the case further in *The Dynamics of Neuroses and Psychoanalysis* (Sokolnicka, 1931) and "About a Case of Quick Healing" (Sokolnicka, 1932). In her paper from 1929, "Some Problems of Psychoanalytic Technique," she dealt with the disappearance of libido. She gave a brief outline of the development of the libido and the abnormal libidinal development characterized by fixations and regressions.

Emigration to Paris

In the first weeks of 1921 Sokolnicka, conflicted with Freud and Ferenczi and disappointed by the failure to set up a society in Warsaw, decided to relocate to Paris (Magnone, 2016, vol. II, p. 36). It is often falsely claimed that she did so at Freud's request and as his representative. Freud had hoped she would spread the psychoanalytic movement to France, but the decision to move to Paris was her own. It was dictated by her fluency in the French language—while her German skills prohibited her from working with patients. Secondly, her brother lived in Paris.

In his support for Sokolnicka's decision, Ferenczi tried to help her resettle. He asked Freud for recommendation letters for her, including to a physician and translator, Samuel Jankélévitch, who had been considering translating Freud's books into French. Freud was to also recommend Sokolnicka to his French publisher, Payot. Additionally, Ferenczi insisted that Freud meet with her in person before her departure. Finally, he encouraged other colleagues to send patients her way (Magnone, 2016, 2023). In their correspondence, Freud interpreted Ferenczi's support for their former patient as a manifestation of an unexpressed feeling. Ferenczi continued to emphasize the professional character of his relationship with Sokolnicka and his admiration for her rare psychoanalytical skills. He also stressed the importance of Freud's support for a budding psychoanalyst:

> Now, I think we should offer her the opportunity to restore normal polite relations with you, without which she also cannot exist as an analyst. She is, after all, only waiting for a sign from you, without which her pride forbids her to approach you. If you want to be especially friendly with her, then you will ask her sometime to let off a little steam toward you.
> (Falzeder and Brabant, 2000, p. 49)

Sokolnicka and Freud did meet eventually but the details of the encounter remain lost to history. He did offer to write the recommendation letters requested by Ferenczi, but only after she had already moved to Paris. This lack of support significantly complicated her resettlement and assimilation into the psychiatric circles. If Freud had named her his official representative, it would have been much easier for Sokolnicka to gain respect and promote psychoanalysis in France where it was still largely unrecognized at the time (Roudinesco, 1994). In French medical circles, "Freudian thinking was only known at that point through a number of purely theoretical critical studies which did not really enable one to judge its effectiveness" (Geissmann and Geissmann, 1998, p. 137).

Parisian literary-artistic circles were more open to psychoanalysis, especially surrealists gathered around André Breton. Unwelcomed in the psychiatric circles, also due to her non-medical status, Sokolnicka joined the group organized around the influential literary magazine *La Nouvelle Revue Française* established in 1909. She organized a psychoanalytic seminar "The Club of the Repressed" (Fr. Club de refoulés) for the bunch, which included the editor-in-chief, Jacques Riviére, and André Gide, André Breton, Jean Schlumberger, and Gaston Gallimard. They met once a week at her home. Sokolnicka's arrival, her status of the former analysand of Freud and Ferenczi, and her seminars, gave an impulse to the development of French psychoanalysis, first in literary circles. In April 1921 the first article on the use of psychoanalysis in literary interpretation was published in *La Nouvelle Revue Française* (Thibaudet, 1921). The medical establishment remained rather hostile to psychoanalysis. However, a group of young psychiatrists, including René Allenby, Angélo Hesnard, René Laforgue, and Eugène Minkowski, became interested in psychoanalysis. In 1925 they founded a psychoanalytically oriented journal, *L'Évolution Psychiatrique* (Psychiatric Evolution), which was a meeting point between medial psychiatry and psychoanalysis. The group later founded the Psychiatric Evolution Society and, together with Raymond and Ariane de Saussure, Eduard Pichon, and Adrien Borel, organized the first Conference of the French-Speaking Psychoanalysts, in 1926 in Geneva. In her *Freud's Emissaries: The Transfer of Psychoanalysis Through the Polish Intelligentsia to Europe 1900–1939* (2023), Lena Magnone made a claim that virtually all of the first-generation French psychoanalysts (with the sole exception of Marie Bonaparte) were introduced into psychoanalysis by Sokolnicka, including Françoise Dolto and Rudolf Loewenstein (who later became the analyst of Jacques Lacan).

In the winter of 1922, Sokolnicka briefly analyzed André Gide. Possibly only interested in acquiring material for his new novel, he interrupted the treatment after only six sessions. At the time he was working on the psychological novel *The Counterfeiters*, published in 1925. It tells a story of a 13-year-old boy, Boris, in therapy with a Polish physician, Mme Sophroniska. The treatment can be designated as child analysis. The patient suffers from similar symptoms to the "boy from Minsk," described in Sokolnicka's study from 1920. In the novel, Doctor Sophroniska is clearly mocked: "she has few doubts and is totally absorbed with her subject, which seems to give her both therapeutic satisfaction and triumphant excitement" (Geissmann and Geissmann, 1998, p. 146).

In 1922 or 1923 physician and child psychiatrist Georges Heuyer invited Sokolnicka to participate in the weekly meetings at the Sainte-Anne Psychiatric Hospital, during which psychiatrists presented case studies. Due to her non-medical status, her contributions to the discussions were largely disregarded by other participants, who showered her with questions to discredit her (Groth, 2015). After just three months she was either uninvited by the new director of the hospital, Henri Claude, or resigned herself.

After leaving Sainte-Anne, Sokolnicka, still the only analyst qualified to teach in Paris, became a training analyst. She taught, among others, psychiatrist René Laforgue and pediatrician Édouard Pichon. She was one of the founders of the Paris Psychoanalytical Society in November 1926, serving as its vice president for two years, while her former student, Laforgue, was named president. Sokolnicka was also a member of the Polish Socialist Party (PPS) in France (Magnone, 2016, p. 9).

Later Life and Death

Following her analysis with Freud in 1925, Princess Marie Bonaparte became his official envoy in France. Although, like Sokolnicka, she was also a lay analyst, she enjoyed a welcoming reception in Paris. Bonaparte's entrance into French psychoanalytical circles marks the disappearance of Sokolnicka from Freud's correspondence with his colleagues.

Sokolnicka became visibly less active on the French psychoanalytic scene since 1930. She published less and saw fewer patients. She once more struggled financially. When the first training institute of psychoanalysis opened in France in January 1934, she joined it as a training analyst, while Freud's favorite, Marie Bonaparte, was named its director. We know that in

Figure 11.1 Eugenia Sokolnicka, early 1930s.
Copyright: Revue Française de Psychanalyse.

May 1934 Sokolnicka was supposed to teach a short course on the psychoanalysis of character disorders, but we don't know if the course even started. On May 19, at the age of 58, Sokolnicka took her own life by gas poisoning. It is impossible to known if her decision was affected by the sociopolitical situation in Europe. At the time of her death, Hitler was already in power in Germany and had slowly initiated the devastation of the Jewish population.

After her untimely death, Sokolnicka was largely forgotten as a pioneer psychoanalyst. At the same time, she was immortalized in a ridiculed way in Gide's famous novel. It appears that only one of her French contemporaries, her former analysand and lifelong friend, Eduard Pichon, publicly acknowledged her contributions toward introduction of Freud's doctrine in France and psychoanalytic training:

> A great void has suddenly been created in the Paris Psychoanalytical Society with the unexpected death of Mme Sokolnicka. She was the first to bring true psychoanalytical culture and direct clinical knowledge of

psychoanalytical methods. Although she did not have a medical degree, she was the only one who could train future psychoanalysts. [. . .] For us, French psychoanalysts, the arrival of Mme Sokolnicka in Paris, in 1921, is a memorable date. Before psychoanalysis was known only through purely theoretical studies that hardly allowed us to judge the efficient value of Freud's concepts. With Mme Sokolnicka came a psychologist who has learned from the best sources, and a specialist able to effectively apply the method to specific cases. [. . .] The Paris Psychoanalytic Society owes a lot to Mme Sokolnicka not only because she was the first one to introduce psychoanalysis to France but also because of her didactic activity, which has shaped many of us.

(Pichon, 1934, pp. 588, 597–598, 603)

Sokolnicka's biography became more well known in the 1990s and early 2000s, as part of the wave of interest in early female psychoanalysts, most importantly thanks to the efforts of a Polish psychoanalyst, Jarosław Groth.

Sophie Morgenstern: Childhood, Early Life, and Education

Around 1924 Eugenia Sokolnicka started treating an acquaintance of hers, Sophie Morgenstern. The two women had met as students, at the Burghölzli Hospital. The details of the analysis remain unknown.

Sophie Morgenstern was born Zofia Kabatschnik on April 1, 1875, in Grodno (now Hrodna in Belarus) then in Russian-occupied Poland formally known as the Congress Kingdom of Poland, to a Jewish family. Little is known about her familial background or her upbringing, education, and early life in general. At an unknown time, she married Abraham Morgenstern and had a daughter with him, Laure, in 1897.

More is known about her university education. In 1906, at the age of 31, Morgenstern began to study medicine at the University of Zurich. During that period, she met and married Abraham Morgenstern. Her time at the Zurich university overlaps with Sabina Spielrein, one of many Russian Jewish female students there, but no record of their possible interactions exists. Morgenstern took her medical degree in 1912, a year after Spielrein, based on a dissertation "About Some Mineral Components of the Thyroid Gland" (Matrikeledition, Universitätat Zürich). After graduation, she traveled to Russia to obtain a state medical diploma required to practice medicine in Russia, including the Congress Kingdom of Poland (Parcheminey, 1947).

Emigration to Zurich

In the 1915–1917 period, Morgenstern returned to Zurich to work under Eugen Bleuler at the Burghölzli Clinic. It seems that the director valued her work, as she was gradually promoted from the position of a voluntary assistant to the first assistant. Finally, she was appointed the assistant doctor at another psychiatric hospital, in Münsterlingen (Parcheminey, 1947), famous for being the place of activity of Hermann Rorschach in the early 1910s. Bleuler's son, Manfred, remembered Morgenstern to be a "vivacious woman, interested in all sort of things, charming and intelligent" (qt. in Geissmann and Geissmann, 1998, p. 148).

At the Burghölzli, Morgenstern acquainted herself with psychoanalytic ideas. She met and befriended there a Polish-born psychiatrist and psychiatric phenomenologist, Eugène Minkowski. After completing his studies in medicine, Minkowski joined the Burghölzli Clinic as Bleuler's assistant at the outbreak of the First World War. His wife, Polish physician and psychiatrist Françoise Minkowska-Brokman, also studied under Bleuler. Around the same time that she befriended Minkowski and Minkowska-Brokman, Morgenstern first met Eugenia Sokolnicka. All three left Zurich for Paris in the early 1920s. This might have influenced Morgenstern's decision to relocate there around 1924. About her decision to move to France, Claudine Geissmann and Pierre speculated: "perhaps she even thought she would join this woman [Sokolnicka] with whom she had much in common" (Geissmann and Geissmann, 1998, p. 149).

Emigration to Paris

After arriving in Paris, Morgenstern started an analysis with Sokolnicka. We may only assume that Morgenstern felt less isolated in France thanks to that analysis—with a Polish woman, an immigrant, and in her mother tongue.

In 1925, physician and child psychiatrist Georges Heuyer co-founded, with a Polish-born psychologist, Jadwiga Abramson, a Clinic of Pediatric Neuro-Psychiatric in Paris and took up the position of its director (Guey and Boussion, 2010). A year after she arrived in Paris and until her death in 1940, Morgenstern worked as his assistant "carrying out work in the laboratory and at the psychoanalysis outpatient's clinic" (Geissmann and Geissmann, 1998, p. 149). Like Bleuler before him, Heuyer greatly appreciated Morgenstern's work. Differently from Sokolnicka, he had known her for 15 years. In the preface to Morgenstern's book, *Child Psychoanalysis*, from 1937, he claims that Morgenstern used psychoanalysis to successfully solve psychological problems in children who had very complicated and seemingly insoluble family situations (Heuyer, 1937).

Morgenstern joined the Paris Psychoanalytical Society (SPP) in 1929 as its full member. Her series of lectures on "The Structure of Neuroses Where the Ego Is Prevalent" (Geissmann and Geissmann, 1998, p. 150), scheduled for 1940, were cancelled due to the war. Morgenstern worked as a training analyst at the SPP institute from its establishment in 1934 until her death in 1940, teaching on the subject of infantile neurosis. The institute was shut down in the spring of 1940 due to the Nazi occupation.

Pioneer of Child Analysis in France

Possibly inspired by her former analyst, Sokolnicka, Morgenstern became one of the very first child analysts in France. Between 1927 and 1939, she authored 15 papers, in French and German, mostly in the field of child analysis. She published two books, both in French: *Psychanalyse infantile. Symbolisme et valeur clinique des créations imaginatives chez l'enfant* or *Child Psychoanalysis, Symbolism and Clinical Value of Imaginative Creations in Children* (in 1937) and *La Structure de la personnalité et ses déviations* or *The Structure of Personality and Its Deviations* (in 1939).

According to Morgenstern, infantile neurosis was always strongly connected to a family conflict: "The personalities of the father and the mother, and their behavior towards their child, play a primary role in infantile neurosis" (Morgenstern, 1937, p. 169).[2] The goal of the analysis was to first resolve or at least minimalize the family conflict, and then to allow the young patient to overcome the neurosis. She recommended an intense treatment consisting of everyday meetings, but short—about eight-months long (Aliprandi and Pati, 1999, p. 200). Children were to remain with their families during the therapy. One benefit of this was that since the child's inner conflicts were embedded in the family situation, being at home helped them understand the roots of their symptoms. Second, this allowed treatment of the conflicts emerging during the therapy. Morgenstern also encouraged parents of neurotic children to undergo psychoanalytic treatment.

In an article from 1930, "La Psychanalyse infantile et son rôle dans l'Hygiène mentale" or "Child Psychoanalysis and Its Role in Mental

Hygiene," Morgenstern examined the difficulties that accompany the treatment of young patients.

> By becoming aware of the diversity of the many different pathologies in our little neurotics, of the family constellation, of the fact that it is not of his own volition that the child comes to undergo psychoanalytic treatment, and above all of the fact that he has not yet reached the formation of his personality with the mechanism of the superego well organized [...] we will understand the special difficulties of the task of child analysis. It is a new field, a science in the process of being developed, without the advantages of the directives of adult psychoanalysis.
>
> (pp. 153–154)

She concluded that since children felt that therapy had been imposed on them by their parents, they did not understand the purpose of it.

Like her former analyst Sokolnicka in her case of the boy from Minsk (1920, 1922), Morgenstern also stressed the fundamental importance of building a solid, trust-based relationship with young analysands. Both women believed that only after an analyst understands what is going on with the child can a healthy transference develop (a projection of feelings about someone else onto the therapist). "In the child, the feeling that he is in the presence of someone who understands his conflicts is the greatest help in creating the transference [which in some cases] played the main role in healing" (Morgenstern, 1930, p. 159).

In another article, "La Pensée magique chez l'enfant" or "The Magical Thought in Children" (1934), Morgenstern posed a question about the most appropriate language for a successful communication with young patients. She encouraged child analysts to try to understand their patient's magical thinking—the idea that one's thoughts influence the physical world, described by Sabina Spielrein (2019b/1923) and Jean Piaget (1930). It can be found "in all countries and among all peoples, in neurosis, in infantile thought and in dreams" (Morgenstern, 1934, p. 102). Young children use magical thinking to find answers and explanations to the most difficult questions about childbirth or death. "When a child is faced with phenomena, he is unable to understand with the means at his disposal, his curiosity is fully satisfied by magical thinking, which helps him create a world of his own" (p. 107).

Differently from Sokolnicka, Morgenstern believed in the benefits of play therapy.

> The greatest area of magical thinking in the child is play, which allows him to fulfill all his desires, to give free rein to his instincts. Only where the child creates his own game and even the objects he uses in his game, he shows full satisfaction. The most ingenious, but ready-made toys amuse him only for the first few days and remain out of use afterwards, because they prevent the child from drawing on his imagination and playing the role of the great magician who animates objects, subjects them to many tests, makes them correspond with his emotional needs at the given moment. This is why a child likes to play at home, at school and [why] he takes up the role of father, mother, child, servant, teacher, or student. The child even manages to rid himself of his family conflicts or to mimic these conflicts in his play.
> (Morgenstern, 1934, p. 101)

Morgenstern's main contribution to psychoanalysis was the use of drawing, sculpting, playing games, fantasizing, and storytelling into child analysis. Starting in 1926 with a mute nine-year-old boy, Jacques, she employed the technique of drawing when working with children younger than ten, who found the method of free associations to be too difficult (Morgenstern, 1927). Sabina Spielrein also used drawings in her pioneering work with children. In "Children's Drawings With Eyes Open and Closed," Spielrein used numerous case examples to compared drawings made with eyes open and "blind" ones (2019a/1931).

Morgenstern's research led her to believe that children express their inner conflicts through drawing, allowing the analyst to penetrate more deeply their unconscious tendencies. The deeper and more repressed the conflicts, the more elaborate and original the drawings and the more hidden the symbols (Morgenstern, 1927). Her 11-year-long study of drawings, dreams, games, and storytelling (1933) led to an investigation of children's imaginative creations published in her 1937 book, *Psychanalyse infantile. Symbolisme et valeur clinique des créations imaginatives chez l'enfant* or *Child Psychoanalysis, Symbolism and Clinical Value of Imaginative Creations in Children*.

Figure 11.2 Sophie Morgenstern (middle), speaking with Charles Odier and Odette Codet, 15th Congress of the International Psychoanalytical Association, Paris, 1938.

Copyright: Bourgeron—Rue des Archives/GRANGER.

Some argue that Morgenstern's interest in creativity, magical thought, images, myths, fairy tales, and drawings aligned with some of Jung's ideas.

Morgenstern is also sensitive to the exploration of human creativity and its relation to pathology. The emphasis which in those years is put onto the assumption of similarity/continuity between mentally ill people and children [. . .] is present also in her thinking and makes her prioritize the study [. . .] of the characteristics of magical thought in a way that resents assonances with Jung's theories.

(Aliprandi and Pati, 1999, p. 196)

The Case of Jacques

One of her most famous cases was that of the aforementioned Jacques, published in "Un Cas de Mutisme Psychogène" or "A Case of Psychogenetic

Mutism" in 1927. They started treatment four months after the boy had stopped speaking, on November 4, 1926. After seeing his informative drawings made at home, and "struck [. . .] by the anxious expressions of the people depicted" (Morgenstern, 1927, p. 493), Morgenstern encouraged him to continue drawing during sessions:

> Having noticed that Jacques's only means of expression was drawing, I used it for the treatment. From the first session on I had him draw. I gave these drawings interpretations that Jacques approved or disapproved of with nods. This is how I managed to help him express his unconscious conflicts. I asked him if he had a sorrow, when he answered affirmatively to my question, I said to him: "Draw it for me."
>
> (p. 494)

Jacques's conflict was rooted in the family situation. Morgenstern attributed his silence to "the fear that his tongue would be cut out to punish him for having touched himself, and to the need to be punished for his desire for the death of his father" (p. 503).

The method chosen by Morgenstern proved highly successful. Jacques started to go away and his attitude toward the analyst gradually changed from hostile to friendly. Finally, on January 23, 1927, after less than three months of therapy, he started speaking again. "At first, he only answered in a low voice and with very abrupt words. But, little by little, he managed to express himself aloud" (p. 500). Morgenstern went over all of his drawings with him, confirming her earlier interpretations.

Morgenstern attributed the success of therapy to healthy transference and the use of drawings:

> We have seen in our case what role the transference that Jacques effected on his psychoanalyst had played. As soon as this transfer took place, Jacques had no more difficulty in revealing his deepest conflicts to us. [. . .]. The drawings of our patient contain all the psychological mechanisms noted by Freud: condensation (coitus and castration in the same drawing); transposition from bottom to top: the patient's tongue, head, hands are cut off, being only symbols of the sexual organ; identification: Jacques identifies my person with his own and that of his mother and makes me suffer all the horrors with which he believed his mother and himself were threatened; overdetermination: Jacques represents the same

subject to us several times, and in the most different forms; and finally the transference, which played the main role in the cure of our patient.

(pp. 504, 503)

Another one of her analysands and future well-known psychoanalyst, Françoise Dolto, developed the technique of drawing in therapy further, most importantly in her *The Unconscious Image of the Body* (1984). According to her, children's drawings represent their bodies. It is mainly through drawings that an analyst can reach infantile unconsciousness and understand inner conflicts, as young children are not yet able to conduct free associations.

Later Life and Death

The sociopolitical situation of the late 1930s deeply impacted Morgenstern's life. According to her former analysand turned colleague, Françoise Dolto, Morgenstern was experiencing "a dramatic internal situation" in the final years of her life (qt. in Mons, 2017, p. 186). Her husband died sometime before the Second World War, in unknown circumstances. She had likely been affected by the fact of Sokolnicka's death in 1934. Two years later her only daughter, Laure, a gifted art historian, died from a complication during surgery. She must have had the fate of her family—in the Nazi-occupied Poland—on her mind. In 1940 the psychanalytic training institute in Paris closed. Morgenstern, who reportedly had very few friends outside the psychoanalytic community, became isolated. Furthermore, it is very likely that as a result of the 1940 Vichy government anti-Jewish laws depriving Jews of the right to hold public office, it became harder for Morgenstern to regularly meet with her young patients. Still, she refused to flee Paris with Dolto to the south of France where the latter had friends able to help them (Mons, 2017, p. 186).

Morgenstern committed suicide either on June 13, 1940, a day before the Nazis marched into Paris (Parcheminey, 1947; Nölleke, 2007–2023), or on June 16, two days after they occupied the city (Geissmann and Geissmann, 1998). She was only 55 years old.

Eugenia Sokolnicka and Sophie Morgenstern: Émigrés

Sokolnicka and Morgenstern both left Poland and resettled to Paris voluntarily, regardless of the sociopolitical situation of the time. Nevertheless, every emigration is a form of internal exile that usually precludes return.

The hope of return or nostos is impossible. An exile belongs "to no place, neither departure nor arrival" (Prete, 1996, p. 27). In this "non-place" between departure and arrival, an immigrant has to go on with their difficult life. It seems that both Sokolnicka and Morgenstern left Poland, but never really "arrived" in France. They experienced uprooting, probably nostalgia for Poland, and isolation. Their immigration had a component of a loss of language. Like many early pioneers of psychoanalysis from East Central Europe, Sokolnicka and Morgenstern were fluent in German. This allowed them to study in Zurich and undertake analyses in German with Freud and Ferenczi (Sokolnicka) or work at the Burghölzli Clinic in Switzerland (Morgenstern). Furthermore, their proficiency in German allowed them to read psychoanalytic literature, then predominantly written in German. Interestingly, however, not untypically for Polish analysts of the period, neither of them published any psychoanalytic works in Polish (Sokolnicka published a Polish textbook). Sokolnicka wrote her paper on the case of the boy from Minsk in German despite communicating with her patient in Polish. It is known that Sophie Morgenstern treated several Polish children in Paris in the Polish language, but she also did not publish in her mother tongue, hence, did not contribute in this way to the development of psychoanalysis in Poland. Possibly, their complex and painful experiences of immigration played an important role in their decisions to take their lives. Or maybe, as stated by Emmanuel Levinas, "suicide appears as the final recourse against the absurd" (Levinas, 1987, p. 50).

Notes

1 I would like to thank Klara Naszkowska for her help in researching and editing this chapter, and especially for directing me toward Polish sources.
2 For texts where no English translation exists, such as this one, the quotations were translated by Klara Naszkowska.

Archival Sources

16764. Matrikeledition, Universitätat Zürich, "Morgestrern (geb. Kabatschnik) Frau Sophie."

Reference List

Aliprandi, M. and Pati, A. M. (1999). *L'albo della psicoanalisi infantile*. Milano: Feltrinelli.
Bleuler, E. (1913). Kritik der Freudschen Theorie. *Internationale Zeitschrift für Psychoanalyse*, 2(1), 62–66.

Ellenberger, H. (1970). *The Discovery of the Unconscious. The History and Evolution of Dynamic Psychiatry*. New York: Basic Books.

Falzeder, E. and Brabant, E. (Eds.) (2000). *The Correspondence of Sigmund Freud and Sándor Ferenczi, Vol III: 1920–1933*. P. T. Hoffer (Trans.). Cambridge and London: Belknap Press.

Ferenczi, S. (2019). *Further Contributions to the Theory and Technique of Psychoanalysis*. J. I. Suttie (Trans.). London: Routledge (Orig. publ. 1926).

Freud, S. (1953). *Analysis of a Phobia in a Five-Year-Old Boy*. J. Strachey (Trans.). In J. Strachey (Ed.), *SE, Vol. X: The Case Histories* (pp. 3–149). London: Hoggard Press (Orig. publ. 1909).

Geissmann, C. and Geissmann, P. (1998). *A History of Child Psychoanalysis*. London and New York: Routledge.

Graf-Nold, A. (2001). The Zürich School of Psychiatry in Theory and Practice. Sabina Spielrein's Treatment at the Burghölzli Clinic. *Journal of Analytical Psychology*, 46, 73–104.

Groth, J. (2015). Eugenia Sokolnicka. A Contribution to the History of Psychoanalysis in Poland and France. *Psychoanalysis and History*, 17(1), 59–86.

Guey, E. and Boussion, S. (2010). Le fonds Georges Heuyer (1884–1977): un XXe siècle scientifique à l'orée de la psychiatrie infantile et de ses ramification. *Revue d'historie de l'enfance "irrégulière." Le Temps de l'historie*, 12, 215–229.

Hesnard, A. and Laforgue, R. (1925). Aperçu l'historique du mouvement psychanalytique en France. *L'Évolution Psychiatrique*, 1, 11–26.

Heuyer, G. (1937). *Introduction to Morgenstern, S. Psychanalyse infantile. Symbolisme et valeur clinique des créations imaginatives chez l'enfant*. Paris: Denoel.

Hug-Hellmuth, H. (1919). *A Study of the Mental Life of the Child*. J. Putnam and M. Stevens (Trans.). Washington, DC: Nervous & Mental Disease Pub. Co. (Orig. Publ. 1913).

Kallivayalil, R. A. (2016). The Burgholzli Hospital: Its History and Legacy. *Indian Journal of Psychiatry*, 58(2), 226–228.

Levinas, E. (1987). *Time and the Other*. R. A. Cohen (Trans.). Pittsburg, PA: Duquesne UP.

Lieberman, E. J. and Kramer, R. (Eds.) (2012). *The Letters of Sigmund Freud and Otto Rank. Inside Psychoanalysis*. Baltimore, MD: John Hopkins UP.

Magnone, L. (2016). *Emisariusze Freuda. Transfer psychoanalizy do polskich sfer inteligenckich przed drugą wojną światową, Vol. II*. Kraków: Universitas.

Magnone, L. (2023). *Freud's Emissaries: The Transfer of Psychoanalysis Through the Polish Intelligentsia to Europe 1900–1939*. T. Bhambry (Trans.). Lausanne: Sdvig Press.

May, U. (2007). Freud's Patient Calendars: 17 Analysts in Analysis with Freud (1910–1920). *Psychoanalysis and History*, 9(2), 153–200.

Mons, I. (2017). *Donne dell'anima. Le pioniere della psicoanalisi*. Roma: Viella Editrice.

Morgenstern, S. (1927). Un Cas de Mutisme Psychogène. *Revue Française de Psychanalyse*, 1(3), 492–504.

Morgenstern, S. (1930). La Psychanalyse infantile et son rôle dans l'Hygiène mentale. *Revue Française de Psychanalyse*, 4(1), 136–162.
Morgenstern, S. (1933). Quelques aperçus sur l'expression du Sentiment de culpabilité dans les Rêves des Enfants. *Revue française de psychanalyse*, 6, 155–174.
Morgenstern, S. (1934). La Pensée magique chez l'enfant. *Revue Française de Psychanalyse*, 7(1), 98–115.
Morgenstern, S. (1937). *Psychanalyse infantile. Symbolisme et valeur clinique des créations imaginatives chez l'enfant*. Paris: Éditions Denoël.
Morgenstern, S. (1939). *La Structure de la personnalité et ses déviations*. Paris: Éditions Denoël.
Nölleke, B. (2007–2023). *Psychoanalytikerinnen. Biografisches Lexikon*. Online at www.psychoanalytikerinnen.de/. Accessed Mar. 10, 2023.
Nunberg, H. and Federn, E. (Eds.) (1975). *Minutes of the Vienna Psychoanalytic Society, Vol. III: 1910–1911*. M. Nunberg (Trans.). New York: International Universities Press.
Parcheminey, G. (1947). Sophie Morgenstern. Notice parue. *L'Évolution Psychiatrique*, 1, 12–13.
Piaget, J. (1930). *The Child's Conception of Physical Causality*. New York: Harcourt Brace.
Pichon, E. (1934). Eugénie Sokolnicka (14 juin 1884–19 mai 1934). *Revue Française de Psychanalyse*, 7(4), 589–603.
Prete, A. (1996). *Nostalgia*. Milano: Cortina Raffaello.
Roudinesco, É. (1994). *Historie de la psychanalyse en France. Vol I: 1885–1939*. Paris: Fayard.
Sokolnicka, E. (1906). *Kurs elementarny Zoologji, Botaniki i Mineralogji*. Łódź: Wydawnictwa Pedagogiczne Księgarni Ludwika Fiszera.
Sokolnicka, E. (1920). Analyse einer infantilen Zwangsneurose. *Internationale Zeitschrift für Psychoanalyse*, 6(3), 228–241.
Sokolnicka, E. (1922). Analysis of an Obsessional Neurosis in a Child. *The International Journal of Psychoanalysis*, 3, 306–319.
Sokolnicka, E. (1931). Les dynamismes des névroses et la psychanalyse. *Prophylaxie mentale*, 6, 417–425.
Sokolnicka, E. (1932). Sur un cas de guérison rapide. *Revue Française de Psychanalyse*, 5(5), 440.
Spielrein, S. (2019a). Children's Drawings with Eyes Open and Closed. J. Gresh and P. Cooper-White (Trans.). In P. Cooper-White and F. Kelcourse (Eds.), *Sabina Spielrein and the Beginnings of Psychoanalysis. Image, Thought, and Language* (pp. 330–366). London and New York: Routledge (Orig. publ. 1931).
Spielrein, S. (2019b). Some Analogies between Thinking in Children, Aphasia and the Subconscious Mind. J. Gresh et al. (Trans.). In P. Cooper-White and F. Kelcourse (Eds.), *Sabina Spielrein and the Beginnings of Psychoanalysis: Image, Thought, and Language* (pp. 301–322). London and New York: Routledge (Orig. publ. 1923).
Thibaudet, A. (1921). Psychanalyse et critique. *La Nouvelle Revue Française*, 91, 467–481.

Chapter 12

Thinking Cure
Jewish Psychoanalyst Alberta Szalita, From Warsaw to New York

Ewa Kobylińska-Dehe

What Happened in 1943?

> Not a single member of my family had survived. All had perished, shot by Germans or Ukrainians. Among the dead from our household were my husband, Zonia Zenoby; his father, Dr. Friedmann Pemow, and his mother, Rosa, as well as Rosa's sister, Eva [. . .]. I had also lost my father and mother, my maternal grandfather, my four sisters, Sara, Esther, Mina and Fanny [. . .], my older brother and his wife [. . .], three sisters [of my mother], my Aunts Rivka, Ester and Mania. There were two uncles, Isaak and Berish, as well. They, as well as their spouses and children were dead. In total, 21 family members were murdered in Lutsk.
>
> (Szalita, 2005, pp. 95–96)

The terrible news reached Alberta Szalita in the fall of 1943, in Moscow, when she received a letter from Warsaw. She wrote, "I felt like something was switched off in my head [. . .]. [I]t was as if I were *afraid* to think" (Szalita, 2005, pp. 96–97, original emphasis). I found this memory in a little book published in 2005 by a 95-year-old Szalita, a Warsaw doctor and New York City psychoanalyst. "[I]t was as if I were *afraid* to think" was the sentence that got engraved in my memory for good.

Why have I decided to tell her life story and how do I intend to do that? I can readily answer the first question: it is an effort to bring back from oblivion the unsung and forgotten Polish psychoanalysts. The answer to the second question, "How to tell such a story?" is more complex. The Holocaust voided preexisting meanings, narratives, and theories (cf. Rüsen, 2020, 2021). Since then, historians, artists, and psychoanalysts have been searching for new ways to cope with this collapse of meaning. They have faced an unavoidable dilemma. On the one hand, notions and ideas have a cognitive function. Without them, thinking does not exist. Additionally, naming

DOI: 10.4324/9781003455844-17

has a containing purpose. However, on the other hand, generalization and narrative structures may divert attention from an individual experience of extreme trauma. Trauma can even be stigmatized by being "encapsulated" in a concept. Let us consider, for example, William G. Niederland's "a death engram" that marked the survivors of death camps (Niederland, 1980, p. 232, cf. 1968).

The dilemma becomes more extreme when we are dealing with totalities; when we confront the totality of a concept or narrative with the imperative of the unspeakable or even silence often bordering on a prohibition against thinking. Still, the limits and forms of what can be expressed vary. Historian Friedhelm Boll, who conducted many interviews with Holocaust survivors and victims of Stalinism, believes that people are too eager to accept some things as untellable because they are resistant to hearing about them and because the survivors are reluctant to speak (Boll, 2001).

In the 1980s, historians developed an interesting new method of microhistory. It focuses on collecting all available bits and pieces of information from multiple sources with the goal of telling a detailed story recreating unique, individual experiences and opposing the reductionist power of generalization. While this may be consistent with the paradigm of the "memory turn," excessive "microscopization" may cause truth and universality to split into tiny fragments and particularities. Microhistory resembles the attempts of present-day psychoanalysis to capture and describe microprocesses. Differing from historiography, however, clinical psychoanalysis has at its disposal a certain tool enabling access to the experience of the other through transference and "scenic understanding" (cf. Lorenzer, 2016).

As a psychoanalyst, I value the method of micro-storytelling (despite having some reservations). It has turned out to be a fruitful tool in Holocaust Studies as well. Recently, while reading *Night Without End* (Engelking and Grabowski, 2022) devoted to the fate of Polish Jews during the Second World War, I became aware of the fact that by telling a story of an individual in a thorough way, we make a considerable contribution to the restorative practice of remembering. At the same time, I realized that the method of micro-storytelling helps uncover more general psychological mechanisms from the perspective of a victim (p. 17). However, it is not just about capturing these mechanisms while preserving the singularity of an individual fate. It is also about universalism in the ethical sense; to the confrontation with Primo Levi's "If this is a man," a dilemma which concerns us all (Levi, 2003/1947).

The viewpoint described earlier sets a framework for this biographical essay about a woman whose life was marked by the Holocaust trauma. I will try to give justice to the uniqueness of her life while not excluding her important theoretical contributions. I owe it to Alberta Szalita who perceived psychoanalysis not only as a talking cure, but also as a thinking cure, and who believed that the core of a person lies in the courage to think "without a banister" (Arendt, 2018).

Surely, I am also not free of the dilemma outlined previously, trying to consider both universality and particularity. While searching for Szalita's traces in published materials, I repeatedly came across the following descriptions: a Polish psychoanalyst who lost her entire family in the Shoah—as if there had been no Szalita without the Holocaust. The reduction irritated me. On the other hand, I kept on asking myself almost obsessively: what are the psychological mechanisms enabling one to survive the trauma of the Shoah?

As I was reading the Foreword to Szalita's autobiography by Darel Benaim, I was moved by another thing. Benaim writes:

> This is not a holocaust story. [. . .] [This] is a tale of individual courage, audacity and determination. [. . .] [T]his memoir has the key elements of a good action story: a constant sense of danger in a world where a single false move could have fatal consequences.
>
> (Benaim, 2005a, p. 7)

This is an "amazing story." When giving me the book, Szalita's last analysand, affiliated with the Alanson White Institute in New York City, used similar words. Why are they stressing this? An entire family was murdered and all I hear is, "This is not a story about the Holocaust; this is an amazing story." It would be oversimplifying to see in this position only a common defensive reflex, which is what I first thought of until I realized something else. I understood that, for Szalita, an "amazing story" was a form of a rescue fantasy when she was separated from her family. The thought that one day she would be able to tell her loved ones about her experiences was consoling and calming. She decided to publish her story 60 years later, at the end of her life. I want to respect the wish of the 95-year-old Alberta Szalita and tell a story of survival, instead of a story of death (p. 7).

Figure 12.1 Alberta Szalita at home, Central Park & 85th West Street, New York City, 1992.
Reproduced with permission of Aviva Gitlin and Saul Szalita Gitlin.

"Amazing Story"?

Alberta Szalita was born in 1910 in Vladimiretz near Lutsk in present-day Ukraine (then Włodzimierzec near Łuck). She ends her memoir with a fantasy, in which she dreams of returning to that small town in Western Ukraine, remembered as the "paradise lost":

> For all the tragedies and triumphs of my life—my wartime trials and survival, the respect my psychiatric practice and writings have brought to me, my intriguing travels across the world, my two marriages, and even the apartment I've lived in for nearly 50 years [in New York City], with its view of the water and the city lights—some part of me [. . .] has longed to return to that splendid but simple home on the square [in Vladimiretz].
> (Szalita, 2005, p. 103)

Like many small towns in the region of Volhynia, Vladimiretz was a melting pot of languages, religions, and cultures. Tony Judt emphasizes the vibrant multiculturality of these places, while pointing out that we must not idealize them, since they had been regularly shaken by pogroms and riots (Judt, 2006, p. 22). Szalita remembers the place she grew up in the following way: "Each of the six schools I attended before university is linked in my memory with a specific melody. [. . .] These sound memoirs include Greek Orthodox prayers, Russian revolutionary songs, the Polish national anthem and a Catholic prayer still fresh in my mind" (Szalita, 2005, p. 13). However, she sees the cacophony of cultures as a reflection of the instability of these times. When Szalita was growing up, conflicts between Jews, Ukrainians, and Poles were quite mild in Volhynia, but in as little as 13 years—between 1932 and 1945—the region transformed into one of Timothy Snyder's "bloodlands":

> In the middle of Europe in the middle of the twentieth century, the Nazi and Soviet regimes murdered some 14 million people. The place where all of the victims died, the bloodlands, extends from central Poland to western Russia, through Ukraine, Belarus, and the Baltic States. [. . .] [M]ass violence of a sort never before seen in history was visited upon this region. The victims were chiefly Jews, Belarusians, Ukrainians, Poles, Russians, and Balts.
>
> (Snyder, 2010, pp. vii–viii)

As we know, there were victims but also many eager accomplices among residents of the "bloodlands."

In 1910 there were two churches on the main street of Vladimiretz: one Catholic and the other Eastern Orthodox. Szalita's impressive family home stood close by. It had two porches and a fruit and vegetable garden, and it was maintained by four servants. Among the second row of houses there was a Jewish synagogue and two Hassidic houses of prayer. Orthodox Hassidim shaped the image of the town. Streets resounded with Yiddish; Szalita's family also spoke Russian and Hebrew. Her parents were *Mitnagdim* or enlightened Jews, followers of the Vilna Gaon. Szalita's father was very well educated in Hebrew, the Bible, and the Talmud. He maintained high ethical standards and he raised his children in accordance with them: honesty, composure, clarity, discipline, and respect. Lying was considered a fundamental sin, and weaknesses were forbidden. Her father knew how to instill values in his children in a compelling way. He had at his disposal a never-ending repertoire of stories concealing subtle messages. Her mother's warmth and tenderness complemented his educational approach. Up until her death, Szalita felt her mother's loving gaze watching over her. Her mother knew how to advise, support, and comfort her neighbors. Szalita had an older brother and four younger sisters. Her family expected both boys and girls to study. Private tutors gave four-year-old Szalita her first Bible and Hebrew lessons, while her mother taught her to read Russian literature.

On the eve of the First World War, Russian officers moved into the Szalita family home and warned them of a bloody German invasion coming to Vladimiretz. Her parents decided to flee to Rostov-on-Don in southern Russia to save their six children. They stayed there for six years amidst the brutal Bolshevik Revolution. When her parents were arrested in 1918, eight-year-old Szalita had to take care of her younger siblings.

When the Polish-Soviet War was over in 1920, the entire family returned to Vladimiretz. As Russian immigrants, Szalita's parents were granted Polish citizenship that they kept until their deaths. Since Vladimiretz did not have a high school or *Gymnasium*, the family moved to Volodymyr (then Włodzimierz). Szalita graduated from a Polish state high school in 1929. Both she and her sister Sara dreamt of studying at the University of Warsaw. Szalita enrolled in medicine; Sara in Polish studies. Out of 400 Jews seeking to study at the university, only 20 were accepted. Only in passing Szalita mentioned harassment, the "bench ghetto," and the unwritten rule of *numerus clausus* limiting the number of Jewish students. Jewish medical students were treated worse than others. For example, they were allowed to perform autopsies only on children's corpses, which impeded their learning process.

After suffering financial losses, Szalita's father was unable to support her any longer. She minimized her expenses, tutored, rented little nooks in other people's living rooms and stores, and served as a night watchman to secure a few hours of sleep on a cot. Nonetheless, she wrote in her memoir, "I did well in school and grew to love Warsaw" (Szalita, 2005, p. 14). She fell in love with Warsaw as a student despite living in poverty and having to handle antisemitic harassment. In her second year of medical school, she met her future husband, Zonia Pemow. He was a student at the Gdańsk University of Technology, spending the summer holiday with his parents in Lutsk (then Łuck). Zonia's father, Doctor Pemow, was the director of the hospital in Lutsk, where Szalita volunteered. He instilled in her his passion for medicine.

After qualifying as a doctor in the spring of 1936, she started working at the Piłsudzki Neurological Clinic, and then, until the war broke, at the Berson and Bauman Children's Hospital in Warsaw under a brilliant Jewish physician, Anna Braude-Heller. The most immediate "medical" problem to be solved in September 1939 was to acquire gas masks for the ill children, while the city was under constant bombardment.

Fleeing Warsaw

When the war broke, Zonia wanted to leave Warsaw. Szalita initially wanted to stay but finally decided to flee with him to Lutsk, leaving the heavily bombarded city behind. On the way they learned that on September 17, 1939, Lutsk became part of the Soviet Union as a result of the Molotov-Ribbentrop Pact.

A new health care system was being organized in Lutsk. Szalita received a well-paid job in a local office of the Soviet Health Administration. Her position enabled her to save her family from deportation to Siberia. That was the fate that befell Polish intelligentsia, especially those who, like Szalita's parents, refused to hand over their Polish passports. At that time there was no way of knowing that Siberia might have been a safer place for them than Ukraine under the German occupation, considering the later extermination of Volhynian Jews.

On June 14, 1941, Szalita flew to Odessa by herself to attend a conference on avitaminosis. A week later Nazi Germany invaded the Soviet Union. Szalita got cut off from her family. Volhynia was under German occupation since the beginning of July 1941. Escape was virtually impossible. The German troops were moving faster toward the east than the refugees. In 1939 many Jews fled from the west of Poland to the eastern regions that had belonged to Poland before 1939, hoping to find refuge among the Jewish communities there, including in Volhynia. Further east (beyond the Polish border of 1939) there was no organized Jewish life, and Volhynian Jews had no illusions regarding the Soviet rule. As a result, the vast majority of Jews remained. They might have suspected that the Nazi occupation would be worse than the Soviet one. However, according to Snyder, at that time it was impossible to foresee the almost total annihilation.

A special action force, *Einsatzgruppe C*, commanded by Dr. Otto Rasch, encouraged the local population in Volhynia and the entire eastern front to rid the region of Jews and Bolsheviks, as part of the "self-cleansing action";

the killings were often initiated by local collaborators. Since the summer of 1942, German and Ukrainian police officers were murdering Jews near their homes (Snyder, 2007). Jewish inhabitants from Lutsk and Volodymyr were taken to a forest where pits had already been dug. They were told to get undressed and lay on the ground; 17,000 people were shot, including the entire Szalita family.

Cut off from the possibility of return home, Szalita found out that that she was pregnant. She was excited about the prospect of motherhood. Then, a Soviet medical committee decided that her abdomen was too large and that the pregnancy had to be terminated. At the same time, they didn't believe that Szalita was pregnant and decided to open her uterus. As a result, the baby (a boy) had to be removed and so did her womb. However, an incidentally detected tumor was left inside and it caused serious problems several decades later, in the States. For the first time since childhood Szalita cried inconsolably for days. She had wanted to have six children, like her parents. At the same time, she felt ashamed: no one ever cried in her family.

Working in the Gulag and Uzbekistan

Meanwhile, Szalita found a job as a physician in a gulag in Siberia. Horrific BBC news reports, the harsh winter, and the grim atmosphere of the place made her want to move closer to the western border . . . and to her family whose fate was still unknown to her. She wrote in her memoir about her undying will to live, to "tell her story later." She managed to get to Uzbekistan. At that time, thousands of refugees were fleeing war-stricken territories to Tashkent, including many physicians from Moscow, Odessa, and Leningrad (now Saint Petersburg). The only places where doctors were able to work were collective farms (kolkhoz).

With time, Szalita learned the Uzbek language and gained popularity as a doctor. She provided home visits, arriving in a carriage drawn by a mare named Rosa Luxemburg and assisted by a young girl, Oktabrina, named after the October Revolution. During home visits, while tending to her patients, Szalita, then 32 years old, always honored Uzbek traditions, cultural practices, and rituals. While applying drugs to accelerate wound healing, she assured her patients that she had put a frog on them—the most popular local remedy, believed to be infallible. She later used these experiences in her work with schizophrenics. She knew, for example, how to calm a triggered, paranoidal patient who believed himself to be Jesus. She assured him by saying she had nothing against the fact that he was Jesus. Szalita earned the respect of the village elders and the priest. When he greeted her with "Salaam-Aleikum," she replied "Aleikum a Salaam" and placed the flower he had presented to her behind her ear. She tried to avoid conflicts and to share responsibilities. Keeping kolkhoz workers healthy, she wrote, was her contribution against the war. She was lucky: no one died in the kolkhoz under her watch, which earned her a lot of respect among the locals. She writes in her memoir:

> Despite my good fortune, my seemingly interminable separation from my loved ones, total ignorance of what was happening to them, and inability to communicate with them continued to haunt me. My concern deepened when accounts of German atrocities in Poland and the Ukraine began to be reported in the press and on the radio. I tried to ignore these reports.
>
> (Szalita, 2005, p. 85)

Metropol Hotel

In the summer of 1943, an order came to the Uzbek Ministry of Health to send 20 physicians to Moscow. Szalita did not hesitate for a second. In Moscow, she stayed with distant relatives with whom she shared a room and hope: Ukraine at that time was already mostly liberated from the Germans. There, in the fall of 1943, she received the tragic news: her entire family had perished. "I felt like something was switched off in my head. [. . .] [I]t was as if I were *afraid* to think" (pp. 96–97, original emphasis).

In 1944 Szalita traveled to the city of Lublin in Poland with Dr. Emil Sommerstein, the head of the Central Committee of Polish Jews (CKŻP) responsible for providing repatriation assistance to Polish Jews in the USSR. At that time, the Polish communist government was being established in Lublin, on Soviet orders. Szalita became involved with the Health Care Organization of the CKŻP (Towarzystwo Ochrony Zdrowia Ludności Żydowskiej w Polsce, TOZ), an equivalent of the Society for the Protection of the Health of the Jews (OSE) in Poland.

In 1944–1945 she taught medical students at the University Clinic in the city of Łódź in Poland and helped organize the health care sector in the country. Her task was to take care of Nazi concentration camp survivors, mainly from Auschwitz and Majdanek near Lublin. She conducted a series of interviews with children who survived Majdanek. She later recalled that all of the children were completely devoid of emotions and exhibited "affective anesthesia," as Eugène Minkowski later labelled the phenomenon (Minkowski, 1948). The children were not in the state of apathy. They were active and capable of taking care of themselves and of taking chances, but they were helpless when it came to having an emotional reaction to others. Emotional denial allowed them to mobilize the energy they needed to survive. Thirty years later, Szalita would write about the need for temporary denial to slow down the process of confrontation with the reality of trauma. A loss of a parent cannot be mourned in early childhood. Grief comes much later. On the other hand, a long-lasting denial can lead to permanent dissociation and emptiness.

An American psychoanalyst, Paul Friedman, encouraged Szalita to establish a psychoanalytic clinic for survivors in Łódź. It would have been the first institution of this kind in the world. At that time, the psychological consequences of being imprisoned in a concentration camp were completely ignored. Szalita refused, explaining that psychoanalysts, with their heads in the clouds, ignored the most pressing needs of former prisoners for medical care. Her viewpoint was commonly shared at that time.

More than 200,000 Jews returned to Poland right after the war, including 160,000 from the Soviet Union. Almost all of them subsequently decided to leave the country for a number of reasons. Some did not want to live in the vast cemetery that postwar Poland had become, others had already experienced the brutality of the Soviet communist regime, while a handful wanted to help build a new homeland in Israel. The (often bloody) shadow of antisemitism fell on all these motives (cf. Krajewski, 2014). Szalita briefly commented on her decision to leave Poland: "I couldn't stand the anti-Semitism" (Szalita, 2005, p. 101). She immigrated to Paris in 1946 to become a medical director at OSE. Her responsibilities included organizing medical care for Jewish survivors, mainly from USSR and Poland, in several European countries and in displaced persons camps. A year later, she received a scholarship from the American Jewish Joint Distribution Committee (JDC) to study public health in America.

"I Ran From Grief; Grief Ran and Overtook Me"

"I ran from grief; grief ran and overtook me"—Szalita described her mental condition with the words of an English poet, Francis Quarles, written in

1635 (Szalita, 1974, p. 5; Quarles, 1861/1635, p. 115). She was functioning well on the outside, but felt internally torn into pieces. She was unable to focus and to study. A friend encouraged her to consult a fellow émigré psychoanalyst Frieda Fromm-Reichmann. At first, Szalita reportedly strongly rejected the idea: "There's no point; I'm not interested" (Benaim, 2005b, p. 105). She felt humiliated and angry at the thought that she might need help. Nevertheless, she soon entered psychoanalysis with Fromm-Reichmann's friend, Marjorie Jarvis, of the Washington-Baltimore Center for Psychoanalysis.

Szalita finally described her grieving process 30 years later in *Grief and Bereavement* (1974), where she used an example of her patient who had had parallel experiences. We may assume that Szalita herself was also the patient. In the book, the patient is a 34-year-old nurse whose entire family had been murdered by their Ukrainian neighbors, on the order of the Germans. During the massacre, the patient, just like Szalita, was two thousand miles away, with her husband and three-year-old son. Although she was aware of the atrocities happening in Ukraine and Poland, she rejected the thought that such things might happen to her family. Immediately after receiving the tragic news, she felt the following: "'[s]omething snapped in my head', she said. 'It was as if a curtain had fallen down on a part of my brain and chopped off part of it'" (Szalita, 1974, p. 11). The patient told Szalita that she felt nothing, while simultaneously keeping busy all the time. She was unable to focus. Listening to music brought her relief, but she didn't understand the meaning of words. She became fearful and irritable. She desperately avoided thinking about her family. Whenever she did think about what happened to them, she felt she would either go mad or take her own life. On her commute to work, she would sometimes choose an empty subway car and scream her lungs out. She avoided all conversations about the Holocaust.

Three torturous years later the patient finally sought out therapeutic counselling. During psychoanalytic therapy she carefully reviewed her relationships with each of her family members. At first, she identified herself totally with each one of them, one by one. She mimicked their gestures, facial expressions, and their manners of speaking and behaving. Upon discovering that she was angry at them for abandoning her, she started having suicidal thoughts. She was fighting a pressing urge to punish herself and to self-harm, for example, by "accidentally" self-inflicting cigarette or boiling-water burns. Each of her loved ones maintained a life of their own within her. She conducted endless conversations with all of them; repeatedly asking each of them for forgiveness. A lot of time had to pass for her to accept the reality of their deaths.

On the basis of her own and her patient's experiences, Szalita distinguished three stages in the mourning process: (1) complete identification with a deceased family member. Some people stop at this phase. For the rest of their lives, they continue to try to fulfil the wishes of the deceased and thus avoid guilt. (2) A splitting of the identification leads to a conflict between submission and rebellion. (3) Finally, a review of the relationship with the deceased family member, with neither idealization nor blame, enables a necessary detachment. Szalita believed that it is highly possible for a person who underwent the process of mourning to feel more integrated and to come back to life. The process is not about accepting the loss, but about calming feelings that are too intense. It is not indifference but a kind of detachment, which can only happen if a mourner is separated enough from the lost object and has a life of his own. The process of mourning is similar to the analysis of transference. It is also a kind of mourning where one struggles to gain independence from parental figures, while attempting to integrate internal conflicts and ambivalences.

Szalita believed that not all who bereaved need therapy. The decisive issue is to establish a connection with an isolated introject, with or without therapy. According to Szalita,

> there are few psychiatric conditions that may not mask a delayed, unfinished, or absent mourning. Such a view may be challenged as an extreme oversimplification, for it virtually reduces the whole of psychiatry except schizophrenia to the pathology of mourning. Nevertheless, it is no oversimplification to assert that every human being has to face death in those close to him and his own death, and that the human condition is afflicted with sorrows, to which the schizophrenic is no less immune.
> (Szalita, 1974, p. 29)

In July 1949, while still in analysis, Szalita started to see her first psychotic patients at Chestnut Lodge in Rockville, Maryland, 18 miles from Washington, DC. The establishment of the Chestnut Lodge psychoanalytically oriented clinic for the treatment of psychotics, spearheaded by Frieda Fromm-Reichmann, was possible under the auspices of the broad-minded Washington-Baltimore Center for Psychoanalysis, of which Szalita was a member. While the psychoanalytic societies in New York City and Boston, mainly shaped by orthodox Freudians who emigrated from Vienna, were conservative and authoritarian, in the 1940s the Washington-Baltimore Psychoanalytic Society was open to experimentation. There was a spirit of the left-wing Berlin Institute of Psychoanalysis there, founded by Karl Abraham in 1910, where high standards of training went hand in hand with open-mindedness to innovative ideas, such as the so-called Child Seminar (Germ. *Kinderseminar*), the establishment of the Psychoanalytic Polyclinic in 1920, free-of-charge psychoanalytic treatment for workers and poor patients, and attempts at treating psychotic patients. Abraham, despite exhibiting some stiffness, must have been rather receptive to new psychoanalytic ideas since his three most prominent analysands, namely Melanie Klein, Karen Horney, and Frieda Fromm-Reichmann, spearheaded three very different psychoanalytic schools of thought (Hornstein, 2000, p. 32).

In Chestnut Lodge clinic Szalita found a "facilitating environment" (Winnicott, 1984). It was also a good place to hide from antisemitism and anti-German resentments spreading wide in America in the late 1940s.

Szalita had the ability to create and shape an environment, in which she and everyone around her felt safe, whether in a gulag, a kolkhoz, or a Muslim village. She respected all cultural customs and had organizational skills. All these traits came in handy at Chestnut Lodge: she became known as the Polish physician who knew how to connect and communicate with psychotic patients.

Many years after Szalita left Chestnut Lodge in 1953, legitimate questions have been raised regarding the rules of intense psychotherapy implemented by Frieda Fromm-Reichmann, who was a committed opponent of administering drugs. Today, psychoses are treated with a multifactorial therapy model. Still, therapists at Chestnut Lodge tried to give their patients a bit of hope and to build relationships with them.

In the early 1950s the attitude of both psychoanalysts and psychiatrists toward Chestnut Lodge—and Frieda Fromm-Reichmann personally—was becoming increasingly hostile. This has triggered traumatic memories in Szalita. Refugees who, like her, had lost their entire families and friends to murder deeply feared social condemnation and rejection. It might have been the reason behind Szalita's initial decision to reject Clara Thompson's invitation to conduct seminars on intensive psychotherapy at the William Alanson White Institute in New York. She changed her mind in 1953 and decided to move to New York for personal reasons, after meeting and then falling in love with a Polish chemist, Meier Mendelsohn, who was pursuing scientific research in the city. They met through a common Warsaw friend, psychoanalyst Gustav Bychowski (Kobylinska-Dehe, 2018, p. 179). Szalita later worked with Bychowski at the Institute for the Crippled and Disabled in New York. For the next 50 years she worked as a training and supervising analyst at the White Institute and the Columbia University Psychoanalytic Center.

Three months after her wedding to Mendelsohn on January 2, 1954, Szalita was diagnosed with lymphosarcoma. She refused the treatment: "if I have to die, I have to die" (Benaim, 2005b, p. 107). Around the same time her husband developed lung cancer. Nine years later, after Mendelsohn's death, Szalita spent a year in Israel, at the invitation of her psychiatrist colleagues. She was surprised by the absence of psychotherapeutic services in the Israeli hospitals and the lack of training programs in psychotherapy in the country. She developed such a program, supervised many Israeli psychiatrists, and finally co-founded the Tel Aviv Institute of Psychotherapy in 1971. For the next 30 years, Szalita taught and supervised candidates in Oslo.

Figure 12.2 Alberta Szalita with colleagues of the Abarbanel Mental Health Center, Bat Yam, Israel, March 1965.

Reproduced with permission of Aviva Gitlin and Saul Szalita Gitlin.

Psychosis, Trauma, and the Holocaust

Szalita shared a sense of social isolation and loneliness with her schizophrenic patients. They also felt completely alone with their experiences and excluded from the world. Inner loneliness is a state in which a person is unable to imagine that someone could share part of his or her experience, that there could be an empathic object. It is like falling out of the world or belonging to another species. Szalita had experienced this herself, when she was going through the states of a quasi-psychotic fragmentation and deep dissociation. In analysis, she was able to work through her own traumatic experience and transform it into an extraordinary sensitivity, later used to help the "lonely ones," as she called the schizophrenic patients.

From the viewpoint of contemporary psychoanalysis, it is astounding to realize the extent to which postwar metapsychology precluded many psychoanalysts from working with externally caused traumatic losses but focusing exclusively on intrapsychic conflicts (Kuriloff, 2014, p. 155). By turning their backs on the perished world of yesterday, these analysts employed a powerful defense mechanism, allowing them to start life anew. They could not have predicted that all that was dissociated would become a difficult legacy to overcome for the next generation. As we know today, children of both, Holocaust victims and Holocaust survivors, were often burdened with an ineffable load they were unable to carry.

Differently from many psychoanalysts who fled Europe and did not allow themselves the thought of confronting the trauma in clinical and theoretical work, Alberta Szalita addressed bereavement in her work. It opened her to her own experiences of pain and loss. This, in turn, allowed her patients and supervisees to face the traumas endured by their parents.

New York analyst Emily Kuriloff, who interviewed many psychoanalysts who were children of survivors, has suggested a possible conjunction between their capability to connect with psychotic patients and having worked through their own extreme trauma (Kuriloff, 2014). In any case, Szalita repeatedly stressed the importance of her own traumatic Holocaust experiences in her work with psychotic patients, as well as the profound impact of this work on her personally (Szalita, 1968).

Szalita learned from her own experiences that earlier loses are often overshadowed by more severe later losses. Patients who had lost their loved ones in the Shoah were ashamed and guilt-ridden when talking about a painful loss of their childhood dog or doll. Szalita created a mental space for these earlier losses. Evelyn Hartman, a Holocaust survivor from Kraków and Szalita's student, wrote about learning from her mentor about many different ways of connecting with traumatized patients. "Alberta taught me," said Hartman, "to listen more carefully, more subtly to myself, not just to the patient" (qt. in Kuriloff, 2014, p. 153).

Postwar psychoanalysis in America focused on autonomy, as opposed to an immature, symbiotic dependency. As Kuriloff has described (2014), mourners were treated as pariahs incapable of separation. Many of them felt that they had been excluded from the psychoanalytic community because of that (p. 155). In her paper "Reanalysis," Szalita wrote:

> Mourning and confrontation with death are not too popular themes in many analyses. [. . .] The tendency to avoid feelings and thoughts on death is natural to man. It brings out the deepest helplessness in his destiny. [. . .] I don't believe it is possible to think freely about life if one excludes death and denies it. Only too often both the analyst and the patient are in complicity about this omission.
> (Szalita, 1968, p. 97)

Epistemological Approach

Szalita was a highly respected therapeutic clinician. Her innovative theoretical concepts are less known. Her ideas, dismissed in the 1950s as unorthodox, today belong in mainstream psychoanalysis.

When traumatized Szalita arrived in the Unites States in 1946, she didn't know anyone. She found a mentor and friend in Frieda Fromm-Reichmann and a home at Chestnut Lodge. Possibly for this reason, she had remained reserved when discussing the nature of schizophrenia up until the end of her life. Then, she finally admitted that she did not believe at any time in the psychogenic nature of schizophrenic disorders. There is no "schizophrenic mother" as described by Frieda Fromm-Reichmann (1948). One of the conditions for successful therapy is to relieve parents of the etiological responsibility for their child's illness and get them as partners in the therapeutic process.

According to Szalita, successful therapy depends on many factors, including of intense exploration of the thinking process in therapy within the therapeutic relationship, which leads to structural changes in the patient's mind.

Integrating verbal and nonverbal communication leads to new connections in the brain, which in turn affect mental development.

Of course, in the 1950s Szalita could not prove scientifically what she had intuitively anticipated. This was at least two decades before neuroscientists, including 2000 Nobel Prize recipient Eric Kandel discovered and proved the neuroplasticity of brain structures as a result of interaction with the environment.

Szalita believed that psychotherapy helps to revise patients' self-perception and their understanding of the world around them, even if a psychotic process is irreversible. This, in turn, strengthens the healthier components of patients' personality, enabling them to better cope with their limitations.

Hence, Szalita discovered the process of changing the perspective, while acknowledging prior experiences that cannot be revoked. Her student, Marc Blechner, named the process "epistemological approach" (1997). Our experiences have a lasting impact that cannot be undone. However, by thinking and talking about them, and recontextualizing them, one can create new meanings that modify the preexisting ones, and change a perspective (Szalita and Kelman, 1964). Even schizophrenics are capable, to some extent, of learning how to think and applying the epistemological approach to their delusions and hallucinations. Similar concepts can be found in the work of Wilfred Bion and 30 years later in the work of Otto F. Kernberg.

Szalita was convinced that a therapist should not question the experiences of patients, even the delusional ones. If a patient said: Someone is hiding behind a tree, Szalita answered, "Let us suppose you were right. Why were you so frightened?" (Blechner, 2001, p. 68). In this way, a thought process can be initiated without having to question the perception of the patient. Reflection reduces fears, as patients are treated seriously and shielded from their own delusions. According to Szalita, schizophrenia consists mainly of a disruption of the ability to self-correct (Szalita, 1958). Psychotics are incapable of self-correction because, trapped in the immediacy of a concrete experience, they are paralyzed by unimaginable fear.

Psychoanalysis as the Thinking Cure

Contemporary psychoanalysis seems to be more interested in adaptation and regulation than self-knowledge and truth. The practice of self-discovery has been relegated to the background. Let us recall that Szalita understood psychoanalysis as a "thinking cure" rather than a "talking cure" (cf. Antonovsky, 1978, p. 398). She knew how to combine empathic listening and nonverbal communication used to reach deeply disturbed patients with an epistemological approach. Thinking was not an intellectual exercise for her. It belonged to spiritual life; it was an effort to think into oneself. When working with her psychoanalytic patients, Szalita focused on reinforcing a "capacity to look into themselves, to be with themselves" (Issacharoff, 1997, p. 628), rather than on helping them with internal, psychodynamic conflicts.

Thinking has to "graduate from a school of life." It starts by accepting things as they are. According to Hannah Arendt, highly respected by Szalita, philosophizing is the quintessence of being alive. It is not about theories but about internal balance. Szalita described it with her own term, "psychointegration." Szalita would say, in line with Winnicott, that what is needed is a "facilitating environment" in which the measure of things is not lost. The source of destructiveness is hybris, the loss of the measure of things (Szalita, 1994).

For Szalita, to think is to be able to shift perspectives and to survive loss, which is part of every psychoanalytic process. Her way of thinking corresponds with one of Hannah Arendt's most important reflections. On September 28, 1959, upon receiving the city of Hamburg's Lessing Prize, she said that "mastering" the past is impossible: "The best that can be achieved is to know precisely what it was, and to endure this knowledge, and then to wait and see what comes of knowing and enduring" (Arendt, 1968, p. 20). Szalita also believed that wounds could never heal completely. But one can have a meaningful relationship with them.

Intuition and Psychointegration

While in the 1950s psychoanalytic thinking was dominated by the Freudian concept of repression of unwanted or shameful content, Szalita started to discuss the splitting of the ego into "islands" as the main defense mechanism in psychopathology (1958, p. 47). Therapists help patients establish communication between the parts, the "islands" of feelings, thoughts, and behaviors, which were unconsciously split apart, to avoid fear. The reconnection of the "islands," called psychointegration, leads to the reduction of symptoms and reinforcement of the sense of continuity of oneself (Szalita, 1994).

Unlike John Rosen, who believed that a patient should view a defeated illness or a past psychotic episode as a foreign corpse, Szalita argued for continuity between the sick and the recovering person. They are one and the same. It is important that patients see their illnesses as part of themselves and integrate them like any other experience.

Szalita's understanding of psychointegration is twofold: first, it means increasing the patient's integrative capacity for mental integration as a result of the relationship with the therapist, which, in turn, leads, she assumed, to neurological changes in the brain; and second, the therapist's eclectic integration of various clinical and theoretical approaches. Her openness to different cultures, rituals, and languages influenced her preference for the idiosyncratic therapeutic style. While identifying as a Freudian, she also believed that one cannot live wisely according to a single theory; no single theory has solved the mystery of human mind and thinking (Szalita, 1994). In 1994 she wrote that present-day students of psychoanalysis are very familiar with theories but don't appreciate the importance of learning from one's experiences and of being a humanist. They forget that the main sources of our knowledge about the human soul are literature, philosophy, and history, not science (p. 109).

What a mind can do after experiencing loss is to tell a story, one of many that will live on. Such story has an embedded substance. No philosophical theory, analysis, or even the most profound aphorism matches a well-told story in terms of intensity and richness of meanings. The abundance of educational Hassidic tales told by Szalita's father comes to mind. Surely, storytelling and psychoanalysis have different narrative strategies. What they have in common is the act of talking to another human being.

Literature was an endless source of inspiration for Szalita in clinical work. She treated it as a precise cognitive tool, as resourceful as any other learning technique. Her seminars on literature at Columbia University became famous.

Personal analysis is not a sufficient or exclusive path to increasing empathy. A psychoanalyst or psychiatrist should learn from experience, especially from other people's experiences about themselves. Empathy is a specific instrument that allows one to deepen knowledge of another. It "is not a method; it is rather a skill to be used selectively [and] responsibly" (Szalita, 1981b, p. 19). Szalita's student Mark Blechner recalled:

> We read Ibsen's *The Wild Duck*, which deals very much with the issue of intent and effect that Szalita discusses in her essay on empathy. The play

raises the question, How much truth does anyone need? When is truth-telling valuable and when is it destructive?

(2001, p. 69)

Szalita used Dostoyevsky's character, Prince Myshkin, from his novel *The Idiot* as an example of destructive use of empathy—an obsessive need to always tell the truth regardless of the situation—to use it as a weapon against another human being. The need to comprehend and be understood transforms unnoticeably into the need to be right, not to be confused with love for truth.

Szalita stresses that since we, the analysts, make statements with a therapeutic goal in mind, we should use spontaneity in a disciplined way. Therapists, like artists, have a capability of eliciting emotions. However, unlike artists, they must be held accountable for the effects of their words: "I came to the conclusion that you cannot equate intention with effect; that's when I started to be different in my interpretations or whatever I had to say" (Issacharoff, 1997, p. 624). A successful therapy depends on the therapist's ability to recognize the needs of the patient, find a common language, and put his or her own needs aside.

Blechner recalled that Szalita gave her students space to work and made only sporadic comments, with her unforgettable Polish-Russian accent. Her colleagues called her the queen of one-liners. She communicated her observations in a single concise sentence while paying close attention to her patients. She was an expert at finding out what was most important. Like many other clinically talented psychoanalysts, she was unable to explain what she did but knew how to describe it in writing, like Frieda Fromm-Reichmann in *Principles of Intensive Psychotherapy* or Sándor Ferenczi in his *Clinical Diary*.

Together with Harold Searles, Harry Stack Sullivan, and Gregory Bateson, she belonged to the Chestnut Lodge study group on intuition. Intuition was for them a creative process of using a spontaneous, yet subtle, observation that evokes recollections from the past life and prior clinical situations. Szalita wrote about the importance of intuition in work with schizophrenics in her 1955 paper, "The 'Intuitive Process' and Its Relation to Work with Schizophrenics." All thoughts are produced in the process of "dreaming in waking life." Visual images help condense thoughts. Following a chain of complex steps, images continuously combine to create new forms. Some images reveal themselves in dreams. Therefore, a dream is not only a laboratory for the intuitive process, but also space in which thought is produced.

The direction of the dream is determined by desires; they are the organizing force. Intuitive processes are not that different from other thinking processes (Szalita-Pemow, 1955).

What to us is a dream is reality to a schizophrenic. The boundary between the conscious and the unconscious is permeable like in a dream. When working with schizophrenics, we have direct access to "dreaming in waking life" and can observe the process of thought development. Their productions are created following the principle described by Sigmund Freud as the "primary process": a free flow of contradictions, thoughts, and desires, repeating, and suddenly stopping (Freud, 1953/1900). It is very challenging for therapists. They must have the ability to temporarily loosen their own defense mechanisms and allow the permeability of their own boundaries. Therapists must be capable of listening to the patient, developing the images based on what the patient had said, translating the images into thoughts (namely abstract them from their literalness), binding anxiety, and finally presenting them to the patient in an appropriate form. These very complex operations are only possible intuitively. Intuitive understanding enables therapists to follow their patients. Szalita believed that in the case of schizophrenic patients, their distorted perception of the world should be regarded as an immediate expression of their realities, not interpreted as metaphorical. Hence, the objective of the therapist is to relate to the patient at the level of reality nearest to the patients' reality.

Szalita had a talent for understanding deeply disturbed people. I would like to illustrate it with clinical evidence. Here is the first session with Ms. N., a young, very aggressive schizophrenic patient who gave Szalita a similarly sounding nickname, "Chiquita," possibly because it was easier for her to pronounce.

> She threw a careful look at me, and said, "I've heard that you are from Bulgaria. Is it true?" "No," I replied, "I am from Poland." "That is the same thing," she answered angrily. [. . .] I smiled and said, "Possibly." She then proceeded, "Frieda [Fromm-Reichmann] told me that you were in France, and you talk Paris. France, Paris, Paris, France. . . . Is the Rue des Capucines all right to live in?" [Szalita meditated briefly how to answer]. "It is a somewhat noisy street, but it is quite all right to live in."

Szalita must have sensed that the patient was giving her a second chance. Ms. N. was content: "That is exactly what I felt about it. [. . .] My brother was of a different opinion." Until now the patient was sitting on the floor. Now she got up and sat down in an armchair facing the therapist, saying, "I'd better be nice to this nice little lady." A plane passed over the veranda and the umbrella making a sound: "Did you ever fly?" asked N., to which Szalita nodded. N: "'I was always afraid to fly [. . .] and my brother chose to be a flier during the war.' Her facial expression changed, and she mumbled, 'Uniform . . . medal d'or . . . buttons . . . ten buttons.'"

It seemed that she had forgotten Szalita's existence. The therapist watched the patient calmly while her thoughts drifted to the war time, when she listened to the sounds of bomber engines to assess how far they were. N. muttered something unintelligibly. Her face darkened and she repeated: "Isle de France . . . Isle de France . . . a dancer with an umbrella." She looked at the therapist with a begging gaze. Szalita replied, "'Are you trying to tell me that you had suicidal thoughts on the Isle de France?' [. . .] She said, 'Ye-e-es'. [. . .] [S]he appeared surprised and relieved" (Szalita, 1981b, pp. 10–11).

At first Szalita struggled to explain to her colleagues how she had arrived at the idea. She didn't know then that Ms. N. had come back from a trip to Europe at a critical point in her life, and soon after had to be hospitalized in a psychiatric clinic. Szalita sensed her enormous suffering and her call for help. Only later was she able to recreate the components that contributed to the thought of suicide. Ms. N.'s silent begging for help reminded her of her own helplessness when watching planes coming over the defenseless Warsaw. She imagined the dancer with an umbrella as a balancing acrobat endangered by losing equilibrium at any moment. All these components combined into a sense of despair and suggested suicidal thoughts.

Szalita applied the epistemological approach in therapy with schizophrenic patients but she was also open to nonverbal communication. She was convinced that gestures and facial expressions carry information on thoughts reflecting prior experiences. She believed that therapists should not rush to interpretation because psychotics, who indulge in magical thinking, attach too much importance to interpretation. Bizarre behaviors should be tolerated unless they are too destructive. When patients feel enough protected in a relationship with a therapist, they diminish narcissistic defenses and attempt to establish a communication with the world. A therapist must be able to recognize nonverbal signals. Schizophrenics communicate in a very subtle way, with an altered facial expression or body position. A responsive therapist should take these signals into consideration.

Figure 12.3 Alberta Szalita, on her way to Le Havre and Paris, S.S. *Liberté*, 1960. Reproduced with permission of Aviva Gitlin and Saul Szalita Gitlin.

Figure 12.4 Alberta Szalita with her best friend, Szyfra, Paris, date unknown. Reproduced with permission of Aviva Gitlin and Saul Szalita Gitlin.

Szalita developed a mimetic technique. She would imitate her patient's gesture for her own sake. There is a lot of discussion today of how much information on mental state a gesture can carry and whether a mimetic behavior is more beneficial in approaching a patient than a reflection. If we assume that complex affects, cognitions, expressions, and perceptions are correlated, and that people are all influencing one another, or "intertwining" and "overlapping" in the context of Maurice Merleau-Ponty's "common corporeality," we will understand why a mimetic repetition of a patients' gestures may be a way of accessing their inner world (Merleau-Ponty, 2012/1945).

Wisdom of the Aged: How to Become and Remain a Psychoanalyst?

In a conversation with Amnon Issacharoff from 1997, Szalita talked about what was most important to her in psychoanalysis and how she had changed during her 60 years of practice (Issacharoff, 1997). Over a decade earlier, in an acceptance speech on the occasion of receiving the Frieda Fromm-Reichmann Award, she said that a sufficiently talented analyst should be similar to a sufficiently talented patient: "narcissistic enough to be curious about himself [. . .] hysterical enough to discover and prove the psychoanalytical theory, and obsessional enough to ensure persistence and endurance, which the process requires" (Szalita, 1981a, p. 15).

As she got older, Szalita grew more detached from her own and her patients' experiences, which only made her a better listener:

> I am more concerned about the patient, and at the same time I am more distant and more indifferent. [. . .] My response now is more to what the patient needs at a given moment, not whether I agree with him or disagree with him. [. . .] [T]he distance now is easier for me, it is a form of detachment. [. . .] Detachment sometimes makes for miracles in therapy. [. . .] [M]ost of the things that I say to a patient can be something that, one time or another in my work as a psychoanalyst, I said to myself.
>
> (Issacharoff, 1997, pp. 617, 622, 630, 619)

She learned how to be freer and more open with her patients, to ask them about their own ideas regarding therapy, and to ask for feedback. She would say, "I'm asking you a question, you have a right to find out why I asked you this question, so that you know what I am about" (p. 619). This way she created a sense of partnership.

Szalita often stressed that to understand a patient, one has to go beyond psychoanalytic knowledge. A therapist must take cultural differences into consideration. She often read romance books and detective stories that her patients read, listened to the songs they listened to, and watched Muhammed Ali's boxing matches, all to understand them better (Szalita, 1985).

Szalita considered psychoanalysis to be hard work on oneself, requiring an exercise in mindfulness and discipline of thought. She listened attentively to her patients and expected them to listen to her. She made use of her talent of keeping others calm, acquired during the Bolshevik revolution and her escape from Warsaw under bombardment. Even her most disturbed patients benefited from the atmosphere of cooperation, respect, and calmness.

The most beneficial modifications of the classic analytic technique are, according to Szalita, more freedom to use one's own subjectivity, being more responsive to patients, and engaging in a real dialogue with them. Free association is something different from a free stream of words. Analysis is not just an interpretation or just a free conversation. Many patients are incapable of listening to themselves, incapable of paying attention to what they are saying. The most important thing, therefore, is to learn to listen actively: to the patient and to oneself. Interpreting is less important, and if it is, the process of interpretation is a struggle for emotional meaning, not an intellectual operation. And for this, one needs, according to Szalita, to trust in the force, work, and life of the unconscious mind.

Burning Bridges?

After coming to the United States Szalita severed all ties with Poland. Looking back, at the age of 95, she wrote:

> Two lives, two beginnings. [. . .] [M]y life is divided almost equally in half. My early life, the first half, is in Europe. The half I am living now is here in the States, in America. The gulf, the abyss that divides them, is the Second World War.
>
> (Szalita, 2005, p. 5)

Undoubtedly, antisemitism, as well as the profound rupture between her former and later life, prevented her from bridging the gap over the "abyss,"

Figure 12.5 Alberta Szalita, later in life, possibly upstate New York.
Reproduced with permission of Aviva Gitlin and Saul Szalita Gitlin.

despite decades-long work on psychointegration. Poland became her family's grave and remained so until the end.

Alberta Szalita died on November 10, 2010, at the age of 100. She is one of the great, yet forgotten, women psychoanalysts of the twentieth century.

Reference List

Antonovsky, A. M. (1978). The Thinking Cure—Some Thoughts on Thinking in Psychoanalysis. *Contemporary Psychoanalysis*, 14(3), 388–404.
Arendt, H. (1968). On Humanity in Dark Times: Thoughts about Lessing. In H. Arendt (Ed.), *Men in Dark Times* (pp. 3–31). New York: Harcourt, Brace & World.
Arendt, H. (2018). *Thinking Without a Banister: Essays in Understanding, 1953–1975*. New York: Schocken Books.
Benaim, D. (2005a). Foreword. In A. Szalita (Ed.), *The Force of Destiny* (pp. 7–8). New York: Jay Street Publishers.
Benaim, D. (2005b). Epilogue: The Second Half-Century. In A. Szalita (Ed.), *The Force of Destiny* (pp. 103–111). New York: Jay Street Publishers.
Blechner, M. (1997). Psychoanalytic Psychotherapy with Schizophrenics, Then and Now: Discussion of Ann Silver. *Contemporary Psychoanalysis*, 33(2), 251–262.

Blechner, M. (2001). Clinical Wisdom and Theoretical Advances: Alberta Szalita's Contributions to Psychoanalysis. *Contemporary Psychoanalysis*, 37(1), 63–76.
Boll, F. (2001), *Sprechen als Last und Befreiung. Holocaust-Überlebende und politisch Verfolgte zweier Dikataturen.* Bonn: Dietz J.H.
Engelking, B. and Grabowski, J. (Eds.) (2022). *Night Without End: The Fate of Jews in German-Occupied Poland.* A. Brzostowska et al. (Trans.). Indiana: Indiana UP.
Freud, S. (1953). Interpretation of Dreams (Second Part). J. Strachey (Trans.). In J. Strachey (Ed.), *SE, Vol. V: The Interpretation of Dreams (Second Part) and On Dreams* (pp. 339–628). London: The Hogarth Press. (Orig. publ. 1900).
Fromm-Reichmann, F. (1948). Notes on the Development of Treatment of Schizophrenics by Psychoanalytic Psychotherapy. *Psychiatry*, 11(3), 263–273.
Hornstein, G. A. (2000). *To Redeem One Person Is to Redeem the World: The Life of Frieda Fromm-Reichmann.* New York: Other Press.
Issacharoff, A. (1997). A Conversation with Dr. Alberta Szalita. *Contemporary Psychoanalysis*, 33(4), 615–632.
Judt, T. (2006). *Postwar: A History of Europe Since 1945.* New York: The Penguin Press.
Kobylinska [Kobylińska]-Dehe, E. (2018). Von Warschau nach New York: Gustav Bychowski: Ein jüdischer Psychoanalytiker aus Polen zwischen Alter und Neuer Welt. In E. Kobylinska-Dehe, P. Dybel and L. Hermanns (Eds.), *Zwischen Hoffnung und Verzweiflung: Psychoanalyse in Polen in polnisch-deutsch-jüdischen Kulturkontext 1900–1939* (pp. 167–192). Gießen: Psychosozial-Verlag.
Krajewski, S. (2014). Powojnie od 1944 do dziś. In *Polin. 1000 lat historii Żydów polskich* (pp. 351–400). Warszawa: Polin.
Kuriloff, E. (2014). *Contemporary Psychoanalysis and the Legacy of the Third Reich.* New York: Routledge.
Levi, P. (2003). *If This Is a Man. The Truce.* S. Woolf (Trans.). London: Abacus (Orig. publ. 1922).
Lorenzer, A. (2016). Language, Life Praxis and Scenic Understanding in Psychoanalytic Therapy. *The International Journal of Psychoanalysis*, 97(5), 1399–1414.
Merleau-Ponty, M. (2012). *Phenomenology of Perception.* D. A. Landes (Trans.). New York: Routledge. (Orig. publ. 1945).
Minkowski, E. (1948). Les conséquences psychologiques et psychopathologiques de la guerre et du nazisme. *Schweizer Archiv für Neurologie Psychiatrie*, 61, 280–301.
Niederland, W. G. (1968). The Problem of the Survivor. In H. Krystal (Ed.), *Massive Psychic Trauma* (pp. 8–22). New York: International Universities Press.
Niederland, W. G. (1980). *Folgen der Verfolgung: Das Überlebenden-Syndrom, Seelenmord.* Frankfurt am Main: Suhrkamp.
Quarles, F. (1861). *Emblems.* London: James Nisbet & Co. Berners Street (Orig. publ. 1635).
Rüsen, J. (2020). Czy można uhistorycznić Holokaust? O sensie i bezsensie doświadczenia historycznego. In E. Kobylinska-Dehe (Ed.), *W cieniu wojny i zagłady* (pp. 29–44). Kraków: Universitas.

Rüsen, J. (2021). *Humanism: Foundations, Diversities, Developments*. New York: Routledge.
Snyder, T. (2007). Leben und Sterben der Juden in Wolhynien. *Osteuropa*, 57(4), 123–142.
Snyder, T. (2010). *Bloodlands: Europe between Hitler and Stalin*. New York: Basic Books.
Szalita, A. B. (1958). Regression and Perception in Psychotic States. *Psychiatry*, 21(1), 77–94.
Szalita, A. B. (1968). Reanalysis. *Contemporary Psychoanalysis*, 4, 83–102.
Szalita, A. B. (1974). *Grief and Bereavement*. New York: Basic Books.
Szalita, A. B. (1981a). Acceptance Speech on the Occasion of Receiving the Frieda Fromm-Reichmann Award. *Journal of the American Academy of Psychoanalysis*, 9(1), 11–16.
Szalita, A. B. (1981b). The Use and Misuse of Empathy in Psychoanalysis and Psychotherapy. *Psychoanalytic Review*, 68, 3–21.
Szalita, A. B. (1985). On Becoming a Psychoanalyst: Education or Experience. *Contemporary Psychoanalysis*, 21(1), 130–142.
Szalita, A. B. (1994). The Dilemma of Therapeutic Changes in Psychotherapy: Psychointegration. *The Israel Journal of Psychiatry and Related Sciences*, 31(2), 106–114.
Szalita, A. B. (2005). *The Force of Destiny*. New York: Jay Street Publishers.
Szalita, A. B. and Kelman, H. (1964). Discussions. *American Journal of Psychoanalysis*, 24(2), 174–183.
Szalita-Pemow, A. (1955), The "Intuitive Process" and Its Relation to Work with Schizophrenics. *Journal of the American Psychoanalytic Association*, 3, 7–18.
Winnicott, D. W. (1984). *The Maturational Process and the Facilitating Environment: Studies in the Theory of Emotional Development*. New York: Routledge.

Chapter 13

Olga Wermer

From Galician Archives to Memory and Postmemory

Klara Naszkowska

This is the story of Olga Wermer, one of many Jewish women doctors and psychoanalysts left out of the recorded past. The reconstruction of her biography, using long-forgotten archival materials and present-day interviews with family members, reveals another story: of the "vanishing" of the multicultural, multireligious, non-national "kingdom" of Galicia (Davis, 2011), with its Jewish populace and their Yiddish language, customs, schools, institutions of philanthropy, and religion. All of which also contains the end of Poland's epoch as home to the largest Jewish population to date, of some 3.3 million. Finally, Wermer's is a story of the shaping of historical records by historical events, contemporary beliefs, and the works of memory, which create some narratives while erasing others.

Family History Before the Holocaust (a Reconstruction)

Olga Wermer, who died in 1993 after a long career in endocrinology, gynecology, and psychoanalytically oriented psychotherapy, was born Olga Speranza Plachte, in Zurich, Switzerland, on September 3, 1913. Her father, Leon Plachte (1888–1943?), a Polish Jewish civil engineer, was then overseeing construction of the Hauenstein railway tunnel in the small town of Olten, 40 miles west of Zurich. Leon worked in the field of large-scale infrastructure, with a focus on tunnels and bridges. He must have been a sought-after expert, as the Swiss government hired him from Tarnau, a midsize Polish town almost 1,000 miles away, then under Austrian rule. The Hauenstein tunnel, opened in January 1916, was the first base tunnel in Switzerland to be built through a mountain pass. It remains one of the busiest railway tunnels in the country (Ribeli, 2022).

Leon and his wife, Jadwiga (1889–1942?), returned to Tarnau with their newborn daughter sometime before July 1914 and the outbreak of the First

DOI: 10.4324/9781003455844-18

World War. Olga's sister, Irena (also Irene; d. 1987), was born on January 9, 1917, in Vienna, where Leon was then reportedly overseeing construction of a bridge. The family returned to Tarnau shortly after the war ended (HW).[1]

From around the age of four, Olga lived in Tarnau. Founded in southern Poland in 1330 as Tarnów, it was "a famous city from the past" (Kahane, 1954–1968, p. 189). By 1913, its name had assumed the German spelling and was a key center in Austrian Galicia, a region that was "fundamentally non-national" (Wolff, 2010, p. 6) and had been created in 1772 with the first partition of Poland from lands annexed into the Hapsburg Empire. Over more than a century of Austrian rule, until 1918, when Galicia was removed from the map, the region's Jewish population increased sixfold. As Olga was growing up, her hometown had Galicia's fourth largest Jewish (Ashkenazi) population. After the town had been liberated from occupying forces on the night of October 30, 1918, the Jewish population of the town—now Tarnów again—continued to grow. That year, its 15,000 Jews comprised a little over 40 percent of the townspeople. The community was vibrant, with highly influential Hasidic and Zionist movements. There were two large synagogues, around 40 smaller places of prayer and study (shuls, shtibls, and kloyzn) (Bartosz, 2007, p. 2), and its Jewish cemetery was the oldest and largest in Poland.

On the eve of German invasion in September 1939 and the Soviet Union's conquest of its eastern regions, Poland was home to the largest Jewish population in the world: over 3.3 million people, about 10 percent of the country's population, largely concentrated in the east. Then the Tarnów Jewish community numbered 25,000, almost half of the town's population (Gelber, 2008).

In the interwar period, the Plachte family belonged to the town's affluent, intellectual-cultural elite. They led a "luxurious cultural life" on a large estate on the outskirts "with horses and livestock" (HW). Next to the estate stood a spirits refinery supplying Tarnów residents with products, including vodka and mead (a regional specialty beverage made by fermenting honey), as well as vinegar. It had belonged to Olga's wealthy maternal great-grandparents, Avraham (also Ascher) Schwanenfeld and Rachel (née Schonwetter). According to a list of properties in a claim submitted by Olga's aunt, Marie Frisch, the Schwanenfelds also owned a house in Baden bei Wien, a renowned spa town 15 miles south of Vienna, along with "gardens, courts, adjoining property on either side of road." Property plans from 1919 reveal holdings of almost 7,000 acres with factory buildings, a brewery, warehouses, and workers' lodgings. "The Szwanenfeld's liqueur factory" building survived the German occupation (Kornilo, 1954–1968, p. 318).

One of Avraham and Rachel's children was Leon (or Leib) Schwanenfeld (1856–1941?)—Olga Wermer's maternal grandfather. He had been an "architect," a "master builder," and a "building contractor" based in Tarnau. His wife, Rozalia (also Rosalia, Ruda, or Roze, née Siódmak or Schudmak; 1868–1942?), daughter of Löbel and Sprynca Siódmak, was "a grand lady [. . .] always in sable and diamonds" (H. Wermer, 1974/1975). Among the very few items Olga Wermer would bring from Europe to the United States was one of her grandmother's earrings encrusted with pearls and rubies. She would have it made into a brooch, which she wore frequently (HW).

Rozalia and Leon Schwanenfeld were observant Jews. They went on to have seven daughters, five of whom survived into adulthood: Zofia (also Sara; 1888–1942?), Jadwiga (1889–1942?), Irena (1895–1942?), Olga (1900–1942?), and Marie (also Marya, Maria; 1901–1983). Their only son, Henryk (b. 1892), died at the age of two. Olga Wermer's mother, Jadwiga, the second eldest, was born in Tarnau on December 11, 1889, with the help of a midwife, Debora. To date, nothing is known of her education. Most likely, she attended the same elementary school as her sister, Irena, which was named for the writer Maria Konopnicka and opened in the 1879–1880 school year, headed by an experienced pedagogue, Jan Ruszczyński. Jadwiga was a gifted classical pianist and a homemaker, "a superb cook and seamstress" (H. Wermer, 1974/1975).

About Jadwiga's sisters we know that the oldest, Zofia, became a social activist involved with organizations including the Jewish National Fund (Pl. Żydowski Fundusz Narodowy) (Gawron, 2009, p. 311), which was devoted to buying land in Palestine for Jewish settlement. She married Hersch (also Hersz, Herman) Syrop (also Sirop; 1875–1942), a lawyer and Zionist activist from Neu Sandez (now Nowy Sącz, Poland). They had three children: Rut (also Ruta), Rafael Elizer (also Elizezar) (Gawron, 2009, p. 311), and Adam Theodore (b. 1910) (KB). Hersch practiced law from 1906 to 1940 in Nowy Sącz (Gawron, 2009, p. 33). As a member of the multi-factional Kraków Association for Helping Political Prisoners (Krakowski Związek Pomocy dla Więźniów Politycznych), Hersch represented Vladimir Lenin, who had been arrested in 1914 by the Austrian authorities, accused of espionage as a Russian citizen, and jailed in the town of Nowy Targ from August 8 to 19 (Rice, 1990, pp. 127–128). Another of Jadwiga's sisters,

Olga, received a PhD in art history from the University of Vienna. She married Aleksander Aleksandrowicz and had a son, Aleksander (KB). About Irena we know that she held a PhD in botany from the University of Vienna. She married Alfred Holländer (or Hollaender, changing his name to the Polish-sounding Holiński in 1936) and had a daughter, Marja Stanislawa Magda, born in Vienna in 1926. The youngest sister, Marie, the only one to survive the war, received her doctorate from the Faculty of Philosophy of the University of Vienna in 1927 and was a chemist. She married Zygmund (also Siegmund; 1902–1986), originally from Kolomea (now Kolomyia, Ukraine), also a chemist. They had no children.

Leon Plachte, Olga Wermer's father, came from a less affluent family. Born on May 29, 1888, he was the first child of the newlyweds Curtel (née Schollem; 1866–1940s?) and Max (also Majer, Mase, Maximilian; 1863–1940s?) Plachte. He had two sisters, Bronisława (1889–1941/1942) and Franciszka (also Franziska, 1890–1942?). All three children attended

Figure 13.1 Family photograph, Tarnów, ca. 1925. Back row, from left to right: unknown man, Olga Aleksandrowicz or Irena Holländer, Leon Plachte, Marie Frisch, Olga Wermer, Rut Syrop. Little girl in front—Irena Borecka. Front row, from left to right: possibly Zofia Syrop, Rozalia Schwanenfeld, Leon (Leib) Schwanenfeld, Jadwiga Plachte. The child in front, unknown.

Reproduced with permission of Margaret Wermer.

secondary public schools in Tarnau. Leon completed a *realschule*, a six-year boys' vocational school. A *realschule*, ranked below an eight-year high school oriented to the humanities (or *Gymnasium*), provided technical education focused on practical skills instead of a comprehensive academic-level education. Its goal was to prepare students for work in branches of local trade and industry, rather than university preparation (Pelczar, 2022). Leon graduated in 1904, at 16, with no record of further education.

Bronisława, remembered as "a brilliant, very strong, bossy woman" (H. Wermer, 1974/1975), completed a four-year school for girls, also with an emphasis on practical education, and graduated in 1905, at 16. While Austro-Hungarian universities, including those in Galicia, started to accept women in the late 1890s, applicants were required to have taken their *matura*, a rigorous written and oral exit exam. The problem that arose was that only those leaving a high school could take the *matura*, and for girls in Galicia there were no public or private high schools until the interwar period (Domus, 2016). Since the school she had completed did not qualify her for university enrollment, it may be assumed that Bronisława studied on her own for the *matura* and the entrance exam that universities required of applicants who had not attended a high school. And as a woman, she had to request special permission to take them. Helene Deutsch, another Galician-born psychoanalyst faced with a similar situation, had studied with the help of private tutors and was admitted to the medical school at the University of Vienna in 1907 (cf. Deutsch, 1973, pp. 30–47).

Bronisława enrolled in the medical school at the Jagiellonian University in Krakau (Kraków) in the 1908/1909 academic year (Stopka, 2011, p. 438). Established in 1364, the Jagiellonian remains the second oldest university in Central-East Europe (the Charles University in Prague was founded in 1348). Women then comprised a little over 10 percent of all first-year medical students (Sikora, 2007, pp. 254–255). When medical schools in Austro-Hungary began accepting women in 1900, Jewish women promptly came to make up a high proportion of their students (cf. Friedenreich, 1996). Of 55 women in Bronisława's first-year class, 55 percent were Jewish (Sikora, 2007, p. 259).

The preponderance of Jewish women among medical students in the first years of the twentieth century came about due to a combination of socioeconomic and cultural factors. University education was expensive and scholarships were very rarely given to women. Most female students came from well-off families of merchants, industrialists, teachers, and clerks

(Suchmiel, 1997). Hence, their parents, less worried about the need for their daughters to marry for material support, could afford to educate them well. Typically, the fathers had some form of college-level or practical education and valued its benefits. Additionally, education holds special value among Jews. This principle of educating children included endowing them with something that could not be taken away, in the way that possessions, citizenship, even life could. As a result, Jewish women frequently had their parents' financial as well as moral support in pursuing university education and professional careers, especially in practical professions, including medicine.

Bronisława qualified as a doctor in 1914 (Stopka, 2011, p. 438) and began practicing internal medicine and stomatology, most likely in Tarnau. The next year she married a lawyer and Zionist leader from Tarnau, Wolf Israel Mendel Szenkel (also Schenkel; 1888–1942). The ceremony took place in Vienna's largest synagogue, the Leopoldstädter Temple, later destroyed by the Nazis during Kristallnacht, on November 10, 1938. After the wedding, Bronisława and Wolf Szenkel settled in Tarnau, an important Zionist center: "[I]f one can speak of an atmosphere, that rules in a given city, about the moods of the streets in a given city, about the spirit of the city, everyone would have to agree, that Jewish Tarnow was a city thoroughly and almost 100 percent Zionist" (Berkelhamer, 1954–1968, p. 349). The Schenkels lived on Wałowa Street, in the part of town where houses of the Jewish community holding rights of autonomous organization (kehilla) and the Great Synagogue stood. Both were actively involved in social work and invested in the Jewish community. Wolf headed the town's oldest philanthropic organization, Bikur Cholim or Society to Aid the Sick, which provided free medical and mental-health assistance. Additionally, he was on the managing committee of the town's Jewish orphanage for those who lost parents in the First World War. These children would be murdered by the Germans during the Second World War (Chomet, 1954–1968b, p. 733). He helped establish and then manage a coed Jewish high school. The school, founded in 1923 by the Safa Berura Society, responsible for protection of the Hebrew language, had strong Zionist leanings (Chomet, 1954–1968a, p. 678; cf. Juśko, 2020) and received financial support from many community members. Names of 37 generous donors were engraved on a memorial tablet, including those of Leon Plachte and Wolf Szenkel (Chomet, 1954–1968a, pp. 685–687). Bronisława and Wolf had three children: Leon Teodor (also Theodore; 1917–2002), Adam (1920–1948/1949), and Gizelle

(1926–1942?). Adam attended the Safa Berura school. When the parents' council was elected in 1929, "Mrs. Dr. Bronislava Szenkel" was named "chairwoman" (Chomet, 1954–1968a, p. 680).

Of Franciszka Plachte's education, I have only found that she attended a newly opened four-year elementary school for girls, named for the Romantic-era poet Juliusz Słowacki. She went on to become a successful dressmaker and entrepreneur. Her atelier, opened shortly after the First World War, was prominently located in the central town square, at the heart of newly liberated Tarnów and situated on the ground floor of the prestigious Nikielson Townhouse. The building's history provides a vivid glimpse of the region's turbulent history. Built in the mid-sixteenth century for a Scottish family, the Nikielsons, it collapsed in the mid-1770s after a series of fires and was rebuilt by new owners, the Sanguszkos, an aristocratic Polish-Lithuanian family. In Galicia under Austrian rule, it was a courthouse and then was taken over by the Tarnau bishopric. From 1912, the Nikielson Townhouse belonged to the mayor, Tadeusz Tertil, who had it transformed into apartments with ground-floor commercial spaces. Currently under renovation, the building is meant to house an Experimental Park (Park Doświadczeń, in Polish) focused on science.

Franciszka, at 35, married Lipa Hirsch Goldstein (in 1925), very late for her era. They had two daughters, Rachela and Mirka, when Franciszka was 36 (in 1926) and 39 (in 1929), respectively (KB). It was truly unconventional in the 1920s for Franciszka to become a mother so well into her thirties.

Olga Wermer's Education: Tarnów, Kraków, Vienna, Bologna

Olga grew up in a "secular, nonkosher Jewish home" (HW). It can be gleaned from available sources that her parents had strong Polish identities, and she did not receive a Jewish upbringing. She "was raised Polish" (HW) and the family spoke Polish at home, perhaps with "a few Yiddish words included" (HW). As with Jadwiga's parents, she and Leon gave their daughters the popular Slavic names Olga and Irena, originally Ruthenian and Greek, respectively. I have come across no record of their Hebrew names. Olga means happy and healthy and Speranza, her middle name, means hope, while Irena means peace. In Jewish tradition, a child's name is significant to forming an identity. Were Jadwiga and Leon trying to conjure up a safe future for their children by choosing these names? On the other hand, Olga and Irena may have been named after their two aunts, in accordance with a Sephardic tradition of naming babies for living people.

Most likely Olga received her early education at home, as was then the custom. When she reached school age, in 1921 or 1922, there were still no public high schools for girls in Tarnów. She was enrolled in the town's oldest private high school for girls, named after the novelist Eliza Orzeszkowa (est. 1908). To the best of my knowledge, it was the only nondenominational option, with around 30 percent of students being Jewish (Ruta, 1990, p. 95). One alternative was a girls' *realschule* being run by the Ursulines; the second was a private teachers' seminary for girls named after the thirteenth-century saint known as Blessed Kinga.

After graduating in 1930, Olga, then 17, wanted to study at the University of Vienna's renowned medical school. Her choice might have been influenced by Bronisława Szenkel, her path-breaking aunt. Her parents reportedly wanted her to wait a year after graduating before leaving to study

Figure 13.2 Olga Wermer at the age of 20, Vienna, 1933.
Photograph by Trude Fleischmann. Reproduced with permission of Hedy Wermer.

in Vienna (HW), almost 350 miles from Tarnów. Instead, she enrolled in the Jagiellonian University, only 45 miles away. Olga initially chose the philosophy department and then transferred to the law department just a few weeks later, on October 27, 1931 (written communication from Marcin Baster, 2022). She reportedly found law studies "boring" and was eager to begin medical studies (HW). She completed her first year and then transferred again, this time to Vienna and medical school. She was almost 19 when she began the 1932/1933 winter semester.

Olga's sister, Irena, studied chemistry at the Jagiellonian University from 1935 to 1937 and then transferred to Warsaw (1937–1939), where her studies were interrupted by the outbreak of war (KB).

At medical school, Olga met her future husband, Henry Wermer (né Heinz; 1913–1968). Henry came from a Viennese Jewish family. His mother, Sonja Sophie (or Sofie, née Goldstern; 1874–1927), originally from Odessa (now Odesa) in Ukraine, was a translator of Russian books into German (H. Wermer, 1974/1975). His father, Leopold Wermer (1865–1939/1940), a dentist, came from Trnava (Tyrnau) in Slovakia. Henry's older brother, Paul (1897–1975), was also a medical doctor, specializing in endocrinology. Paul Wermer gained renown in the US in 1954 after describing a rare genetic disorder, multiple endocrine neoplasia type I (MEN I), or the Wermer syndrome.

Henry qualified as a doctor on December 22, 1936. Olga, despite being his age peer, was a year and a half behind him due to her stint at the Jagiellonian University and possibly due to studies at the University of Bologna over the 1933–1934 academic year (medicine, surgery). She was set to graduate in Vienna in the spring of 1938. However, she and around 2,700 Jewish students were expelled from university within weeks of Austria's annexation into the Third Reich on March 13.

Austria's "collective amnesia" has conveniently ignored the actual reception of the Anschluss since the war ended and would have us believe the nation had been Nazi Germany's first victim (cf. Brook-Shepherd, 1996). In fact, Austria had been a stronghold of antisemitism and racial violence well before the annexation. Since the 1880s, politicized antisemitism had grown markedly in the Austro-Hungarian Empire, under the conservative Christian Social Party and its populist leader, Karl Lueger. As mayor of Vienna (1897–1910), Lueger led Europe's largest antisemitic movement (cf. Pauley, 1992). In the period of Austrofascism (1933–1938), the university's medical school became infested with Nazi policies of eugenics and racial hygiene. The relentless process of "de-Judification" of Austro-German medicine led to the dismissal of some 36 percent of its non-Aryan professors and lecturers, replaced with political adherents to National Socialist principles (cf. Zeidman, 2020).

After the Anschluss, the expulsion of Jewish faculty and students was a "remarkably smooth and quick running [. . .] operation" with "little opposition voiced by colleagues remaining in the Faculty" (Ernst, 1995, p. 750). Just three days after the annexation, Eduard Pernkopf, an ardent member both of the NSDAP and of the SA paramilitary wing (the Brownshirts), was named dean of the medical school. Under Pernkopf's leadership, all remaining Jewish faculty were quickly laid off. Professors had to submit proof of their Aryan descent (birth certificates of parents and spouses) and "give an oath of loyalty to Hitler" (Ernst, 1995, p. 750). The large majority of the dismissed Jewish faculty (around 125) managed to escape, mostly to the United States. The rest were deported to concentration camps, with many committing suicide (Taschwer, 2020).

Pernkopf went on to have a successful career during and after the war until his death in 1955, as president of the University of Vienna (1943–1946) and as the author of a monumental *Atlas of Topographical Human Anatomy* (Pernkopf, 1963). He was never charged for complicity with the Nazi regime and served just two years at labor in the Marcus W. Orr labor camp in Austria (Malina, 1998). It took until the mid-1980s before Pernkopf's pro-Nazi past was brought to light (Weissmann, 1985; Williams, 1988). This led to a Yad Vashem investigation, which revealed that he and his collaborators, all of them committed Nazis, almost certainly used cadavers of executed prisoners in their research and "decorated" the *Atlas* with Nazi symbols. Nonetheless, since the first volume Pernkopf's *Atlas* appeared in 1937 until the present, the work has been the standard anatomy book for medical students worldwide. In the 1960s, Nazi symbols and commentary were airbrushed out; the rights' holder, Urban & Schwarzenberg, stopped publishing it in 1994, but second-hand copies, including US editions, remain in circulation (cf. Hubbard, 2002).

Emigration to the US: Between Agency and Assimilation

On July 21, 1938, Henry embarked on a ship to the United States, leaving behind Vienna, plunged into post-annexation antisemitic violence. He traveled on a quota immigrant visa (QIV) issued on June 2. The quota system was part of the 1924 Immigration Act, designed to curb the arrival of "undesirable" immigrants including Jews, Asians, and Africans. The Ku Klux Klan influenced the passage of this legislation (cf. Simins, n.d.). As of July 1, 1929, anyone arriving in the US had to present a visa stamped in their passport. The total quota cap for immigrants from Europe was 164,667, an 80 percent decrease from the average before the First World War, which was then further reduced to 153,879. Meanwhile, the 1882 Asian Exclusion Act, virtually banning immigrants from Asia, was upheld and extended to all groups of immigrants (remaining in force until the Immigration and Nationality Act was passed in 1965). Additionally, the "national origins quota" was set at 2 percent of a given country's total number of individuals already residing in the US, calculated using US Census data. Congress, reacting to changing immigration trends, used the 1890 data that showed lower totals of resident immigrants from Eastern and Southern Europe, instead of the most recent 1910 census. Thus, Congress favored Northern and Western Europeans from Scandinavia, the UK, and Germany, perceived as white, arriving to join communities that had largely assimilated into the general population. They filled around 85 percent of available quota slots. This rendered the mass migration of the largest community of Jewry impossible: those from Eastern Europe. Additionally, the 1924 Immigration Act set up a system for deportations of immigrants.

This racist, antisemitic, xenophobic, and exclusionary system reflected the country's widespread sentiment in the 1930s and beyond. According to the 1938 Gallup poll, conducted two weeks after the Kristallnacht pogroms, which were widely reported on in the domestic press (cf. *Life Magazine*, November 28, 1938), 72 percent of respondents opposed any increase of quotas that would permit more Jews seeking asylum into the country (Davie, 1947, pp. 369–390; Brody, 1956).

As Nazi German persecution in Europe intensified, the State Department did not increase quotas to aid Jewish refugees. Indeed, a recalculation of national quotas based on the 1920 census led to the German quota being halved. After Austria was annexed in March 1938 and the occupation that September of Czechoslovakia's Sudetenland, that annual quota, capped at 27,370, covered all German-occupied territories. In 1939, Jews numbered around 318,000 in Germany (Blau, 1950, pp. 161, 162); in 1938, about 190,000 lived in Austria (Holocaust Encyclopedia, USHMM), with some 24,500 in Sudetenland late that same year (Bazyler et al., 2019). This total of about 530,000 Jewish people, including Henry Wermer, was eligible for a little over 27,000 slots per year (shared with all others across what was then deemed German lands). Moreover, since the State Department viewed quotas as limits, not as goals, the German quota was filled only once, in 1939 (Holocaust Encyclopedia, USHMM).

Along with quota limits, more and increasingly expensive requirements and further restrictions were imposed on visa applicants. An "affidavit of support" from a US sponsor had to be submitted with each application. After the war began, additional moral affidavits had to be provided, attesting to an applicant's identity and good conduct. After September 1940, a second financial affidavit was required. Prospective refugees had to purchase a berth on a ship and obtain costly transit visas for all countries they would travel through to reach their port of departure. This all had to be finalized prior to an interview at a US consulate. During interviews, consuls refused visas to those who were "likely to become public charges" (unable to support themselves), "lunatics," or "idiots." Preference was given to skilled applicants with employment invitations. In July 1941, the "relatives' rule" came into effect: visas were denied to individuals whose close relatives (including elderly parents and grandparents) remained in German-occupied territory. Visas were valid for just four months.

It is often emphasized that the US admitted more refugees fleeing German persecution than any other country. However, only around 132,000 Jewish refugees were accepted between 1933 and 1945 (cf. Breitman and Kraut, 1987). This number could have been significantly higher had Congress modified existing antisemitic immigration laws.

Given all this, once Henry was granted his visa, in June 1938, he had no choice but to leave Nazi-dominated lands. He simply couldn't risk staying with Olga in Vienna and losing the visa. Left in annexed Vienna, she was reportedly "chased at bayonet point by the Nazis" (HW), an example of street-level violence on the rise in Austria after the Anschluss.

Olga received her visa that October, under the Polish quota capped at 6,524, a limit imposed on what was the world's largest interwar Jewish population by far. According to the Ellis Island Passenger Records, Olga traveled to the US three times in 1938 and 1939. Her first embarkation took place on December 17, 1938, from Le Havre in Normandy. She crossed the Atlantic on the SS *Normandie*, acclaimed as the greatest, most elegant ocean liner in history. Olga arrived in New York Harbor five days later, on December 22.

Even upon their arrival, visa holders could be refused entry by Immigration and Naturalization Service officials, who could also detain them at the Screening and Quarantine Station on Ellis Island. Every foreigner was subjected to a physical and mental examination conducted by their ship's surgeon. The *Normandie*'s manifest recorded Olga's health as "good," her profession as "student," and her "race of people" as "Hebrew." The history of newly arrived Eastern European Jews is revealing, in terms of accepted racial status. While first regarded as non-whites, many were then seen as whites after they had culturally assimilated into American society. This "becoming white" and entering the middle class remains a complicated issue. "Did Jews [. . .] become white because they became middle class? That is, did money whiten? Or did being incorporated in an expanded version of whiteness open up the economic doors to a middle-class status?" (Sacks, 1994, p. 86). It does seem that in this process in which a newly arrived person may "become white," the émigrés were erasing their Jewish identities and pasts, likely in an attempt to forget, start anew, and reestablish and reinvent themselves in the "promised land." It also points to the issue of Black Jews, which to date has been largely neglected.

There is also a larger issue of identifying Jews as a race or ethnicity and of antisemitism as racism. This classification is often rejected as antisemitic, as it was used by the Third Reich (following the example of Hungary and its head of state, Miklós Horthy). However, as David Baddiel writes on the issue, "we live in a time—luckily—when ethnicity is something to be celebrated, not hidden. It is indeed a key part of the struggle against discrimination that this is so" (Baddiel, 2021, p. xvii). In fact, for Holocaust survivors, and their children and grandchildren affected by the intergenerational transmission of trauma, the sense of Jewishness as a race or ethnicity is often rooted in antisemitic violence and Nazi persecution. This rings true for Olga Wermer. As Hedy Wermer told me, her mother did have "an ethnic Jewish identity," which was "important to her because of the Holocaust" (HW). As Baddiel adds: "Identity, particularly ethnic identity, is created in the story of survival against the odds" (Baddiel, 2021, pp. xviii–xix).

The classification of Jews as "Hebrew race" upon arrival from Nazi-occupied Europe in the 1930s and 1940s certainly has negative echoes. On the other hand, so does the fact that there has never been an ethnicity box for Jews on the US census. The latest, in 2020, added an optional "origins" box that gave an opportunity to enter, for example, Jewish, Ashkenazi, and so on, after checking one of the main boxes: White, Black or African American, American Indian or Alaska Native, Asian, Native Hawaiian and Pacific Islander, or "Some Other Race."

Under "purpose of visit," Olga declared "permanent." Five days after this arrival, she married Henry in New York City "in what was most likely a very simple civil ceremony with no religious aspects" (HW). On September 18 of that year, she filed a Declaration of Intention to become a US citizen. The prescribed waiting period was five years, and Olga would be granted her citizenship on April 10, 1944.

According to the Ellis Island Records, Olga then traveled to Europe twice in early 1939. During the last of these return voyages, from March 3, 1939, she lived there for five months, just at the cusp of the war. She spent most of that time in relatively peaceful Switzerland at the University of Lausanne, completing her interrupted medical studies. This return to Europe had been planned before departing the first time for the US. She filled out enrollment forms for the 1938/1939 winter semester in October 1938 (possibly right after she received her US visa). She completed the summer semester in May 1939, and took her medical doctorate that October, based on her dissertation, *Clinical Contribution to the Knowledge of Thallium Poisoning* (Plachte-Wermer, 1939). Thallium is a highly toxic chemical element, then in common use in rat and ant poisons. Olga told her daughter, Hedy, that before returning to the US to stay, she visited Tarnów hoping to persuade her family to join her. Despite her pleas, her parents decided to remain and take care of their elderly parents who were too frail to make the transatlantic journey (HW). Another family member pointed out that in August of 1939, Olga's parents and sister could not have known what was coming (KB). Additionally, to join her in the US, they would have needed visas. In any case, Olga embarked alone on the SS *Manhattan* on August 10, 1939, three weeks before the Germans invaded Poland.

The quota system still exists in the US, and mistreatment of refugees continues. The current total annual quota for permanent employment-based individuals, including their spouses and dependents, is 140,000. Additionally, the national quota is capped at 7 percent of the total number of immigrants per fiscal year (Oct. 1 to Sept. 30). The numerical ceiling for refugee admissions is determined by the president. The Biden administration set the 2023 limit at 125,000; however, the projected arrivals are at less than half of that – 60,100 (Report to Congress on Projected Refugee Admissions for Fiscal Year 2024, November 3, 2023). Both numbers are a considerate improvement in comparison to the previous years. In one telling example, the US officially recognizes as genocide the persecution of Uyghurs by the Chinese, yet does not provide emigration relief for those of that mostly Muslim Turkic ethnic minority who are fleeing China, where most of around 13.5 million Uyghurs live. The US admitted no Uyghur refugees in the fiscal year of 2021 (Prude and Wilt, October 21, 2021).

The Shoah

Almost the entire extended Plachte and Schwanenfeld families perished in the Holocaust. In the first days of the German invasion of Poland, many Tarnów Jews managed to flee east, including Olga Wermer's sister, Irena, her future husband, the engineer Jerzy Borecki (né Waksman; 1914–2011), Jadwiga and her frail parents, Rozalia and Leon Schwanenfeld, and two of Olga's aunts, Irena and Olga, with their children, Marja and Aleksander and a yet unidentified boy of 15. They left Tarnów on September 1 or 2, traveling rather comfortably in a rented bus to Busko-Zdrój, a spa town only 40 miles north. They rented rooms in a hotel there (KB). Olga's father, Leon, made the decision to stay in Tarnów, to care for his frail parents (HW) or, according to a different source, with the intention of joining his family in Busko-Zdrój in a few days (KB). Before he could, the group split in two. On September 4, the majority (Jadwiga's parents, Olga's aunts Irena and Olga and their children) returned to Tarnów, while the others (Olga's sister Irena, Jerzy, Jadwiga, and the unidentified boy) continued east (KB).

None of those who returned to Tarnów survived the war. Their particular circumstances have largely been lost to history. The historical circumstances were the following: German troops occupied Tarnów on September 8, 1939, and immediately began persecuting Jews, destroying their property and local cultural and religious institutions. As early as October 20, Tarnovian Jews were forced to wear Star of David armbands. On November 8, the Great Synagogue was set ablaze, then blown up and dismantled. Its bimah, the platform from which the Torah is read, has survived and remains a commemorative site today (Wirtualny Sztetl, POLIN). In March 1941, the Tarnów ghetto was officially established. Across Poland, once the war had ended, approximately 380,000 Jews remained alive (Yad Vashem). As with all those communities, Tarnovian Jews had been obliterated, most all of their cultural and religious buildings razed, and their institutions destroyed (Komet, 1954–1968).

Nothing is known of the circumstances of the deaths of Leon Plachte and his parents, Curtel and Max. His father-in-law, Leon Schwanenfeld, died in September 1941 from natural causes (a letter from Rozalia to Marie

Frisch; KB). Rozalia Schwanenfeld was reportedly murdered in the Shoah. In his letter to Marie Frisch, Adam Theodore Syrop asserted that she died in 1942 in a "death camp in Poland." I was unable to see that letter.

Leon's sister, Franciszka Plachte, her husband and both daughters lived in the Tarnów ghetto (KB). The remaining Jewish population there was executed or deported by Germans between June 1942 and September 1943. Franciszka, her husband, and children, as well as Bronisława Szenkel and her daughter, Gizelle, were likely deported in September 1942 to Bełżec, with about 8,000 people, and then murdered in the gas chambers (YIVO). In 1941 or 1942, Wolf Szenkel, then a leader of Tarnów's Jewish Council (Judenrat) and a member of "the Tarnow spiritual elite" (Goldberg-Klimek, 1954–1968, p. 250), was ordered by "the Germans [. . .] to march through the Tarnow streets with his hands raised and shouting: 'The Jews are guilty of the war'" (Komet, 1954–1968, p. 819). He was then deported to Auschwitz on February 26, 1942, in a group of 28 prisoners, and murdered there on March 9 (Mączka, 2004, p. 60).

Jadwiga's two sisters, Irena and Olga, their children, Marja Stanislawa Magda and Aleksander, and Olga's husband, Aleksander, all perished in the Shoah.

As noted earlier, I have been unable to confirm the circumstances of Leon Plachte's death. Olga told her daughters that the Germans tried to force him to provide them with his extensive knowledge and expertise on Polish bridges and tunnels. When he refused, they executed him (HW). I have yet to corroborate the source of this information, which may be family legend. A letter from Leon survived, dated July 20, 1943, possibly his final letter (KB). The undated fact of Leon's death is recorded in *The Tarnów Yizkor Book* (List of Holocaust Victims, 1954–1968, p. 358).

After leaving Busko-Zdrój on September 4, 1939, Olga's sister, Irena, Jerzy, Jadwiga, and the unidentified boy made a harrowing journey by carriage and foot until they reached Lemberg (now Lviv, Ukraine), almost 150 miles away (KB). They most likely stayed there until mid-1941. Irena and Jerzy continued their studies and lived in a dorm, while Jadwiga stayed with family. Following Germany's invasion of the Soviet Union on June 22, 1941, Irena and Jerzy made the difficult decision to continue eastward, to Siberia.

The details of Jadwiga's death are also lost to history. The last known communication from her was on October 1942, in a letter to her husband (KB). She most likely died in occupied Ukraine shortly after, at the hands of Germans or Russians. We know that she decided not to leave with Irena and Jerzy for Siberia. There is a possibility that she traveled southwest instead, to join her sister Zofia Schwanenfeld in Sambir (now in Ukraine) (KB), about 45 miles away. Zofia, her husband, Hersch Syrop, and their two children, Rut and Rafael Elizer, fled Nowy Sącz in September 1939 with many Jewish and other refugees. In mid-1942 the Germans began forced deportations of Jews to the killing center in Bełżec, established in the first phase of the "Operation Reinhard," the plan engineered to commit genocide across the German zone of occupation, the General Government, which included the broad region of Galicia. The Syrop family was most likely among them (Tabaszewski, 2014, pp. 56, 68, 87). Their names are on the recently unveiled Nowy Sącz Holocaust Victims Memorial, with those of some 12,000 of town's Jews killed in the Shoah.

Irena and Jerzy survived the war in Siberia and returned to Poland shortly after fighting ended, in 1945 or early 1946. They settled in Warsaw,

Figure 13.3 Remains of the Schwanenfeld factory and the family estate. Tarnów, shortly after the Second World War ended.

Reproduced with permission of Krystina Borecka.

where their children were born: Krystina (later Borecka; b. 1949) and Alexander (1954–1976). Other survivors included Marie Frisch and her husband, Zygmund, who fled Vienna on November 18, 1938, aboard the SS *Europa*. Despite Marie's profession and educational background, she was listed in the ship's manifest below Zygmund, as "his wife." Initially they settled in New York City, and then moved to Lancaster, Pennsylvania (after 1950, as the census that year places them in New York). They had no children.

Both sons of Bronisława and Wolf Szenkel survived the war. The older, Leon Teodor (also Theodore; 1917–2002), an engineer, immigrated to Melbourne, Australia, in 1949 with his wife, Barbara Carolina, and son, Piotr (also Peter). Adam (b. 1920), who completed the Safa Berura school, was among "only a few graduates and students [who] survived and arrived to Israel [then] fell defending the homeland in the War of Independence" fought in 1948–1949 (Argov, 1954–1968, p. 777).

Also surviving were Olga's cousin, Adam Theodore Syrop (later Solak), an engineer, and his wife, Teresa, survived the war, reportedly in Warsaw (Frisch, 1946). They moved to New York City on March 6, 1951, traveling aboard the RMS *Queen Mary* from Southampton, England. They were recorded as "stateless" ("Polish" had been crossed out), traveling to join "Dr. Frisch." Another survivor was Alfred Holländer, widower of Olga's aunt, Irena Schwanenfeld (KB; Frisch, 1946). Finally, Paul Wermer, his wife, Eva (née Raudnitz; 1899–1966), a dentist and an aspiring opera singer, and their son, Hans (later John; 1927–2022), had fled the invasion to the United States on November 25, 1939 (Wermer, Feb. 25, 2002).

From after Olga's emigration in August 1939 through 1946, she reportedly believed her entire family perished in the Holocaust, with the sole exceptions of her aunt and uncle, Marie and Zygmund Frisch. She didn't know that her sister, Irena, had survived, as had her two cousins, Adam and Leon Theodore Szenkel (HW). Their names were not on the *Sh'arit ha-pl'atah* list of survivors of the occupation, published by the Central Committee of Jews in Bavaria in 1946 (*Sh'arit ha-pl'atah*, Holocaust Encyclopedia, USHMM). We can only imagine how disturbing it must have been for Olga to know neither if, when, where, nor how her mother, father, sister, and other close family members had died, or if their remains had been buried. Judith Kestenberg, another Tarnów-born Jewish psychoanalyst and Olga's age peer who also lost both parents in the Shoah, has stressed the significance of not having that knowledge. Kestenberg, who conducted thousands of interviews with Holocaust survivors, wrote:

> Many who did not accept the finality of their relatives' deaths suffered from a split between knowing and not knowing. It was not right to say Kaddish [the ritual prayer] for them without being sure of their death. It was not right to mourn. Energies were concentrated on building a new life, on adjusting to a new country, [. . .] on studies, and making a career.
> (Kestenberg, 1989, p. 401)

In 1946, Olga received a letter from her sister, Irena, writing from communist Poland across the Iron Curtain (KB). The sisters and their children had to wait another decade to meet, in the picturesque Austrian village of St. Gilgen. They then met regularly, at least once a year, and talked on the phone very frequently (KB).

Physician and Abortion Practitioner

Olga's first career in the US was in endocrinology and gynecology. To receive a state-issued medical license, she had to pass a comprehensive state-board exam, a requirement for émigré physicians regardless of their existing degrees and qualifications. The examination was in English. This must have been a serious hurdle for Olga: while fluent in six languages upon her arrival in the US—Polish, German, Italian, French, Latin, and Greek—"she didn't speak any English" (HW). She reportedly learned from her new patients. In 1939–1943, Olga completed internships at Chapin Hospital in Providence, Rhode Island, then at Lutheran Hospital in Omaha, Nebraska, and at Mount Sinai Hospital in Milwaukee, Wisconsin. When her residencies were complete, she trained as a Fellow of Medicine at the Boston Dispensary (now Tufts Medical Center), founded to provide relief to the poor (1943–1946), and as a Fellow in Endocrinology at the Nebraska Medical Center in Omaha (1946–1949) (*McLean Hospital clipping*, 1962). In 1949, she opened a private practice in endocrinology and medical gynecology in Boston (*McLean Hospital clipping*, 1962).

In 1943, Olga and Henry moved to Boston (HW). It was then home to the second-largest émigré psychoanalytic community, after New York City. A few years later, they bought a 1920 four-bedroom Tudor-style house in suburban Newton (in Waban Village), described as a "small brick English-type house" by Olmsted Associates, the landscape-architecture firm the Wermers hired in August 1949 (founded by Frederick Law Olmsted, codesigner with Calvert Vaux of Central and Prospect Parks in New York City). Then, in 1953 or 1954, they bought a seven-bedroom Tudor-style country manor closer to Boston, in the wealthy Chestnut Hill suburb. The house stands by Chestnut Hill Reservoir, a park Olmsted created in 1870.

One room in the Chestnut Hill house was set up for gynecological exams and treatment. In the 1950s and 1960s—the pre-*Roe* era in the US—Olga used it to perform safe medical abortions in secrecy for her existing patients (HW), risking arrest and possible prison (cf. Goodwin, n.d.). In the States, the anti-abortion movement is rooted in and continues to be motivated by misogyny, racism, and white supremacy. Through the end of the Civil War, abortions and contraceptives had been legal for white citizens, though not for enslaved Blacks. Terminations were typically performed by midwives, half of whom were Black. In the 1860s, intent on destroying midwifery,

Figure 13.4 Olga Wermer and Henry, USA, 1941.
Reproduced with permission of Hedy Wermer.

white gynecologists of the American Medical Association, which barred women and Black people from membership, started a racist, misogynistic smear campaign. Their goal was to dominate the field of reproductive health, medicalizing and monetizing it while establishing control over women's bodies, as Michele Goodwin details in her book *Policing the Womb* (2020). Gynecologists wielded considerable political and social influence in pushing for total bans on midwifery and abortion. After slavery was abolished with the Thirteenth Amendment's ratification in 1865, states began passing anti-abortion laws; by 1910, it had been banned nationwide. It took over 60 years to decriminalize abortion, with the Supreme Court's 1973 ruling in *Roe v. Wade*. Due to systemic racism built into disproportionate practices and policies—the Hyde Amendment, for example, which restricts uses of federal funds for abortion—reproductive rights remained less accessible to people of color (Goodwin, n.d.). Since the Supreme Court overturned *Roe v. Wade* in June 2022, 24 states have already passed new, total, or near-total abortion bans (Nash and Guarnieri, 2023).

Moving Into Psychoanalysis and Psychiatry

In the mid-1950s, Olga enrolled in a training program at the Boston Psychoanalytic Society and Institute (BPSI), graduating in 1957 (*Bulletin of the American Psychoanalytic Association*, 1957, p. 721) and joining BPSI. It is likely that she became interested in psychoanalysis through her husband and their mutual friends. Another, much earlier experience might have informed Olga's interest in mental-health care. When she was a girl, her father would reportedly often bring her with him to check in on his mentally ill cousin and bring her food, telling Olga that it was "important to take care of those who were unwell and needed help" (HW). Additionally, as an adult "she found the personal lives of her patients and their desire to discuss emotional issues more interesting than the practice of gynecology" (HW). According to Margaret Wermer, a lawyer, her mother's decision to switch to psychiatry might also have been connected with Henry's deteriorating health, perhaps as an attempt at securing financial stability for their family through a more lucrative type of practice (MW). Indeed, Henry suffered his first heart attack in 1958; a series of eight more coronaries and two episodes of congestive heart failure continued until his death on the night of November 4–5, 1968 (HW; *New York Times*, November 8, 1968).

Olga completed her psychiatric residency at Beth Israel Hospital and McLean Hospital in Belmont, Massachusetts (HW), two teaching hospitals of the Harvard Medical School. At Beth Israel, she completed a three-year program of "intensive psychiatric training" and then "special training in a program of obstetrical and psychiatric research" (Psychiatric Service of the Beth Israel Hospital, 1959, p. 7). She became an associate in psychiatry there in 1956 (*McLean Hospital clipping*, 1962). A year earlier, Grete Bibring was named psychiatrist-in-chief; Bibring was later the first woman to be appointed full clinical professor at Harvard Medical School (cf. Naszkowska, 2023). In 1959, with three of her colleagues, Olga was made responsible for developing a five-year Clinical Course in Medical Psychology for Physicians of the Endocrine and Fertility Clinics, aimed at "permitting the attending practitioners to integrate psychological concepts and techniques into their work" (Psychiatric Service of BIH, 1959, p. 7). She was also an instructor in medicine at Harvard Medical School (p. 7). She was staff psychiatrist in student-health services at the Massachusetts Institute of Technology in Cambridge from 1963 until her retirement from MIT in 1976 (*MIT Tech Talk*, June 16, 1993). During this period, after the American Public Health Association had agreed in 1959 to introduce sex education into schools, Olga participated in the 1965 Marriage Lecture Series at Wellesley College, a liberal women's school in Massachusetts, with the lecture "Sexuality and Guilt" (Wellesley College News, March 4, 1965).

Despite her training at BPSI, she "did not identify as an analyst but rather as a psychoanalytically oriented psychotherapist" (HW). Indeed, she specialized in treating deeply disturbed patients, who typically were no longer being treated by classical psychoanalysts. In her second career, Olga conducted a private psychiatric practice for adult patients in an office in her home. Following the prewar Freudian principle of making therapy accessible to all and as a "staunch non-elitist," Olga reportedly "offered substantially reduced fees to needy patients" (HW). In the model of the first training institute established in 1920 in Berlin, treatment of patients without fees had been included. Analysts at the Berlin Training Institute were even required to treat at least one patient without charge (Danto, 2007). This commitment among European psychoanalysts to bring the benefits of therapy to the poor and to the working classes had generally been abandoned in the US, and psychoanalysis was a lucrative, elitist practice (cf. Jacoby, 1983). To the best of my knowledge, Olga Wermer did not have a connection to the interwar psychoanalytic community in Vienna, but she had lived in progressive, left-wing Red Vienna before it was abolished by the rise of Austrofascism in 1934. Additionally, she was raised in a family that adhered to the Jewish principle of giving back to the community through philanthropic work, social activism, and investing in education.

Trauma, Memory, Postmemory

Olga had a complex relationship with her past, with Poland and Polishness, and with her Jewish heritage. According to her oldest daughter, Hedy Wermer, a clinical psychologist working with female trauma victims, Olga was deeply affected by the experience of the war, especially by the loss of her family. "She nonetheless managed to cope and function impeccably without evidence of pathological trauma," Hedy stated (HW). On the other hand, Olga was surely aware of the impact of her traumatic experiences on her wellbeing, and shortly after arriving in the US, she entered analysis with another Jewish Galician émigré, Edward Bibring. She made a decision to postpone motherhood until after her analysis was complete (HW). Hedy, born in 1949, was named after Olga's mother, Hedwig, using the German version of that name instead of the commonly used Polish one, Jadwiga. Olga's second daughter, Margaret, was born two years later.

She stayed home with her infant children; once they were in school, she worked only part-time for several years, to spend time with them in the afternoons. They remember her as "an exceptionally perceptive, loving, affectionate, creatively playful, and sensible mother" (MW) who was "warm, affectionate, playful, funny, and interesting but also sensible, and not too strict" (HW).

Despite the analysis with Bibring, Olga remained reluctant to talk about aspects of her personal history. She "didn't volunteer about the past" and, as Margaret Wermer has more recently realized about her relations with her mother, while the latter was alive, she "didn't ask enough" in their discussions (MW). Hedy reports that Olga did tell many stories about her childhood but spoke little about wartime experiences: "There was relatively little talk about the loss of the family although Olga did discuss her growing up and early family life in rich detail" (HW).

It was very typical of Jews who had been refuges in the 1930s and 1940s to avoid conversations with children and grandchildren about their pre-war and interwar lives, the war, and their deceased relatives and to repress their painful, traumatic experiences (cf. Kuriloff, 2014; Naszkowska, 2022, 2023). Issues of trauma and loss connected with the Holocaust were generally absent from the psychoanalytic literature until the pioneering work of Henry Krystal and William Niederland (cf. Krystal, 1968; Krystal and Niederland, 1971) and of Judith Kestenberg in the late 1960s (cf. Kestenberg, 1986). About the general approach of mental-health professionals toward survivors in the first decades after the war, Kestenberg wrote, "The 'cure all' was to forget the past and build the future. A prohibition against discussing the past [. . .] was for many survivors a continuation of the prohibition against divulging their Jewishness" (Kestenberg, 1989, p. 386). As one of Kestenberg's younger colleagues and followers, Robert Prince, has pointed out, "Despite its central European origins, the historical impact of the Holocaust on psychoanalysis had been seriously neglected. This silence of psychoanalysis bears striking parallels to the silence found in survivor families" (Prince, 2009, p. 180).

It seems that Olga held on to her European identity by creating a "nonhuman environment" through the continued use of the German and Polish languages at home and through objects that reminded her of her upbringing, along with some European customs (cf. Grinberg and Grinberg, 1984). The Wermer celebration of Christmas was "European, nonreligious, and festive, with a decorated tree, a sumptuous family meal and presents" (HW). In the States, Olga continued to be very elegant and wore fashionable dresses for work (HW). She had brought with her a few linens, handkerchiefs, napkins, and a small amount of family jewelry, including the pearl-and-ruby earring of her grandmother's that she wore as a brooch. She also brought a white sweater knitted by her mother, Jadwiga, and wore it frequently for years, repairing it many times and finally dyeing it purple to cover stains.

Additionally, Olga transported a collection of family photographs across the Atlantic. These she kept secret for over 50 years. After Olga's death, in 1993, her daughter Hedy discovered the photo trove hidden in a cupboard (HW). The cache included one from 1933, taken in the Vienna studio of Trude Fleischmann (1895–1990), a leading portrait photographer of the era (see Figure 13.2). Fleischmann fled Vienna and settled in New York City; her portraits included prominent intellectuals, artists, and activists from Albert Einstein, Eleanor Roosevelt, and Max Reinhardt to Stefan Zweig, Claire Bauroff, Arturo Toscanini, and Hedy Lamarr.

Her daughters both stated independently that Olga "thought of herself as Polish" (HW; MW). Yet she didn't teach them Polish (MW). Hedy learned a bit of the language from her mother, mostly social expressions and greetings, such as "good morning" (*dzień dobry*) and "thank you" (*dziękuję*). Olga sometimes used Polish in comments to their dog, such as "come here" (*chodź tu*) and "good boy" (*dobry pies*) (HW). It might have been an attempt to recall her beloved dog, Telli, left behind in Tarnów in 1939 and reportedly shot by Germans during the occupation. The standard language used in their home was English. Olga retained a "strong Eastern European accent," though her grammar and vocabulary were "essentially perfect" (HW). Finally, Olga and Henry used German as their secret language, not understood by their young daughters. Olga's sense of identity may well have been rooted in and interspersed among all of these languages.

Olga remained unwilling to visit Poland after the war. To the best of Margaret's knowledge, she also didn't seek out the circumstances of her parents' death (MW). A friend or family member—no one remembers who—visited Tarnów and took a photograph of the ruined family house. Olga also deferred from visiting Germany and from buying a car or other products that were made there (MW; KB). Atypically among Jewish refugees, who often felt personally betrayed by Austria and refused to go there, Olga visited the country several times.

As to her Jewish identity, she had been driven from Europe by Nazi-led antisemitism and violence, and almost her entire family perished in the Shoah, so Jewishness was certainly an important component of her life story. Hedy believed that Olga did have "an ethnic Jewish identity" (HW). Still, it appears that Olga did not maintain a strong religious, cultural, or familial Jewish identity. As Nancy Chodorow discovered in her interviews with early women psychoanalysts, Jewishness and gender were not key identity components in general for Jewish women psychoanalysts who fled Hitler to the States (Chodorow, 1989; cf. Naszkowska, 2022, 2023). Olga was agnostic and did not bring up her daughters as Jews, didn't teach them Jewish traditions, customs or rituals, didn't bat mitzvah them. Yet since early childhood, they both had been aware of being Jewish (MW).

It can be deduced that Olga's distress manifested in a considerable shift in her social habits. In interwar Vienna, she was reportedly very social and popular; once in the US, she kept a small, intimate group of women friends. Her best friend was Malvina "Mila" Stock (née Malbinah Shtok; 1915–1980), a psychoanalyst originally from Galicia who also lost her family in the Shoah. Stock, who lived ten minutes from the Wermers, was a "very close friend" for decades, and was considered a "family member." Between them, the two women spoke Polish (HW).

Olga Wermer worked until her untimely death in a car crash at 79, on April 21, 1993. Her name has been lost to official histories because she was a psychotherapist and clinician first and foremost, prioritizing her work with patients over holding public positions or publishing papers. Recorded history tends to omit the experiences and voices of minorities, and she was both a woman and a Jew. Additionally, it prioritizes "success stories," and Olga's life doesn't encourage neat simplifications, despite her highly successful career.

Yet the arc of her life is important, revealing, and relevant for us today. Her earliest experiences were of growing up Polish in an occupied land that had not existed for over a century on the geopolitical map, and later, of being Jewish in newly liberated Poland, where antisemitism held increasing sway after authoritarian rule was established by the initial chief of state, Józef Piłsudzki. Living and studying in socially progressive Red Vienna, she then witnessed its collapse as Austrofascism prevailed and Austria embraced

Figure 13.5 Olga Wermer and Henry, USA, ca. 1964.
Reproduced with permission of Hedy Wermer.

annexation to Hitler's Germany. She lost both parents and many close family members in the Shoah, after departing from Poland mere weeks before the Second World War struck Europe.

Once in the United States, the experience of necessary perseverance became Olga's, as a first-generation migrant needing to promptly reestablish and reinvent herself, adjusting to a new environment and a new language, while raising a family and bearing heartbreaking losses. Deeply present in Olga's story is the story of the erasure of the deeply rooted Jewish populace across the region that had formed the historic Galician, and across all Polish lands. Olga Wermer's story, along with those of other Jewish female psychoanalysts, helps us illuminate the importance of remembering and discussing interconnectivities in history and contemporaneity, in particular in the connections between women, immigration, racist (antisemitic) violence, and other of humanity's ongoing, age-old achievements and often traumatic difficulties.

Note

1 I would like to express my deepest thanks to Hedy Wermer, Margaret Wermer, Krystina Borecka, Alex Wermer-Colan, and Malkah Topin Notman, each of whom were kind enough to talk to me at length and share their knowledge, memories, documents, and photographs. For communications with Krystina Borecka (March 10, 2022; April 22, 2023; May 24, 2023), Margaret Wermer (March 11, 2022), and Hedy Wermer (March 11, 2022; March 9, 10, and 13, 2023), I have designated their contributions with the abbreviations KB, MW, and HW, respectively.

Due to space limitations, archival sources are listed at the end of this chapter and not referenced in the text.

Archival Materials

AT—UAW, Eintrag in das Rigorosenprotokoll, PH 59.25, Prot.—Nr. 4602. "Irene Schwanenfeld."

AT—UAW, Eintrag in das Rigorosenprotokoll PH 59.31, Prot.—Nr. 9693. "Olga Schwanenfeld."

AT—UAW, Nationale der Medizinischen Fakultät, SS 1918—WS 1921/22. "Wermer, Paul."

AT—UAW, Nationale der Medizinischen Fakultät, WS 1931/32—WS 1936. "Wermer, Heinz."

AT—UAW, Nationale der Medizinischen Fakultät, WS 1932/33—SS 1933. "Plachte, Olga."

AT—UAW, Nationale der Medizinischen Fakultät, SS 1934—SS 1938. "Plachte, Olga."

AT—UAW, Rigorosenakt PH RA 4602. "Irene Schwanenfeld."

AT—UAW, Rigorosenakt PH RA 9693. "Olga Schwanenfeld."
AT—UAW, M 33.11, Promotionsprotokoll Mediziner, P—Nr. 1407. "Wermer, Paul."
AT—UAW, M 33.13, Promotionsprotokoll Mediziner, P—Nr. 3220. "Wermer, Heinz."
AT—UAW/PH, Nationale der Philosophischen Fakultät, Buchstabe "F", WS 1920/21 bis SS 1924. "Siegmund Frisch."
AT—UAW/PH, Nationale der Philosophischen Fakultät, Buchstabe "S", WS 1920/21 bis SS 1925. "Marie Schwanenfeld."
AT—UAW/PH, Rigorosenakt, RA 9147. "Marie Schwanenfeld."
AT—UAW/PH, Rigorosenakt, RA 9016. "Siegmund Frisch."
AT—UAW/PH, Rigorosenprotokoll der Philosophischen Fakultät, 59.29, Prot.—Nr. 9147. "Marie Schwanenfeld."
AT—UAW/PH, Rigorosenprotokoll der Philosophischen Fakultät, 59.29, Prot.—Nr. 9016. "Siegmund Frisch."
Austrian Property Declarations. 1938. File 44181. "Schwanenfeld, Rosalie." Österreichische Staatsarchiv. Archiv der Republik. Vienna, Austria.
Commercial and Craft Activities Database (1912–1914, 1916). Austrian Ministry of Trade and Industry. Fond 308. File 75, pp. 113–132. The Central Archive of Historical Records (AGAD), Warsaw. "Plachte, Franziska."
Central Database of Shoah Victims' Names. Yad Vashem.
Database of Jewish Refugees Arriving in Australia via Melbourne between 1946–1954. Unites States Holocaust Memorial Museum.
Demande d'immatriculation. Semestre d'hiver 1938–1939. Université de Lausanne. UNIRIS.
Diplôme de docteur en médecine. No. 1283. Registre des grades. Université de Lausanne. UNIRIS.
Documentary heritage. Student archives. File 8704. Historical Archive of the University of Bologna. Faculty of Medicine. "Plachte, Olga."
DÖW: Jewish Deportations from Austria. Serial 48739, Döwid 88223. "Rosalia Schwanenfeld." Dokumentationsarchiv des österreichischen Widerstandes.
Galicia Business Directory. 1891. Tarnow. "Szwanenfeld, Leon." JewishGen.
Inscription de cours. Semestre d'été 1939. Université de Lausanne. UNIRIS.
Karta wpisowa dla kwestury. 1931/32. Uniwersytet Jagielloński. S II, 382. "Plachtówna, Olga."
Karta wpisowa dla dziekanatu. 1931/32. Uniwersytet Jagielloński. WF II, 448; WP II 345. "Plachtówna, Olga."
Kolomyya AGAD Births. 1902. Akt 150, sygn. 2263. "Frisch, Zygmunt."
Krakow Births. June 12, 1889. Akt 369. "Plachte, Bronisława." Akta stanu cywilnego Izraelickiego Okręgu Metrykalnego w Tarnowie. Archiwum Narodowe w Krakowie, oddział w Tarnowie.
Krakow Births. Aug. 20, 1890. Akt 571. "Plachte, Franciszka." Akta stanu cywilnego Izraelickiego Okręgu Metrykalnego w Tarnowie. Archiwum Narodowe w Krakowie, oddział w Tarnowie.
Krakow Births. May 29, 1888. Akt 325. "Plachte, Leon." Akta stanu cywilnego Izraelickiego Okręgu Metrykalnego w Tarnowie. Archiwum Narodowe w Krakowie, oddział w Tarnowie.

Krakow Births. Feb. 22, 1917. Akt 69, sygn. 1201. "Schenkel, Leon Theodor." Akta stanu cywilnego Izraelickiego Okręgu Metrykalnego w Tarnowie. Archiwum Narodowe w Krakowie, oddział w Tarnowie.

Krakow Marriages. Nov. 27, 1887. Akt 122. "Leib/Leon Schwanenfeld, Ruda/ Rozalia Shudmak." Akta stanu cywilnego Izraelickiego Okręgu Metrykalnego w Tarnowie. Archiwum Narodowe w Krakowie, oddział w Tarnowie.

Krakow Marriages. Aug. 22, 1887. Akt. 108. "Plachte, Majer; Schollem, Curtel." JRI-Poland.

Krakow, Poland, Census Records. 1870. "Scholem, Curtel."

Księga małżeństw. Akta stanu cywilnego izraelickiego okręgu metrykalnego w Tarnowie. "Zofia Schwanenfeld," 1909. 33/276/0/—/42. Archiwum Narodowe w Krakowie. Oddział w Tarnowie.

Księga urodzin. Akta stanu cywilnego izraelickiego okręgu metrykalnego w Tarnowie. "Zofia Schwanenfeld," 1888. 33/276/0/—/8. Archiwum Narodowe w Krakowie. Oddział w Tarnowie.

List or manifest of Alien Passengers for the United States Immigrant Inspector at port of arrival. 1938. The Statue of Liberty—Ellis Island Foundation, Inc. "Plachte, Olga."

List or manifest of Alien Passengers for the United States Immigrant Inspector at port of arrival. 1938. The Statue of Liberty—Ellis Island Foundation, Inc. "Wermer, Heinz."

List or manifest of Alien Passengers for the United States Immigrant Inspector at port of arrival. 1939. The Statue of Liberty—Ellis Island Foundation, Inc. "Wermer, Olga."

Liste des étudiants de l'Université de Lausanne. Semestre d'hiver 1938–1939. Université de Lausanne. UNIRIS, p. 34.

Liste des étudiants de l'Université de Lausanne. Semestre d'été 1939. Université de Lausanne. UNIRIS, p. 31.

Frisch, M. (1946). Correspondence relating to claims and queries. Claim A—346. 74386488. National Archives.

McLean Hospital clipping (1962). Olga S. Wermer, M.D.

Memorial Book for the Victims of National Socialism. University of Vienna. 1938.

Olmsted Associates Records: Job Files, 1863–1971; Files; 9854; Wermer, Henry; Waban, Mass., 1949. Library of Congress.

Polish Business Directories Database. 1926, Tarnów, Kraków, Krakowska 783, "Plachte, Leon." JewishGen.

Polish Business Directories Database. 1926. Tarnów. Rynek 4. "Plachte, Franciszka." JewishGen.

Polish Martyred Physicians. Record no. 1655, p. 433. "Plachte-Schenkel, Bronislawa." JewishGen.

Tarnow Marriages. 1925. Akta 98, sygn. 22/276/116. "Plachte, Franciszka."

Tarnow Schools 1873–1915. III Liceum A. Mickiewicz. 1899/1900; 1900/1901; 1901/1902; 1902/1903; 1904/1905. "Leon Plachte." JRI-Poland.

Tarnow Schools 1873–1915. Juliusz Słowacki. 1897/1898, 1898/1899, 1899/1900, "Plachte, Franciszka." JRI—Poland.

Tarnow Schools 1873–1915. Juliusz Słowacki. 1897/1898, 1898/1899, "Plachte, Bronisława." JRI-Poland.

Tarnow Schools 1973–1915. Maria Konopnicka. 1894/1895, "Schwanenfeld, Zofia." JRI-Poland.
Tarnow Births. "Henryk Schwanenfeld," 1892. Akta 542, sygn. 33/276/52. JRI-Poland.
Tarnow Births. "Irena Schwanenfeld," 1895, Akta 308, sygn. 33/276/10. JRI-Poland.
Tarnow Births. "Jadwiga Schwanenfeld," 1889. Akta 480, sygn. 33/276/8. JRI-Poland.
Tarnow Births. "Marya Schwanenfeld," 1901, Akta 320, syg. 33/276/15. JRI-Poland.
Tarnow Births. "Olga Schwanenfeld," 1900. Akta 316, sygn. 33/276/14. JRI-Poland.
The Psychiatric Service of the Beth Israel Hospital. (1959). Ruth and David Freiman Archives at Beth Israel Deaconess Medical Center.
Tarnow Births. "Szenkel, Wolf Mendel. 1888. Akta 258, sygn. 33/276/8. JRI-Poland.
The JewishGen Yizkor Book Necrology Database—Krakow. Tarnów. "Plachteh, Leon the engineer and family."
Vienna Births. Jan. 9, 1917. Book 1917, vol. 1917, no. 35. "Plachte, Irene." JewishGen.
Vienna Births. Dec. 7, 1927. Book 1927, Vol. 1927, no. 1397. "Lewenberg, Ilse." JewishGen.
Vienna Marriages. 1929. No. 346. "Frisch, Zygmund, Dr.; Szwanenfeld, Marya, Dr." JewishGen.
Vienna Marriages. 1915. No. 659. "Schenkel, Wolf M., Dr.; Plachte Dr. Bronisława." JRI-Poland.
Vienna Marriages. 1927. No. 9. "Lewenberg, Nusyn L.; Plachte, Franziska." JRI-Poland.
Wermer, H. (1974/1975). Unpublished notes.
Wermer, J. (Feb. 25, 2002). Long Letter from John. Providence, Rhode Island. Unpublished.

Reference List

Argov, R. (1954–1968), Memories of a Graduate of the "Safa Berura" High-School in Tarnow. S. Mages (Trans.). In A. Chomet (Ed.), *Tarnow; The Life and Destruction of a Jewish City (Tarnów, Poland), Vol. I* (pp. 774–778). Tel Aviv: Association of Former Residents of Tarnów.

Baddiel, D. (2021). *Jews Don't Count: How Identity Politics Failed One Particular Identity*. London: TLS Books.

Bartosz, A. (2007). *Żydowskim szlakiem po Tarnowie*. Tarnów: Muzeum Okręgowe w Tarnowie, S-CAN Wydawnictwo.

Bazyler, M. J., et al. (2019). *Searching for Justice after the Holocaust: Fulfilling the Terezin Declaration and Immovable Property Restitution*. New York: Oxford UP.

Berkelhamer, V. (1954–1968). Tarnow in the Geography of Zionism. In Lieu of an Introduction. G. Schaechter-Viswanath (Trans.). In A. Chomet (Ed.), *Tarnow; The Life and Destruction of a Jewish City (Tarnów, Poland), Vol. I* (pp. 248–350). Tel Aviv: Association of Former Residents of Tarnów.

Blau, B. (1950). The Jewish Population of Germany 1939–1945. *Jewish Social Studies*, 12(2), 161–172.

Breitman, R. and Kraut, A. M. (1987). *American Refugee Policy and European Jewry, 1933–1945*. Bloomington: Indiana UP.

Brody, D. (1956). American Jewry. The Refugees and Immigration restriction (1932–1942). *Publications of the American Jewish Historical Society*, 45(4), 219–247.

Brook-Shepherd, G. (1996). *The Austrians: A Thousand-year Odyssey*. New York: Carroll & Graf Publishers.

Bulletin of the American Psychoanalytic Association (1957). 13, 720–740.

Chodorow, N. (1989). Seventies Questions for Thirties Women: Gender and Generation in a Study of Early Women Psychoanalysts. In N. Chodorow (Ed.), *Feminism and Psychoanalytic Theory* (pp. 199–218). New Haven and London: Yale UP.

Chomet, A. (1954–1968a). About the Jewish Cultural System in Tarnow. G. Berkenstat Freund (Trans.). In A. Chomet (Ed.), *Tarnow; The Life and Destruction of a Jewish City (Tarnów, Poland), Vol. I* (pp. 671–713). Tel Aviv: Association of Former Residents of Tarnów.

Chomet, A. (1954–1968b). Charitable Unions and Committees in Tarnow. G. Berkenstat Freund (Trans.). In A. Chomet (Ed.), *Tarnow; The Life and Destruction of a Jewish City (Tarnów, Poland), Vol. I* (pp. 733–762). Tel Aviv: Association of Former Residents of Tarnów.

Danto, A. (2007). *Freud's Free Clinics. Psychoanalysis and Social Justice, 1918–1938*. New York: Columbia UP.

Davie, M. R. (1947). *Refuges in America. Report of the Committee for the Study of Recent Immigration from Europe*. New York: Harper & Brothers Publishers.

Davis, N. (2011). *Vanished Kingdoms: The Rise and Gall of States and Nations*. New York: Penguin Books.

Deutsch, H. (1973). *Confrontations with Myself. An Epilogue*. New York: W.W. Norton & Company.

Domus, K. (2016). Krakowskie gimnazja żeńskie przełomu XIX i XX wieku. *SPI*, 19(2), 87–103.

Dr. Henry Wermer, Child Psychiatrist (November 8, 1968). *The New York Times*, 47.

Ernst, E. (1995). A Leading Medical School Seriously Damaged: Vienna 1938. *American College of Physicians*, 122, 789–792.

Friedenreich, H. P. (1996). Jewish Women Physicians in Central Europe in the Early Twentieth Century. *Contemporary Jewry*, 17(1), 79–105.

Gawron, E. (2009). Syrop, Hersch (Hersz, Herman). In A. Romanowski (Ed.), *Polski słownik biograficzny, Vol. XXXXVI* (p. 311). Kraków: Wydawnictwo Towarzystwa Naukowego Societas Vistulana.

Gelber, N. M. (2008). Tarnow. *Encyclopaedia Judaica*. Online at www.jewishvirtuallibrary.org/tarnow-poland. Accessed Feb. 2, 2023.

Goldberg-Klimek, R. (1954–1968). A Collection of Memories of the Hitlerist Hell. G. Berkenstat Freund (Trans.). In A. Chomet (Ed.), *Tarnow; The Life and Destruction of a Jewish City (Tarnów, Poland)*, *Vol. I* (pp. 248–257). Tel Aviv: Association of Former Residents of Tarnów.

Goodwin, M. (2020). *Policing the Womb: Invisible Women and the Criminalization of Motherhood*. Cambridge: Cambridge UP.

Goodwin, M. (n.d.). *The Racist History of Abortion and Midwifery Bans*. Online at www.aclu.org/news/racial-justice/the-racist-history-of-abortion-and-midwifery-bans/. Accessed Feb. 2, 2023.

Grinberg, L. and Grinberg, R. (1984). A Psychoanalytic Study of Migration: Its Normal and Pathological Aspects. *Journal of the American Psychoanalytic Association*, 32, 13–38.

Holocaust Encyclopedia. *United States Holocaust Memorial Museum (USHMM)*. Online at www.ushmm.org/. Accessed June 25, 2023.

Hubbard, C. (2002). Eduard Pernkopf's "Atlas of Topographical and Applied Human Anatomy": The Continuing Ethical Controversy. *The Anatomical Record*, 265(5), 207–211.

Jacoby, R. (1983). *The Repression of Psychoanalysis. Otto Fenichel and the Political Freudians*. Chicago: University of Chicago Press.

Juśko, E. (2020). Edukacja dzieci Żydowskich w Tarnowie w okresie II Rzeczypospolitej. *Resovia Sacra*, 27, 319–342.

Kahane, A. (1954–1968). Tarnow—A Center of Torah, Hasidus, Zionism and Culture. G. Berkenstat Freund (Trans.). In A. Chomet (Ed.), *Tarnow; The Life and Destruction of a Jewish City (Tarnów, Poland)*, *Vol. I* (pp. 189–231). Tel Aviv: Association of Former Residents of Tarnów.

Kestenberg, J. S. (1986). Ein Requiem für die Verluste der Psychoanalyse in der Nazizeit. Eindrücke vom Hamburger IPA-Kongreß. *Psyche—Zeitschrift für Psychoanalyse*, 40(10), 881–883.

Kestenberg, J. S. (1989). Coping with Losses and Survival. In D. R. Dietrich and P. S. Shabad (Eds.), *The Problem of Loss and Mourning: Psychoanalytic Perspectives* (pp. 381–403). Madison, CT: International Universities Press.

Komet, A. (1954–1968). The Annihilation of the Jews in Tarnov. Y. D. Shulman and G. Berkenstat Freund (Trans.). In A. Chomet (Ed.), *Tarnow; The Life and Destruction of a Jewish City (Tarnów, Poland)*, *Vol. I* (pp. 808–836). Tel Aviv: Association of Former Residents of Tarnów.

Kornilo, Y. (1954–1968). What Remained of Our Jewish Tarnow. G. Berkenstat Freund (Trans.). In A. Chomet (Ed.), *Tarnow; The Life and Destruction of a Jewish City (Tarnów, Poland)*, *Vol. II* (pp. 315–325). Tel Aviv: Association of Former Residents of Tarnów.

Krystal, H. (1968). *Massive Psychic Trauma*. New York: International Universities Press.

Krystal, H. and Niederland, W. G. (1971). *Psychic Traumatization: Aftereffects in Individuals and Communities*. Boston: Little, Brown & Company.

Kuriloff, E. A. (2014). *Contemporary Psychoanalysis and the Legacy of the Third Reich: History, Memory, Tradition.* New York: Routledge.
Life Magazine (November 28, 1938).
List of Holocaust Victims. (1954–1968). S. Bronstein (Trans.). In A. Chomet (Ed.), *Tarnow; The Life and Destruction of a Jewish City (Tarnów, Poland), Vol. II* (pp. 343–368). Tel Aviv: Association of Former Residents of Tarnów.
Mączka, S. (2004). *Żydzi Polscy w KL Auschwitz. Wykazy imienne. Polish Jews in KL Auschwitz. Name Lists.* Warszawa: Żydowski Instytut Historyczny.
Malina, P. (1998). Eduard Pernkopf's Atlas of Anatomy or: The Fiction of Pure Science. *Wien Klin Wochenschr*, 110(4–5), 193–201.
MIT Tech Talk (June 16, 1993). 37(36).
Nash, E. and Guarnieri, I. (2023). Six Months Post-Roe, 24 US States Have Banned Abortion or Are Likely to Do So: A Roundup. *Guttmacher Institute.* Online at www.guttmacher.org/2023/01/six-months-post-roe-24-us-states-have-banned-abortion-or-are-likely-do-so-roundup. Accessed Apr. 5, 2023.
Naszkowska, K. (2022). Psychoanalyst, Jew, Woman, Wife, Mother, Emigrant: The Émigré Foremothers of Psychoanalysis in the United States. *European Judaism*, 55(1), 112–137.
Naszkowska, K. (2023). Help, Health, Husbands, and Hutzpah: The Lives of Five Women Analysts. In A. Harris (Ed.), *The Émigré Analysts and American Psychoanalysis: History and Contemporary Relevance* (pp. 56–91). New York: Routledge.
Open Marriage Lecture Has Brand New Forms, Functions (March 4, 1965). *Wellesley College News.*
Pauley, B. (1992). *From Prejudice to Persecution. A History of Austrian Anti-Semitism.* Chapel Hill, NC: University of North California Press.
Pelczar, R. (2022). Niższe szkoły realne w Galicji w latach 1842–1873. *Zeszyty Naukowe Uniwersitetu Jegiellońskiego, Prace Historyczne*, 149(1), 97–122.
Pernkopf, E. (1963). *Atlas of Topographical and Applied Human Anatomy.* Philadelphia and London: W.B. Saunders Co.
Plachte-Wermer, O. S. (1939). *Klinischer Beitrag zur Kenntnis der Thalliumvergiftung.* Lausanne: Imp. C. Risold & Fils.
Prince, R. (2009). Psychoanalysis Traumatized: The Legacy of the Holocaust. *The American Journal of Psychoanalysis*, 69, 179–194.
Prude, H. and Wilt, H. B. (Oct. 21, 2021). U.S. Admitted Zero Uyghur Refugees in Fiscal 2021. *The Dispatch.* Online at https://thedispatch.com/newsletter/uphill/us-admitted-zero-uyghur-refugees/. Accessed Apr. 19, 2023.
Report to Congress on Projected Refugee Admissions for Fiscal Year 2024 (November 3, 2023). *U.S. Department of State.* Online at https://www.state.gov/report-to-congress-on-proposed-refugee-admissions-for-fiscal-year-2024/. Accessed Nov. 29, 2023.
Ribeli, M. (2022). *A Major Project in Tumultuous Times. Swiss National Museum.* Online at https://blog.nationalmuseum.ch/en/2022/01/hauenstein-base-tunnel/. Accessed Apr. 19, 2023.

Rice, C. (1990). *Lenin: Portrait of a Professional Revolutionary*. London: Cassell Illustrated.
Ruta, Z. (1990). *Prywatne szkoły średnie ogólnokształcące w Krakowie i województwie krakowksicm w latach 1932–1939*. Kraków: Wydawnictwo naukowe WSP.
Sacks, K. B. (1994). How Did Jews Become White Folks? In S. Gregory and R. Sanjek (Eds.), *Race* (pp. 78–102). New Brunswick, NJ: Rutgers UP.
Sh'arit ha-pl'atah. Unites States Holocaust Memorial Museum, USHMM.
Sikora, K. (2007). Pierwsze kobiety na Uniwersytecie Jagiellońskim. *Annales Acaemiae Paedagogicae Cracoviensis, Studia Politologica*, 3(46), 248–268.
Simins, J. W. (n.d.). American First: The Ku Klux Klan's Influence on Immigration Policy in the 1920s. *Re-Imagining Migration*. Online at https://reimaginingmigration.org/historical-context-the-ku-klux-klan-influence-on-immigration-policy-in-the-1920s/. Accessed June 28, 2023.
Stopka, K. (Ed.) (2011). *Corpus Studiosorum Universitatis Jagellonicae in Saeculis XVIII—XX, Vol. III: O—Q 1850/51–1917/18*. Kraków: Archiwum Uniwersytetu Jagiellońskiego.
Suchmiel, J. (1997). *Żydówki ze stopniem doktora wszech nauk lekarskich oraz doktora filozofii na Uniwersytecie Jagiellońskim do czasów II Reczpospolitej*. Częstochowa: WSP.
Tabaszewski, R. K. (2014). *Adwokaci Nowego Sącza do 1945 roku*. Nowy Sącz: Biblioteka "Rocznika Sądeckiego."
Taschwer, K. (2020). The 1938 Anschluss and the Decline of the University of Vienna's Medical School. *Ethics, Medicine and Public Health*, 12, 1–5.
Weissmann, G. (1985). Springtime for Pernkopf. *Hospital Practice*, 20(10), 142–168.
Williams, D. (1988). This History of Eduard Pernkopf's Topographische Anatomie des Menschen. *Journal of Biocommunication*, 15(2), 2–12.
Wirtualny Sztetl. *Muzeum Historii Żydów Polskich POLIN*. Online at https://sztetl.org.pl/pl/miejscowosci/t/625-tarnow/112-synagogi-domy-modlitwy-mykwy/89308-stara-synagoga-w-tarnowie-ul-zydowska. Accessed Feb. 2, 2023.
Wolff, L. (2010). *The Idea of Galicia: History and Fantasy in Habsburg Political Culture*. Stanford, CA: Stanford UP.
Zeidman, L. A. (2020). *Brain Science under the Swastika. Ethical Violations, Resistance, and Victimization of Neuroscientists in Nazi Europe*. Oxford: Oxford UP.

General Bibliography

Appignanesi, L. and Forrester, J. (1996). *Freud's Women*. New York: Other Press.
Mijolla, A. de (Ed.) (2005). *International Dictionary of Psychoanalysis, Vol. I–III*. New York, NY: Macmillan Reference.
Nölleke, B. (2007–2023). *Psychoanalytikerinnen. Biografisches Lexikon*. Online at www.psychoanalytikerinnen.de/. Accessed Mar. 10, 2023.
Thompson, Nellie L. (1987). Early Women Psychoanalysts. *International Review of Psycho-Analysis*, 14, 391–406.
Young-Bruehl, E. (2000). *Subject to Biography: Psychoanalysis, Feminism, and Writing Women's Lives*. Cambridge, MA: Harvard UP.

Abraham, Hilda

Bental, V. (1971). In Memory of Dr. Hilda Abraham. *Israel Journal of Psychiatry and Related Sciences*, 9(3), 265–266.

Balint, Enid

Ruszczynski, S. (1996). Enid Balint and the Beginning of the Psychoanalytical Understanding and Treatment of the Marital Relationship. *Bulletin of the Society of Psychoanalytical Marital Psychotherapists*, 3, 4–7.

Benedek, Therese

Borgos, A. (2021). *Women in the Budapest School of Psychoanalysis: Girls of Tomorrow*. Abingdon and New York: Routledge.
Schmidt, E. (2004). Therese Benedek. Shaping Psychoanalysis from Within. *Annual of Psychoanalysis*, 32, 217–231.

Bibring, Grete

Naszkowska, K. (2023). Help, Health, Husbands, and Hutzpah: The Lives of Five Women Analysts. In A. Harris (Ed.), *The Émigré Analysts and American Psychoanalysis: History and Contemporary Relevance* (pp. 56–91). New York: Routledge.

Bick, Esther

Briggs, A. (2002). The Life and Work of Esther Bick. In A. Bick (Ed.), *Surviving Space. Papers on Infant Observation* (pp. xix–xxx). London and New York: Routledge.

Bonaparte, Marie

Bertin, C. (1982). *Marie Bonaparte*. New York: Harcourt Brace Jovanich.
Stein-Monod, C. (1966). Marie Bonaparte 1882–1962. The Problem of Female Sexuality. In F. Alexander et al. (Eds.), *Psychoanalytic Pioneers: A History of Psychoanalysis as Seen Through the Lives and the Works of Its Most Eminent Teachers, Thinkers, and Clinicians* (pp. 399–414). New York: Basic Books.
Thompson, N. (2003). Marie Bonaparte's Theory of Female Sexuality. Fantasy and Biology. *American Imago*, 60, 343–378.

Bornstein, Berta

Alvarez, A. (2014). Discussion of Berta Bornstein's "The Analysis of a Phobic Child". *Psychoanalytic Study of the Child*, 68, 144–151.
Blos, P. (1974). Berta Bornstein, 1899–1971. *Psychoanalytic Study of the Child*, 29, 35–39.
Galatzer-Levy, R. M. (2014). A Nonlinear Lens on Berta Bornstein's "Frankie". *Psychoanalytic Study of the Child*, 68, 177–190.
Harrison, A. (2014). Co-Creativity and Interactive Repair: Commentary on Berta Bornstein's "The Analysis of a Phobic Child". *Psychoanalytic Study of the Child*, 68, 191–208.
Hoffman, L. (2014). Berta Bornstein's "Frankie:" The Contemporary Relevance of a Classic to the Treatment of Children with Disruptive Symptoms. *Psychoanalytic Study of the Child*, 68, 152–176.
Magnone, L. (2023). *Freud's Emissaries: The Transfer of Psychoanalysis Through the Polish Intelligentsia to Europe 1900–1939*. T. Bhambry (Trans.). Lausanne: Sdvig Press.

Bornstein, Steff

Magnone, L. (2023). *Freud's Emissaries: The Transfer of Psychoanalysis Through the Polish Intelligentsia to Europe 1900–1939*. T. Bhambry (Trans.). Lausanne: Sdvig Press.

Burlingham, Dorothy

Burlingham, M. J. (1989). *The Last Tiffany. A Biography of Dorothy Tiffany Burlingham*. New York: Behind Glass.
Kennedy, H. (1980). Dorothy Burlingham, 1891–1979. *Psychoanalytic Quarterly*, 49, 508–511.

Buxbaum, Edith

www.edithbuxbaum.com/

Cassirer-Bernfeld, Suzanne

Benveniste, D. (2006). The Early History of Psychoanalysis in San Francisco. *Psychoanalysis and History*, 8(2), 195–233.

Deming, Julia

Umansky, O. (2021). Women Histories in Photos—Julia Deming. *BPSI Library Newsletter* (Spring).

Deri, Frances

Kitlitschko, S. (2013). The Prague Psychoanalytic Study Group 1933–1938: Frances Deri, Annie Reich, Theodor Dosužkov, and Heinrich Löwenfeld, and Their Contributions to Psychoanalysis. *International Journal of Psychoanalysis*, 94(6), 1196–1198.

Naszkowska, K. (2022). Psychoanalyst, Jew, Woman, Wife, Mother, Emigrant: The Émigré Foremothers of Psychoanalysis in the United States. *European Judaism*, 55(1), 112–137.

Deutsch, Helene

Magnone, L. (2023). *Freud's Emissaries: The Transfer of Psychoanalysis Through the Polish Intelligentsia to Europe 1900–1939*. T. Bhambry (Trans.). Lausanne: Sdvig Press.

Naszkowska, K. (2022). Psychoanalyst, Jew, Woman, Wife, Mother, Emigrant: The Émigré Foremothers of Psychoanalysis in the United States. *European Judaism*, 55(1), 112–137.

Naszkowska, K. (2023). Help, Health, Husbands, and Hutzpah: The Lives of Five Women Analysts. In A. Harris (Ed.), *The Émigré Analysts and American Psychoanalysis: History and Contemporary Relevance* (pp. 56–91). New York: Routledge.

Roazen, P. (1985). *Helene Deutsch: A Psychoanalyst's Life*. Garden City, NY: Anchor Press/Doubleday.

Fabian Roth, Michalina

Menninger, K. (1970). In memory of Michalina Fabian Roth, MD (1900–1969). *Bulletin of the Menninger Clinic*, 34(1), 31–32.

Feibel, Charlotte

Menaker, E. (1988). Early Struggles in Lay Psychoanalysis. New York in the Thirties, Forties, and Fifties. *Psychoanalytic Review*, 75(3), 373–379.

Frankl, Liselotte

Pakesch, N. (2019). Liselotte Frankl and Hans Herma. Two Candidates of the Vienna Psychoanalytic Society in 1938. In V. Blüml et al. (Eds.), *Contemporary Perspectives on the Freudian Death Drive in Theory, Clinical Practice and Culture* (pp. 163–172). London: Routledge.

Frenkel-Brunswik, Else

Freidenreich, H. (n.d.). Else Frenkel-Brunswik. *The Shavi/Hyman Encyclopedia of Jewish Women*. Online at https://jwa.org/encyclopedia/article/frenkel-brunswik-else. Accessed June 15, 2023.

Freud, Anna

Edgcumbe, R. (2000). *Anna Freud: A View of Development, Disturbance and Therapeutic Techniques*. London: Routledge.
Young-Bruehl, E. (1988). *Anna Freud: A Biography*. New Haven and London: Yale UP.
Young-Bruehl, E. (2004). Anna Freud and Dorothy Burlingham at Hampstead. The Origins of Psychoanalytic Parent-Infant Observation. *Annual of Psychoanalysis*, 32, 185–197.

Friedländer, Kate

Lantos, B. (1966). Kate Friedländer. Prevention of Juvenile Deliquency. In F. Alexander et al. (Eds.), *Psychoanalytic Pioneers: A History of Psychoanalysis as Seen Through the Lives and the Works of its Most Eminent Teachers, Thinkers, and Clinicians* (pp. 508–518). New York: Basic Books.

Fromm-Reichmann, Frieda

Bateson, G. (1958). Language and Psychiatry: Frieda Fromm-Reichmann's Last Project. *Psychiatry*, 21, 90–100.
Bruch, H. (1982). Personal Reminiscences of Frieda Fromm-Reichmann. *Psychiatry*, 45, 98–104.
Hoff, S. G. (1982). Frieda Fromm-Reichmann. The Early Years. *Psychiatry*, 45, 115–120.
Hornstein, G. A. (2000). *To Redeem One Person Is to Redeem the World: The Life of Frieda Fromm-Reichmann*. New York: Free Press.
Weigert, E. (1958). In Memoriam: Frieda Fromm-Reichmann, 1889–1957. *Psychiatry*, 21, 91–95.

Geleerd Löwenstein, Elisabeth

Tartakoff, H. (1970). Obituary—Elisabeth Geleerd Löwenstein. *International Journal of Psychoanalysis*, 51, 71–73.

Gincburg-Oberholzer, Mira

Magnone, L. (2023). *Freud's Emissaries: The Transfer of Psychoanalysis Through the Polish Intelligentsia to Europe 1900–1939*. T. Bhambry (Trans.). Lausanne: Sdvig Press.
Naszkowska, K. (2022). Psychoanalyst, Jew, Woman, Wife, Mother, Emigrant: The Émigré Foremothers of Psychoanalysis in the United States. *European Judaism*, 55(1), 112–137.

Gutmann-Isakower, Salomea

Kirsner, D. (2007). Saving Psychoanalysis: Ernest Jones and the Isakowers. *Psychoanalysis and History*, 9, 83–91.

Naszkowska, K. (2022). Psychoanalyst, Jew, Woman, Wife, Mother, Emigrant: The Émigré Foremothers of Psychoanalysis in the United States. *European Judaism*, 55(1), 112–137.

Hann-Kende, Fanny

Borgos, A. (2021). *Women in the Budapest School of Psychoanalysis: Girls of Tomorrow*. Abingdon and New York: Routledge.

Mészáros, J. (2014). *Ferenczi and Beyond: Exile of the Budapest School and Solidarity in the Psychoanalytic Movement During the Nazi Years*. London: Routledge.

Happel, Clara

Naszkowska, K. (2022). Psychoanalyst, Jew, Woman, Wife, Mother, Emigrant: The Émigré Foremothers of Psychoanalysis in the United States. *European Judaism*, 55(1), 112–137.

Hartmann, Dora

Bernard, V. W. (1974). Dora Hartmann, M.D. (1902–1974). *Psychoanalytic Quarterly*, 43(4), 661–662.

Naszkowska, K. (2023). Help, Health, Husbands, and Hutzpah: The Lives of Five Women Analysts. In A. Harris (Ed.), *The Émigré Analysts and American Psychoanalysis: History and Contemporary Relevance* (pp. 56–91). New York: Routledge.

Heimann, Paula

Rolnik, E. (2008). "Why Is It That I See Everything Differently?" Reading a 1933 Letter from Paula Heimann to Theodor Reik. *Journal of the American Psychoanalytic Association*, 56(2), 409–430.

Hermann, Alice

Borgos, A. (2021). *Women in the Budapest School of Psychoanalysis: Girls of Tomorrow*. Abingdon and New York: Routledge.

Horney, Karen

Quinn, S. (1987). *A Mind of Her Own. The Life of Karen Horney*. New York: Summit Books.

Zimerman Vizzi, I. (2022). Pioneer Women in Psychoanalysis: Subjectivity, Intersubjectivity and the Fates of the Primitive Object. *Psychoanalytical Inquiry*, 42(7), 523–543.

Hug-Hellmuth, Hermine

Balsam, R. H. (2003). Women of the Wednesday Society. The presentations of Drs. Hilferding, Spielrein, and Hug-Hellmuth. *American Imago*, 60(3), 303–342.

Larson, W. (2011). The Freudian Subject and the Maoist Mind: The Diaries of Hermine Hug-Hellmuth and Lei Feng. *Psychoanalysis and History*, 13, 157–180.
Plastow, M. (2011). Hermine Hug-Hellmuth, the First Child Psychoanalyst: Legacy and Dilemmas. *Australasian Psychiatry*, 19(3), 206–210.

Isaacs, Susan

Gardner, D. E. M. (1969). *Susan Isaacs. The First Biography*. London: Routledge.
Graham, P. (2009). *A Biography of Susan Isaacs. A Life Freeing the Minds of Children*. London: Routledge.
Rickman, J. (1950). Susan Sutherland Isaacs. *International Journal of Psychoanalysis*, 31, 279–285.
Smith, L. A. (1985). *To Understand and to Help. The Life and Work of Susan Isaacs (1885–1948)*. Cranbury, NJ: 1st Associated Universities Press.

Jacob, Gertrud

Fromm-Reichmann, F. (1940). In Memoriam Gertrud Jacob, 1893–1940. *Psychoanalytic Quarterly*, 9, 546–548.
Silverberg, W. V. (1941). The Art of Gertrud Jacob, 1893–1940. Portraits of Psychotics. *Psychiatry*, 4, 157–160.

Jacobson, Edith

Kronold, E. (1980). Edith Jacobson 1897–1978. *Psychoanalytic Quarterly*, 49, 505–507.

Kardos, Erzsébet

Borgos, A. (2021). *Women in the Budapest School of Psychoanalysis: Girls of Tomorrow*. Abingdon and New York: Routledge.

Kestenberg, Judith

Brenner, I. (2000). Obituary. Judith Kestenberg (1910–1999). *International Journal of Psychoanalysis*, 81, 815–817.
https://kestenbergmovementprofile.org/
Kormos, J. (2021). History and the Psychoanalytic Foundations of the Kestenberg Movement Profile. *Body, Movement and Dance Psychotherapy. An International Journal for Theory, Research and Practice*, 17(2), 101–116.
Naszkowska, K. (2023). Give me Permission to Remember: Judith S. Kestenberg and the Memory of the Holocaust. In L. Henik (Ed.), *Psychoanalysis and Jewish Life*. New York: Routledge.

Klein, Melanie

Grosskurth, P. (1986). *Melanie Klein: Her World and Her Work*. New York: Knopf.
Kristeva, J. (2002). *Melanie Klein*. New York: Columbia UP.

Likierman, M. (2002). *Melanie Klein: Her Work in Context*. London and New York: Continuum.
Segal, H. (1980). *Introduction to the Work of Melanie Klein*. New York: Basic Books.
Segal, H. (1980). *Melanie Klein*. New York: Viking Press.
Zetzel, E. (1961). Melanie Klein 1882–1960. *Psychoanalytic Quarterly*, 30, 420–425.

Kraus, Flora

Naszkowska, K. (2022). Psychoanalyst, Jew, Woman, Wife, Mother, Emigrant: The Émigré Foremothers of Psychoanalysis in the United States. *European Judaism*, 55(1), 112–137.

Kris, Marianne

Naszkowska, K. (2023). Help, Health, Husbands, and Hutzpah: The Lives of Five Women Analysts. In A. Harris (Ed.), *The Émigré Analysts and American Psychoanalysis: History and Contemporary Relevance* (pp. 56–91). New York: Routledge.
Neubauer, P. (1981). In Memoriam. Marianne Kris. *Psychoanalytic Study of the Child*, 36, 14–17.
Nunberg, H. (1983). In Memoriam. Marianne Kris. *Psychoanalytic Study of the Child*, 38, 1–7.
Solnit, A. (1981). In Memoriam. Marianne Kris. *Psychoanalytic Study of the Child*, 36, 9–14.

Lázár, Klára

Borgos, A. (2021). *Women in the Budapest School of Psychoanalysis: Girls of Tomorrow*. Abingdon and New York: Routledge.
Lazar Geroe, C. (1982). A Reluctant Immigrant. *Meanjin*, 41(3), 352–357.

Mahler, Margaret

Bond, A. H. (2008). *Margaret Mahler. A Biography of the Psychoanalyst*. London: McFarland, Jefferson, N.C.
Mahler, M. (1988). *The Memoirs of Margaret S. Mahler*. P. E. Stepansky (Ed.). New York: Free Press.

Olden, Christine

Naszkowska, K. (2022). Psychoanalyst, Jew, Woman, Wife, Mother, Emigrant: The Émigré Foremothers of Psychoanalysis in the United States. *European Judaism*, 55(1), 112–137.

Perls, Laura

Litt, S. (2000). Laura Perls (1905–1990): Co-Founder of Gestalt Therapy. *Positive Health Magazine*, 50.

Reich, Annie

Jacobson, E. (1971). Obituary. Annie Reich (1902–1971). *International Journal of Psychoanalysis*, 52, 334–336.

Kitlitschko, S. (2013). The Prague Psychoanalytic Study Group 1933–1938: Frances Deri, Annie Reich, Theodor Dosužkov, and Heinrich Löwenfeld, and Their Contributions to Psychoanalysis. *International Journal of Psychoanalysis*, 94(6), 1196–1198.

Kronold, E. (1971). Annie Reich M.D. 1902–1971. *Psychoanalytic Quarterly*, 40, 708.

Riviere, Joan

Bower, M. (2019). *The Life and Work of Joan Riviere. Freud, Klein and Female Sexuality.* London and New York: Routledge.

Butler, J. (1999). Lacan, Riviere and the Strategies of Masquerade. In J. Butler (Ed.), *Gender Trouble. Feminism and the Subversion of Identity* (pp. 59–77). London and New York: Routledge.

Hughes, A. (Ed.) (1991). *The Inner World and Joan Riviere, Collected Papers: 1920–1958.* London: Karnac Books.

Rotter, Lillián

Borgos, A. (2021). *Women in the Budapest School of Psychoanalysis: Girls of Tomorrow.* Abingdon and New York: Routledge.

Schmideberg, Melitta

Cassullo, G. (2016). The Psychoanalytic Contributions of Melitta Schmideberg Klein. More than Melanie Klein's Rebel Daughter. *American Journal of Psychoanalysis*, 76(1), 18–34.

Shapira, M. (2017). Melitta Schmideberg. Her Life and Work Encompassing Migration, Psychoanalysis, and War in Britain. *Psychoanalysis and History*, 19(3), 323–348.

Spillius, E. (2009). Melitta and Her Mother. *Psychoanalytic Quarterly*, 78(4), 1147–1166.

Seglow, Ilse

Herman, N. (1989). Ilse Seglow in Her Time. Reflections on Her Life and Work. *British Journal of Psychotherapy*, 5, 431–441.

Sharpe, Ella Freeman

Netzer, C. (1982). Annals of Psychoanalysis: Ella Freeman Sharpe. *Psychoanalytic Review*, 69(2), 207–219.

Payne, S. (1947). Ella Freeman Sharpe. An Appreciation. *International Journal of Psychoanalysis*, 28, 54–56.

Wahl, C. W. (1966). Ella Freeman Sharpe, 1875–1947. In F. Alexander et al. (Eds.), *Psychoanalytic Pioneers: A History of Psychoanalysis as Seen Through the Lives and the Works of Its Most Eminent Teachers, Thinkers, and Clinicians* (pp. 265–271). New York: Basic Books.

Whelan, M. (Ed.) (2005). *Mistress of Her Own Thoughts. Ella Freeman Sharpe and the Practice of Psychoanalysis.* North Melbourne: BookSurge Australia.

Waelder-Hall, Jenny

Gifford, S. (2017). Jenny Waelder-Hall and the Early Child Analysis. *American Imago*, 74(4).

Naszkowska, K. (2023). Help, Health, Husbands, and Hutzpah: The Lives of Five Women Analysts. In A. Harris (Ed.), *The Émigré Analysts and American Psychoanalysis: History and Contemporary Relevance* (pp. 56–91). New York: Routledge.

Umansky, O. (2021). Women Histories in Photos—Jenny Waelder-Hall. *BPSI Library Newsletter* (Winter).

Winnicott, Clare

Kanter, J (2000). The Untold Story of Clare and Donald Winnicott. How Social Work Influenced Modern Psychoanalysis. *Clinical Social Work Journal*, 28(3), 245–261.

Kanter, J. (Ed.) (2004). *Face to Face with Children. The Life and Work of Clare Winnicott*. London and New York: Routledge.

Kanter, J. (2004). "Let's Never Ask Him What to Do." Clare Britton's Transformative Impact on Donald Winnicott. *American Imago*, 61, 457–481.

Index

abortion 2, 8, 79–80, 94–97, 316–318
Abraham, Karl 59, 216, 282; *see also* Berlin Institute of Psychoanalysis
Adler, Alfred 5, 20–22, 38, 79, 92–93, 119; and psychoanalysis 33; *see also* individual psychology
American Psychoanalytic Association (APsA) 207, 233
Andreas-Salomé, Lou 6, 37–56
Anschluss 97, 306–309, 324
antisemitism: and boycotts 4; history of 2–3, 7, 58, 86–88, 310; and laws 3, 132–134, 147, 266, 308–309; and violence 97, 100, 146–147, 275, 303, 307–310; *see also* Austrofascism
aphasia 26–33
Arendt, Hannah 272, 287
Ashkenazi Jews 3, 299, 310
association experiments 27, 31, 118, 161–162, 167, 238; *see also* Jung, Carl Gustav
Auschwitz concentration camp 9, 99, 149, 278, 313
Austrofascism 2–3, 306–307, 320, 323
Austro-Hungarian Empire 2–3, 58, 82, 85, 156, 302–306

Bálint, Alice 7, 229–230, 233, 236, 239–240; and the Budapest School of Psychoanalysis 131, 135; and child analysis 137, 224–225
Bálint, Mihály (Michael) 230, 235–237, 240–241
Berlin Institute of Psychoanalysis 187, 197, 211, 233, 319; and "Aryanization" 190–193, 252; founding of 216, 282; *see also* Göring Institute
Bernfeld, Siegfried 69, 228
Bibring, Edward 239, 320

Bibring, Grete 319, 332
birth control 95–96, 144; *see also* abortion
Bleuler, Eugen (*also* Burghölzli Clinic) 15, 20, 161, 250, 260; *see also* Zurich psychoanalysis
Boehm, Felix 187, 190–195, 252
Bolshevik Revolution 4, 114–116, 123, 275–277, 294; *see also* Russia
Bonaparte, Marie 239, 256–257, 333
Boston Psychoanalytic Society and Institute 68, 282, 318–319
British psychoanalysis 190, 204–205, 207–210, 212–213, 217
Budapest Psychoanalytic Polyclinic 224, 235
Budapest School of Psychoanalysis *see* Hungarian psychoanalysis

Chestnut Lodge 281–282, 285, 289; *see also* Fromm-Reichmann, Frieda
child analysis: Anna Freud's seminars on 68, 212; and the Case of a Boy from Minsk 253–255, 257, 262, 267; and drawings 30–31, 263–266; history of 105, 117, 209, 224, 249, 261–266; and *Symposium on Child-Analysis* 212
child linguistics 23–25
child psychiatry 178, 199, 201
Child Seminar (*Kinderseminar*) 187, 228, 282; *see also* Fenichel, Otto
circular letters (*Rundbriefe*) 187–189
Claparède, Éduard 14–15, 27, 250
class 81–83; middle class 81, 224–227, 236, 239, 310; working class 2, 83–84, 87, 93–95, 99, 319
collective amnesia 2, 306
communism 3, 7, 116, 226–227, 278–279, 316; Hungarian Communist Party 149

Darwin, Charles 19–21, 25–27
depression 69, 112, 122, 179, 182, 186
Deutsch, Helene 57, 67–69, 72, 302, 334
drive: sexual drive 16, 118, 137; and Spielrein, Sabina 16–21; theory 46, 88, 118, 124, 137

Eckstein, Emma 87–88
Eitingon, Max 65, 113, 193, 216, 235; *see also* Berlin Institute of Psychoanalysis
equality 83, 114, 142, 160, 237
ethnicity 4, 310–312, 322; *see also* race

Farkas, Erzsébet 2–3, 5, 7, 129–152
February Revolution 4, 105, 114
feminism 63, 66, 83, 96, 99, 142
Fenichel, Otto 187–192, 193–198, 228; *see also* Child Seminar; circular letters
Ferenczi, Sándor 13, 38, 65, 207, 289; and active technique 254; and Bálint, Alice 230; and Budapest School of Psychoanalysis 131, 142, 224; and Karpińska-Woyczyńska, Ludwika 165–168; and Kovács, Vilma 231–241; and Sokolnicka, Eugenia 251–256, 267
First World War 1, 180, 232; and aphasia 29; and Austria 2; and Great Britain 208–209; and Hungary 131, 142; and Karpińska-Woyczyńska, Ludwika 167–170; and Low, Barbara 206–209; and Morgenstern, Sophie 260; and Poland 3, 58–59, 71, 298–299; 303–304; and Sokolnicka, Eugenia 252–253; and Spielrein, Sabina 14; and Szalita, Alberta 275; and Waal, Nic 196
France and psychoanalysis 5, 255–261
Freidenreich, Harriet Pass 59, 81–82, 85–86, 129
Freud, Anna 39, 214, 335; and Klein, Melanie 199, 204–205, 211–214, 217; and Rosenthal, Tatiana 110–111, 117–118; and seminars on child analysis 68, 212; and Sokolnicka, Eugenia 253; and Spielrein, Sabina 13, 21; and Waal, Nic 191–193, 195
Freud, Sigmund 87–88; and Adler, Alfred 22, 92; analysis with 250–251, 257, 267; and Andreas-Salomé, Lou 37–43, 45–46, 48, 51; and *Beyond the Pleasure Principle* 13, 17, 19, 120, 233, 238; and case of Little Hans 253–254; criticism of 20, 51, 181–182; and Jung, Carl Gustav 5, 13, 16, 23–24, 207–208, 250; and Karpińska-Woyczyńska, Ludwika 161–166; and Low, Barbara 204–207, 210–215, 219; and Marx 4, 105, 113; and Morgenstern, Sophie 265; and primary process 290; and Rank, Beata 5–6, 57–60, 65, 70–71; Rosenthal, Tatiana 105, 110, 113, 118–119; and Sokolnicka, Eugenia 250–251, 254–256, 258–259; and Spielrein, Sabina 15–17, 20, 33; and *Totem and Taboo* 61–64; *see also* hysteria
Fromm-Reichmann, Frieda 280–282, 285, 289–290, 293, 335; *see also* Chestnut Lodge

Galicia (Poland) 4, 57–58, 72, 165, 298–304, 314–324
gender: discrimination 100, 160; identity 1, 322; issues 82, 144, 178; roles 180, 224, 239; violence 8; *see also* equality; misogyny
German Psychoanalytic Society (DPG) 187, 190–193, 195, 252
Gestapo 97–99, 190–191, 196; *see also* Nazism
Gide, André 256–258
Gincburg-Oberholzer, Mira 67–68, 335
God 44–45, 52–53, 95, 115, 182–186; death of 45
goddess 63–64
Göring Institute 189, 193–195, 252
grief 8, 240, 279–281, 284–285
Gymnasium (high school) 58, 82, 132, 157, 249, 275, 302
Gyömrői, Edit (Ludowyk) 7, 130, 135, 225, 227–229

Hajdu, Lilly 7, 225–226, 233
Hampstead Clinic 117, 228
Hermann, Alice 135, 224, 233, 241
Hilferding, Margarethe (Hilferding-Hönigsberg) 2, 5–7, 22, 79–103
Hilferding, Rudolf 80, 86–87, 99
Holocaust: children of Holocaust victims and survivors 284, 310; death in 4–5, 13, 79, 131; experience 2, 69, 105, 131, 312–315; Holocaust Studies 271; and loss 272, 284–285; and psychoanalysis 8, 321; and silence 270–272, 280, 321–324; survivors 9, 130, 226, 285, 310, 316; and trauma 150, 271–273

homosexuality 62, 90, 187, 215
Hug-Hellmuth, Hermine 88, 215, 254, 336–337
Hungarian psychoanalysis 7, 142, 227, 230, 242; and education 135–136; Hungarian Psychoanalytical Society 130–131, 224–226, 232, 237, 241, 251; Hungarian method of supervision 239–240; *see also* Ferenczi, Sándor
Hungarian Soviet Republic 3, 227
Hungary (*also* Kingdom of Hungary): and antisemitism 130–134, 146–149, 310; history of 3, 7–8, 226–230; Hungarian Soviet Republic 3
hysteria 105, 117, 161; *Studies on Hysteria* 87–88

Imago (journal) 39, 60–64, 69, 230, 237
individual psychology 61, 92–93, 120; Association for Individual Psychology 92; *see also* Adler, Alfred
International Psychoanalytical Association (IPA) 165, 178, 192, 208, 250–251, 254; *see also* Jones, Ernest
interwar: Europe 225; Jewish population 3–4, 309; period 1, 168–171, 299, 302; Poland 3–4; Vienna 9, 322
intuition 72, 287, 289
Irigaray, Luce 63

Jacobson, Edith 188–195, 228, 337
Jagiellonian University 58–59, 70–71, 166, 302, 306
Jekels, Ludwik 57, 70, 162–163, 166–167
Jews: and ancestry 87–88, 109, 130, 133–134, 143–145, 147; and community 81–82, 258, 276–277, 298–299, 303, 308–309; and education 82, 134, 142–143, 301–305; and family 81, 224–231, 249, 259, 304–306; and identity 80–82, 87, 131–134, 146, 310, 322; Jewish students 85–86, 223–226, 275, 305–307; Jewish women students 58–59, 104–105, 112–113, 259, 302–305; and tradition 81, 133, 139, 144, 320
Jones, Ernest 64, 166, 187, 190–195, 207–214, 217
Judaism 81, 131–134, 141–146; Hassidim 274
Jung, Carl Gustav 31–33, 105, 161–163, 167–168, 264; and Spielrein, Sabina 13–17, 20–21; *see also* association experiments; Freud, Sigmund, and Jung, Carl Gustav

Kardos, Erzsébet 224, 233, 337
Karpińska-Woyczyńska, Ludwika 2–3, 5, 7, 155–177
Kempner, Salomea 187
Kestenberg, Judith 315–316, 321, 337
Klein, Melanie 117, 189, 212–213, 282, 337–338; and Rosenthal, Tatiana 111–112; and Spielrein, Sabina 13, 21; *see also* Freud, Anna, and Klein, Melanie
Kovács, Vilma 2–3, 7, 130, 134, 223–245
Kristeva, Julia 91–92
Kuriloff, Emily 69, 284–285, 321

lay analysis 38, 224, 233–234, 238, 257
Lévy, Kata 130–131, 135–141, 224
libido 40–49, 62, 118, 216, 255
London Psychoanalytical Society (LPS) 207–208
Low, Barbara 5, 7, 19, 202–222

magical thinking 262–263, 291
Malinowski, Bronisław 63–64, 190
Marx 7, 87, 94, 181, 189–191, 228; *see also* Freud, Sigmund, and Marx
matricide 61–63
medicine: study of 13–14, 27, 58–59, 79, 311, 319; *see also* Jews, and education; Jews, Jewish students; Jews, Jewish women students
memory 69, 201, 260, 270–274; collective memory 150; Memory Studies 150, 298, 302, 320–324; remembering 49, 132, 141, 183–185, 232, 324; remembering inadequately 6–8, 57, 79–80, 166, 173, 210–211; and trauma 194, 234, 240, 282
migration 1, 97, 147, 187, 223, 315; and exile 7–8, 266–267; experience of 69, 115, 157, 191, 255, 260; migration crisis 8–9; and the United States' laws 8–9, 307–312, 315
Minkowski, Eugène 256, 260, 279
misogyny 5, 9, 86–88, 317
Morgenstern, Sophie 1, 3, 5, 7, 249, 259–270
mother-child relationship 64, 135–137, 142
motherhood 6, 86, 89–94, 142, 320; and pregnancy 64, 91, 94, 144, 277
mother-infant relationship 91, 224, 230
motherly love 89–93

narcissism 19, 39–45, 47–54
Nazism: and Austria 97–99, 196, 303, 306–307, 309–310; and France 261, 266; and Germany 3–4, 97–99, 187–191, 212, 276, 308–310; and Hungary 146–147, 149; and Norway 196–197; and persecution 79, 97, 274, 310, 322; and Poland 266–268; and psychoanalysis 191, 195–196; see also Göring Institute
New York City 8, 270–273, 283, 309–311, 315–317, 321
New York Psychoanalytic Society (NYPS) 207, 282
Niederland, William 271, 321
Nietzsche, Friedrich 37–38, 44–45, 124–125
Nin, Anaïs 57, 65–66
Nirvana principle 205, 210–211, 219; see also Low, Barbara
numerus clausus 223, 275, 132–134

Oslo: University of 182, 187

Paris Psychoanalytical Society (SPP) 257–259, 261
Piaget, Jean 15, 24, 262
Piłsudzki, Józef 3–4, 250, 323
Poland: and antisemitism 266, 274, 276, 278–280, 322–324; and communism 278–279, 314–316; history of 3–8, 168, 172–173, 253; and identity 294–295, 320; and Jewish community 298–300, 311–314; and partitions 299; and Polish Socialist Party 160; and psychoanalysis 60, 65, 155, 162–173, 252, 267; Russian-occupied Poland 3, 156–158, 249, 259
postmemory 8, 320
postwar period 7, 199; and Austria 2–3; and metapsychology 284; and Poland 279, 322; and psychoanalysis 285, 319–321
psychoanalysis and education 210, 213, 216–218, 224, 230

race 97, 134, 160, 310; see also ethnicity
racism 2, 8–9, 310, 317–318
Rank, Beata (Tola) 3, 5–6, 57–76
Rank, Otto 57, 59–60, 63–66, 70–71, 251–253
Red Vienna 2, 94–95, 320, 323
Reich, Annie 188, 228
Reich, Wilhelm 187, 189–191, 193, 195, 198–200, 228
repression (in psychoanalysis) 46, 51, 88, 256, 287, 320; Sex and Repression 63–64; sexual 237

Rilke, Rainer Maria 52–53
Riviere, Joan 207, 212, 215, 339
Rosenthal, Tatiana 4, 6–7, 104–128
Rostov-on-Don 5, 15, 275
Rothschild Hospital 97–98
Rotter, Lillián 135, 224, 339
Russia: history of 4, 8, 15, 28–29, 104–122, 156–159; and psychoanalysis 106–107, 119, 123; Soviet Russia 4, 7, 123, 172, 189, 278–279; see also Poland, Russian-occupied Poland

Sachs, Hans 211, 216, 230
schizophrenia 225–226, 277, 281, 284–286, 289–291
Schmideberg, Melitta 218, 339
Schmidt, Vera 117, 188–189
Second World War 1–2; and Hilferding, Margarethe 79–80, 97–99; and Hungary 3, 130, 142, 149, 226–228; and Poland 57, 271, 303, 324; and Szalita, Alberta 5–6, 276–279, 291, 294; and Waal, Nic 193–196; and Wermer, Olga 311–315, 320
sexual abuse 185
sexual development 51, 88, 116, 129, 143
sexual difference 62–63
sexual education: and Bálint, Alice 230; and Farkas, Erzsébet 141, 144; and Hilferding, Margarethe 2, 94–95; and Norway 179; and Rosenthal, Tatiana 116–117; Sokolnicka, Eugenia 254; Wermer, Olga 319
sexual freedom 79, 179–180
sexuality 19–21, 92, 117, 144, 218; and Andreas-Salomé, Lou 39–40, 46–50; exploration of 180, 182; and guilt 319; and men 237, 254; and mother 6, 90–91; and taboo 179; and women 91, 120, 142, 209
sexual masochism 17
Sharpe, Ella Freeman 210–212, 217, 339
Snyder, Timothy also bloodlands 4, 274, 277
Sokolnicka, Eugenia 1, 3, 5, 7, 173, 249–269; and Karpińska-Woyczyńska, Ludwika 168
Spielrein, Sabina 1, 4–6, 13–36, 120; and child analysis 262–263; and Fenichel, Otto 188–189; and Rosenthal, Tatiana 104–105, 112–113, 122; and Zurich 259
Stock, Malvina 322–323
Szalita, Alberta (Szalita-Pemow) 3–8, 270–297
Szenkel, Bronisława 304–305, 313, 315
Szenkel, Wolf 303, 313, 315; see also Zionism

Theresienstadt 97–99
trauma 9, 119, 122, 224; and childhood 184, 279; intergenerational transmission of 310; *The Trauma of Birth* 63–64; and war 6, 213, 284–285, 320–321; *see also* Holocaust, and trauma; memory, and trauma

Ukraine: history of 4, 8, 273–278, 280, 301–306, 313–314

Vienna: University of 2–3, 86–88, 301–302, 305, 307
Vienna Psychoanalytic Society: and Andreas-Salomé, Lou 38; and Hilferding, Margarethe 2, 5, 22, 79; history of 20, 88; Karpińska-Woyczyńska, Ludwika 163, 168; and Rank, Beata 60; and Rosenthal, Tatiana 105, 109, 112; and Sokolnicka, Eugenia 252; Spielrein, Sabina 17, 112

Volhynia 4, 273–276

Waal, Nic 2, 6–7, 178–203
Warsaw: University of 157, 171, 275
Washington-Baltimore and psychoanalysis 280–282
Wermer, Henry 306–311
Wermer, Olga 3–4, 6, 8, 298–331
Wermer, Paul 306, 315
Winnicott, Donald 91, 282, 287
women and education 156, 180, 206, 208, 224
women's emancipation 72, 84, 94, 131, 142–144, 179–180

Yiddish 274, 298, 304

Zionism 206, 208, 216, 299–303
Zurich: University of 109, 112–113, 160, 259
Zurich psychoanalysis 15, 238, 250

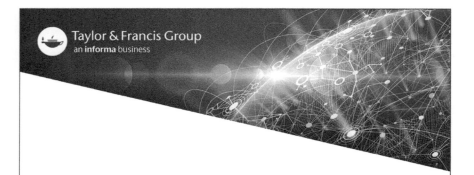